Metacognition in Literacy Learning

Theory, Assessment, Instruction, and Professional Development

Metacognition in Literacy Learning

Theory, Assessment, Instruction, and Professional Development

Edited by

Susan E. Israel
Cathy Collins Block
Kathryn L. Bauserman
Kathryn Kinnucan-Welsch

 LAWRENCE ERLBAUM ASSOCIATES, PUBLISHERS
2005   Mahwah, New Jersey   London

Lawrence Erlbaum Associates, Inc., Publishers
10 Industrial Avenue
Mahwah, New Jersey 07430
www.erlbaum.com

Cover design by Tomai Maridou

Library of Congress Cataloging-in-Publication Data

Metacognition in literacy learning : theory, assessment, instruction, and professional
development / edited by Susan E. Israel . . . [et al.].
      p.   cm.
Includes bibliographical references and index.
ISBN 0-8058-5229-8 (cloth : alk. paper)
ISBN 0-8058-5230-1 (pbk. : alk. paper)
    1. Reading.   2. Reading, Psychology of.   3. Metacognition in children.   I. Israel, Susan E.

LB1050.M46   2005
428.4—dc22
                                                                        2005045498
                                                                        CIP

Books published by Lawrence Erlbaum Associates are printed on acid-free paper,
and their bindings are chosen for strength and durability.

Printed in the United States of America
10 9 8 7 6 5 4 3 2 1

Contents

Preface

In 1979, Flavell coined the term *metacognition*. In his landmark paper on meta-cognition he stated, "Increasing the quantity and quality of children's metacognitive knowledge and monitoring skills through systematic training may be feasible as well as desirable" (p. 906).

The purpose of this book on metacognition and literacy learning is threefold. First, it is meant to help reading educators develop higher level thinking and reading strategies in their classrooms. Second, it is a response to current research that demonstrates how metacognition can improve both students' and teachers' thought and reading processes with the goal of improving reading achievement. Third, it is a response to the call to increase the quality and quantity of children's metacognitive knowledge, and monitoring skills and approaches for instructional change.

This book is important in the field of literacy and education because there are no comprehensive volumes published on the topic of metacognition and literacy learning. *Mosaic of Thought* (Keene & Zimmerman, 1997) focused on strategy application in a Reader's Workshop and begins to develop the notion of metacognition. This book goes beyond isolated metacognitive strategies by taking an integrated approach in reading and literacy. Learning to incorporate metacognition is a challenging task for all teachers, especially those who teach literacy and reading instruction. Therefore, the recommended audience of the book will be reading teachers, reading specialists, reading researchers, and a text to be used in graduate level reading courses.

This book is a comprehensive volume that includes four significant areas. The first part summarizes the theoretical foundation of metacognition. The second part provides a variety of assessment tools to measure metacognition. The third part builds on how assessment drives instruction, using the new and innovative instructional strategies and models of how metacognition can be integrated with instruction. The final part is devoted to professional development with reading teachers, reading professionals, and preservice teachers.

Each chapter has special features to help the reader develop metacognitive thoughts while engaged in the text. The features of each chapter are as follows:

- **Metacognitive Teacher Reflection:** Reflections at the beginning of each chapter illustrate what teachers are thinking about the topic discussed in the chapter. Teacher reflections activate the reader's prior knowledge about the topic, and they set the stage for reader expectations.
- **Metacognitive Connections:** Closing each chapter is a metacognitive connection that links the prior chapter's discussion with the current chapter, and gives the reader an idea of what they can expect to learn about in the next chapter. Metacognitive connections help the learner connect the new information gained with previous learning. This special feature also provides a model that demonstrates how metacognition is applied to authentic learning situations.

When the authors were contacted to contribute to the volume, they responded with overwhelming support and interest. As the book progressed, the interest and support extended far beyond a professional level. Many contributors took a very personal interest in the completion and success of the publication. One memorable conversation occurred during the 2004 International Reading Association's 49th Conference in Reno, Nevada. I made it a point to introduce myself to Jay S. Samuels, a contributor in chapter 3, after his presentation. After a brief introduction, Jay commented, "The book will be a true contribution to the field of reading and literacy. I am truly impressed with the level of commitment from such notable scholars who have made contributions to your volume on metacognition." As our conversation continued, I provided him with an update on the status of the book and the chapters. Being curious, Jay asked me if all the chapters had in fact been written. I responded, "All but one author who needed a short extension due to many commitments." Jay continued to press me for information about the delayed chapter and the author's identification. After some trepidation, I revealed the contributor(s). Jay said, "That chapter is worth the wait."

The overwhelming response by the contributors to this volume affords us the opportunity to provide a path for metacognition to "be feasible as well as desirable" for literacy teachers who wish to develop metacognition in literacy learning. For that, I am personally grateful. We think our book on metacognition and literacy learning is long overdue, but it has been "worth the wait."

Susan E. Israel
Assistant Professor, University of Dayton

REFERENCES

Flavell, J. H. (1979). Metacognition and cognitive monitoring: A new area of cognitive developmental inquiry. *American Psychologist, 34*(10), 906–911.

Keene, E., & Zimmerman, S. (1997). *Mosaic of thought: Teaching comprehension in a reader's workshop.* Portsmouth, NH: Heinemann.

Acknowledgments

The intention of this volume is to open awareness to metacognition and literary learning by bringing together research findings from reading, linguistics, psychology, and education. The editors of this volume wish to thank, first and foremost, all the contributors. Their commitment to the publication of a book on metacognition exceeded our expectations. In addition, we would like to express our gratitude and appreciation to the senior editor, Lane Akers, whose enthusiasm and interest in the project expedited the volume's publication. We are also grateful to Dixie Massey, of North Carolina A & T State University, and Kelly Cartwright, of Christopher Newport University, for assisting us with the collection of metacognitive teacher reflections. Dr. Kathryn Kinnucan-Welsch would like to thank Anna L. Fohmin, Graduate Assistant in the Matas Program in Early Childhood Education at the University of Dayton, for her assistance with the organization of Part IV. We would also like to thank our family members, who provided us with support and love during the genesis of the book. We would like to express our gratitude for your support and positive response to what we think will be a classic book in the field of literacy and education. Lastly, we would like to thank John Flavell, the pioneer in metacognition, for writing the review that highlights the depth of knowledge on metacognition that has emerged since his first landmark publication on the subject.

—Susan E. Israel
Cathy Collins Block
Kathryn L. Bauserman
Kathryn Kinnucan-Welsch

About the Editors

Susan E. Israel is the graduate reading coordinator and assistant professor at the University of Dayton. In addition, she has served the Alliance for Catholic Education at the University of Notre Dame, where she has taught language arts courses and supervised graduates who learn how to teach and serve in under-resourced Catholic Schools around the country. She was awarded the teacher researcher grant from the International Reading Association, where she has served and been a member for over a decade. Her most recent research involves understanding developmental aspects of reading comprehension, metacognition, as well as research in neuroscience as it relates to reading processes.

Cathy Collins Block is a professor of education at Texas Christian University. She was elected to serve on the board of directors of the International Reading Association from 2002–2005. She has served, or is presently serving, on the board of directors of the National Reading Conference, Nobel Learning Communities, IBM Educational Board of Directors, and the National Center for Learning Disabilities. She presently serves on the editorial boards for the *Journal of Educational Psychology, Reading Research Quarterly, The Reading Teacher, National Reading Conference Yearbook, and America Tomorrow*. She has written more than 30 books relative to reading comprehension and teacher education. She has also served on authorial writing teams for elementary reading curriculum materials, and has published more than 90 research articles.

Kathryn L. Bauserman is an assistant reading professor at Indiana State University, teaching graduate and undergraduate classes in the areas of emergent reading, literacy integration in the curriculum, and reading intervention strategies based on assessment. She is an active member of several organizations that promote reading: the International Reading Association, serving as a reviewer, and the National Reading Conference, serving on the field council committee. Recent areas of research and writing include metacognition and vocabulary.

Kathryn Kinnucan-Welsch is associate professor of education and chair in the department of teacher education at the University of Dayton. She is currently working with literacy coaches in a statewide literacy professional development initiative, and is a member of the Governor's Literacy Partnership. Her research and publications have focused on the professional development of practicing teachers.

About the Contributors

Peter Afflerbach, PhD, Department of Curriculum and Instruction, University of Maryland, College Park, MD

Linda Baker, PhD, Department of Psychology, University of Maryland, Baltimore, MD

Kathryn L. Bauserman, PhD, Department of Education, Indiana State University, Terre Haute, IN

Connie L. Bowman, PhD, Department of Teacher Education, University of Dayton, Dayton, OH

Cathy Collins Block, PhD, School of Education, Texas Christian University, Fort Worth, TX

Carrice Cummins, College of Education, Louisiana Tech University, Ruston, LA

Stephen J. Donndelinger, MA, Alliance for Catholic Education, University of Notre Dame, Notre Dame, IN

Gerald G. Duffy, PhD, William E. Moran Distinguished Professor of Reading and Literacy, University of North Carolina, Greensboro, NC

Kari-Ann M. Ediger, Department of Educational Psychology, University of Minnesota, Minneapolis, MN

Jonathan Flukes, Department of Psychology, University of Michigan, Ann Arbor, MI

Malena Galvez-Martin, PhD, University of South Florida, St. Petersburg, FL

Priscilla L. Griffith, PhD, Department of Instructional Leadership and Academic Curriculum, University of Oklahoma, Norman, OK

Elena L. Grigorenko, PhD, Child Study Center and PACE Center, Yale University, New Haven, CT, USA; Department of Psychology, Moscow State University, Russia

Susan E. Israel, PhD, Department of Teacher Education, University of Dayton, Dayton, OH

Laurice M. Joseph, PhD, College of Education, Ohio State University, Columbus, OH

Kathryn Kinnucan-Welsch, EdD, Department of Teacher Education, University of Dayton, Dayton, OH

Dixie D. Massey, PhD, School of Education, North Carolina A&T State University, Greensboro, NC

Kevin Meuwissen, Department of Curriculum and Instruction, University of Maryland, College Park, MD

Margaret Morrison, PhD, Assistant Visiting Professor, The Ohio State University, Columbus, OH

Theresa J. Palumbo, Department of Educational Psychology, University of Minnesota, Minneapolis, MN

Scott G. Paris, PhD, Department of Psychology, University of Michigan, Ann Arbor, MI

Michael Pressley, PhD, Department of Teacher Education, Michigan State University, East Lansing, MI

Judi Randi, PhD, Department of Education, University of New Haven, New Haven, CT

Victoria J. Risko, EdD, Department of Teaching and Learning, College of Vanderbilt University, Nashville, TN

Kathleen Roskos, PhD, Department of Education and Allied Studies, John Carroll University, Cleveland, OH

Catherine A. Rosemary, PhD, Department of Teacher Education, John Carroll University, Cleveland, OH

Jiening Ruan, PhD, Assistant Professor of Instructional Leadership and Academic Curriculum, University of Oklahoma, OK

S. Jay Samuels, EdD, Department of Educational Psychology, University of Minnesota, Minneapolis, MN

Maribeth Cassidy Schmitt, PhD, Literacy and Language Education, Purdue University, West Lafayette, IN

Fredric J. Schreiber, PhD, Haskins Laboratories, Yale University, New Haven, CT

Paige A. Smith, MA, Alliance for Catholic Education, University of Notre Dame, Notre Dame, IN

Robert J. Sternberg, PhD, PACE Center, Yale University, New Haven, CT

Margaret T. Stewart, PhD, Louisiana State University, Baton Rouge, LA

Carol Vukelich, PhD, Delaware Center for Teacher Education, University of Delaware, DE

Jennifer R. Willcutt, Department of Educational Psychology, University of Minnesota, Minneapolis, MN

I

Metacognition and Theory

The foundation of this book rests on the theoretical foundations of metacognition. This section discusses the foundation of metacognition and puts theory in context with literacy learning. Metacognition is defined within the context of cognitive structures within a reading framework. In part I the guiding theoretical principles explain the automatic processes of reading, the role of comprehension in conjunction with metacognition and literacy learning, and the developmental aspects of metacognition. Part I is distinctive in that the theoretical framework of metacognition explains monitoring functions of learning through metacognition and strategy instruction. A range of metacognitive models—some never before published and some that are newly updated and improved—have been included.

Part I provides an excellent classroom resource for the foundational scaffolds that can be used to guide metacognitive assessments, instruction, and professional development that are later described in the corresponding chapters. Griffith and Ruan's chapter 1 contains a definition of metacognition and what is involved in skilled reading, and touches on the relation between reader interests and metacognition. Randi, Grigorenko, and Sternberg (chap. 2) discuss how the process of comprehension can help increase metacognitive awareness and strategic processes. This chapter is guided by the theoretical foundations of comprehension and explains the role of metacognition in the application of instruction. Chapter 3, by Samuels, Ediger, Willcutt, and Palumbo, focuses on the theoretical foundations of automaticity and metacognition, as well as instructional strategies that develop automatic processes of metacognition. This chapter is unique in that a new model of automaticity and metacognition have been explained. After the reader has developed a theoretical foundation of metacognition, Baker (chap. 4) places metacognition in perspective with a child's developmental differences.

Once literacy learners have gained a solid understanding of the theoretical foundations of metacognition and how this relates to developmental differences, they are ready to better understand how assessment tools can be used to identify areas of metacognition. Therefore, part II summarizes the area of metacognition and assessment.

1

What Is Metacognition and What Should Be Its Role in Literacy Instruction?

Priscilla L. Griffith
Jiening Ruan
The University of Oklahoma

If only there was a book called "What Students Think" with a how-to-guide, then everyone would want to be a teacher. But of course that's our challenge! Chapter 1 is essential for every educator because the more we understand the thought processes in our students the better we as teachers can instruct our lessons to reflect all the ways our students are decoding what the heck we are trying to teach! If we can read up-to-date research on how our students are thinking and how they are learning about what they're thinking we can adjust our delivery accordingly and frequently.

There is exemplary information on decoding strategies and ways for teachers to elicit think out louds, but we need concise research on metacognition. We need to know the different ways our children are self-monitoring a lesson on Shakespeare, the Civil War, or ladybugs. So we as teachers can "teach to their brain." A book solely devoted to this concept and a chapter specifically targeted to what has been studied gives a great helping hand to our further understanding of metacognition; research gives us the confidence to use strategies in our classroom.

I hope to find in this chapter research to give credit to what I am doing in my classroom, but more importantly let me see other successful methods. If I can peer into my student's mind with the help of chapter 1, hopefully I can continue my quest in being an exemplary reading teacher.

—Lindsey M. Hale

In 1979, John Flavell published "Metacognition and Cognitive Monitoring: A New Area of Cognitive-Developmental Inquiry." He defined metacognition as "knowledge and cognition about cognitive phenomena" (p. 906) and tied the term to self-regulated learning through the phrase "cognitive monitoring."

Flavell (1979) described a model of cognitive monitoring that incorporated metacognitive knowledge and metacognitive experiences. In this model, metacognitive knowledge is characterized as combinations of information around three knowledge variables—self, task, and strategies—that will be effective in achieving the goals of the task. Metacognitive experiences are "items of metacognitive knowledge that have entered consciousness" (p. 908), and may include an evaluation of where one is in completing a task, or perhaps just a sense of confusion on which the person may or may not act. According to Flavell, metacognitive experiences alter a person's metacognitive knowledge base. We provide an example from our own reading of Flavell's article to illustrate how metacognition impinges on reading.

As we read, we asked ourselves, just what does Flavell's definition mean? *Webster's New Collegiate Dictionary* (1973) became our source of information about key terms in that definition:

- Knowledge—the fact or experience of knowing something with familiarity gained through experience or association
- Cognition—the act or process of knowing including both awareness and judgment
- Phenomenon—fact or event

Putting the terms together, we constructed our definition: Awareness and judgment about an event gained through experience. We compiled enough information about the term to enable us to continue reading with meaning.

What we have described in this brief example of our own reading is how metacognitive processes actually work during ongoing reading. We realized that some parts of the text were confusing. We were monitoring. Metacognition was being defined using cognition, a word that was part of the term. We needed a clarification before reading much further. We self-regulated, that is, we stopped our reading to get more information. Consulting a dictionary had worked well for us in the past, and that is what we tried this time. We deployed a strategy. We put together an understanding of the term, which we checked by rereading the text. Our constructed definition was adequate and we continued reading. (An aside: How close was our definition to that of Harris and Hodges', 1995, in *The Literacy Dictionary: The Vocabulary of Reading and Writing*? Close enough, we believe, for comprehension to occur. Harris and Hodges defined metacognition as "awareness and knowledge of one's mental processes such that one can monitor, regulate, and direct them as a desired end; self-mediation," p. 153.)

Since Flavell's article, the notion of metacognition has been applied to learning across the content areas. The goal of this chapter is to clarify and expand understanding of the role of metacognition in literacy. The chapter has four main sections. It begins with a survey of the research on metacognition and reading. Next it examines the current state of metacognitive and literacy instruction. The third section is a discussion of metacognitive literacy instruction and practice, that is, the role of metacognition in literacy instruction. Finally, directions for future research on metacognitive literacy instruction are considered.

RESEARCH REVIEW

The focus of this chapter is the grounding of metacognitive research within literacy instruction. As we surveyed the research literature, our own metacognitive abilities led us to construct pertinent questions around which we organized the information on metacognition. Our questions are as follows:

- What is involved in skilled reading and what is the role of metacognition in skilled reading?
- How has metacognition been described as it applies to reading?
- What is a reading strategy? What is a reading skill?
- What is the relation between reader interest and metacognition?

What Is Involved in Skilled Reading and What Is the Role of Metacognition in Skilled Reading?

Skilled reading consists of the interaction of macro- and microprocesses with prior knowledge that results in the reader constructing a mental picture of the text (Irwin, 1991; Kintsch & van Dijk, 1978; van den Broek & Kremer, 2000). At the macrolevel, the reader relies on summarization and the author's organizational structure to construct a coherent representation of the text. Working at the sentence, or microlevel, the reader attempts to make sense of individual idea units, first by grouping words into meaningful phrases and then by tying together the idea units. At both the macro- and microlevels, the reader must connect the information in the text to concepts in background knowledge. Along the way, the reader makes inferences and elaborations that make sense based on prior knowledge and information in the text (Pearson & Johnson, 1978; Raphael, 1986; Reder, 1980). Fluent reading and a well-developed meaning vocabulary facilitate this process (Pressley, 2002). Figure 1.1 represents this ongoing process.

The execution of any complex skill requires the coordination of many component processes. Attention plays a crucial role in this coordination. Yet, human attentional capacity is limited (LaBerge & Samuels, 1985; van den Broek & Kremer, 2000). Readers must constantly make decisions that impinge on their comprehension of text: when to reread a portion of text, when and what type of inference to make, what information of importance to retain in memory and what information of lesser importance to discard, when to move on in the reading of text and at what rate. Each of these decisions requires selective allocation

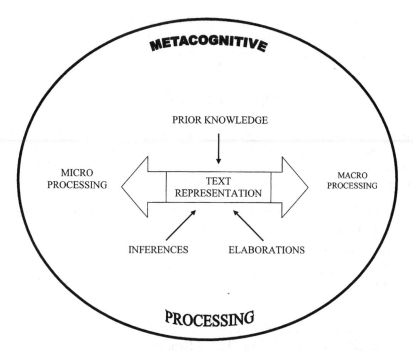

FIG. 1.1.   The ongoing process of skilled reading.

of cognitive resources, for example, making a determination to focus attention on text that is important or hard to understand (Wade, Schraw, Buxton, & Hayes, 1993). Readers use metacognitive information to monitor their comprehension for success or failure, and to distribute attentional resources. Note in Fig. 1.1 that we have embedded the cognitive processes of skilled reading within the frame of metacognition because skilled reading breaks down without ongoing monitoring.

Frequently, a reading event is depicted in three phrases: preparing to read, constructing meaning while reading, and reviewing and reflecting on reading (Paris, Wasik, & Turner, 1991). Pressley (2002) described the actions of a skilled reader during each phase. Figure 1.2 summarizes the characteristics of a skilled reader.

How Has Metacognition Been Described as It Applies to Reading?

A. L. Brown (1985) and Baker and A. L. Brown (1984) built on Flavell's model to discuss the relation between metacognitive skills and reading. According to Baker and Brown, metacognition consists of two interrelated clusters of information, which they referred to as *knowledge of cognition* and *regulation of cognition*.

Preparing to Read
- Is clear about the goals for reading
- Skims the text to get information about the length and structure of the text
- Activates prior knowledge

Constructing Meaning While Reading

- Reads selectively, reading quickly irrelevant information or rereading important, difficult, or interesting text
- Identifies main ideas
- Predicts
- Makes inferences
- Interprets and evaluates
- Integrates ideas into a coherent representation of the text
- Monitors understanding

Reviewing and Reflecting on Reading

- Self-questions for understanding
- Invokes strategies to review the text and comprehension
- Summarizes
- Continues to process the text based on reading goals

FIG. 1.2.   The characteristics of a skilled reader. Compiled from "The Development of Strategic Readers" in *Handbook of Reading Research* (pp. 609–640), by S. G. Paris, B. A. Wasik, and J. C. Turner, 1991, New York: Longman; and "Metacognition and Self-Regulated Comprehension" in *What Research Has to Say About Reading Instruction* (pp. 291–309), by M. Pressley, 2002, Newark, DE: International Reading Association.

Knowledge of cognition is stable and statable. It is the knowledge readers have about their own cognitive resources, about the reading task, and about the compatibility between the two. Paris, Lipson, and Wixson (1994) described this as the "that," the "how," the "when," and the "why" of metacognition. To illustrate, the readers could know *that* prior knowledge is important for reading comprehension, *how* to use previewing strategies to tap into prior knowledge, and *when* and *why* to adjust their reading rate to achieve the goals set for the reading event. Once this type of information has been established, it will continue to be known, and can be discussed.

The second cluster, the regulatory mechanisms used to solve a problem with comprehension during reading, includes the deployment of a remedy that involves "checking the outcome of [strategy use,] planning one's next move, monitoring the effectiveness of any attempted action, and testing, revising and evaluating one's strategies for learning" (Baker & A. L. Brown, 1984, p. 354). Regulatory mechanisms are not necessarily stable skills. Older children and adults typically use them, but younger children may also use regulatory mechanisms if the task is simple enough. In contrast, an older child or adult, faced with a task that is too hard, might not be able to put any regulatory mechanisms into operation (A. L. Brown, 1985).

Metacognition is considered to be a late-developing skill. Not many high school graduates and beginning college students are metacognitively mature with respect to reading. Flavell (1979) reported that preschool and elementary school-children, when asked to study a set of items until they were sure they could recall them, said they could remember the items when they usually could not do so. Paris and Myers (cited in Paris & Winograd, 1990) reported that 10-year-olds failed to identify many scrambled phrases and nonsense words while reading. According to A. L. Brown (1985), college students and older high school students are better at planning ahead than younger children. They are more sensitive to fine gradations of importance in text, and in their ability to summarize.

What Is a Reading Strategy? What Is a Reading Skill?

The notion of strategy plays an important role in any discussion of reading and metacognition. Strategic readers are distinguished by their ability to match appropriate strategies to the reading situation (Paris et al., 1991). The terms *strategy* and *skill* both emerge in reviews of the reading process and reading instruction (i.e., a strategic reader, skilled reading). These terms have been used indiscriminately without regard to differential meaning, interchangeably, or quite distinctively to describe different types of processes during reading. This chapter adopts the notion of strategy employed by Paris and colleagues (Paris et al., 1994; Paris et al., 1991). According to Paris et al. (1994), an action becomes strategic when it is selected from among alternatives to attain an intended goal. Thus, the use of a strategy is intentional and purposeful. In contrast, Paris et al. (1991) described a skill as an automatic process applied unconsciously. However, they suggested the interchangeability of skills and strategies by saying that "an emerging skill can become a strategy when used intentionally" (p. 611), and that a strategy can become a skill. "Indeed, strategies are more efficient and developmentally advanced when they become generated and applied as skills" (Paris et al., 1991, p. 611).

Wade, Trathen, and Schraw (1990) took an interesting view of a strategy as being a configuration of different tactics used to meet a particular goal and monitored for effectiveness. They tested this theory by devising a list of study tactics that fell under three categories: text noting, mental learning, and reading. Undergraduate students reported retrospectively on their study methods after reading a large segment of text. Using the self-report information from the students, these researchers identified six categories of study tactics.

Wade et al.'s (1990) Good Strategy User was the closest to other characterizations of skilled, metacognitive readers (Presley, Borkowski, & Schneider, cited in

Wade et al., 1990). A Good Strategy User employed a diverse set of tactics flexibly, showed the greatest use of text-noting tactics (e.g., highlighting, paraphrasing in notes, and diagramming), but also used reading tactics (e.g., reading slowly, skimming, rereading selected portions of the text). Good Strategy Users also used mental integration (mental-learning tactic) to draw connections between ideas in the text and to mentally summarize.

However, the Good Strategy User was not the only category identified. Other skillful users of strategies included Information Organizer, Flexible Reader, Text-Noter, Mental Integrator, and Memorizer. This finding is consistent with Dole, K. J. Brown, and Trathen's (1996) assertion that higher achieving readers comprehend more when they use their preferred strategies. Although lower achievers may benefit from learning specific strategies, better readers benefit more from becoming metacognitively skillful at deploying strategies they do use.

What Is the Relation Between Reader Interest and Metacognition?

Interest is related to attention, deeper processing, and learning (Wade, Buxton, & Kelly, 1999). Deci (cited in Wade, Buxton, & Kelly, 1999) equated interest with intrinsic motivation, or behavior that is characterized by concentration and motivation. Using think-aloud protocols to examine reader interest, Wade et al. (1999) identified text characteristics associated with undergraduate readers' interest. These characteristics were labeled importance/value, unexpected, and reader's connections. Texts that contained information the reader valued, but had not known before, were rated as interesting. Likewise, texts containing information that was different from their prior knowledge, assumptions, or beliefs, or that could be related to their own personal experiences, were also rated interesting.

Wade et al. (1999) also found some text characteristics that were negatively associated with interest. Typically, these characteristics made the text difficult to process, for example: text that did not contain adequate explanations for important concepts (essentially a text that did not have sufficient background information); text that was not well organized or did not flow, preventing the reader from constructing a coherent macrostructure; or text with difficult vocabulary. According to Flavell (1979), metacognitive experiences can affect a reader's metacognitive knowledge base. In some cases, the result is an elaboration of metacognitive strategies. However, experiences with difficult or poorly constructed text may have a negative effect as well. Paris and Winograd (1990) emphasized that self-appraisal and self-management are personal assessments that have an affective component. According to Paris and Winograd, "Expectations, perceptions of the task, and attributions for success and failure can all be regarded as emotionally charged metacognitions" (p. 25).

CURRENT STATE OF METACOGNITIVE
AND LITERACY INSTRUCTION

Metacognitive studies have provided literacy educators with greater understanding of reading comprehension processes and compensatory strategies that successful readers employ to support text understanding. These studies have also generated a plethora of ideas for effective comprehension instruction.

Although a careful review of current literature on metacognition reveals an overwhelming amount of information on metacognition and reading comprehension, less information can be found on how metacognition is related to writing, early literacy, and critical literacy.

Metacognition and Writing

There is a corollary between the phases of reading and stages in the writing process. That is, reading and writing may be thought of as complimentary processes involving the use of similar cognitive strategies, including planning and goal setting, tapping prior knowledge, organizing ideas, constructing a gist, monitoring, applying fix-up strategies, revising meaning, and evaluating (Booth, 2003; Tompkins, 2003). Although connected, the two processes require deployment of strategies in somewhat different ways. Langer (cited in Booth, 2003) indicated that formulating meaning occurs more recursively during writing because the writer must constantly generate new text. In addition, whereas readers are involved in adapting their representation of the text to fit the author's message, the writer is engaged in a process of fitting the text to "the needs of another person, a reader, and to the constraints of formal prose" (Flower & Hayes, cited in Booth, 2003, p. 15). We suggest that an important role in metacognitive literacy instruction is helping students determine how cognitive strategies are used during reading and writing.

Metacognition and Early Literacy

Early literacy is an extremely important area in literacy research and instruction. Although metacognition concerns higher level cognitive operations and processes and is generally found in more mature and older students (Baker & A. L. Brown, 1984; Paris & Winograd, 1990), there is evidence that young children are also able to monitor and regulate their cognitive processes during reading and writing activities (Brenna, 1995; Cox, 1994; Rowe, 1994; Ruan, 2004).

Metacognitive research should expand its current focus to cover early literacy. Modeling and teaching developmentally appropriate metacognitive skills to young children can greatly enhance their abilities to acquire early literacy skills and empower them to become problem solvers and independent readers. A lesson learned from the highly successful Reading Recovery program is that young children and immature readers can benefit greatly from metacognitive training. The children receiving Reading Recovery tutoring are taught to monitor their reading by constantly asking themselves whether or not what they have read makes sense, sounds right, or looks right. They are also taught to use a list of highly successful fix-up strategies when they encounter difficulties during reading. These strategies include using semantic cues (pictures, background knowledge, context, etc.), syntactic cues (knowledge of sentence structure), and graphophonemic cues (knowledge of sound–letter relation) to decode an unfamiliar word, cross-checking their decoding attempts with all three cuing systems (i.e., rereading, skipping the word, and reading on), and asking for help from others, to name a few. Most students are able to develop a self-monitoring and self-regulating mechanism at the completion of the tutoring.

Young children who are developing phonemic awareness can also benefit from metacognitive training. They can be taught to self-report how they identify rhyming words, syllables, and individual sounds. They can also be taught to verbalize their concepts about print.

Metacognition and Critical Literacy

Critical literacy goes beyond traditional literacy, which emphasizes literal text comprehension. According to McDaniel (2004), "Critical literacy transcends conventional notions of reading and writing to incorporate critical thinking, questioning, and transformation of self or one's world" (p. 474). Critical literacy researchers and scholars take into account the sociocultural aspect of literacy practices and call for readers to carefully examine texts for hidden agenda and assumptions held by the authors or the society in general. From the critical literacy stance, it is not enough that readers comprehend what they have read. They have to critically analyze the social structure and power relationship reflected in texts and ultimately to take actions to achieve social equity and justice (Luke & Freebody, 1997).

Because of the unique emphasis that critical literacy places on questioning and evaluating texts for potential biases and inequality, readers who exercise critical literacy have to closely monitor their reading. In addition to gaining literal understanding of the text, they have to use their own sociocultural knowledge and resources to inform their decision-making about the text, that is, to negotiate the discrepancies in different ideologies, to identify with, or to challenge the author's messages.

Although no existing literature specifically points out the connection between metacognition and critical literacy, the two are closely related to each other. Readers with critical literacy knowledge and skills are most likely to employ metacognitive strategies for text understanding and critiquing. Metacognitive research can generate important implications concerning how we support readers in developing critical literacy.

METACOGNITIVE LITERACY INSTRUCTION AND PRACTICE

In light of the critical role of metacognition in skilled reading, we propose that metacognitive instruction should be a much-valued component in literacy instruction. The goal of metacognitive literacy instruction is for students to develop metacognitive awareness and self-regulatory mechanisms to support problem solving when they are engaged in literacy related activities. This instruction aims at supporting students in forming a learning system that aligns assessment of one's cognitive resources with its allocation and the execution of the task-specific strategies in different learning situations.

Because metacognitive studies have their roots in comprehension studies, most instructional strategies in this area focus on supporting reading comprehension. In particular, research in the past three decades suggests that teaching students to monitor their reading is crucial to success in reading comprehension (Baker & A. L. Brown, 1984). The self-monitoring process can range from goal setting (Baker & A. L. Brown, 1984) to self-questioning (Andre & Anderson, 1978–1979), using mental imagery (Gambrell & Bales, 1986; Pressley, 1976), and deploying fix-up strategies.

These strategies are applicable to both reading and writing activities. For example, goal setting in reading entails the readers setting a purpose for reading, reading for information or for pleasure, and indicating the type of information most valued by the reader. In writing, goal setting can also lead to success of the writing effort. It is related to audience awareness and purpose for the writing (e.g., to inform or to entertain).

Several instructional methods have been demonstrated effective in promoting students' metacognitive development. They are more closely related to supporting the development of reader self-regulation. The strategies include Reciprocal Teaching (Palincsar & Brown, 1984), think-alouds (Baumann, Jones, & Seifert-Kessell, 1993), and Question–Answer Relationships (Raphael, 1986), among others. These instructional strategies generally focus on processes such as questioning, predicting, clarifying, and summarizing and promote student interactions with text and self-monitoring for greater understanding. They also involve powerful teacher modeling and student guided practices, which are keys to successful learning.

Beyond the identification of specific learner strategies and instructional strategies, metacognitive literacy research also points to the close interrelation between reader's interest and reading comprehension. Because reader interest decides the allocation of cognitive resources (Wade et al., 1993), in order for successful reading to occur, the reader has to show and maintain interest during the reading. Metacognitive instruction should teach students to assess their interest and be able to sustain their interest throughout the reading.

For successful reading to happen, both reader strategies and background knowledge have to be in place (Baker & A. L. Brown, 1984). It is ineffective to focus on strategy use without helping students build sufficient background knowledge.

Teaching for strategies should be emphasized over teaching isolated skills and bits and pieces of knowledge. Strategy use implies a process involving careful and deliberate selection of strategies to accomplish a set purpose (Wade et al., 1990). Teaching students to use strategies for problem solving during reading and writing activities also implies that teachers should teach students to develop metacognitive awareness, knowledge that allows them to understand the task nature/demand, steps to take to complete the task, and under what conditions (contexts). These are generally referred to as metacognitive declarative, procedural, and conditional knowledge (Jacobs & Paris, 1987).

Research has also suggested that instruction on using specific strategies benefits low performing readers, more than high performing readers, with their reading comprehension. Therefore, helping learners become metacognitive about the use of strategies in their current repertoire is more effective than asking them to learn to use different and new strategies (Dole et al., 1996). An implication from this research highlights the significance of support to learners in assessing and taking an inventory of strategies that are currently in use effectively in various learning situations.

One aspect that influences learners' ability to deploy self-regulatory mechanisms for problem solving is the level of task difficulty. Active control of one's cognitive resources occurs when the learner encounters "tasks of intermediate difficulty" (Baker & A. L. Brown, 1984, p. 354). Learners could fail to mobilize their self-regulatory mechanism when the task difficulty level is too high or when the learning situation does not pose much challenge and there is therefore no need to activate the cognitive resources. When supporting students in their development of metacognitive knowledge and control, carefully selected reading materials should be considered.

Based on the review of literature, successful metacognitive literacy instruction should address the following components: student background knowledge and schema development, knowledge and practice of a set of developmentally appropriate metacognitive strategies, knowledge of the conditions for the deployment of compensatory strategies. Teacher modeling and scaffolding are extremely important for students to develop self-regulatory mechanisms.

The two scenarios that follow demonstrate how teachers can support the development of regulatory mechanisms with beginning and developing literacy learners. The first scenario is about self-regulation focusing on metalinguistic knowledge; the second is about self-regulation focusing on writing. In each case, the teacher scaffolds instruction by analyzing the task to be carried out by the students, determining what part of the task might be difficult for the students, and providing practice with strategies that enable the students to successfully complete the task (Booth, 2003).

In the first scenario, we see a first-grade teacher sharing a big book, *Old McDonald Had a Farm*, with a group of first graders at the beginning of the school year. The teacher is focusing on helping students develop metalinguistic awareness, the ability to talk about language as an object of learning (Goodman, 1986). Metalinguistic awareness is a critical indicator of young children's metacognitive knowledge. During the read-aloud and the before and after reading phases, the teacher constantly uses metalinguistic terms such as *letter*, *sound*, *word*, and *sentence*. Several times during the reading, the teacher asks some children to identify those elements of language while she provides praise and informative feedback. The teacher gives each student a card with icons that represent letter, word, sound, and sentence and an example for each. After the teacher read-aloud, the children are given their own little books to read. The teacher checks on individual students. They are asked to identify each element of language as she frequently models and to share an example of each with her. When the students get stuck, she reminds them to look at the card and visualize each object. After several sessions of practice, the students are able to master the metalinguistic terms. This instructional practice helps to develop in young children various levels of awareness and understanding about language.

In the second scenario, a group of fourth graders are asked to write an essay helping their first grader book buddies use the library computer to search for books they want. In the class, the teacher has just finished his mini-lesson on how to write instructions. He shares with the class an essay on planting tulip bulbs in his garden. He discusses with the class the text structure and language features of instructions. As a class, they construct a chart with major elements of the text structure identified. They also highlight the language features/wording choices that most frequently appear in this type of text. He tells the students that when they write their essay, if they encounter a problem, they can refer to the chart for help. The teacher then asks the students to make a checklist of things they should pay attention to when they write their instructions. Next he sends his students to the library to investigate the steps it takes to find a book they want in the school's library system and to record the steps they identify. He reminds them that if they have difficulty, they can refer to the checklist and look up the chart on text structure and wording choices displayed on one of the classroom walls. Many students do exactly what he said. They plan what their essays should include, monitor their own progress during the writing, and evaluate and revise the draft against the chart to produce satisfactory essays.

DIRECTIONS FOR FUTURE RESEARCH

Research efforts in the past three decades have produced a plethora of findings important to the understanding of literacy and teaching. However, several issues demand further research:

1. To what extent should metacognitive instruction be promoted within a literacy curriculum? In most literacy curricula in use across the country, metacognitive literacy instruction is not promoted or emphasized. Although many literacy educators advocate that teachers should emphasize teaching for strategies instead of teaching isolated skills and facts (Fountas & Pinnel, 1996), limited research has been conducted to assess the effect of a literacy curriculum focusing on strategies versus traditional literacy instruction focusing on skills and knowledge.

2. How can teachers support students in developing self-regulation mechanisms? Currently, there is no coherent body of literature on what self-regulatory mechanisms are like, how they operate, or on the efficient orchestration of various metacognitive strategies. According to Baker and A. L. Brown (1984), there are five indexes of self-regulatory mechanism, namely, checking, monitoring, testing, revising, and evaluating. How a reader or writer decides what processes to mobilize and under what circumstances remains an unanswered question. Information on how different mechanisms manifest themselves in learners with different learner characteristics is needed. Part of the difficulty results from the wide variety of literacy learning situations that demand different mechanisms. More substantive information on how self-regulatory mechanisms operate in various learning situations is necessary.

3. Teacher knowledge of metacognition and metacognitive literacy instruction should be investigated. Limited substantive research could be found in this regard. In order for teachers to be successful in implementing metacognitive literacy instruction, an adequate knowledge base on metacognitive literacy instructional practices should be identified for teachers. This knowledge base could also facilitate teacher self-analysis and support teacher learning in developing the expertise necessary for effective metacognitive literacy instruction.

4. Reader threshold for incoherence and ambiguity is another area for investigation. Readers have to notice comprehension failure in order to regulate and deploy fix-up strategies. The way mature and immature readers establish their threshold for activating mechanisms for using compensatory strategies should be more carefully researched.

5. The transfer of metacognitive strategies among different areas of literacy, for example, from reading to writing, or from decoding to comprehension should be studied. Raphael, Englert, and Kirschner (1989) found evidence that upper elementary school students were able to apply their metacognitive knowledge about writing to a reading situation. However, limited research can be found in relation to metacognitive knowledge transfer among different areas of literacy.

6. Past research has identified a number of strategies that support good reading comprehension, and has established that a good reader is able to deploy a variety of strategies (Wade et al., 1990) depending on the interest level, background knowledge, and difficulty level of the text. However, there is no clear understanding of if and how some strategies are chosen over others. The question

remains as to whether or not there is a set of strategies that is more readily activated by the reader and how.

7. Much research has been conducted to explore metacognition and reading. Because of the important role of writing in making a literate person, it is important to investigate the relation between metacognitive knowledge and control and writing development. In addition, how metacognitive instruction can benefit students' writing development also demands more attention from metacognitive researchers.

CONCLUSIONS

Metacognition is a key to successful learning. Learners with high levels of metacognitive abilities are able to monitor and regulate their learning processes to accomplish the learning goals they set. More importantly, supporting learners in developing self-regulation mechanisms should be an important aspect of metacognitive literacy instruction.

Although Baker (2002) argued that metacognition should not be the focus of reading instruction, it should be the goal of literacy instruction if we want to support learners' movement toward independence and success. Teachers should place metacognitive instruction at the center of instruction for all learners, albeit at different levels and with different strategy components.

Consider three cautionary points. We do not intend to make the term into a buzzword or a bandwagon. The term is used to help conceptualize the type of instruction that has its distinctive strengths and focus. Second, because metacognitive abilities involve higher level cognitive processes, teachers should be more aware of their students' cognitive abilities and basic knowledge/skills development. Different students might have different self-regulation mechanisms with different sets of metacognitive strategies closely related to their own cognitive facilities and knowledge/skill base. Metacognitive literacy instruction expecting all students to develop the same type of mechanisms could be an act of hit and miss. Third, the ultimate goal of literacy instruction is to develop lifelong readers and writers who enjoy literacy activities and use literacy to better themselves and their society. Therefore, metacognitive literacy instruction should be a means instead of an end to literacy instruction.

METACONNECTION FOR CHAPTER 1

Chapter 1 defines metacognition and literacy learning relative to theory. Skilled reading strategies are discussed in relationship to metacognitive strategy application. The following chapter guides us as we learn more about the relationship between reading comprehension and metacognition.

REFERENCES

Andre, M.D.A., & Anderson, T. H. (1978–1979). The development and evaluation of a self-questioning study technique. *Reading Research Quarterly, 14,* 405–623.

Baker, L. (2002). Metacognitive comprehension instruction. In C. C. Block & M. Pressley (Eds.), *Comprehension instruction: Research-based best practices* (pp. 77–95). New York: The Guilford Press.

Baker, L., & Brown, A. L. (1984). Metacognitive skills and reading. In P. D. Pearson, R. Barr, M. L. Kamil, & P. Mosenthal (Eds.), *Handbook of reading research* (pp. 353–394). New York: Longman.

Baumann, J. F., Jones, L. A., & Seifert-Kessell, N. (1993). Using think alouds to enhance children's comprehension monitoring abilities. *The Reading Teacher, 47*(3), 184–193.

Booth, C. B. (2003). *The reading/writing connection: Strategies for teaching and learning in the secondary classroom.* Boston: Allyn & Bacon.

Brenna, B. A. (1995). The metacognitive reading strategies of five early readers. *Journal of Research in Reading, 18*(1), 53–62.

Brown, A. L. (1985). Metacognition: The development of selective attention strategies for learning from texts. In H. Singer & R. B. Ruddell (Eds.), *Theoretical models and processes of reading* (3rd ed., pp. 501–526). Newark, DE: International Reading Association.

Cox, B. E. (1994). Young children's regulatory talk: Evidence of emergent metacognitive control over literary products and processes. In R. Ruddell, M. Ruddell, & H. Singer (Eds.), *Theoretical models and processes of reading* (4th ed., pp. 733–756). Newark, DE: International Reading Association.

Dole, J. A., Brown, K. J., & Trathen, W. (1996). The effects of strategy instruction on the comprehension performance of at-risk students. *Reading Research Quarterly, 31,* 62–88.

Flavell, J. H. (1979). Metacognition and cognitive monitoring: A new area of cognitive-developmental inquiry. *American Psychologist, 34,* 906–911.

Fountas, I., & Pinnel, G. S. (1996). *Guided reading: Good first teaching for all children.* Portsmouth, NH: Heinemann.

Gambrell, L. B., & Bales, R. J. (1986). Mental imagery and the comprehension-monitoring performance of fourth- and fifth-grade poor readers. *Reading Research Quarterly, 21,* 454–464.

Goodman, Y. (1986). Children coming to know literacy. In W. Teale & E. Sulzby (Eds.), *Emergent literacy: Writing and reading* (pp. 1–14). Norwood, NJ: Ablex.

Harris, T. L., & Hodges, R. E. (Eds.). (1995). *The literacy dictionary: The vocabulary of reading and writing.* Newark, DE: International Reading Association.

Irwin, J. W. (1991). *Teaching reading comprehension processes* (2nd ed.). Boston: Allyn & Bacon.

Jacobs, J. E., & Paris, S. G. (1987). Children's metacognition about reading: Issues in the definition, measurement, and instruction. *Educational Psychologist, 22,* 255–278.

Kintsch, W. M., & van Dijk, T. A. (1978). Toward a model of text comprehension and production. *Psychological Review, 95*(2), 163–182.

LaBerge, D., & Samuels, S. J. (1985). Toward a theory of automatic information processing in reading. In H. Singer & R. B. Ruddell (Eds.), *Theoretical models and processes of reading* (3rd ed., pp. 689–718). Newark, DE: International Reading Association.

Luke, A., & Freebody, P. (1997). Shaping the social practices of reading. In S. Muspratt, A. Luke, & P. Freebody (Eds.), *Constructing critical literacies: Teaching and learning textual practices* (pp. 185–225). Cresskill, NJ: Hampton Press.

McDaniel, C. (2004). Critical literacy: A questioning stance and the possibility for change. *The Reading Teacher, 57*(5), 472–481.

Palincsar, A. S., & Brown, A. L. (1984). Reciprocal teaching of comprehensive-fostering and comprehension-monitoring activities. *Cognition and Instruction*, *1*, 117–175.

Paris, S. G., & Winograd, P. (1990). How metacognition can promote academic learning and instruction. In B. F. Jones & L. Idol (Eds.), *Dimensions of thinking and cognitive instruction* (pp. 15–51). Hillsdale, NJ: Lawrence Erlbaum Associates.

Paris, S. G., Lipson, J. Y., & Wixson, K. K. (1994). Becoming a strategic reader. In R. B. Ruddell, M. R. Ruddell, & H. Singer (Eds.), *Theoretical models and processes of reading* (4th ed., pp. 778–810). Newark, DE: International Reading Association.

Paris, S. G., Wasik, B. A., & Turner, J. C. (1991). The development of strategic readers. In R. Barr, M. L. Kamil, P. B. Mosenthal, & P. D. Pearson (Eds.), *Handbook of reading research* (Vol. 2, pp. 609–640). New York: Longman.

Pearson, P. D., & Johnson, D. D. (1978). *Teaching reading comprehension*. New York: Holt, Rinehart & Winston.

Pressley, M. (1976). Mental imagery helps eight-year-olds remember what they read. *Journal of Educational Psychology*, *68*, 355–359.

Pressley, M. (2002). Metacognition and self-regulated comprehension. In A. E. Farstrup & S. J. Samuels (Eds.), *What research has to say about reading instruction* (3rd ed., pp. 291–309). Newark, DE: International Reading Association.

Raphael, T. E. (1986). Teaching question–answer relationships revisited. *The Reading Teacher*, *40*, 516–522.

Raphael, T. E., Englert, C. S., & Kirschner, B. W. (1989). Students' metacognitive knowledge about writing. *Research in the Teaching of English*, *23*(9), 343–379.

Reder, L. M. (1980). The role of elaboration in the comprehension and retention of prose: A critical review. *Review of Educational Research*, *50*, 5–53.

Rowe, D. (1994). *Preschoolers as authors: Literacy learning in the social world of the classroom*. Cresskill, NJ: Hampton Press.

Ruan, J. (2004). Bilingual Chinese/English first graders developing metacognition about writing. *Journal of Literacy*, *38*(2), 106–112.

Tompkins, G. E. (2003). *Literacy in the 21st century* (3rd ed.). Upper Saddle River, NJ: Merrill.

Van den Broek, P., & Kremer, K. E. (2000). The mind in action: What it means to comprehend during reading. In B. M. Taylor, M. F. Graves, & P. van den Broek (Eds.), *Reading for meaning: Fostering comprehension in the middle grades* (pp. 1–31). New York: Teacher's College Press.

Wade, S. E., Buxton, W., & Kelly, M. (1999). Using think alouds to examine reader-text interest. *Reading Research Quarterly*, *34*, 194–216.

Wade, S. E., Schraw, G., Buxton, W. M., & Hayes, M. T. (1993). Seduction of the strategic readers: Effects of interest on strategies and recall. *Reading Research Quarterly*, *28*, 92–114.

Wade, S. E., Trathen, W., & Schraw, G. (1990). An analysis of spontaneous study strategies. *Reading Research Quarterly*, *25*, 147–166.

Webster's new collegiate dictionary. (1973). Springfield, MA: Merriam.

2

Revisiting Definitions of Reading Comprehension: Just What Is Reading Comprehension Anyway?

Judi Randi
University of New Haven

Elena L. Grigorenko
Robert J. Sternberg
Yale University

It is important and vital to measure student's awareness of strategic comprehension processes in order to know the problems which students are having with understanding what they are reading and to identify decoding strategies which they may be misapplying or not using at all.

When children fail to understand what they read, this impacts on how well they will perform in every academic study area. A science teacher related to a class I attended that he was instructed to write his objectives on the board for each lesson he taught. It was illogical for him to do this since these students he was teaching science to did not have the ability to read the objectives and as a result would have no understanding of what he wrote. These students are obviously having problems with processing what they are reading and need help to rectify their comprehension processing.

To be made aware of students' strategic comprehension processes would enable teachers to cater to the instructional level of the child. Identifying and addressing problems students are having with comprehension processes, would enable teachers to increase the understanding of students and their ability to problem solve. This would result in higher order thinking culminating in self directed learning.

—Cecelia Batson

In her observational study, Durkin (1978) examined reading comprehension instruction in the upper elementary grades and found surprisingly little of it going on. Since then, there has been much interest in providing teachers with the knowledge and skills necessary to teach reading comprehension effectively. Research on reading instruction began to focus teachers' attention on the cognitive processes good readers use to comprehend text, providing detailed descriptions of what effective readers do. Reading comprehension research has identified more than 30 cognitive and metacognitive processes involved in reading comprehension (see, e.g., Collins Block & Pressley, 2002).

Although theories of reading comprehension abound, in practice, there appears to be little teaching of reading comprehension. In 1998, researchers published a study providing evidence that there may be more testing of reading comprehension than there is instruction guiding students in processing text in ways that contribute to understanding (Pressley, Wharton-McDonald, Mistretta-Hampton, & Echevarria, 1998). Teachers typically assess reading comprehension by asking "comprehension questions." But assessment is no substitute for instruction, especially if the questions are intended to assess literal comprehension. Moreover, if students are able to answer such questions, then does it necessarily mean they *understand* what they have read? Exactly what does it mean to "comprehend" what one reads?

This chapter explores different definitions of reading comprehension that have informed reading comprehension research, reading instruction, and assessment practices. How has reading comprehension been defined by researchers, teachers, and those interested in assessing reading comprehension? Has there ever been a single definition of reading comprehension? To answer these questions, the discussion first revisits theoretical conceptions of reading comprehension that have guided the study, teaching, and assessment of reading comprehension. Next, it reviews the research base on reading comprehension instruction, including research on the cognitive processes that make readers' thinking visible. Reading comprehension research has typically focused on the cognitive processes thought to be components of reading comprehension. In this program of research, the goal has often been to identify the skills readers need to "comprehend" or make sense of the text to arrive at commonly agreed on meanings. Assessments consistent with this conception of reading comprehension evaluate the component processes used to comprehend text at the literal level. More contemporary assessments of reading comprehension, however, are informed by a different conception of reading comprehension that takes into account how readers interact with the text to construct meaning and to interpret the text in personally relevant ways (Rosenblatt, 1978). This chapter argues that a unifying definition of reading comprehension is essential both to the teaching and the testing of reading for understanding. It concludes by describing a componential approach to reading comprehension instruction that contributes both to the literal and interpretive understanding of text as well as to personal enjoyment of reading.

DEFINITIONS OF READING COMPREHENSION

One early definition of reading comprehension viewed "reading as a process of communication by which a message is transmitted graphically between individuals" (Kingston, 1967, p. 72). Kingston argued that reading comprehension depends on the reader's interpretation of the written symbols conveyed by the author, much as in the interpretation of an abstract painting. He noted that, given how unlikely it is for all individuals to attach identical associations to any given symbol, reading comprehension is often measured by the degree to which readers conform to some authority figure's interpretation (e.g., teacher or test constructor).

Reading comprehension is a complex process that is difficult to define, much less teach and assess. For more than two decades, researchers have attempted to identify the processes effective readers use. The goal is that teachers articulate those strategies to novice readers. Pioneering research in this area described a set of comprehension-monitoring strategies students could practice in a reciprocal teaching format (Palincsar & Brown, 1984). Readers' intentional use of these cognitive strategies, which include summarizing, generating questions, clarifying unfamiliar vocabulary, and making and revising predictions, has been found to improve reading comprehension (Rosenshine & Meister, 1994).

Although reading comprehension research has identified individual cognitive processes efficient readers use, it is less clear how these strategies work together to contribute to comprehension, and which skills are essential for comprehension to occur. For example, if a reader cannot summarize a passage concisely, does that indicate poor reading comprehension or lack of summarization skills? The answers may depend on the definition of reading comprehension.

If meaning resides in the text, then comprehension involves summarizing and recalling what is stated in the text; generating a unique interpretation consistent with one's own experiences may be inappropriate for arriving at the meaning agreed on by the majority of readers. Winograd and Johnston (1987) called attention to this distinction between personally constructed and socially constructed meaning. They argued that research has tended to view reading comprehension as an end convergent on a single meaning perhaps best achieved through the use of strategies. They called for an expanded definition of reading comprehension that recognizes both the personal and social construction of meaning. Personally constructed meaning arises from the interaction between reader and text and reading is a generative activity that results in unique interpretations of the same text by different readers (Rosenblatt, 1978). In this view, readers' prior knowledge and experiences serve more central roles and readers' interpretations are more likely to be different than convergent on one traditional meaning. Reading comprehension is thought to occur when readers bring to bear their prior knowledge and experiences to make sense of text, often rendering the author's ideas, the reader's (Pearson & Fielding, 1991).

This is a transactional view of reading comprehension that assumes the reader's active meaning-making role in dialogue with the author (Rosenblatt, 1978). Transactional strategy instruction, including teaching students to take active reader roles, helps students make predictions about stories, associate what they read with their prior knowledge, and construct mental images. It has been found to be effective in increasing reading achievement (Pressley & El-Dinary, 1997). But, as Winograd and Johnston (1987) pointed out, reading for enjoyment is not typically prompted by purpose setting strategies, such as reading to confirm predictions.

Rosenblatt (1978) distinguished "aesthetic reading" for the purpose of enjoyment from "efferent reading" for the purpose of information seeking. Other researchers (Guthrie & Mosenthal, 1987) have distinguished descriptive definitions of reading from pragmatic definitions. These researchers explained that theorists typically create descriptive definitions of reading that embody particular ideologies. For example, theorists may define features of reading materials that imply that meaning resides in the text. The pragmatic approach, on the other hand, is concerned with studying how people read in different settings and for different purposes. Building on the pragmatic approach, Guthrie and Mosenthal drew a distinction between reading comprehension and reading to locate information, arguing that reading for information is more strategic and goal directed. Reading comprehension research, however, has tended to take a theoretical approach to defining reading and has tended to view all reading as strategic.

READING COMPREHENSION RESEARCH

Reading comprehension is a complex cognitive process. Metacognition, or thinking about the cognitive processes involved in reading, has been a primary focus of reading comprehension research (see Baker, 2002, for a review of metacognition in comprehension instruction). One important defining feature of metacognition is that it can be made "public" (Jacobs & Paris, 1987). A goal of reading comprehension research has been articulating the cognitive processes used by effective readers. Defining these processes, however, risks reducing reading to an algorithm that may not be appropriate for different situations and different purposes.

Reading Comprehension Processes

Much research on reading comprehension has focused on identifying skills that may account for poor readers' deficits. Cain, Oakhill, and Bryant (2003) characterized poor comprehenders as a heterogeneous group whose difficulties are likely to derive from a variety of cognitive deficits, including weakness in understanding vocabulary and syntax. They summarized the reading comprehension deficits of poor comprehenders at the discourse level: difficulty making inferences, regardless of prior knowledge; lack of ability in identifying referent pronouns; lack of skill in using context clues, especially when abstract thinking is involved; weak comprehension monitoring skills and lack of ability to repair comprehension or vary strategy to purpose; and incomplete understanding of text structure. This research has focused on skills readers use to comprehend the literal meaning of text.

Kintsch (1988) identified similar processes used in text comprehension. At the sentence level, readers decode words and use knowledge of syntax to construct the meaning of sentences. At another level, relational processes are used to make connections across sentences or paragraphs. Other comprehension skills include making inferences and interpreting author's words and phrases that have been omitted.

Winograd and Johnston (1987) argued that conditional knowledge is necessary for reading comprehension and the teaching of reading comprehension can be advanced by understanding the conditions under which particular strategies are appropriate. They further argued that there are a limited variety of strategies in the reading comprehension research base and these strategies are not sufficient for understanding and interpreting text at more than a superficial level. Some reading comprehension programs have focused on helping students understand when to use particular strategies. Process-based comprehension instruction models strategies during the reading process at times when particular processes are called for (Collins Block, Schaller, Joy, & Gaine, 2002). In this model, students are encouraged to think about why the authors wrote as they did. Students are also encouraged to describe their own comprehension processes as they are used at particular times, rather than memorizing separate strategies to be applied universally.

Knowing when to use different comprehension processes to make sense of text may assist struggling readers in answering comprehension questions on reading achievement tests. One study analyzed reading comprehension errors made by 10 sixth-grade students on the Qualitative Reading Inventory (P. Dewitz & P. K. Dewitz, 2003). Consistent with Kintsch's comprehension processes and Cain et al.'s research on poor comprehenders, this study found that students' errors could be attributed to failure to make relational inferences (linking ideas across passages), failure to make causal inferences, failure to parse syntax correctly, inappropriate use of prior knowledge, or failure to know a key vocabulary word. The researchers hypothesized why strategy instruction may not solve the kinds of reading comprehension problems described in this case study. For example, some strategies may conflict with other strategies, such as drawing on prior knowledge to make a prediction and looking for connections across sentences and paragraphs to make causal inferences. The researchers also pointed out that strategies typically packaged in strategy instruction programs, such as reciprocal teaching, do not specifically match students' comprehension problems and students would benefit from learning when and which strategies to use, depending on the text and the purposes of reading.

Some classroom teachers have also questioned the appropriateness of strategy instruction. Villaume and Brabham (2002) described teachers' listserv discussions on teaching reading comprehension. Some teachers noted students' perfunctory use of strategies rather than the thoughtful interactions that strategy instruction is intended to promote. Other teachers described a different kind of strategy instruction in which teachers modeled their own thinking about text and encouraged students to generate and share their own strategies they use to interpret text. In these classrooms, students demonstrated more engagement and thoughtfulness. Nonetheless, whether reading comprehension strategies are applied universally or as the text demands, such strategies alone may not be sufficient for reading beyond the literal level. In classrooms that emphasize reading in authentic contexts, teachers and students may take a more pragmatic view of reading. Considering the complexity of reading comprehension, the research base may offer little guidance for teachers interested in promoting thoughtful interactions with text (Snow, 2002).

Research on Reading Comprehension Instruction

The research base on reading instruction has been the focus of several recent publications that have aimed to disseminate research findings about effective literacy instruction to educators. The National Reading Panel (2000) investigated studies of 16 categories of reading comprehension instruction. Of these, the panel identified 7 methods that appeared to have a scientific research base for concluding that they are effective in improving reading comprehension (pp. 4–42). The seven methods include comprehension-monitoring strategy instruction, cooperative learning, graphic organizers, discovering and describing story structure, question answering, question generating, and summarization. In addition, the panel concluded that many of these strategies have been used effectively in combination where readers and teachers interact with texts.

Although the National Reading Panel Report reported research on reading comprehension, teachers may not find the research base adequate for making informed decisions about how to teach reading comprehension effectively (Snow, 2002). The report of the Rand Reading Study Group (Snow, 2002) attempted to organize the research base on reading comprehension to identify gaps in the knowledge base. Reviewing the research, the Rand Study Group formulated a three-dimensional definition of reading comprehension that synthesized transactional, social, and functional theories of reading comprehension. Defined as "the process of simultaneously extracting and constructing meaning through interaction and involvement with written language," reading comprehension includes three elements: the reader, the text, and the activity or purpose for reading (p. 33). Whereas the National Reading Panel Report (2000) focused on interactions between text and reader, the Rand Study Group added the functional and social dimensions. From a social perspective, reading comprehension is a process of constructing meaning through interactions in particular settings, such as classrooms (Bloome & Egan-Robertson, 1993). From a functional perspective, comprehension focuses on the purposes of reading, such as for gathering information or for enjoyment, which often involves imagination or creative processes (Heath, 1980).

The Rand Study Group described reading comprehension as developmental and multifaceted. The Rand Group called for further research on reading comprehension strategy instruction, the conditions in which strategy instruction leads to improved reading comprehension, and the role of direct strategy instruction in inquiry-based content areas, such as science and history. The Rand Group also called for research on reading comprehension assessments, citing the need for more authentic reading assessments, implying that comprehension as measured on "tests" is of a different nature than comprehension in real-life contexts.

READING COMPREHENSION INSTRUCTION IN PRACTICE

Thus, widely differing conceptions of reading comprehension have guided reading comprehension research. These different conceptions of reading may also explain differences in instructional practices. A review of reading research and instruction suggests that those researchers finding little comprehension instruction in classrooms (Durkin, 1978; Pressley et al., 1998) may have been looking for direct instruction of comprehension strategies. Teachers, however, may have been prompting different types of comprehension processes through questioning and the facilitation of interactions with text. These teaching practices suggest that teachers may have a different conception of what constitutes reading comprehension—a conception that may be informed by observing their students' interactions and engagement with text, rather than focusing on discrete cognitive processes.

Looking for strategy instruction in the classroom, Pressley and his colleagues observed fourth- and fifth-grade language arts classrooms in upstate New York and found little actual teaching of comprehension processes (Pressley et al., 1998). These researchers found that teachers provided students with opportunities to interpret the text and discuss literature, but much of the interaction around the text was prompted by questions, rather than direct instruction in how to comprehend the text. But teachers ask questions both to assess and scaffold instruction (see, e.g., Dillon, 1988).

Teachers (and standardized achievement tests) regularly assess "reading comprehension," typically by asking "comprehension questions." But such questions are also used during instruction and classroom activities, often as the basis for literary discussions. Some research has found that classroom questioning is primarily at the literal level and students are not encouraged to interpret the text based on their prior experiences (M. D. Applegate, Quinn, & A. J. Applegate, 2002). Moving away from traditional text-based strategies, such as vocabulary instruction, however, other teachers encourage readers to bring their background knowledge to the text and engage in a dialog with the author (Borasi & Siegel, 2000). The questions these teachers ask may prompt engagement with the text in ways that promote more than a superficial understanding of text at the level of literal comprehension. In either case, however, teachers may ask questions more often than they provide explicit strategy instruction.

One reason for the lack of direct instruction in reading comprehension strategies may be that the comprehension strategies described in the literature thus far, even when "bundled" in programs such as reciprocal teaching or transactional strategy instruction, are insufficient for prompting interactions between the text and the reader in ways that promote understanding. For example, if a reader can summarize a passage, does that necessarily mean the reader comprehends the passage? One study, for instance, found that poor readers who could not answer inferential questions could answer other questions correctly simply by restating ideas in the text (P. Dewitz & P. K. Dewitz, 2003). Teachers interested in promoting more in-depth understanding of text may not see any value in training students in the procedural use of strategies that promote literal comprehension, without the need for thoughtful interactions with text. Moreover, this research found that certain strategies, such as drawing on prior knowledge, could actually interfere with higher level comprehension and interpretation as measured on reading achievement tests. Again, the question becomes which strategies are appropriate for which definition of reading comprehension.

Assessing Reading Comprehension

Traditional multiple-choice reading assessments are often intended to assess low level comprehension strategies rather than imaginative and interpretive stances. In a lecture delivered at Teacher's College, Hill (2000) described the tensions between low level operations and the more constructivist responses, which the distracters on multiple-choice tests often stimulate. Hill interviewed children about the choices they selected and the children were often able to substantiate a logical interpretation for choosing a distracter above the "right" answer. After all, this is the kind of thinking teachers tend to promote in children when they invite original interpretations and ask children to support their thinking with evidence from the text. Thus, in contrast to "comprehension questions" asked on traditional reading comprehension assessments, teachers' questions may be intended to prompt engagement and interaction with the text, rather than "the answers" typically expected on traditional reading comprehension assessments. Some teachers' classroom practices may be encouraging a more authentic "reading comprehension" than can be measured on traditional assessments. In other classrooms, "comprehension questions" of a more literal nature may focus students' attention on arriving at the meaning that most readers would assign, directed at preparing students for success on traditional assessments of reading comprehension (M. D. Applegate et al., 2002).

Some contemporary assessment programs, in contrast to more traditional multiple-choice assessments, include open-ended questions that require children to interpret the text and defend their interpretations, as well as demonstrate understanding at the literal level. These contemporary assessments, such as the National Assessment of Educational Progress (NAEP) and state assessments based on the NAEP frameworks (National Assessment Governing Board, 2002), typically include both traditional "one right answer" multiple-choice items and open-ended items requiring explanation. These different types of items require different levels of thinking and different approaches to reading comprehension (M. D. Applegate et al., 2002). Preparing students for success on such assessments may pose a dilemma for teachers attempting to promote personal engagement with text and original, thoughtful interpretations at the same time that they are accountable for ensuring that students select the "one right answer" for those questions requiring students to arrive at the commonly held interpretation.

READING COMPREHENSION: MAKING SENSE OF MIXED MESSAGES

In authentic reading situations, in contrast to testing situations, readers are more likely to adjust their reading strategies for different purposes. For example, individuals reading a novel for enjoyment may not be concerned about commonly held interpretations. This is what Rosenblatt (1978) described as an "aesthetic" stance, which teachers and parents promote when they read aloud stories, offer children a variety of reading selections that appeal to their interests, and encourage children to imagine being transported into the stories themselves (see also Winograd & Johnston, 1987). Furthermore, there is evidence that reading materials at home and at school are more likely to be different than they are the same. Some research has found that reading in school emphasizes different genres than reading at home and that few genres overlap (Duke & Purcell-Gates, 2003). Although children's books were commonly used both at school and at home, these researchers found that other reading materials, such as names, labels, newspapers, and correspondence were more common at home than at school. On the other hand, reading materials such as worksheets, journals, descriptive text, charts, and poems were more likely to be read in school than at home.

Similarly, in authentic contexts, when individuals read for information or what Rosenblatt (1978) termed "efferent" reading, readers skim the text for the information they need, and skilled readers remember less about what they read for information than poorer readers who read every word in informational text in search of "comprehension" (Cain, 1999). In short, reading in authentic contexts may make different demands on readers than reading in test situations. Nonetheless, even contemporary reading assessments that aim to simulate reading in more natural situations include items that assess literal comprehension and discrete skills.

Thus, teachers and students experience different aspects of reading comprehension, depending on the contexts for reading. Students hear different messages about what it means to read, including reading for convergent and divergent meanings, reading for information and reading for enjoyment, and reading in school and reading at home. At home, there are no journal entries, no comprehension questions, and no one to question personal interpretation. Multiple conceptions of what it means to read not only require students to understand that reading for information is different from reading for enjoyment but also that reading in school may be different than reading at home, and reading for tests may require different skills again.

A Componential Definition of Reading Comprehension

There is an approach to reading comprehension that prepares students for success on the test as well as for success in reading in authentic contexts. It is a componential theory of reading comprehension that synthesizes, integrates, and balances three aspects of reading comprehension, which in addition to memory (prior knowledge), work together to contribute to an understanding of text in almost any situation (see Sternberg, Grigorenko, & Jarvin, 2001).

Based on Sternberg's (1985, 1997) triarchic theory, *componential reading comprehension* is an instructional approach that encourages students to capitalize on their strengths to learn important content, including what they come to understand through integrating the analytical, creative, and practical aspects of reading text. For more than a decade, Sternberg's research group at Yale University has been investigating how Teaching for Successful Intelligence, an instructional approach based on Sternberg's triarchic theory, can be applied in classrooms to help children develop skills that will allow them to be successful in school as well as in life.

One current TSI research program is investigating the impact of TSI applied to language arts, science, and mathematics instruction in fourth-grade classrooms nationwide (Sternberg & Grigorenko, 2002a, 2002b). Our work in the area of language arts and reading informs the componential approach to reading comprehension presented here. Rather than teach isolated facts and skills, a componential approach to reading comprehension encourages students to integrate three aspects of intelligence that, in addition to memory, are needed for success both in and beyond the classroom: *analytical abilities*, characterized by cognitive processes such as analysis, evaluation, or comparison; *practical abilities*, characterized by application of knowledge in situation-specific tasks; and *creative abilities*, characterized by original thinking, invention, or imagination.

Triarchic instruction (TSI), for several reasons, is especially appropriate for teaching reading comprehension (Grigorenko, Jarvin, & Sternberg, 2002). First, this componential approach affords students opportunities to encode information in three different ways (analytical, practical, and creative) as well as for memory. In addition, students are encouraged to rehearse the information multiple times. Second, this approach may be especially motivating because it enables students to capitalize on their strengths and compensate for their weaknesses and it makes the material more interesting to students when they are able to "make the text their own" with personal connections and original interpretations. Third, this approach balances traditional memory-based skills instruction and analysis of text structure with opportunities for students to interact with text in personally relevant and creative ways, thus preparing students for success on the test, as well as success in authentic reading contexts.

Using Componential Reading Comprehension Skills in Authentic Reading Contexts

Componential reading comprehension is easily embedded into classroom environments that aim to simulate authentic reading contexts. Our approach seems consistent with the kinds of questioning some teachers use to prompt engagement and interpretation. For example, asking students to compare two characters requires analytical thinking. Asking students to imagine what might happen if a character had behaved differently requires creative thinking. Asking students if literary characters remind them of anyone they know is a practical question.

Analytical Comprehension and Instruction. Most language arts teachers provide instruction and learning experiences that require students to think analytically as part of the regular language arts curriculum. It is likely that, in most traditional language arts programs, analytical thinking is emphasized over practical or creative thinking. Most teachers will recognize examples of prompts for analytical thinking skills: compare and contrast (characters, plots, settings, word meanings), sequence or organize (sentences, paragraphs, events in a narrative), differentiate fact from opinion, give your opinion of/evaluate (this book, this idea, this information, different reference sources, your own work), use context clues to infer meaning of new vocabulary, and identify the cause and the effect.

In addition to teaching and prompting for specific skills, teachers also use instructional strategies that require analytical thinking. For example, semantic feature analysis (Anders & Bos, 1986) is a categorization strategy based on how individuals organize knowledge. Described in "teacher friendly" terms as "word sort," this strategy is commonly used to encourage students to identify and classify word patterns (see, for example, Cunningham, 2000). In word sorts, students group together words that have the same spelling patterns, the same definitions, the same phonetic sounds, the same roots or affixes, and so forth. Although semantic feature analysis has been used to promote vocabulary development, this analytical-based strategy can also be applied to study of literature (Readance & Searfoss, 1980). Students, for example, can be asked to categorize types of characters, plot structures, and other literary elements. Another analytical-based instructional strategy that has long been used to help students categorize information is the advanced organizer (Ausubel, 1978). Today, graphic organizers such as semantic maps, flow charts, or Venn diagrams are common examples of classroom tasks that require analytical thinking.

Practical Comprehension and Instruction.   Language arts teachers continually encourage students to describe their initial reactions to literature and to make text-to-self connections. Effective language arts instruction includes teaching students to interact with text as they read, asking questions, noting similarities between what they read and what they experience in their own lives, and interpreting the author's theme or message (Langer, 1992). Teaching for practical intelligence can provide students with opportunities to explore literature from a personal perspective. In fact, language arts teachers may intuitively draw on practical activities to encourage children to make personal connections to the text. Combining such practical activities with explicit instruction in "practical intelligence" promotes student metacognition. When students are aware of their own thinking, they are more likely to call on those cognitive processes while they are reading independently, in situations beyond the classroom. After all, in "real life," readers are not prompted by a teacher's set of comprehension questions, but are left to question, interpret, and construct meaning from text in ways that are personally relevant. Providing students with a set of "practical" questions to ask themselves while they read promotes engagement with the text.

Creative Comprehension and Instruction.   When language arts teachers think of creative learning experiences, the first type of task that comes to mind is creative writing. But creative intelligence is an aspect of reading as well as writing. For example, when students predict a story's events (imagine what might come next), they are using creative thinking. Students can be taught to interact with the text as they read by imagining what they might say to a character or imagine what a character might do differently. Vocabulary may also be acquired creative thinking. Other creative tasks include coining new words by combining prefixes and roots taught, inventing events that might precede and follow events in a narrative, inventing similes to describe characters, and creating different titles or endings.

The following are examples of literacy tasks that require creative thinking: brainstorm a list of (words, ideas, sentences, ways one might use . . .); invent a new (title, ending, plot sequence, character, etc.); invent a new (simile, metaphor, idiom, or other figure of speech); imagine what might happen if (the plot, a grammatical rule, conventional spelling) were changed; or create a (dictionary, puzzle, story problem, game).

Componential Reading Comprehension Skills in Assessment Contexts

Our approach to reading comprehension instruction is also consistent with the aspects of reading assessed on the National Assessment of Educational Progress (NAEP). The National Assessment Governing Board (2002) developed a framework for the NAEP reading comprehension assessment that includes four different aspects of reading: forming a general understanding (literal comprehension), developing an interpretation (generating an idea), making reader/text connections (personal relevance), and examining content and structure (analysis). Table 2.1 illustrates how components of TSI align with the aspects of reading assessed on NAEP reading assessments. Notably, although forming a general understanding requires primarily literal comprehension, the other components of TSI, in addition to memory, work together to help students form even a general understanding of the text. In the other NAEP aspects of reading, the TSI components serve a critical role in scaffolding students toward higher levels of comprehension, including making personal connections and supporting unique and unusual interpretations of text.

Our approach to reading comprehension instruction also assists students in adjusting reading strategies for different purposes. For example, the NAEP framework assesses reading in different contexts: reading for literary experience, reading for information, and reading to perform a task. In all these situations, TSI skills are applicable. Table 2.2 illustrates the kinds of questions and instructional tasks that prepare students for reading in different contexts.

How the Components Work Together

The componential approach to reading comprehension encourages students to draw on all three aspects of TSI, in addition to memory. In other words, the three aspects of intelligence work together to contribute to a complete understanding of text in ways similar to the symbiotic relationship of reading to writing. For example, if students are learning what makes a good mystery, they might be asked to read and evaluate mysteries based on criteria (analytical), relate the text to their own experiences (practical), and create a text of their own (creative). Figure 2.1 illustrates how the components work together to facilitate a personal understanding of the text.

A componential approach to reading comprehension is consistent with classroom instruction and reading in authentic contexts and also supports students' success in testing situations. As the Rand Reading Study Group (Snow, 2002)

TABLE 2.1
TSI and NAEP Aspects of Reading

NAEP Aspects of Reading	TSI Skills	Examples of Instructional Tasks
Forming a General Understanding: Readers demonstrate a general understanding of the text by stating the topic, purpose, or theme of the text	**Memory Skills:** Readers identify main ideas, recognize the author's purpose, and provide summaries **Analytic Skills:** Readers interpret the theme, citing evidence from the text **Practical Skills:** Readers provide advice for characters or friends, based on the author's message or lessons learned from the text **Creative Skills:** Readers generate titles for stories, poems, or other texts	Draw an illustration for each paragraph; caption each illustration with one sentence (summarizing its main idea) What is the author's message about friendship? Cite evidence from the text to support your answer. Based on what you learned about the qualities of friendship, describe your best friend and why you consider that person your friend. After reading a poem with title and key words missing, students generate a title and the missing words. The title and the missing words must be related and convey a possible theme in the poem.
Developing Interpretation: Readers extend initial impressions to develop a more complete understanding, draw conclusions, and make inferences	**Memory Skills:** Readers attend to the sequence of events or ideas **Analytic Skills:** Readers compare and contrast, analyze cause and effects, and evaluate the importance of ideas **Practical Skills:** Readers anticipate effects of their own actions in situations similar to those in the text **Creative Skills:** Readers develop unique interpretations of the text and seek novel applications of the content	Develop a timeline of the key events in the (narrative, biography, social studies text) Using a graphic organizer, show the causes and effects of the invention of the printing press (after reading an article on inventions) Describe a device you would invent and anticipate its effects on your life and the lives of your contemporaries Imagine what might have happened if the printing press were never invented
Making Reader/Text Connections: Readers connect information in the text with knowledge and experience	**Practical Skills:** Readers make text-to-self and text-to-world connections **Creative Skills:** Readers imagine themselves as characters in the text	How does (character) remind you of someone you know? If you were (character), what would you say to the other characters in the book and how might they reply to you? Draw a cartoon showing the dialog you imagine.

(Continued)

TABLE 2.1
(Continued)

NAEP Aspects of Reading	TSI Skills	Examples of Instructional Tasks
Examining Content and Structure: Readers evaluate texts, including language and structure; make comparisons within and across texts for the purpose of evaluation/critique	**Memory Skills:** Readers learn to recognize literary conventions (e.g., figures of speech, rhetorical devices) **Analytic Skills:** Readers analyze how literary conventions contribute to the meaning; readers analyze criteria for excellence in the various genres **Practical Skills:** Readers compare the author's point of view with their own views **Creative Skills:** Readers produce symbolic texts; readers create book reviews	Identify the similes in the poem. Draw the image you "see" in the simile How is a snowflake like a grain of sand? What is the author trying to say by comparing a snowflake with a grain of sand? Do you agree or disagree with the author? What experiences in your own life may have influenced your viewpoint? Imagine a snowflake falling in outer space. Generate similes you might write to help others visualize the "snowflakes" you see. Elaborate the similes (e.g., "drifting like a lunar module floating away ever so slowly from the mother ship").

TABLE 2.2
TSI and NAEP Reading Contexts

NAEP Reading Contexts	TSI Skills	Examples of Instructional Tasks
Reading for Literary Experience: Readers bring their experience and knowledge to the text in such activities as anticipating events, picturing settings, predicting consequences, and considering the language of literary works.	**Memory Skills:** Readers learn basic story elements; describe settings, characters, events. **Analytic Skills:** Readers analyze characters and events in the story. **Practical Skills:** Readers make text-to-self connections and interpret events in the story in light of their own experiences. **Creative Skills:** Readers become authors and create various types of literary texts (e.g., short stories, poems, folktales, biographies).	Retell/rewrite stories, identify characters, settings. Develop open-minded portraits showing character's point of view. Become the character's friend; help characters solve their problem. Each unit culminates in a writing task as a direct assessment of reading comprehension (students produce original text in the literary style/genre studied in the unit).

(Continued)

TABLE 2.2
(Continued)

NAEP Aspects of Reading	TSI Skills	Examples of Instructional Tasks
Reading for Information: Readers gain information to understand the world by reading materials such as magazines, newspapers, essays.	**Memory Skills:** Readers learn basic elements of expository text structure. **Analytic Skills:** Readers evaluate expository texts for accuracy, bias, and other appropriate criteria. **Practical Skills:** Readers read for information that is personally relevant. **Creative Skills:** Readers become authors and create various types of expository text in print and nonprint media.	Identify the signal words for various text structures (e.g., "first," "second" for sequence; "therefore" for cause and effect). Analyze the author's credentials and sources and make a judgment about the probable accuracy of the information. Read the weather charts and decide on the best days next week for outdoor activities. Brainstorm all the possible ways/formats you might present information to the community about (issue under study).
Reading to Perform a Task: Readers apply what they learn from reading materials such as train schedules, directions for games, maps.	**Practical Skills:** Readers apply functional literacy skills in authentic contexts, including simulations. **Practical/Creative Skills:** Readers participate in simulated real-world experiences, such as job interviews, after reading classified ads; readers become authors of functional literacy materials, such as writing directions for a game they create.	Read employment ads. With a partner, prepare a list of interview questions and answers; participate in a simulated interview. Create an original game and write directions for the game. Play the game with a partner.

suggested, there may be a serious mismatch between reading comprehension as assessed on "tests" and reading comprehension in more authentic contexts. Comprehension instruction in classroom learning environments that promote reading as a "real life" task may be inconsistent with the kind of reading comprehension that can be assessed by measures of discrete skills. The componential approach to reading instruction prepares readers for success in classroom situations and on traditional and contemporary reading comprehension measures as well as for success in authentic contexts.

Our approach works. To illustrate, in a study of 871 middle school students and 432 high school students, we taught reading either triarchically or through

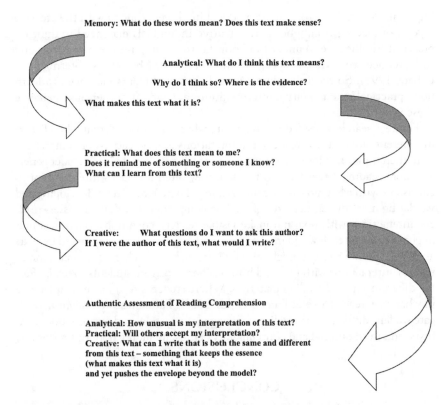

Memory: What do these words mean? Does this text make sense?

Analytical: What do I think this text means?

Why do I think so? Where is the evidence?

What makes this text what it is?

Practical: What does this text mean to me?
Does it remind me of something or someone I know?
What can I learn from this text?

Creative: What questions do I want to ask this author?
If I were the author of this text, what would I write?

Authentic Assessment of Reading Comprehension

Analytical: How unusual is my interpretation of this text?
Practical: Will others accept my interpretation?
Creative: What can I write that is both the same and different
from this text – something that keeps the essence
(what makes this text what it is)
and yet pushes the envelope beyond the model?

FIG. 2.1.   A componential approach to reading comprehension.

the regular curriculum. At the middle school level, reading was taught explicitly. At the high school level, reading was infused into instruction in mathematics, physical sciences, social sciences, English, history, foreign languages, and the arts. In all settings, students who were taught triarchially substantially outperformed students who were taught in standard ways (Grigorenko et al., 2002).

In addition, students are also prepared for success on direct assessments of reading comprehension that integrate reading and writing. For example, by writing an original mystery of their own, students are demonstrating an understanding of what constitutes a mystery and are creating bound by the parameters of what makes a mystery a mystery. Reading serves as a model for writing and the creative act of writing becomes a way of communicating understanding. So the writing is both an assessment of understanding and a new product.

This direct assessment itself also demands a balance of practical, analytical, and creative skills. Creativity often requires individuals to generate original and novel products within certain parameters (Sternberg & Lubart, 1995). In other words, a mystery is a mystery and writing an original mystery requires creativity bound by the parameters of what constitutes mystery. Thus, it may be important for students to develop practical intelligence along with the creative aspects of reading comprehension. Creative individuals may need to draw on practical intelligence to understand how far they can push the parameters and still produce work that is accepted and appreciated by others (Sternberg & Lubart, 1995). So too in reading comprehension, students may need to learn how "practical" their creative interpretations are and how others may perceive these interpretations.

Future research is needed to investigate what it means to "comprehend" text in different situations. If readers' interpretations are indications of comprehension, then it may be more important to count the number of ideas a reader generates from reading a text than to measure how often a reader's interpretation is consistent with what most readers understand. There is a need for developing and validating more direct measures of reading comprehension that can assess readers' interactions with text and make visible readers' cognitions. Such measures might include interviews, journal entries, and original writing prompted by texts as models. Future research might also investigate how teachers' questions prompt readers' interactions with text and how teachers motivate students to read, offering different types of reading materials. Where students read makes a difference in what they read (Duke & Purcell-Gates, 2003). Future research might investigate student differences in reading achievement in school and out-of-school contexts, and in traditional and contemporary genres, including nonprint forms.

CONCLUSIONS

In sum, rather than train particular comprehension strategies, the componential approach to reading comprehension uses questions and tasks that promote interaction with the text in different ways and for different purposes, as readers do in real-life contexts. The memory component develops students' literal comprehension and encourages students to draw on their prior knowledge (what they remember). The analytic component develops students' interpretive skills based on evidence in the text. The practical component encourages students to draw on their own experiences to make text-to-self connections and understand that reading has different purposes. The creative component allows for unique interpretations and encourages students to dialog with the author and imagine new ideas. In short, through the creative component, teachers encourage readers to become authors, facilitating students' understanding of the connection between reading and writing and text as symbolic communication. But the practical component may be necessary for assuring that others accept students' creative interpretations. Students may also need the practical intelligence to understand that there is little room for creative interpretation on traditional assessments of reading comprehension. In more contemporary reading assessments that demand both literal and interpretive stances, students may need to draw on all aspects of

TSI to help them determine what is expected of them as well as what the text means. Most important, in life, readers may need to draw on TSI to understand as well as to comprehend, to produce as well as to consume information, and to enjoy reading as well as to learn from it.

METACONNECTION FOR CHAPTER 2

In chapter 1, the theoretical foundation of metacognition and literacy learning was discussed. Now in chapter 2, we have a better understanding of the foundations of reading comprehension and the role of metacognition. We are provided with the TSI model, which discusses a framework for how to imbed metacognition within a comprehensive model of reading comprehension. As this part progresses, Samuels et al. will help us understand the automatic processes of metacognition in chapter 3.

ACKNOWLEDGMENTS

Preparation of this chapter was supported by Grant No. REC-9979843 from the National Science Foundation (NSF) and by a grant under the Javits Act Program (Grant No. R206R00001) as administered by the Institute for Educational Sciences, U.S. Department of Education. Grantees undertaking such projects are encouraged to express freely their professional judgment. This chapter, therefore, does not necessarily represent the position or policies of the NSF, the Institute for Educational Sciences, or the U.S. Department of Education, and no official endorsement should be inferred.

REFERENCES

Anders, P. L., & Bos, C. S. (1986). Semantic feature analysis: An interactive strategy for vocabulary development and text comprehension. *Journal of Reading, 29,* 610–616.

Applegate, M. D., Quinn, K. B., & Applegate, A. J. (2002). Levels of thinking required by comprehension questions in informal reading inventories. *Reading Teacher, 56*(2), 174–180.

Ausubel, D. P. (1978). In defense of advanced organizers: A reply to critics. *Review of Educational Research, 48,* 251–259.

Baker, L. (2002). Metacognition in comprehension instruction. In C. Collins Block & M. Pressley (Eds.), *Comprehension instruction: Research-based best practices* (pp. 77–95). New York: Guilford.

Bloome, D., & Egan-Robertson, A. (1993). The social construction of intertextuality in classroom reading and writing lessons. *Reading Research Quarterly, 28*(4), 304–333.

Borasi, R., & Siegel, M. (2000). *Reading counts: Expanding the role of reading in mathematics classrooms.* New York: Teacher's College Press.

Cain, K. (1999). Way of reading: How knowledge and use of strategies are related to reading comprehension. *British Journal of Developmental Psychology, 17,* 295–312.

Cain, K., Oakhill, J. V., & Bryant, P. E. (2003). The dissociation of word reading and text comprehension: Evidence from component skills. *Language & Cognitive Processes, 18,* 443–468.

Collins Block, C., & Pressley, M. (2002). *Comprehension instruction: Research-based best practices.* New York: Guilford.

Collins Block, C., Schaller, J., Joy, J., & Gaine, P. (2002). Process-based comprehension instruction. In C. Collins Block & M. Pressley (Eds.), *Comprehension instruction: Research-based best practices* (pp. 42–61). New York: Guilford.

Cunningham, P. (2000). *Phonics they use: Words for reading and writing.* New York: Longman.

Dewitz, P., & Dewitz, P. K. (2003). They can read the words, but they can't understand: Refining comprehension assessment. *Reading Teacher, 56*(5), 422–435.

Dillon, J. (1988). *Questioning and teaching: A manual of practice.* New York: Teacher's College Press.

Duke, N., & Purcell-Gates, V. (2003). Genres at home and at school: Bridging the known to the new. *The Reading Teacher, 57*(1), 30–37.

Durkin, D. (1978). What classroom observation reveals about reading comprehension instruction. *Reading Research Quarterly, 14,* 481–533.

Grigorenko, E. L., Jarvin, L., & Sternberg, R. J. (2002). School-based tests of the triarchic theory of intelligence: Three settings, three samples, three syllabi. *Contemporary Educational Psychology, 27,* 167–208.

Guthrie, J., & Mosenthal, P. (1987). Literacy as multidimensional: Locating information and reading comprehension. *Educational Psychologist, 22,* 279–297.

Heath, S. B. (1980). The function and uses of literacy. *Journal of Communication, 30*(1), 122–133.

Hill, C. (2000, December 7). Falling short of the standards—Part I: High stakes testing in American education–the English language arts test–the reading test. *Teachers College Record* (Online Learning). Retrieved September 4, 2001, from http://www.Tcrecord.org

Jacobs, J., & Paris, S. (1987). Children's metacognition in reading: Issues in definition, measurement, and instruction. *Educational Psychologist, 22,* 255–278.

Kingston, A. (1967). Some thoughts on reading comprehension. In L. Hafner (Ed.), *Improving reading comprehension in secondary schools* (pp. 72–75). New York: Macmillan.

Kintsch, W. (1988). The role of knowledge in discourse comprehension. *Psychological Review, 95*(2), 163–182.

Langer, J. (1992). *Critical thinking and English language arts instruction.* Albany: Center for the Learning and Teaching of Literature

National Assessment Governing Board. (2002). *Reading framework for the 2003 National Assessment of Educational Progress.* Retrieved March 17, 2004, from http://www.nagb.org

National Reading Panel. (2000). *Teaching children to read: An evidence-based assessment of the scientific research literature on reading and its implications for reading instruction.* National Institutes of Health NIH Pub No. 00-4754. Washington, DC.

Palincsar, A., & Brown, A. (1984). Reciprocal teaching of comprehension-fostering and monitoring activities. *Cognition and Instruction, 1,* 117–175.

Pearson, D., & Fielding, L. (1991). Comprehension instruction. In B. Barr, M. Kamil, P. Mosenthal, & P. D. Pearson (Eds.), *Handbook of reading research* (Vol. 2, pp. 815–860). New York: Longman.

Pressley, M., & El-Dinary, P. B. (1997). What we know about translating comprehension strategies instruction research into practice. *Journal of Learning Disabilities, 30,* 486–488.

Pressley, M., Wharton-McDonald, R., Mistretta-Hampton, J., & Echevarria, M. (1998). The nature of literacy instruction in ten grade 4/5 classrooms in upstate New York. *Scientific Studies of Reading, 2,* 159–194.

Readance, J. E., & Searfoss, L. W. (1980). Teaching strategies for vocabulary. *English Journal, 69,* 43–46.

Rosenblatt, L. M. (1978). *The reader, the text, the poem: The transactional theory of the literary work.* Carbondale, IL: Southern Illinois University Press.

Rosenshine, B., & Meister, C. (1994). Reciprocal teaching: A review of the research. *Review of Educational Research, 64,* 479–530.

Snow, C. E. (2002). *Reading for understanding: Toward an R&D program in reading comprehension.* Santa Monica, CA: Rand.

Sternberg, R. (1985). *Beyond IQ: The triarchic theory of human intelligence.* New York: Cambridge University Press.

Sternberg, R. (1997). *Successful intelligence.* New York: Plume.

Sternberg, R. J., & Grigorenko, E. L. (2002a). *An evaluation of teacher training for triarchic instruction and assessment.* Technical Report for the National Science Foundation, July 2002.

Sternberg, R. J., Grigorenko, E. L. (2002b, December). *An evaluation of teacher training for triarchic instruction and assessment.* Paper presented at the annual IERI Grantee Meeting, Washington, DC.

Sternberg, R. J., Grigorenko, E. L., & Jarvin, L. (2001). Improving reading instruction: The triarchic model. *Educational Leadership, 58*(6), 48–52.

Sternberg, R. J., & Lubart, T. I. (1995). *Defying the crowd: Cultivating creativity in a culture of conformity.* New York: The Free Press.

Villaume, S., & Brabham, E. (2002). Comprehension instruction: Beyond strategies. *The Reading Teacher, 55*(7), 672–675.

Winograd, O., & Johnston, P. (1987). Some considerations for advancing the teaching of reading comprehension. *Educational Psychologist, 22,* 213–230.

3

Role of Automaticity in Metacognition and Literacy Instruction

S. Jay Samuels
Kari-Ann M. Ediger
Jennifer R. Willcutt
Theresa J. Palumbo
University of Minnesota, Twin Cities

Allowing students the time to master reading builds self-esteem and facilitates their ability to concentrate on developing metacognitive strategies that will aid them in becoming avid readers. In addition, giving students opportunities to develop fluency in their reading cultivates greater interest and passion for reading, which is vital in creating lifelong readers. Particularly in English Language Learners, I have recognized their need to master simpler tasks in order to feel confident enough to conquer more difficult ones. Teachers should celebrate students' successes in the classroom because fond memories of triumphs will encourage students not only to strive to fulfill their goals in literacy and in other academic areas, but also in their personal lives.

—Amber George

This chapter demonstrates that certain components of metacognition can be trained to automaticity. Furthermore, those components that can be brought to the level of automaticity can be developed instructionally. Students can further their metacognitive skills through pre-, during, and postreading activities, such as skimming, goal setting, rereading, questioning, and so on. The purpose is to inform teachers and researchers about the theoretical foundations of automaticity and metacognition, as well as instructional strategies that have been proven to develop the automaticity of metacognition.

Can metacognitive strategies become automatic? What roles do variables such as interest level, attention, and distraction play in metacognitive reading? Do "good readers" apply different metacognitive strategies than "poor readers"? What metacognitive strategies can be implemented before, during, and after reading the passage to enhance understanding? Can texts be designed in such a way that readers are forced to employ metacognitive strategies? These are some of the theoretical questions about the nature of the automaticity of metacognition addressed in this chapter.

METACOGNITION DEFINED

According to Flavell (1971), metacognition refers to knowledge of one's own cognitive processes and products. This definition of metacognition seems to include most theoretical conventions of metacognition, that of "thinking about one's own thoughts" or an awareness or consciousness of whether or not one knows something. Taken as a whole, the idea of metacognition can incorporate many different everyday terms. Therefore, it becomes necessary to redefine this concept in terms of reading processes in order to establish the role of metacognition in the cognitive processes required for reading. The goal in defining metacognition with regard to reading is to interpret this concept in the context of reading instruction. What exactly are we asking of students who are learning to read when we want them to be "metacognitive" readers? Defining this term and clarifying how it can be an important part of the reading process is essential to being able to proceed to teaching metacognition as a skill. The assumption is that if students have an awareness that they are not comprehending what they are reading, then they will be more self-aware and more self-informed, and consequently they will be better prepared to take the necessary and appropriate steps toward achieving understanding. Knowing whether or not the text is making sense is the first step toward taking the necessary action to the ultimate goal of understanding.

Flavell (1971) asserts that metacognitive thoughts are deliberate, planful, intentional, goal-directed, and future-oriented mental behaviors that can be used to accomplish cognitive tasks. In reference to Piaget's work on developmental stages of cognition, Flavell suggests that the achievement of the formal operations stage involves the development of metacognitive skills; and that formal operations constitute a kind of "metathinking," that is, thinking about thinking itself rather than about objects of thinking (Flavell, 1977).

Metacognition consists of three different factors: one's own nature or the nature of another as a cognitive processor; a task, its demands, and how those demands can be met under varying conditions; and strategies that are invoked to monitor the progress of cognitive processes. This knowledge may influence cognition either deliberately through a conscious memory search or unconsciously through automatic cognitive processes. Metacognition also involves monitoring, regulation, and orchestration (checking, planning, selecting, and inferring) (Brown & Campione, 1980), self-interrogation and introspection (Brown,

1978), and interpretation of ongoing experience (Flavell & Wellman, 1977). Once these strategies are recognized as being effective, they will be used more often, resulting in automaticity. Thinking about thinking can also be overlearned by repeated use and become automatized to the point where the individual is unaware they are being metacognitive.

HISTORICAL PERSPECTIVE AND RESEARCH REVIEW

Powerful psychological theories share an important characteristic. They survive for a long time, and during this extended time interval, like the young chick in the incubator, they develop and change. For example, E. L. Thorndike, known today as the father of educational psychology, observed how cats learned to escape from boxes that he put them in. Based on his observations, he developed the "Law of Effect." This law stated that behaviors that led to successful outcomes were stamped in. Years later, this law was modified by B.F. Skinner and was set forth as reinforcement theory. According to Skinner, the function of rewards was to stamp in stimulus–response connections almost like the glue that connects two pieces of wood. Continued research on the functions of reward led to new formulations, so that today reward is viewed primarily as a feedback mechanism that informs the individual that a particular response made in the presence of a specified stimulus sets the occasion for a reward.

Just as reinforcement theory has been altered over time, so too has automaticity theory, especially as applied to reading. When LaBerge and Samuels (1974) first wrote about automatic information processing in reading, they thought of automaticity primarily in terms of how it affected the word recognition–decoding process. It was obvious to them that if the recognition of words could be done automatically (i.e., with little attention or effort), then there would be sufficient cognitive resources available so that the decoding task and the comprehension process could take place at the same time. But in those days little was known about the intricacies of comprehension and, furthermore, it never occurred to them that some important aspects of comprehension might occur automatically. However, during the next two decades, cognitive psychologists and reading researchers realized that many cognitive processes that are involved in comprehension become automated (Thurlow & van den Broek, 1997). These automated processes that make comprehension possible occur so quickly and so effortlessly that we are scarcely aware that automatic inferences are being made. For example, try to understand the following vignette:

On a sunny autumn day a man walked in the woods smoking a cigarette. The forest fire killed many animals.

If you were able to understand this story, then several inferences had to be made and these inferences occurred automatically. You assume, for example, that the man was carrying a lit cigarette, that he dropped the cigarette on the dry grasses, and then the cigarette started the forest fire. The very short text that you were asked to read is actually an unfriendly piece of writing and several important items of information were missing from the text. But, through the process of making automatic inferences that drew on your prior background and knowledge, you were able to understand the passage. Today, it is believed that all comprehension involves making automatic inferences.

We have explained how over the years the role of automaticity applied to reading has been extended, so that today we recognize that automatic processes are involved in comprehension as well as decoding. Now, once again, we are prepared to extend the role of automaticity by showing how metacognitive processing becomes automatic and is a characteristic of fluent reading.

A model of beginning and fluent reading is used to illustrate the role of automaticity in metacognition. At the risk of oversimplification (but isn't that what one does in a model?), assume that four tasks are involved in successful reading. First, the words in the text must be recognized or decoded. Second, words must be comprehended. Third, metacognition must take place. For example, the reader must self-monitor the comprehension process in order to detect a possible breakdown in comprehension, and if this occurs, the reader must engage in fix-up strategies. Fourth, attention, or cognitive effort, is required in order to perform these three tasks.

The use of cognitive effort, or attention, for performing these four essential reading tasks poses a problem. The problem for the beginning reader is that the cognitive resources available for doing these reading tasks are limited, and any single difficult task, such as decoding, can consume so much of the available cognitive resources that the other tasks cannot get done at the same time. In other words, the reading process for the beginning reader entails doing one task at a time and then switching attention to the next task, and so on, until all the tasks are completed. The problem with reading this way is that it places a heavy load on short-term memory and the entire process is slow and difficult. Refer to Figs. 3.1 and 3.2 to see the changing direction of attention for beginning readers as they become more automatic, until that automaticity is extended to metacognition.

NEW IDEAS AND HOW WE CAN
MOVE THE FIELD FORWARD

Model of Automatic Metacognition

Figures 3.1A, 3.1B, and 3.1C provide a model to describe how the beginning reader proceeds to read a text. One of the problems faced by beginning readers is that they find decoding to be difficult. Looking at Fig. 3.1A, notice that because

FIG. 3.1A, 3.1B, and 3.1C. Beginning reading. Decoding is not automatic.

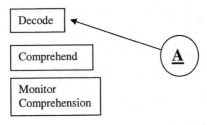

Figure 3.1A.

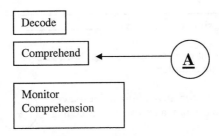

Figure 3.1B.

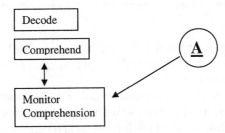

Figure 3.1C.

of the difficulty of decoding, all of the available attention is directed at decoding. Because that single decoding task uses up all of the available cognitive resources, the other tasks (e.g., comprehension and metacognition) cannot be performed at the same time.

As soon as the decoding task is done, however, the reader switches attention to comprehension, as seen in Fig. 3.1B. In general, comprehension is usually a demanding task (even for fluent readers) because meaning has to be constructed

FIG. 3.2.   Fluent reading. Many metacognitive strategies become automatic.

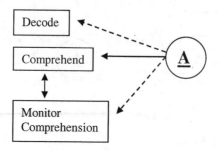

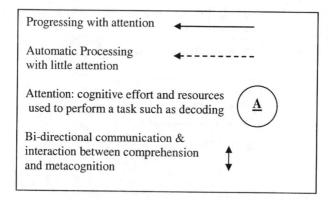

from information provided in the text and knowledge that is in the reader's own mind. So, as seen in Fig. 3.1B, all of the beginning reader's available attention is focused on comprehension.

Having completed the comprehension task, Fig. 3.1C shows how attention is now switched and focused on the metacognitive task. It is at this point that the beginning reader must decide if the level of comprehension is satisfactory. If the level of comprehension is deemed to be satisfactory, then the student can advance to the next text segment and repeat the process. However, if the level of comprehension is not satisfactory, then the student must know what to do in order to correct the problem.

The beginning reading process that was just described is repeated over and over again as the student slowly works through the text. As the beginning reader repeats the process many times over a long period of time, generally ranging from 1 to 3 years, an important change begins to take place. For example, when the same body of high frequency words—such as "the," "it," "boy," and "mother"— appear in the student's text multiple times and in varying contexts, along with literally hundreds of other high frequency words, the student learns to recognize these words automatically. The usual mechanism for developing automaticity is through guided practice. Students can get practice that leads to automatic decoding in a variety of ways, such as reading books independently that are in their zone of proximal development and using the method of repeated reading. This developmental shift from nonautomatic to automatic word recognition has typical characteristics. With the help of instruction, the student becomes accurate, but not automatic, in word recognition. At this stage, word recognition responses are often slow, considerable attention and effort are still required, and when reading orally the student does not read with expression. With considerable practice, the student goes beyond accuracy to automaticity. At the automatic stage, the student is accurate, word recognition occurs rapidly, little attention and effort are required, and there is good oral reading expression and comprehension.

Figure 3.2 shows fluent reading. There are two dotted lines in the figure. The first dotted line goes from attention to decoding, and the second dotted line goes from attention to metacognition. These dotted lines indicate that decoding and metacognition are done automatically. In other words, these two tasks, as the result of years of practice, can be performed with little attention or effort. As a matter of fact, the decoding and the metacognitive tasks require so little attention for their successful performance that there is enough cognitive resources available that the student can do the comprehension task at the same time. As seen in Fig. 3.2, the critical characteristic of fluent reading is that fluent readers can perform all the reading tasks at the same time.

The same mechanisms that explain how decoding becomes automatic are used to explain how metacognition becomes automatic. Usually, teachers help students become aware of the need to self-monitor their own comprehension. If there is a breakdown in comprehension, then the student has to learn several strategies that can restore comprehension to satisfactory levels. At first, the metacognitive strategies are done with accuracy, but considerable attention and effort are required for their execution. With considerable practice, comprehension and fix-up strategies become automatic. Fluent readers automatically monitor their reading and engage in corrective procedures when there is a comprehension problem. In summary, this model of beginning and fluent reading has extended the concept of automaticity so as to include metacognition, which is an essential component of successful reading.

Motivation and Attention

Once the readers' metacognition alerts them to an inconsistency in the text, they must then be motivated or have the will to take an appropriate action to self-regulate their learning. Metacognition is especially relevant in the reading process where learners need to have some self-awareness of whether or not they are comprehending the text in order to maximize the effectiveness of their reading experience.

Attitudes and Beliefs About Reading Ability

To a certain extent, individuals' belief in their self-efficacy can influence whether or not they feel they can be good readers and can learn from a text. If readers believe they can achieve a goal, they are more likely to achieve it. The converse is also true. If readers believe they cannot achieve a goal, then they likely will not achieve it. This is the idea of a self-fulfilling prophecy. People's beliefs in their abilities as readers impact their potential for learning. This could also be true for the extent to which a reader applies metacognition to the reading processes. If readers believe in their ability to deeply process texts, they may be more likely to employ metacognition and implement corrective strategies as snags in comprehension arise in order to enhance their reading experience.

Interest

In order to maximize the amount of return on the investment an individual puts into reading, a high level of interest in the material must be maintained. If readers do not find the text they are reading to be interesting, their attention will stray, comprehension will become unimportant, and metacognition will become disengaged. High interest reading is very motivating for the reader and helps to keep the reader engaged in the task at hand, to direct attentional focus to the reading, to filter out environmental distractions, and to process a text more deeply. High interest level will depend in part on the nature of the text itself (i.e., text structure, expository or narrative, readability level), and in part on the nature of the reader (i.e., the reader's goals, individual preferences, reading ability).

The interest level of a text with regard to a reader affects the amount of attention that is directed toward metacognition, and in turn the automaticity of metacognition. Having a passionate interest area may enable the automaticity of metacognition because it helps to sustain an interest in learning more, to devote attentional resources to the content of the text, to filter out distractions, and to foster a positive attitude toward the content in the text. For readers who have difficulty developing reading fluency, for example, students with reading disabilities, having a passionate interest in a topic might enhance fluency (Fink, 1995) and have further implications for automating the metacognitive process.

Attention

Becoming aware of where readers are directing their attention is the first step toward metacognition. If readers have lost interest in their reading, or have become distracted by something of greater interest, then metacognition has been disengaged. The direction of attention is essential to the metacognitive reading process. Gradually directing more attentional resources to higher order thinking skills allows for the automaticity of metacognition. As lower order thinking skills (LOTS) become more automatic, the student is able to move attentional resources to the higher order thinking skills (HOTS), such as metacognition. The availability of attentional resources due to the automaticity of LOTS is essential for the development of automatic metacognitive reading. If readers can achieve automaticity of the LOTS through repeated reading, highly developed vocabulary, and word recognition skills (i.e., fluent readers), then they are more free to deeply process and comprehend text. From this point, readers will eventually be able to devote more attentional resources toward the conscious direction of their thinking and the awareness, self-monitoring, and good reading skills (i.e., elaborative questioning, summarizing) that constitute the implementation of metacognition.

Distractions

To get the most from reading, individuals need to recognize when distractions are occurring, and change their reading behavior and/or environment in order to improve the ability to direct appropriate attention to immediate reading goals. Distractions are stimuli from the environment that interrupt the process of concentrating attention on reading goals, thus displacing attention from the desired object of comprehending, and thus hindering information from entering the information-processing system where meaning can be actively elaborated. Individual differences exist between learners with regard to an individuals' ability to inhibit distracting stimuli occurring in the environment around them and/or inhibit unnecessary information contained within the body of a text. For example, some people are more sensitive to noises and movement in the environment and therefore require a quieter atmosphere in order to focus their attention on the materials at hand; conversely, they are creating an environmental situation in which there are less distractions needing to be filtered out. Other learners, however, are perfectly comfortable and have no difficulty with the ability of focusing attention, or more to the point, filtering out/inhibiting incoming distractions in environments where there is more movement, action, and noise. If the reading experience is to be successful (i.e., text is deeply processed), then readers need to somehow filter out distractions from the environment either by removing the distracting stimuli, or by removing themselves from the immediately surrounding environment.

Insight

What is the role of insight, or the "Aha!" experience, on automatic metacognition in reading? *Insight* is when people suddenly understand a problem in a new and different way, or the moment when they finally make a connection between what was once obscure and what is now the obvious solution. The fog in thinking suddenly dissipates and concepts become clear in a moment of insight. In a moment of insight, metacognition has become fully automatic and individuals are aware that everything makes sense. There is a sudden meta-awareness of the content or problem as a whole, and the main points of the passage rise to conscious awareness. Questions that individuals ask themselves about the reading have been answered, and they arrive at a new understanding, a higher awareness, and/or a creative idea (Sternberg, 1999).

Overcoming Obstacles to Automating Metacognition

If automating the metacognitive process enables individuals to be better readers and to learn more from what they read, then what is the best method for teaching this process? Are some students more likely to experience problems with automatic metacognition than others? Would the same students that experience difficulty achieving fluency also have difficulty achieving automatic metacognition? If metacognition is part of people's executive functioning, then do students who have difficulty with executive function also experience difficulty with metacognition? This is highly likely. These are further questions to be pursued by research.

SUGGESTIONS FOR INSTRUCTION AND PRACTICE

Readers who are metacognitive can mentally step outside of themselves and view themselves as learners facing a new challenge and opportunity to learn. Readers can take note of whether or not they have prior knowledge about a subject (self-awareness), the task demands of the situation (task knowledge), and the strategies that are helpful in terms of reaching the goal of comprehension (strategy knowledge).

Metacognition can occur not only as a precursor to approaching a text, but additionally throughout the process of reading a text and after completing a passage. If readers come across a word they do not know, then they can employ the strategy of reading ahead to see what happens and then inferring what the unknown word is likely to mean. They can also ask a more knowledgeable individual such as a teacher or parent, or they can look up the word in a dictionary.

If readers have finished a chapter and decide that they still do not understand or recall what they have just read, they can also employ metacognitive strategies following the initial interpretation of information. For example, if they realize that the material did not make sense on the first reading, they can decide to reread the chapter, and read repeatedly until they comprehend the content to their satisfaction. Because using metacognitive strategies takes extra effort until they become automatic, students need to be willing to use these strategies.

Development

Early development of the ability to self-regulate begins as infants when the parents/caregivers assist in the infants' ability to self-regulate their emotions (Sroufe, 1996). This supportive structure later leads to a scaffolding process in which the parent/caregiver helps the child not only with emotional regulation, but also in learning how to solve problems. An example of a problem-solving task for a young child might be putting a puzzle together. The parental figure is a key person in offering the child emotional support, as well as task persistence (Neitzel & Stright, 2003). This individual is there to call the child back if the child gets off-task, offer emotional support if the child becomes frustrated, and additionally, to offer hints and suggestions (i.e., in terms of solving the puzzle). This form of scaffolding provides children with learning cues that help them to understand the process of solving problems, as well as experience the satisfaction and internal reward that come with successfully completing a task. These early processes communicated to the child through the close interaction of the parental figure serve as the foundation on which later metacognitive abilities are constructed.

As the child develops, other important cognitive abilities begin to emerge. For example, according to Kuhn (2000), "by age 3, children have acquired some awareness of themselves and others as knowers" (p. 178). This dawning awareness leads to an understanding of "what" one knows and "how" it came to be known. For example, many children, particularly around age 3 or 4, begin to ask "why" questions—Why is the earth round? How do you know that it is? Why are giraffes so tall? Why are butterflies called butterflies when they don't have any butter in them?—about virtually any idea that their minds come to rest on for more than a moment. This is the stage in which children begin to gain an awareness of knowledge as being "the product of human knowing" (Kuhn, 2000, p. 178). It is this significant factor that creates a stepping stone for the development of metacognition relative to higher order thinking and reasoning processes.

Understanding that knowledge is "the product of human knowing" leads to a transfer of responsibility. That is, children begin to understand that they are in charge of their own knowledge and understanding of the world around them. This period in development of "asking all possible questions" may very well prove to be an interesting prospect in terms of future research. Because the emergence of a stage of inquisition seems to generally appear between age 3 and 4 years, it is uncertain whether or not this may be a sensitive period with regard to the development of metacognition. For example, how would a child whose parent offered support by way of validating the importance of asking questions and thinking critically about the world around them compare with a child whose parent was less engaging and had a tendency to pass off the child's questions as being silly or not important? The ability to ask questions and acquire knowledge for oneself would seem to be of great importance, not only in terms of understanding the source of knowing, but also in terms of expressing a motivation and desire to learn and acquire more information. The opportunity to be validated for one's questioning and reasoning abilities seems more likely to produce an intrinsic motivation to learn in addition to the ability of monitoring what is being learned, or more specifically, the mental representations that one creates as learning occurs. In addition to the scaffolding and support offered by parents during the stages of metacognitive development, teachers can also be a wonderful resource for additional instruction.

Individual Differences

Good readers often use metacognitive strategies while reading to better monitor their comprehension and check for gaps in their understanding. However, children with reading difficulties often do not, or are not able to, implement these metastrategies. These children benefit not only from reading instruction, in general, but show even greater improvements in reading and comprehending ability if explicit instruction in the use of metacognitive strategies and comprehension monitoring are included in the training process (Weir, 1998; Wright & Jacobs, 2003).

Furthermore, it is possible that some learners are more sensitive to certain text characteristics that slow them down (Erlich, Remond, & Tardieu, 1999)—decoding and text inconsistencies, for example—thereby taking up additional cognitive resources that otherwise might be dedicated to building a mental representation and metacognition. This idea further supports the importance of teaching reading to the point of automaticity. Doing this decreases a reader's cognitive load allowing the reader to apply more available resources to metacognition.

Additional evidence suggests that people with low metacognition may tend to focus on actions as opposed to key ideas *behind* the actions (Crawford, 1998). This supports the idea of teaching metacognitive strategies to the point of automaticity, because once a reader is able to successfully decode a text, it then becomes important to learn to recognize how and when a particular strategy is paying off (i.e., paying off in terms of the ability to select relevant information from a text while simultaneously inhibiting any interference either within the text or within a reader's surroundings). For yet other readers, differences between metacognitive abilities and strategy implementation can shift in accordance with comprehension abilities, which means that the better a reader is able to comprehend, the more that person will tend to exhibit flexibility in strategy use (Shore, 2000). It is has also been suggested that children with learning disabilities may have a different conceptual representation of the text (Zambo, 2003).

Taken as a whole, these ideas suggest that metacognitive strategies with regard to reading and reading comprehension should be taught explicitly and practiced to automaticity so that emerging readers will be better equipped to use a meta-strategy at the appropriate time and for the appropriate reading situation. Doing this allows a reader greater freedom from a more burdensome cognitive load with regard to effort in decoding and limited knowledge and application of meta-cognitive strategy use.

Readers' ability to monitor their mental representation of a text might also, then, affect their ability to draw relevant inferences, and therefore create the necessary assumptions needed for inclusion in the gist of the narrative (or other) text. The ability to draw appropriate inferences is essential to the process of understanding the underlying meaning of a text (Van Den Broek, Lorch, Linderholm, & Gustafson, 2001). For example, in reference to the example sentences used earlier in this chapter, a person not only needs to comprehend the meaning of the words—just as they are written—but, also must comprehend the inferred meaning, that is, the unstated meaning that links the two sentences together as a unit of information. Strategies to accomplish this task are discussed in the next section.

THE READING PROCESS

Readers' Goals for Texts

Metacognitive instruction in the classroom begins with setting good and attainable goals. Before a person starts to read, there are strategies that should be implemented to make the task more successful. For example, beginning readers are not aware of the structure and organization of a book. In classrooms, teachers often read stories to emerging readers. However, in addition to reading to students, it is also helpful to have some discussion regarding why a student might want to read a particular text—that is, the teacher can help the learner establish a clear goal. Questions to ask include: Why am I reading this? What is the purpose? Am I reading to clarify a particular point, to obtain new discoveries, for leisure, because it is part of an assignment my teacher gave me to do, or perhaps to prepare for a test? What direction do I want my thinking to take? How much time do I have to complete this task? Answers to these questions will help to guide readers as they proceed through the text, because each question would require a slightly different reading strategy in order to obtain the goal.

For example, when reading for the purpose of studying for a test, it is not hard to imagine that a reader will most likely attend to as much information as possible, making careful decisions as to what information is and is not relevant. Alternatively, people reading for leisure might not be so attentive to all the immediate details and inferences and thereby be more lax in the monitoring of their mental representation of relevant textual information. Especially if the task is for study, individuals create a *standard of coherence*, which they refer back to throughout the reading. A standard of coherence refers to the referential and causal inferences contained within a text. That is, when a text mentions a name, then later refers to the protagonist as "she," the reader must be able to infer who "she" is. Additionally, causal coherence is used to describe the degree to which one idea relates to, or is relevant to, another. For example, in reference to the example passage used at the beginning of this chapter, a reader might ask the following: Does the second sentence make sense in light of the first sentence? How are the two sentences related? Does one sentence provide a setting or contain causality for an action, which was taken in the second sentence? If individuals are reading a novel for relaxation, it is less likely that they would have the desire to extend the extra effort required to perform some of the more strenuous metacognitive skills. On the other hand, if the reading assignment has been received as part of a class requirement and will later be tested on, the students will either effortfully or automatically take the time to raise their level of understanding. Van den Broek et al. (2001) stated that without the construct of the standards of coherence, reader's goals would rely on some unspecified process by which readers constantly check their understanding against an abstract goal. The metacognitive strategies a person uses are different based on the predetermined purpose of the reading. In an experimental study that recorded think-aloud procedures and free-recall, it was shown that if the readers' goal was for study, then the readers did more explaining and predicting; alternatively, if the purpose was for enjoyment, then the readers made more associations and evaluations (van den Broek et al., 2001).

In addition to knowing why a person is reading a text and establishing a clear goal, it is also important to communicate to beginning readers the function of a book's title. A teacher might begin instruction by asking what the title of the book is, and what the students think the book might be about. Asking this requires learners to tap into their background knowledge and begin to prepare their minds for the information to come. For example, if an individual was to read the play *Hamlet* after reading the title of the play, that person could easily guess that the bulk of the play will probably center around a character named Hamlet. An example for younger readers might be *The Pokey Puppy*. It is pretty clear after reading or hearing the title that the main character of the story will be a puppy. Who the puppy meets while on his adventure might also be important, because it relates to the puppy and the puppy's experience. This provides a wonderful learning opportunity within the body of the text because the puppy meets kittens, cows, ducks, and so on, throughout his travels. In both of the previous examples, the title has direct relevance to the theme or main idea of a story and gives an explicit cue as to what will be most important in the story. Titles, in addition to other textual cues inherent in a story, allow a reader to strategically allocate and direct attention toward the more important ideas of a story, which in turn promotes better understanding of the text and better recall after reading (O'Brian &

Meyers, 1987; Trabasso & Sperry, 1995). If these skills, along with more specific metacognitive skills discussed in other areas of this text, are completed often enough through practice and repetition, then these tasks will become automatic.

Monitoring the Emerging Mental Representation

There are four potential aspects to monitoring the intake and culmination of information. First, readers must monitor what is already known in terms of how what they are reading fits with what they already know from their own experiences. Second, they perform inference integration, that is, they figure out how this new bit of information fits together by itself and with previous inferences. Third, they monitor what is already understood in terms of how what they have just read fits with what was previously read in a text. Lastly, they use selection, that is, they decide what information stays, what information goes, what information gets held onto just in case it is needed later, and what information needs to be inhibited.

So, then, what can be done to help those who have difficulty monitoring their comprehension or who are implementing poor strategies with little or no payoff as they monitor their understanding of a text? After determining the goal of reading a particular text, it is important to monitor the construction of incoming information in order to check for coherence and understanding. Repeated reading involves students reading a text multiple times in order to improve reading speed. Repeated reading is an instructional strategy that allows for more opportunities for text comprehension to occur. If students realize they are not fully understanding what happened when they ask themselves questions about what they just read, then they can go back and read the passage until they feel they could adequately summarize or tell a friend about what they just read. More familiarity gives the student a chance to understand the reading, all while taking advantage of their ability to keep the big picture and end goal or purpose for their reading in mind, an intricate part of metacognition.

It is exactly this process of a delay in-between the first and second reading that allows readers to ask themselves questions related to a text, and to check for gaps in understanding. Furthermore, the process of going back to a text for the purposes of rereading may additionally provide opportunities for metacognitive insights.

Metacognitive Assessment Rubric

A method to promote the development of metacognition in students is to ask them to assess their own work. Students who assess their own understanding—by evaluating, regulating, and monitoring their work—will spot areas that need improvement. A *rubric* is a method of assessing how students have performed on a task. A rubric, which includes statements to assess if metacognitive skills have been implemented, is one way to assess if students are implementing metacognitive skills before, during, and after reading, as well as a means for students to assess their work. A rubric to assess metacognitive skills should include analyses, such as: checked my comprehension during reading, reread when it seemed necessary, looked back to make inferences, made predictions of what might come next, checked my memory of what was read, asked questions, self-monitored, and wrote a summary after each page before moving on to the next page. After students assess their understanding, the teacher can also assess the student's understanding, and then compare the two analyses. A teacher may ask the student, "How well do you understand the area covered? What still puzzles you?" At this point, the teacher can give guidance by informing the student of additional metacognitive skills that can be implemented.

DIRECTIONS FOR FUTURE RESEARCH

Can the automaticity of metacognition be measured? Is it possible for readers to be accurate, but not automatic? Can texts with poor standards of coherence be used in classrooms to assess what metacognitive strategies students are using, and then to teach students how to improve their metacognitive skills? Do good readers apply metacognitive strategies automatically, or is it more the case that metacognitive strategies are applied only as readers stop and reflect on reading the passage? With regard to individual differences, it appears as though some people have low metacognitive abilities whereas others have high metacognitive abilities; therefore, what kind of strategies might have a higher pay off for those with lower meta-abilities and what strategies might enhance pay off for those with a higher meta-ability? How might posing questions throughout the body of the text serve to better aid those with lower metacognitive abilities, or would that only be a distraction? Because it is difficult for individuals to report their nonconscious cognitive processes, determining whether or not a strategy is cognitive or metacognitive is puzzling; however, we believe it is possible.

CONCLUSIONS

A good theoretical framework for understanding the nature of metacognition is essential to learning more about how readers process texts. This chapter has discussed the importance of the role of automaticity and fluency in metacognition. It also has covered ideas for developing better methods for the individual learner in terms of instructing emerging learners. Some of these methods include the fact that beginning readers focus all of their attentional resources on decoding a text. As they become accurate and automatic in their reading, their attentional focus gradually shifts to comprehension, and finally to monitoring that comprehension in the form of metacognition. Repeated reading is a tried and true instructional strategy that has been found to be effective in increasing reading automaticity. The concept of automaticity has been extended to metacognition, and the roles of interest, attention, distraction, insight, attitudes and beliefs, and overcoming obstacles have been examined in relation to metacognitive reading. The translation of theory into practice has been addressed in this chapter in terms of instructional strategies that support the development of the automaticity of metacognition in relation to the reader's predetermined goals.

METACONNECTION FOR CHAPTER 3

Randi et al. helped us bridge the gap of theory between metacognition and reading comprehension by placing it in an instructional framework. In chapter 3, Samuels et al. translates theory and places in practice within the classroom summarized strategies that develop the automaticity of metacognition. We will continue building a solid theoretical foundation in chapter 4, where Baker explains the developmental differences among school-aged children. The developmental aspects of metacognition help explain when students are ready developmentally for metacognitive instruction.

REFERENCES

Albrecht, J. E., & O'Brien, E. J. (1993). Updating a mental model: Maintaining both local and global coherence. *Journal of Experimental Psychology: Learning, Memory, and Cognition, 19,* 1061–1070.

Brown, A. L. (1978). Knowing when, where, and how to remember: A problem of metacognition. In R. Glaser (Ed.), *Advances in instructional psychology* (Vol. 1). Hillsdale, NJ: Lawrence Erlbaum Associates.

Brown, A. L., & Campione, J. C. (1980). *Learning to learn: On training students to learn from texts.* Champaign, IL: University of Illinois at Urbana-Champaign, Center for the Study of Reading.

Crawford, S.A.S. (1998). Beyond reading strategies: An investigation of the relationship between academic attributions, achievement motivation and metacognition. *Dissertation Abstracts International, 58*(9-A), 3414. (UMI No.)

Dole, J. A., Duffy, G. G., Roehler, L. R., & Pearson, P. D. (1991). Moving form the old to the new: Research on reading comprehension instruction. *Review of Educational Research, 61,* 239–264.

Erhi, L. C., Nunes, S. R., Willows, D. M., Schuster, B. V., Yaghoub-Zadeh, A., & Shanana, T. (2001). Phonemic awareness instruction helps children to read: Evidence from the National Reading Panel's meta-analysis. *Reading Quarterly, 36,* 250–287.

Erlich, M., Remond, M., & Tardieu, H. (1999). Processing of anaphoric devices in young skilled and less skilled comprehenders: Differences in metacognitive monitoring. *Reading and Writing, 11*(1), 29–63.

Fink, R. P. (1995). Successful dyslexics: A constructivist study of passionate interest reading. *Journal of Adolescent & Adult Literacy, 39*(4), 268–280.

Flavell, J. H. (1971). First discussant's comments: What is memory development the development of? *Human Development, 14*(4), 272–278.

Flavell, J. H. (1976). Metacognitive aspects of problem solving. In L. B. Resnick (Ed.), *The nature of intelligence*. Hillsdale, NJ: Lawrence Erlbaum Associates.

Flavell, J. H. (1977). *Cognitive development*. Englewood Cliffs, NJ: Prentice-Hall.

Flavell, J. H., & Wellman, H. M. (1977). Metamemory. In R. V. Kail, Jr. & J. W. Hagen (Eds.), *Perspectives on the development of memory and cognition*. Hillsdale, NJ: Lawrence Erlbaum Associates.

Hunt, M. (1993). *The story of psychology*. New York: Doubleday.

Kintch, W., & van Dijk, T. A. (1978). Toward a model of text comprehension and production. *Psychological Review, 85*, 362–394.

Kuhn, D. (2000). Metacognitive development. *Current Directions in Psychological Science, 9*(5), 178–181.

LaBerge, D., & Samuels, S. J. (1974). Toward a theory of automatic information processing in reading. *Cognitive Psychology, 6*, 293–323.

LaBerge, D., & Samuels, S. J. (1985). Toward a theory of automatic information processing in reading. In H. Singer & R. Ruddell (Eds.), *Theoretical models and processes of reading* (3rd ed., pp. 689–718). Newark, DE: International Reading Association.

Miller, P. H. (1985). Metacognition and attention. In D. L. Forrest-Pressley, G. E. MacKinnon, & T. Gary Waller (Eds.), *Metacognition, cognition, and human performance: Vol. 2. Instructional practices* (pp. 181–221). New York: Academic Press.

Neitzel, C., & Stright, A. D. (2003). Mother's scaffolding of children's problem solving: Establishing a foundation of academic self-regulatory competence. *Journal of Family Psychology, 17*(1), 147–159.

O'Brian, E. J., & Meyers, J. L. (1987). The role of causal connections in the retrieval of text. *Memory and Cognition, 15*, 419–427.

Samuels, S. J. (1997). The method of repeated readings. *The Reading Teacher, 50*(5), 376–381.

Schreiber, P. A. (1980). On the acquisition of reading fluency. *Journal of Reading Behavior, 12*, 177–186.

Shore, B. M. (2000). Metacognition and flexibility: Qualitative differences in how gifted children think. In R. C. Friedman & B. M. Shore (Eds.), *Talents unfolding: Cognition and development* (pp. 167–187).

Sroufe, L. A. (1996). *Emotional development: The organization of emotional life in the early years*. New York: Cambridge University Press.

Sternberg, R. J. (Ed.). (1999). *Handbook of creativity*. Cambridge, England: Cambridge University Press.

Theide, K. W., Anderson, M.C.M., & Therriault, D. (2003). Accuracy of metacognitive monitoring affects learning of tests. *Journal of Educational Psychology, 95*(1), 66–73.

Thurlow & van den Broek. (1997). Automaticity and inference generation during reading comprehension. *Reading & Writing Quarterly: Overcoming Learning Difficulties, 13*, 165–181.

Trabasso, T., & Sperry, L. L. (1985). Causal relatedness and importance of story events. *Journal of Memory and Language, 24*, 595–611.

Trabasso, T., van den Broek, P. W., & Suh, S. (1989). Logical necessity and transitivity of causal relations in stories. *Discourse Processes, 12*, 1–25.

Van den Broek, P., Lorch R. F., Linderholm, T., & Gustafson, M. (2001). The effects of readers' goals on inference generation and memory texts. *Memory & Cognition, 29*(8), 1081–1087.

Weir, C. (1998). Using embedded questions to jump-start metacognition in middle school re-medial readers. *Journal of Adolescent & Adult Literacy, 41*(6), 458–468.

Wright, J., & Jacobs, B. (2003). Teaching phonological awareness and metacognitive strategies to children with reading difficulties: A comparison of the two instructional methods. *Educational Psychology, 23*(1), 17–45.

Zambo, D. M. (2003). Uncovering the conceptual representations of students with reading dis-abilities. *Dissertation Abstracts International, 64*(3-A), 801. (UMI No.)

4

Developmental Differences in Metacognition: Implications for Metacognitively Oriented Reading Instruction

Linda Baker
University of Maryland, Baltimore County

> *The idea of metacognition in Literacy Instruction is very important. Children need to understand exactly why they are thinking a certain way to learn something. Children need to understand how and why they had to complete the lesson a certain way. By understanding this concept the children can know in the future how to deal with this specific task. A question I have about this is: "If a child does not learn the certain way to do the task, can this affect how the child learns for the rest of their life?"*
>
> —Erin Murray

Ever since metacognition was first introduced by Flavell (1976) and Brown (1978), developmental and educational psychologists have been interested in how it develops. Descriptions of developmental changes in metacognitive skills are widely available, but much less is known about factors influencing those changes. In 1985, Flavell wrote, "School and other life experiences do not advance the child's metacognitive development as fast or as far as might be desirable, and there is a growing feeling that we should try to find ways to teach it more directly and systematically" (p. 263). Despite more than two decades of research on the topic, there is still a lack of information on effective ways to facilitate metacognitive development. As Pressley and Block (2002) put it, "There is just not enough known about how to develop readers who monitor well and who, in turn, self-regulate their comprehension processes well" (p. 387). This chapter presents current theory and research on developmental differences in children's

61

reading-related metacognitive skills, examines sources of influence on metacognitive development, and considers the implications for metacognitively oriented reading instruction.

Because metacognition has been defined in different ways by different researchers, it is important to clarify the definition used here, which encompasses both knowledge about cognition and regulation of cognition. Knowledge about cognition concerns the ability of individuals to reflect on their own cognitive processes and includes knowledge about when, how, and why to engage in various cognitive activities. Regulation of cognition concerns the use of strategies that enable individuals to control their cognitive efforts. These strategies include planning their moves, checking the outcomes of their efforts, evaluating the effectiveness of their actions and remediating any difficulties, and testing and revising their learning techniques (Baker & Brown, 1984). Metacognitive control in the domain of reading includes comprehension monitoring, which entails deciding whether or not individuals understand (evaluation) and taking appropriate steps to correct whatever comprehension problems they detect (regulation).

The first part of the chapter discusses current research on developmental differences in children's reading-related metacognition. It also addresses the extent to which the development of basic cognitive processes contributes to metacognitive development and whether or not metacognition develops spontaneously. These questions about basic processes provide information necessary to address the applied question of when children might benefit from metacognitively oriented instruction. Because school is not the only context relevant to metacognitive growth, the impact of home influences on its development is also considered. The second part of the chapter addresses five questions stemming from the developmental research with direct implications for literacy instruction:

1. How should metacognitive development be assessed?
2. Does metacognition play a role in word recognition as well as comprehension?
3. Should children be given instruction in metacognition and comprehension monitoring before they are fluent readers?
4. At what level are children most likely to benefit from metacognitively oriented strategies instruction?
5. Should students be taught to monitor their comprehension deliberately and routinely?

The chapter closes with a summary and a discussion of directions for further inquiry.

RECENT THEORY AND RESEARCH
ON METACOGNITIVE DEVELOPMENT

Developmental Differences in Children's
Reading-Related Metacognitive Skills

A substantial body of research has accumulated showing better metacognitive knowledge and control among older and higher achieving students (for reviews, see Baker & Brown, 1984; Hacker, Dunlosky, & Graesser, 1998; McCormick, 2003). Despite these developmental improvements, students of all ages are surprisingly poor at monitoring their understanding of text (Baker, 1989). Metacognition thus develops gradually throughout childhood and into adulthood. It cannot simply be asserted that a child "has" or "does not have" metacognitive knowledge or control. Metacognition differs in degree and kind, and its relations with achievement change over time. The evidence is clear that children begin to use simple rehearsal strategies early in elementary school, but complex strategies for understanding text may not develop until middle or high school. Regardless of the strategy in question, there is a common pattern in its development, as Pintrich and Zusho (2002) discussed. Initially, children do not use the strategy spontaneously, then they use the strategy but do not really benefit from it, and finally, after a considerable amount of practice and experience, children show more adaptive and successful strategy use.

An important distinction exists between a child having the competence to use a particular strategy and the child actually using that strategy. Older students become more capable of using strategies, but even if they know how to use them, they still might not do so. This may reflect their failure to realize the strategies are beneficial. But it also may reflect a lack of motivation to put forth the effort required for strategy use. Although research suggests students in middle school are cognitively more prepared to benefit from metacognitive strategies instruction than younger children, another well-established developmental difference may make these students less responsive. At the same time students' ability to evaluate their own learning and performance increases, their intrinsic motivation for learning decreases. In other words, the "self-system" is also implicated. It is not sufficient to focus on metacognition alone as a potential influence on achievement; there are important roles for motivation and attributional beliefs (Borkowski, Chan, & Muthukrishna, 2000; Pintrich & Zusho, 2002).

Most research on developmental changes in metacognition is of a cross-sectional nature. That is, research might compare groups of third, fifth, and eighth graders at the same point in time. This enables statements of the sort that older children are better at monitoring their understanding than younger children, but it provides little insight into the mechanisms of change at the individual level. A number of researchers have called for longitudinal work on students' metacognitive development as they move through the grades (e.g., Pintrich, Wolters, & Baxter, 2000; Simpson & Nist, 2002). A few such studies have been conducted that illustrate stability in metacognition as well as in the relations between metacognition and reading. For example, Roeschl-Heils, Schneider, and van Kraayenoord (2003) followed up an earlier study (van Kraayenoord & Schneider, 1999). Children's metacognition was first examined in grades 3 or 4 in relation to motivation and reading and was subsequently reassessed in grades 7 or 8. Although metacognitive growth was observed, patterns of intercorrelations among the measures were stable over time. Bouffard (1998) conducted a 3-year longitudinal study, beginning when children were in grade 4 and following them into grade 6. She examined interrelations between the self-system (e.g., children's beliefs about themselves as learners), metacognition, and reading and again found similar patterns of relations over time. Both longitudinal studies also provided evidence that metacognitive knowledge predicted reading achievement.

Adolescence is an important developmental period for metacognitive growth. As Pintrich and Zusho (2002) put it, "The active control of cognition may be a rather late-developing phenomenon, coinciding with a developmental shift in adolescence that enables students to have their own thoughts not just as objects of their thinking, but also to control their own thinking" (p. 261). Peverly, Brobst, and Morris (2002) investigated developmental changes in the contributions of comprehension ability and metacognitive control to competence in studying among average and above average 7th- and 11th-grade students. Comprehension and metacognition were both related to the recall of information at both ages, but metacognitive control was more important to the older students than it was to the younger students. Schoonen and Hulstijn (1998) also demonstrated developmental differences across adolescence in metacognitive knowledge of reading and in the relation of metacognitive knowledge to reading comprehension. Metacognitive knowledge concerning text characteristics, reading strategies, and reading goals increased with age across grades 6, 8, and 10. Metacognitive knowledge predicted reading comprehension for the children in grades 8 and 10, but not in grade 6.

To What Extent Does the Development of Basic Cognitive Processes Contribute to Metacognition?

The development of working memory processes, such as attention and executive control, appears to be a factor in the development of self-regulated learning. In addition, the greater degree of background knowledge possessed by older students contributes to their better metacognitive skills. Pintrich and Zusho (2002) argued, "Older students can think about their own thinking and regulate it, not because they are more mature or in a higher developmental stage, but because their cognitive resources are freed up for regulatory tasks in comparison to knowledge search or retrieval processes" (p. 258). Further, they identified an interesting paradox with respect to the development of metacognition:

> It is often suggested that for younger children or novices to become more knowledgeable or skilled, they need to become more metacognitive and regulate their own learning. However, these students are the ones who may have the most difficulty in enacting the various regulatory strategies as use of these strategies will involve working memory at the same time their lack of knowledge also consumes working memory resources. Given this problem, it is not surprising that novices often have to be "other regulated" initially through coaching, instructional supports, and teacher scaffolding before they can be self-regulating. (p. 258)

Does Metacognition Develop Spontaneously, With Age and/or Experience?

What accounts for the differences observed between older and younger readers, between skilled and less skilled readers? Pintrich and Zusho (2002) differentiated two types of developmental trajectories, one associated with age-related maturation and the other with individual task-related expertise. The fact that children of the same age who differ in reading skill also differ in metacognitive knowledge and control lends support to the role of experience. But it has been well-documented that children do not receive differential instruction that might foster such differences. So, does frequent independent reading promote metacognitive awareness and control? Children who read frequently tend to be better readers, but a link between reading frequency and metacognition has not been empirically established. Furthermore, it is not known whether or not independent reading, regardless of its frequency, is sufficient for metacognitive development. The lack of explicit attention to metacognition in the school curriculum has led many researchers to conclude that successful readers spontaneously acquire metacognitive knowledge and control (e.g., Schoonen & Hulstijn, 1998). Perhaps the majority of children first need explicit strategies instruction in order to benefit metacognitively from independent reading.

Home Influences on the Development of Metacognition: Parental Beliefs and Practices

Much current research on early literacy development reveals the powerful contributions of the home environment and the importance of home–school connections (Baker, 1999; Tracey & Morrow, 2002). To what extent might parents help set the stage for metacognitive development with respect to literacy? It is widely agreed that social interaction plays an important role in the development of metacognition (Baker, 1994, 1996). The theoretical underpinnings of this perspective are attributable to Vygotsky (1978), who argued that children develop the capacity for self-regulation through interaction with more knowledgeable others. These individuals initially assume responsibility for monitoring progress, setting goals, planning activities, allocating attention, and so on. Gradually, responsibility for these executive processes is given over to the children, who become increasingly capable of regulating their own cognitive activities. In other words, there is a sequence of development from other-regulation to self-regulation.

Many researchers have suggested that metacognitive growth can be facilitated by the use of socialization practices and instructional strategies that encourage children to plan, to evaluate their progress, and to revise their efforts if unsuccessful. Baker (1994) reviewed research demonstrating that parents do provide scaffolded instruction for their children during problem solving that helps them develop metacognitive awareness and control. Less is known about the extent to which parents foster young children's metacognitive knowledge and control of reading through their spontaneous behaviors during shared book reading.

Borkowski et al. (2000) commented on the likely importance of "an intricate pattern of development-related events . . . (involving consistency in metacognitive based instruction in the home and school over long periods of time)" (p. 34). Paris (2002) also discussed contextual influences on metacognition, noting that different families put more emphasis on talking about thinking and being reflective, as do different teachers and different cultures. He explained that "metacognition is valued, expressed, taught, and supported to different degrees by different communities, and the origins and practices that imbue metacognition with value should be studied" (p. 115).

Davidson and Freebody (1988) provided evidence that children's home experiences before schooling contribute to their metacognitive knowledge about reading, which in turn predicts their subsequent reading development. They assessed children's metacognitive knowledge about person, task, and strategy variables relevant to reading at the beginning of the first year of school, prior to formal instruction. Also assessed were other dimensions of written language knowledge, including concepts about print, letter knowledge, and listening comprehension. Reading in the home (a composite measure that included prevalence of books, amount of adult–child reading and adult reading) predicted the composite measure of written language knowledge (including metacognition). This measure in turn predicted several end-of-year reading competencies, including decoding skills, text comprehension, and knowledge-based comprehension. The demographic variables of socioeconomic status and ethnicity were associated with these various outcomes, but when these variables were controlled, reading in the home still predicted metacognitive knowledge. In other words, what children experience in the home is potentially more important than static social address variables (Serpell, Baker, & Sonnenschein, 2005).

Mothers themselves tend to believe that children acquire metacognitive skills on their own, without direct instruction. This was demonstrated in a study by Sonnenschein, Baker, and Lasaga (1991; cited in Baker, 1996) in which parents of prekindergarten, kindergarten, and first-grade children completed a questionnaire that assessed their beliefs about how children learn specific skills in various domains, including metacognition (planning, comprehension monitoring). Mothers ranked the relative importance of maturation, self-discovery, learning via parents, and learning via teachers as explanations for how children learn the skills within each domain. The item for comprehension monitoring follows:

How do children become able to know whether they understand something?
a. Teachers teach them how to determine whether they understand.
b. Parents emphasize making sure they understand.
c. Children discover through daily experiences whether or not they understand.
d. When children are ready, they are able to determine whether they understand.

The majority of mothers responded that the metacognitive skills of planning and comprehension monitoring were acquired through the child's daily experiences (65% and 50%, respectively), with parental emphasis on the skills also considered important, but less so (31%, 43%). It was striking how few mothers thought teachers were primarily responsible for fostering these skills (1%, 3%).

IMPLICATIONS FOR LITERACY INSTRUCTION

How Should Metacognitive Development Be Assessed?

Many teachers are interested in having information about the metacognitive knowledge and skills of their students. Baker and Cerro (2000) reviewed the literature on the assessment of metacognition in children and adults, with particular attention to the domain of reading. That review critically examined instruments and approaches used in research as well as those that were recommended for teachers. It concluded that few good instruments were available for assessing metacognition, especially among younger students, and that teachers needed to be cautious in the conclusions they drew. Since that time, new standardized measures have been developed. For example, Mokhtari and Reichard (2002) developed a 30-item questionnaire for students in grades 6–12, the Metacognitive Awareness Reading Strategies Inventory. The complete inventory, along with information on how researchers and teachers might use it with students, is included in the published article. Students rate on a 5-point scale how frequently they engage in each strategy. Students can receive a total score and a score for three different types of strategies: global reading strategies (e.g., I have a purpose in mind when I read), problem-solving strategies (e.g., I try to get back on track when I lose concentration); and support reading strategies (e.g., I write summaries to reflect on key ideas in the text). Another instrument for assessing metacognition, adapted from an instrument for adults, is the Jr. Metacognitive Awareness Inventory (Sperling, Howard, Miller, & Murphy, 2002). One version is appropriate for children in grades 3–5 and another for children in grades 6–9. This is a more general measure that applies to academic learning rather than reading per se. Items tap either the knowledge component of metacognition (e.g., I am a good judge of how well I understand something) or the regulation component (e.g., I ask myself questions about how well I am learning while I am learning something new). This instrument, too, is recommended by the authors for use by classroom teachers, and the inventory is included in the published article.

There is still far to go before there are adequate tools for assessing metacognition. One solution to this problem is to use multiple measures with each student (Baker & Cerro, 2000; Juliebo, Malicky, & Norman, 1998). Many investigators do use a combination of measures to obtain converging evidence. The need for converging evidence is perhaps even greater in applied settings, such as in classrooms and schools where the stakes to the student are higher, than it is in basic research. Moreover, there is a need for greater ecological validity in the assessment of metacognition. Paris (1991) advocated using authentic texts and informing students fully about the task. However, the more process-oriented approaches to assessing metacognition are time consuming, and they usually need to be conducted on an individual basis. Questionnaires can be administered quickly, in a group setting, and can still yield useful formative information to guide instruction.

Does Metacognition Play a Role in Word Recognition as Well as Comprehension?

Just as metacognitive knowledge and strategic control contribute to reading comprehension, so too do these play a role in effective word recognition. It is important to teach children when, where, and why particular strategies for recognizing words are advantageous. Students need to be shown strategies for using what they already know about how words work to identify new words. Similarly, students should be taught to use the semantic and syntactic cues provided by the surrounding context to help them decide if they have decoded a word correctly. When children self-correct during oral reading, they show metacognitive awareness that a word does not make sense in the context of the larger passage. Unfortunately, it is not uncommon for beginning and less proficient older readers to believe that good reading is being able to pronounce all of the words correctly.

This impression is more likely to develop in classrooms where there is an emphasis on accurate and fluent decoding rather than comprehension. From the very beginning, children need to understand that word recognition is a means to an end, not the end in itself (Baker, 2000).

Teaching children to reflect on the processes and strategies they use to recognize words is effective, as illustrated by Cunningham (1990). First-grade children who were given information about when, where, and why to use the knowledge of the phonemes they were acquiring performed better on tests of word recognition than those who received phonemic awareness instruction without the metacognitive component. This type of intervention is also effective with older children who are experiencing difficulty learning to read. Wright and Barrie (2003) provided 7- to 10-year-old children who had reading difficulties with phonological awareness instruction in combination with training in metacognitive strategies. These children showed greater benefits in word recognition than those who had phonological awareness training alone or no training. The children were taught planning and other metacognitive skills in the context of decoding rather than comprehension. This type of early metacognitive instruction serves to direct children's attention to a different level of cognitive processing than that targeted in much of the research.

Should Children Be Given Instruction in Metacognition and Comprehension Monitoring Before They Are Fluent Readers?

The research base is now sufficiently strong that there is consensus that metacognition should be fostered in comprehension instruction (Baker, 2002). Two influential national committees analyzed the available empirical research and concluded that metacognition is indeed important to reading comprehension (National Reading Panel, 2000; Snow, Burns, & Griffin, 1998). According to Snow et al., children must have "opportunities to develop and enhance language and metacognitive skills to meet the demands of understanding printed texts" (p. 278). They also indicated that "adequate progress in learning to read English beyond the initial level depends on [among other things] control over procedures for monitoring comprehension and repairing comprehension" (p. 223).

Based on several well-controlled instructional studies, the National Reading Panel concluded that comprehension monitoring can and should be taught (see also Trabasso & Bouchard, 2002). Students improve not only in their ability to monitor their understanding but also in their comprehension. Children have been taught by teacher modeling and guided practice to use self-instruction or think-alouds to monitor their own comprehension during reading. Children have also been taught to regulate their comprehension once an obstacle arises, using "fix-up" strategies such as rereading and reading ahead in search of clarification.

Opinions are diverse with respect to the question of when such instruction should begin. As R. Glaubman, H. Glaubman, and Ofir (1997) pointed out, some developmental theorists would predict that children in kindergarten would be too young to benefit from metacognitively oriented instruction, based on research showing that they have difficulty making the connection between awareness and actual use of the strategies or in distinguishing between thought content and knowledge about thinking processes. But other developmental theorists would contend that young children are capable of deeper knowledge about cognitive functioning; they simply have not had the opportunity to acquire relevant strategies. There is now ample evidence that children as young as 4 years can indeed use simple metacognitive strategies under carefully structured conditions and can reason at a rudimentary level about their thinking and the thinking of others (i.e., they have a "theory of mind").

Many educators, historically, have endorsed the view that children should first learn to decode and only then be taught to comprehend. This perspective would rule out any attempt to foster comprehension monitoring at an early age. Chall and Squire (1991), for example, purported that direct instruction in metacognitive skills related to literacy may be inappropriate during the early years of schooling. The National Research Council (Snow et al., 1998) recommended explicit instruction in monitoring for understanding throughout the early grades, beginning in grade 1. Paris (2002) argued that metacognition is important during the initial acquisition of a skill: "The child, for example, needs to become familiar with the task requirements, the goals, and the tactics that enable completion, whether the task is adding numbers, reading words, or assembling toys" (p. 116). In other words, metacognitive aspects of reading should be emphasized in early instruction. Braunger and Lewis (1998) similarly explained that children learning to read need access to their own reading processes.

Others have objected to early metacognitive instruction not because the initial focus should be on decoding, but rather because direct instruction may be developmentally inappropriate for young children. Cox (1994) endorsed instead "a model in which the child is actively involved in the learning activity and a more knowledgeable other (parent, teacher, or peer) may externalize his or her more expert thinking and reasoning through informal social/verbal interactions while assisting the child in completing the activity" (p. 255). Most instructional interventions with a metacognitive/self-regulation focus do in fact use this type of approach. However, Clay (1998) expressed concern that this popular instructional technique of gradual transfer of responsibility through verbal guidance is not appropriate for the teacher working with beginning readers who are aware of very little: "It is not enough to have children adopt our verbal statements about what they are doing. We want them to think about their thinking and not merely parrot teacher talk" (p. 68).

Strategic reading, including comprehension monitoring, is often seen as something that older readers learn, a view held by preservice teachers studied by

Thomas and Barksdale-Ladd (2000). In a comprehensive survey of elementary reading instruction practices, Baumann, Hoffman, Duffy-Hester, and Ro (2000) found that 88% of 1,207 prekindergarten to grade 5 teachers indicated that one of their goals for reading instruction was to produce readers who were skillful and strategic. Intermediate teachers (grades 3–5) were also asked whether they regularly provided instruction in comprehension strategies and in comprehension monitoring. However, teachers in the primary grades were not asked these questions, perhaps reflecting the "decoding first and comprehension later" perspective.

Several sources of evidence are available, suggesting that children can be taught to monitor their comprehension long before they are fluent decoders. One way to do this is to have children listen to stories read aloud rather than have them read independently. Baker (1984) found that young children could monitor their listening comprehension effectively in an error detection paradigm if specifically told that problems would be present. The processes of monitoring for comprehension are similar in listening and reading situations, and children could be sensitized to the need to check their understanding through such everyday classroom activities as teacher read-alouds. Smolkin and Donovan (2002) emphasized the value of teacher read-alouds with young children for promoting metacognition. By starting early, "readers naturally internalize higher order comprehension processing as the way a reader should approach a text" (Pressley & Block, 2002, p. 385).

Juliebo et al. (1998) conducted an in-depth analysis of a small sample of first graders participating in Reading Recovery. Metacognition was assessed by videotaping the intervention sessions and asking children to describe what they were doing through stimulated recall. Children's behaviors during the intervention session reflected self-regulation, and their responses in stimulated recall showed awareness of reading strategies. A similar type of study revealed self-monitoring in first- and second-grade classrooms (Van Leuvan & Wang, 1997). Cox (1994) reported that children as young as age 4 demonstrated some metacognitive awareness and control of their literacy processes as they dictated stories for other children. Finnish first graders (who are a year older than their American counterparts) were shown to be capable of monitoring their comprehension while reading, but as might be expected, children who were struggling with decoding were less likely to recognize that there were inconsistencies in the texts they were reading (Kinnunen, Vauras, & Niemi, 1998). Not only does facility with word recognition enable comprehension, it also enables comprehension monitoring.

Research efforts to teach metacognitively oriented comprehension strategies to young children are rare, but there is evidence that such instruction can be successful. For example, R. Glaubman et al. (1997) examined the effects of a metacognitive intervention in contrast to an active processing intervention on kindergarten children's self-questioning and story comprehension. Relative to the active processing group, children in the metacognitive condition generated better questions and engaged in higher levels of self-directed learning; children in the active processing condition outperformed those in a no treatment comparison condition.

At What Level Are Children Most Likely to Benefit From Metacognitively Oriented Strategies Instruction?

Several syntheses of the research literature raise questions as to the efficacy of metacognitively oriented strategies instruction with young students. Rosenshine and Meister's (1994) meta-analysis revealed that multiple strategies instruction (reciprocal teaching) is most effective for older students, with consistently significant effects only for grades 7 and 8. They suggested that reciprocal teaching was most suited for grade 4 and above, and that weaker and older readers would benefit the most. Similarly, Haller, Child, and Walberg (1988) concluded that the positive effects of teaching metacognition on reading comprehension do not appear until the 7th grade. Chall, Jacobs, and Baldwin (1990) interpreted these results as support for their stage model of reading, which holds that higher level comprehension processes begin to appear when children are reading at grade levels 7 and 8. Indeed, as discussed earlier, there is evidence that significant metacognitive growth occurs during adolescence.

On the other hand, Trabasso and Bouchard (2002) summarized the evidence compiled by the National Reading Panel and concluded that "training in comprehension monitoring can be used successfully in grade levels 2 through 6" (p. 179). Pearson and Duke (2002) were critical of those who argue that children are not able to benefit from comprehension strategy instruction until the intermediate grades, after they have learned how to decode. They identified several studies showing that effective comprehension strategy instruction can take place in first- and second-grade classrooms (e.g., transactional strategies instruction; Pressley et al., 1994). They pointed out that "to delay this sort of powerful instruction until children have reached the intermediate grades is to deny them the very experiences that help them develop the most important of reading dispositions—the expectation that they should and can understand each and every text they read" (p. 257).

Interventions that reduce some of the processing demands of reading are useful for teaching metacognitive strategies to young children and less successful readers whose decoding skills are weak. Demands on working memory are such that insufficient cognitive resources are available to engage in higher level cognitive processing. As already noted, having a teacher read aloud to the students is one way to address this concern. For example, Ivey (2002) recommended a directed listening thinking activity, an adaptation of Directed Reading-Thinking Activity (DR-TA). With the teacher assuming the responsibility for reading the text, the students can focus on building meaning-based strategies and monitoring their understanding. Through thinking aloud, the teacher models the processes involved in predicting, revising, evaluating, and so on. These comprehension strategies can be transferred from listening to reading. In an experimental investigation, LeFevre, Moore, and Wilkinson (2003) used a tape-assisted reciprocal teaching procedure with 9-year-old students whose decoding skills were weak. Students in the intervention showed improved use of cognitive and metacognitive strategies, as well as improved comprehension, relative to a comparison group. As the authors concluded, this technique can serve as a form of "cognitive bootstrapping" to help poor readers have a more meaningful engagement with reading.

Are some metacognitive strategies easier for children to learn than others, and if so, should they be the focus of early instruction? Are some strategies more foundational than others, such that there is an optimal sequence? Just as memory research has shown that rehearsal strategies are acquired earlier and more easily than organizational strategies, so too might there be an optimal sequence for metacognitive strategies in reading. Pearson and Duke (2002) suggested that relating text to prior experiences may be one such foundational strategy. This suggestion is consistent with evidence that this is an early-developing standard with which children can evaluate their comprehension. Baker (1984) found that children as young as kindergarten were fairly successful in identifying information in simple stories that conflicted with what they already knew (e.g., that ice cream does not grow in gardens), but they were much less successful comparing ideas expressed within the text for consistency (e.g., a rabbit's fur is described as "snow white" in one part of the story and brown in another). In this study using the classic error detection paradigm, children listened to stories read aloud by the researcher so that there were no demands on decoding skill. However, children's limited working memory resources still made it more difficult for them to hold information in memory from different parts of the story, and/or to integrate the propositions, which was necessary to detect inconsistencies internal to the story. Older children, in contrast, were better able to detect this type of inconsistency.

Rubman and Waters (2000) devised a technique for helping children perform the necessary integrations for detecting inconsistencies. Skilled and less skilled readers in grades 3 and 6 were assigned to one of two conditions. They read stories containing either internal inconsistencies or external inconsistencies. Half of the children were instructed to create a storyboard representation of the story as a way of externalizing the integration processes necessary to make sense of the story. Children instructed to use this approach were more likely to detect the inconsistencies, of both types, than children who simply read the stories. The benefit was greatest for less skilled readers at both ages. The third graders performed as well as the sixth graders on this task. The authors commented that schools do not typically provide children with instruction on integrating information within a story to create a coherent representation, and so children do not spontaneously think to evaluate text for consistency. However, the fact that children can be taught this skill relatively easily, as shown in the Rubman and Waters study as well as by Baker and Zimlin (1989), suggests that explicit classroom instruction in text integration is warranted.

Should Students Be Taught to Monitor Their Comprehension Deliberately and Routinely?

Given all of the evidence that comprehension monitoring is beneficial to reading, it might be assumed that the answer to this question should be "yes." But consider Clay's (1998) assertion, "We need to have children successfully monitoring and controlling their literacy acts, but with minimal conscious attention" (p. 68). A model proposed by Butterfield, Hacker, and Albertson (1996) allows for monitoring to take place at two different levels: "Readers can decide consciously which standards to use when monitoring comprehension, or . . . they may decide implicitly and automatically" (p. 277). When the decision is made at a conscious level, it competes for valuable working memory resources that are involved in comprehension per se. Less competent readers will have little capacity available for comprehension monitoring, as shown by Kinnunen et al. (1998); first graders who were struggling with decoding were less likely to detect inconsistencies in the texts they were reading than their more advanced classmates.

When teachers provide instruction in comprehension monitoring, the process must, of course, take place on a conscious level. But the goal would be for this "other regulation" to become internalized as "self-regulation" that proceeds automatically until a problem is detected. As Paris (2002) expressed it, "It is erroneous and presumptuous to think that people constantly try to monitor and control their own thinking" (p. 117). Rather, metacognitive skills come into play during troubleshooting, when a problem is encountered and the individual must attempt to resolve it.

Teachers must take care in their instruction not to focus on metacognition as a decontextualized skill. Brown and Campione (1998) expressed dismay with how reciprocal teaching had been appropriated by teachers and textbook publishers: "The surface rituals of questioning, summarizing, and so forth are engaged in, divorced from the goal of reading for understanding that they were designed to serve. These 'strategies' are sometimes practiced out of the context of reading authentic texts" (p. 177). And as Beck, McKeown, Hamilton, and Kucan (1997) noted, a "potential drawback of strategy-based instruction is that the attention of teachers and students may be drawn too easily to the features of the strategies themselves rather than to the meaning of what is being read" (p. 16). In other words, metacognitive skills should be taught within the context of authentic literacy engagement, and students should be given sufficient practice in their application that they know when, why, and how to use them relatively effortlessly.

CONCLUSIONS AND DIRECTIONS
FOR FURTHER RESEARCH

This chapter has reviewed some current research and theory on developmental differences in metacognition that can inform educators with respect to when metacognitive skills can and should be a focus of literacy instruction. At one level, the answer is simple: from the outset. But at another level, it is more complex, because metacognition is not a unitary skill that develops in an all-or-none fashion. By the time children enter school, they are able to reflect on their thinking at a rudimentary level, and they are able to think about a story with respect to what they already know. Thus, it is quite appropriate to ask kindergarten children to question their understanding of a story that has been read aloud to them as it relates to previous experience. At this early stage, however, they are unlikely to do so spontaneously. Similarly, it is quite appropriate to ask first graders whether or not a word they have just decoded with difficulty makes sense in the context of a sentence. But because word recognition poses considerable demands on children's working memory, they likely will experience difficulty evaluating their understanding of a lengthier passage. Just as the complexity of the memory strategies children can use effectively increases over the early years of schooling, from simple rehearsal to organization to elaboration, so too does the complexity of the reading strategies that can be used effectively increase, from relating text to prior knowledge to identifying main ideas to summarizing. In other words, the sorts of metacognitive demands placed on children should increase with development, just as the cognitive demands do.

Calls for additional research were noted throughout the chapter, such as the need for further study of the mechanisms of metacognitive change over time (Baker, 1994; Pintrich et al., 2000), cultural differences in how metacognition is valued and taught (Baker, 1996; Paris, 2002), and how to assess metacognition in developmentally appropriate ways (Baker & Cerro, 2002). Most of the yes–no questions posed in the subheadings of the chapter were answered in the affirmative, but empirical support remains limited. All of these issues should be further explored. For example, based on my interpretation of the available evidence, I concluded that children should be given instruction in metacognition and comprehension monitoring before they are fluent readers. The rationale is that early exposure will help children develop ways of thinking and reacting to text that will serve them well throughout their lives. However, many people have expressed views to the contrary, arguing that children are not yet ready and therefore instruction would not be helpful. The best way to resolve the controversy is to compare the long-term outcomes of children who receive metacognitively oriented literacy instruction from the outset with those of children who receive more conventional literacy instruction. Important outcomes would include not only reading achievement, but also metacognitive awareness, self-regulation, and motivation for reading.

METACONNECTION FOR CHAPTER 4

In chapter 3, we learned that certain aspects of metacognition can be automatic based on developmental levels and levels of instructional intervention. In chapter 4, by Baker, our understanding of when instruction is appropriate based on developmental levels is explained in relationship to instruction. Early exposure will help children develop ways of thinking, however if children are not yet ready for such instruction, metacognitive instruction will not aid a child in becoming more automatic. Part II will follow with an emphasis on metacognition and assessment.

REFERENCES

Baker, L. (1984). Children's effective use of multiple standards for evaluating their comprehension. *Journal of Educational Psychology, 76*, 588–597.

Baker, L. (1989). Metacognition, comprehension monitoring, and the adult reader. *Educational Psychology Review, 1*, 3–38.

Baker, L. (1994). Fostering metacognitive development. In H. Reese (Ed.), *Advances in child development and behavior* (Vol. 25, pp. 201–239). San Diego: Academic Press.

Baker, L. (1996). Social influences on metacognitive development in reading. In C. Cornoldi & J. Oakhill (Eds.), *Reading comprehension difficulties: Processes and interventions* (pp. 331–351). Hillsdale, NJ: Lawrence Erlbaum Associates.

Baker, L. (1999). Opportunities at home and in the community that foster reading engagement. In J. T. Guthrie & D. E. Alvermann (Eds.), *Engagement in reading: Processes, practices, and policy implications* (pp. 105–133). New York: Teachers College Press.

Baker, L. (2000). Building the word-level foundation for engaged reading. In L. Baker, M. J. Dreher, & J. T. Guthrie (Eds.), *Engaging young readers: Promoting achievement and motivation* (pp. 17–42). New York: Guilford.

Baker, L. (2002). Metacognition in comprehension instruction. In C. C. Block & M. Pressley (Eds.), *Comprehension instruction: Research based best practices* (pp. 77–95). New York: Guilford.

Baker, L., & Brown, A. L. (1984). Metacognitive skills and reading. In P. D. Pearson, M. Kamil, R. Barr, & P. Mosenthal (Eds.), *Handbook of research in reading* (pp. 353–395). New York: Longman.

Baker, L., & Cerro, L. (2000). Assessing metacognition in children and adults. In G. Schraw & J. Impara (Eds.), *Issues in the measurement of metacognition* (pp. 99–145). Lincoln, NE: Buros Institute of Mental Measurements, University of Nebraska.

Baker, L., & Zimlin, L. (1989). Instructional effects on children's use of two levels of standards for evaluating their comprehension. *Journal of Educational Psychology, 81*, 340–346.

Baumann, J. F., Hoffman, J. V., Duffy-Hester, A. M., & Ro, J. M. (2000). The First R yesterday and today: U.S. elementary reading instruction practices reported by teachers and administrators. *Reading Research Quarterly, 35*, 338–377.

Beck, I. L., McKeown, M. G., Hamilton, R. L., & Kucan, L. (1997). *Questioning the Author: An approach for enhancing student engagement with text.* Newark, DE: International Reading Association.

Borkowski, J. G., Chan, L.K.S., & Muthukrishna, N. (2000). A process-oriented model of metacognition: Links between motivation and executive functioning. In G. Schraw & J. Impara (Eds.), *Issues in the measurement of metacognition* (pp. 1–42). Lincoln, NE: Buros Institute of Mental Measurements, University of Nebraska.

Braunger, J., & Lewis, J. P. (1997). *Building a knowledge base in reading*. Newark, DE: International Reading Association.

Bouffard, T. (1998). A developmental study of the relationship between reading development and the self-system. *European Journal of Psychology of Education, 13*, 61–74.

Brown, A. L. (1978). Knowing when, where, and how to remember: A problem of metacognition. In R. Glaser (Ed.), *Advances in instructional psychology* (Vol. 1, pp. 65–116). Hillsdale, NJ: Lawrence Erlbaum Associates.

Brown, A. L., & Campione, J. C. (1998). Designing a community of young learners: Theoretical and practical lessons. In N. M. Lambert & B. L. McCombs (Eds.), *How students learn: Reforming schools through learner-centered education* (pp. 153–186). Washington, DC: American Psychological Association.

Butterfield, E. C., Hacker, D. J., & Albertson, L. R. (1996). Environmental, cognitive, and metacognitive influences on text revision: Assessing the evidence. *Educational Psychology Review, 8*, 239–297.

Chall, J. S., Jacobs, V. A., & Baldwin, L. E. (1990). *The reading crisis: Why poor children fall behind*. Cambridge, MA: Harvard University Press.

Chall, J. S., & Squire, J. R. (1991). The publishing industry and textbooks. In R. Barr, M. L. Kamil, P. Mosenthal, & P. D. Pearson (Eds.), *Handbook of reading research* (Vol. 2, pp. 120–146). White Plains, NY: Longman.

Clay, M. M. (1998). *By different paths to common outcomes*. York, ME: Stenhouse.

Cox, B. E. (1994). At-risk preschoolers' emerging control over literacy: Issues of observation, evaluation, and instruction. *Reading & Writing Quarterly: Overcoming Learning Difficulties, 10*, 259–275.

Cunningham, A. E. (1990). Explicit versus implicit instruction in phonemic awareness. *Journal of Experimental Child Psychology, 50*, 429–444.

Davidson, G., & Freebody, P. (1988). Cross-cultural perspectives on the development of metacognitive thinking. *Hiroshima Forum for Psychology, 13*, 21–31.

Flavell, J. H. (1976). Metacognitive aspects of problem solving. In L. B. Resnick (Ed.), *The nature of intelligence* (pp. 231–235). Hillsdale, NJ: Lawrence Erlbaum Associates.

Flavell, J. H. (1985). *Cognitive development* (2nd ed.). Englewood Cliffs, NJ: Prentice Hall.

Glaubman, R., Glaubman, H., & Ofir, L. (1997). Effects of self-directed learning, story comprehension, and self-questioning in kindergarten. *Journal of Educational Research, 90*, 361–374.

Hacker, D. J., Dunlosky, J., & Graesser, A. C. (Eds.). (1998). *Metacognition in educational theory and practice*. Mahwah, NJ: Lawrence Erlbaum Associates.

Haller, E. P., Child, D. A., & Walberg, H. J. (1988). Can comprehension be taught? A quantitative synthesis of "metacognitive" studies. *Educational Researcher, 17*(9), 5–8.

Ivey, G. (2002). Building comprehension when they're still learning to read the words. In C. C. Block & M. Pressley (Eds.), *Comprehension instruction: Research based best practices* (pp. 234–246). New York: Guilford.

Juliebo, M., Malicky, G. V., & Norman, C. (1998). Metacognition of young readers in an early intervention programme. *Journal of Research in Reading, 21*, 24–35.

Kinnunen, R., Vauras, M., & Niemi, P. (1998). Comprehension monitoring in beginning readers. *Scientific Studies of Reading, 2*, 353–375.

LeFevre, D. M., Moore, D. W., & Wilkinson, I. A. (2003). Tape-assisted reciprocal teaching: Cognitive bootstrapping for poor decoders. *British Journal of Educational Psychology, 73*, 37–58.

McCormick, C. B. (2003). Metacognition and learning. In W. M Reynolds & G. E. Miller (Eds.), *Handbook of psychology: Educational psychology* (Vol. 7, pp. 79–102). New York: Wiley.

Mokhtari, K., & Reichard, C. A. (2002). Assessing students' metacognitive awareness of reading strategies. *Journal of Educational Psychology, 94,* 249–259.

National Reading Panel (2000). *Teaching children to read: An evidence-based assessment of the scientific research literature on reading and its implications for reading instruction.* Bethesda, MD: National Institute of Child Health and Human Development.

Paris, S. G. (1991). Assessment and remediation of metacognitive aspects of children's reading comprehension. *Topics in Language Disorders, 12,* 32–50.

Paris, S. G. (2002). When is metacognition helpful, debilitating, or benign? In P. Chambres, M. Izaute, & P. Marescaux (Eds.), *Metacognition: Process, function and use* (pp. 105–120). Boston: Kluwer.

Pearson, P. D., & Duke, N. K. (2002). Comprehension instruction in the primary grades. In C. C. Block & M. Pressley (Eds.), *Comprehension instruction: Research based best practices* (pp. 247–258). New York: Guilford.

Peverly, S T., Brobst, K. E., & Morris, K. S. (2002). The contribution of reading comprehension ability and meta-cognitive control to the development of studying in adolescence. *Journal of Research in Reading, 25,* 203–216.

Pintrich, P. R., Wolters, C. A., & Baxter, G. P. (2000). In G. Schraw & J. Impara (Eds.), *Issues in the measurement of metacognition* (pp. 43–98). Lincoln, NE: Buros Institute of Mental Measurements, University of Nebraska.

Pintrich, P. R., & Zusho, A. (2002). The development of academic self-regulation: The role of cognitive and motivational factors. In A. Wigfield & J. S. Eccles (Eds.), *Development of achievement motivation* (pp. 249–284). San Diego: Academic Press.

Pressley, M., Almasi, J., Schuder, T., Bergman, J., Hite, S., El-Dinary, P. B., & Brown, R. (1994). Transactional instruction of comprehension strategies: The Montgomery County, Maryland, SAIL program. *Reading & Writing Quarterly: Overcoming learning difficulties, 10,* 5–19.

Pressley, M., & Block, C. C. (2002). Summing up: What comprehension instruction could be. In C. C. Block & M. Pressley (Eds.), *Comprehension instruction: Research based best practices* (pp. 383–392). New York: Guilford.

Roeschl-Heils, A., Schneider, W., & van Kraayenoord, C. E. (2003). Reading, metacognition and motivation: A follow-up study of German students 7 and 8. *European Journal of Psychology of Education, 18,* 75–86.

Rosenshine, B., & Meister, C. (1994). Reciprocal teaching: A review of the research. *Review of Educational Research, 64,* 479–530.

Rubman, C. N., & Waters, H. S. (2000). A, B seeing: The role of constructive processes in children's comprehension monitoring. *Journal of Educational Psychology, 92,* 503–514.

Schoonen, R., & Hulstijn, J. (1998). Metacognitive and language-specific knowledge in native and foreign language reading comprehension: An empirical study among Dutch students in grades 6, 8 and 10. *Language Learning, 48,* 71–106.

Serpell, R., Baker, L., & Sonnenschein, S. (2005). *Becoming literate in the city: The Baltimore Early Childhood Project.* New York: Cambridge University Press.

Simpson, M. L., & Nist, S. L. (2002). Encouraging active reading at the college level. In C. C. Block & M. Pressley (Eds.), *Comprehension instruction: Research based best practices* (pp. 365–382). New York: Guilford.

Smolkin, L. B., & Donovan, C. A. (2002). Oh excellent, excellent question! Developmental differences and comprehension instruction. In C. C. Block & M. Pressley (Eds.), *Comprehension instruction: Research based best practices* (pp. 140–157). New York: Guilford.

Snow, C. E., Burns, M. S., & Griffin, P. (Eds.). (1998). *Preventing reading difficulties in young children*. Washington, DC: National Academy Press.

Sperling, R. A., Howard, B. C., Miller, L. A., & Murphy, C. (2002). Measures of children's knowledge and regulation of cognition. *Contemporary Educational Psychology, 27*, 51–79.

Thomas, K. F., & Barksdale-Ladd, M. A. (2000). Metacognitive processes: Teaching strategies in literacy education courses. *Reading Psychology, 21*, 67–84.

Trabasso, T., & Bouchard, E. (2002). Teaching readers how to comprehend text strategically. In C. C. Block & M. Pressley (Eds.), *Comprehension instruction: Research based best practices* (pp. 176–200). New York: Guilford.

Tracey, D. H., & Morrow, L. M. (2002). Preparing young learners for successful reading comprehension: Laying the foundation. In C. C. Block & M. Pressley (Eds.), *Comprehension instruction: Research based best practices* (pp. 219–233). New York: Guilford.

van Kraayenoord, C. E., & Schneider, W. E. (1999). Reading achievement, metacognition, reading self-concept and interest: A study of German students in grades 3 and 4. *European Journal of Psychology of Education, 14*, 305–324.

Van Leuvan, P., & Wang, M. C. (1997). An analysis of students' self-monitoring in first- and second-grade classrooms. *Journal of Education Research, 90*, 132–143.

Vygotsky, L. S. (1978). *Mind in society*. Cambridge, MA: MIT Press.

Wright, J., & Barrie, J. (2003). Teaching phonological awareness and metacognitive strategies to children with reading difficulties: A comparison of two instructional methods. *Educational Psychology, 23*, 17–45.

II

Metacognition and Assessment

Assessment informs instruction. Because we thoroughly believe this pedagogical foundation, we have included the assessment section before the instruction section. The assessment section is unique in that it includes a variety of metacognitive assessments, some never before published and some that are newly updated and improved. They also run the gamut of age appropriateness: Some assessment techniques are appropriate for elementary students as young as first grade and some are appropriate for junior high and high school students.

This section builds on the theory section in several important ways. After reading part I, we have a more thorough understanding of metacognition and its importance in literacy learning. We have a working definition and explanation of the role of metacognition in chapter 1 (Griffith & Ruan). Chapter 2 (Randi, Grigorenko, & Sternberg) helps us understand the importance of metacognition in literacy learning as we focus on building comprehension processes. In chapter 3 (Samuels, Ediger, Willcutt, & Palumbo), we discover a deeper understanding of the importance of automaticity and fluency as they help us build on our theoretical foundations. Finally, we have a description of the most current research in chapter 4 (Baker) that shapes our understanding of metacognition, as well as directs us into future areas of research.

Part II provides an excellent classroom resource for metacognitive assessments. Block's chapter 5 contains a definition of metacognitive assessments and includes a variety of informal classroom assessments appropriate to a variety of ages. Schmitt's chapter 6 talks about how to assess awareness and control of strategic comprehension processes for younger children. Chapter 7, by Paris and Flukes, focuses on metacognitive assessments for strategic reading with practical examples from grades 1, 4, and 7. Once children have seen metacognitive strategies modeled by teachers, they are ready to move to self-assessment strategies, appropriate for middle school and junior high students, discussed in chapter 8 by Afflerbach and Meuwissen. Finally, in chapter 9, by Bauserman, we learn of a developing model for assessing 11 metacognitive processes, a tool that shows promise for all ages.

Once practitioners have chosen, administered, and analyzed an appropriate assessment tool, they are ready to choose the most beneficial instructional tools for meeting identified student needs. Therefore, this part on assessment is followed by part III, which contains a complete guide to metacognitive instruction.

5

What Are Metacognitive Assessments?

Cathy Collins Block
Texas Christian University

I want to know how to teach and assess my students to the best of my ability. Maybe this chapter could teach me ways of assessment that I had not previously considered. I know that students need to learn how to "think about thinking." As teachers we have to remember that learning is not as natural of a process as it may seem. How will I know when this learning is taking place? Will I evaluate this based on growth, or based on daily reflections and strategies being shown?
    —Michelle Evans-Sapp, Special Education, Grades 7–12, Indiana

This chapter, hopefully, answers some of Michelle's questions about metacognitive assessments.

As the bell rang to end the school year, Ms. Whalen, at St. Mary of the Mills School (Baltimore, MD), said good-bye to her fifth graders. Jeanette was the last to leave. With tears in her eyes, she said she would miss Ms. Whalen, and she handed her this note:

Dear Ms. Whalen,

I liked how you tested my reading comprehension. You always asked me what I wanted to learn next. I liked the new metacognitive tests. Because of them, I have read four times as much as I used to. I think that we should stick with these kinds of tests. This is the best class I've had in all my 5 years at Saint Mary's School. I love you,

Jeanette Montgomery

Can comprehension be better assessed? This question has been asked for several decades. Many assessment issues arise in classrooms everyday. "How often does Roberto imagine?" "Can Mariettalynette infer?" "How often does Peggy engage effective metacognitive processes before, during, and after reading?" "How motivated is Charles to overcome his confusion as he reads?" "How can I be sure that my students are applying what they learned in this text to their lives?"

Unfortunately, research in educational evaluation has not advanced as rapidly as the body of knowledge concerning instructional methodology. Most reading comprehension tests do not incorporate the principles discussed in this book. They are based on brief paragraphs, and do not viably measure students' metacognition. Moreover, such tests assess pupil's background experiences with a topic rather than their ability to initiate metacognitive processes independently. This chapter reports new research-based methods of assessing literacy. It describes 10 metacognitive measures that have been demonstrated to significantly increase students' comprehension (Block & Mangieri, 1996; Stewart, Cummins, Block, & Lewis, 2004), and provides answers to these questions:

1. How can the metacognitive components of reading comprehension be measured?
2. How can we advance the field of metacognitive assessment?
3. How can we assess metacomprehension in beginning readers?
4. What can administrators, teachers, and students document each of individuals' metacognitive success?

HISTORICAL PERSPECTIVE AND RESEARCH

Metacognitive assessment is defined as an evaluation of a reader's awareness and knowledge of the mental processes engaged during reading. It also tests if a reader can monitor, regulate, and direct their thoughts before, during, and after reading to obtain a complete comprehension of text (Block, 2004; Harris & Hodges, 1995). Metacognitive readers know how they comprehend and why, at times, they do not comprehend well. They activate relevant prior knowledge before, during, and after reading, and easily use newly learned information in their lives (Pearson, Roehler, Dole, & Duffy, 1992; Pressley & Afflerbach, 1995). They image and determine the most important ideas in a text (Brown & Palincsar, 1985; Reznitskaya & Anderson, 2001). They ask questions, draw inferences (NICHHD, 2000; NRP, 1999), and use a variety of fix-up strategies (Block, Gambrell, & Pressley, 2003; Garner, 1987).

Unfortunately, such readers are a minority in today's schools. Researchers (as represented in this book) are working diligently to make this minority population the majority. This work has been listed as one of the nation's most pressing needs.

To date, not enough programs have been developed to promote metacognition, much less the assessment instruments that can be used to measure their success. More curricula and evaluative tools must be examined empirically. There is an equal need to identify the factors that contribute to the speed with which above, on, and below grade level students become automatic, metacognitive readers. Do students of variant reading ability levels require different instructional methods to build lifelong automatic use of metacognitive thinking?

Since the last century, teaching comprehension has been dominated by merely providing instruction to read and answer questions over what was read (Durkin, 1976/1977). This must change. Students cannot be left to learn how to think metacognitive on their own. Recitation of facts must be deemphasized. Responsive individualized interactions with text must become commonplace in the classroom. The metacognitive assessments described in this chapter are a first step toward attaining this goal.

The National Reading Panel (1999) and the Rand Reading Study Group (Sweet & Snow, 2002) found that the elementary school years are the most critical years in which educators must diagnose the depths of students' metacomprehension competencies. Unless such determinations are made by third grade, most students will have developed too many defense mechanisms to camouflage their weaknesses. Their shame, guilt, and history of failure as a reader further diminish their desire to make meaning from text. Only very precise and effective assessment instruments can tap these students' metacognitive thought processes while they are engaged in reading so that teachers can assist these readers to disarm this arsenal of defenses. If these students' metacognitions are not developed early, most will develop even more elaborate camouflages of their reading failures, and the chances of ever experiencing pleasure from reading in their lives is significantly decreased (Block, 2004).

Stewart et al. (2004) completed a research project to answer these empirical questions, involving 1,310 students from states in the southwestern United States. Fifty-four experimental and control classrooms of approximately 25 students each were randomly assigned to treatment groups in second-, third-, fourth-, and sixth-grade classrooms. Students represented high, middle, and low socioeconomic levels. Subjects came from Caucasian, African American, Hispanic, Asian, and multiracial backgrounds. All experimental subjects engaged in three metacognitive programs. Method 1 employed structured, charted whole-class discussions. Method 2 utilized post-it note prompts, proceeded by enhanced think-aloud, and guided instruction. Method 3 used visual metacognitive prompts in the form of bookmarks to alert students' to 12 metacognitions that have proven to enhance comprehension at specific points in a text (Block & Israel, 2004).

Following 6 weeks of participation in each method, students were administered a few of the end-of-treatment metacognitive assessments described in this chapter, as well as the Stanford Achievement Vocabulary and Comprehension Subtests. Data from structured weekly oral interviews, and work samples were also collected. Analyses of variance and regression analyses were used to determine the statistical value of these metacognitive programs. Work samples were tallied in three ways, and they were tested through a repeated measures design. Interviews were analyzed qualitatively and quantitatively. Results demonstrated that the three instructional programs and assessment methods significantly increased elementary and middle school students' metacognition in six distinct areas. Students who became metacognitive readers outscored peers who had not developed metacognitive reading abilities, as measured by the metacognitive assessments described in this chapter. The least amount of time that it took for a significant number of students to attain automatic metacognitive reading ability was 6 weeks with students who were not exposed to proper treatments and assessment tools being unable to reach automaticity after 16 weeks of controlled conditions without metacognitive instruction (Block et al., in press).

Other studies are under way to examine the effects new staff development programs designed to enhance teachers' assessment abilities. These are entitled the Best Comprehension Practices Consortium, sponsored by the Institute for Literacy Enhancement (Mangieri, 2004). These training programs are creating new assessment initiatives that enable teachers to "get inside the heads" of students' independent silent reading processes. The work at this institute documented that teachers want new metacognitive assessment tools. They want tests that not only assess what they have taught about comprehension, but also how much students are actively using them to craft their own metacognitively guided meaning. When such measures are developed, it has been argued that children's zones of proximal development (Vygotsky, 1978) and their rates of learning can be advanced. Moreover, of the 12 principles needed to advance the assessment of comprehension, the following 7 relate specifically to how we can assess students' metacognition better (Block, 2004; Tierney, 1998):

- Assessments should lead from behind. They should help students assess themselves, with instruction being delivered to address individual needs after students' metacognitions have been assessed.
- Assessment should extend beyond improving present tests to making new tests that are more conceptually valid.
- Unfortunately, in the past, test developers tried to make tests culture free, which is impossible: "Cultural free assessments afford, at best, only a partial, perhaps distorted, understanding of a student's [meta]comprehension ability" (Tierney, 1998, p. 381).
- Future comprehension tests must allow for different students to have differing amounts of encouragement and support to measure the degrees that they are interrelating metacognitive processes. Some students have the potential to reveal their inner thoughts accurately, others do not, and still others do not process meaning metacognitively as they read. Future tests must tap into this metacognitive knowledge more directly.

- Some things worth assessing cannot be evaluated except through student self-assessment (e.g., self-questioning, self-reported engagement, and degrees of interpretation).
- The interaction between speed, factual literal recall, vocabulary development, inference accuracy, and metacognitive depth must be assessed. Presently, few tests measure such interactions.
- Assessment should be developmentally appropriate. They must contain sustained silent reading rather than "dipstick approaches" to assessment. Instead of measuring all of children's ability in one day, using only a few paragraphs or page-length passages, metacognitive tests should continue for several days, and be calculated through reading for longer than 5 minutes on a specific topic.

NEW TESTS AND HOW TO MOVE THE FIELD FORWARD

Research has demonstrated that teachers can use the following metacognitive assessments to scaffold, support, and document students' self-initiated literacy processes. They evaluate growth more effectively through pinpointing exactly when metacognition becomes an active and self-initiated process by students. These research-based tools are prototypes, and as such can be modified to address the complexity of individual student needs in single classrooms around the world.

Metacognitive Assessment 1: "What Do We Need to Fill in?" Test

Based on the research of Block et al. (in press) and Oakhill and Yuill (1999), one of the most effective metacognitive assessments is a test that allows students to recognize and use their metacognition to resolve inconsistencies that occur in a text. In this test, children describe what needs to be "fixed" in a particular passage so that the information makes sense, and adjacent sentences can be linked seamlessly. Children who need more work in integrating inferences with literal comprehension will not perform well on this test. By administering it, teachers can find out which types of information (literal or inferential) are not being processed metacognitively by individual students.

In kindergarten through grade 3, this test begins with a blank sheet of paper, turned landscape style that has been divided into eight equal size numbered boxes. In each box, students write a sentence, or draw a picture that could be used to complete the idea that you do not read from a page in a text. The information students record in the first box corresponds to the information that you want them to deduce had to occur on the first page at which you stopped your reading.

The second box, progressing horizontally across the page, corresponds to the information that you want them to infer through use of their metacognitive processes that must occur on the second page that you stopped and did not read, and so on. This test allows children to tell what needs to be "fixed" in a particular passage so that the text is complete. These boxes can also be used to assess students' abilities to integrate literal and inferential comprehension processes.

For older students, this test becomes a silent reading test. They read a section of text in which you placed numbered post-it notes over a sentence that communicated vital literal information. Students are to stop at each covered portion of text and record in the boxes marked with the corresponding number on each post-it note the literal sentence that should appear at this spot to make the text coherent.

The "What Do We Need to Fill in?" test can also be given orally and individually. A child can come to your desk to read a passage, similar to the one used in Oakhill and Yuill's research (1999): "A scarecrow was dressed by someone else. A scarecrow is tied down to a pole forever. He is not allowed to turn his head at all. He must stand in the rain without an umbrella all day long. When the winter comes, no one lends him a coat. But a scarecrow's life is all his own" (Modified from *Scarecrow* by Cynthia Ryland, 1998).

When students have read it, they tell what they read in a retelling. Then, you ask: "What do we need to fill in to make this story more complete for others to read?" When children read and tell what needs to be added to make the text easier for others to comprehend, they reveal what it is that they need to comprehend better. As they answer this question, write down as many of their comments as possible in the first box of the "What Do We Need to Fill in" test. Date your entry. Keep a separate boxed test for each child. Administer the assessment four times during the year. When students return to their seats, and the next pupil comes to read the same passage, you diagnose the next type of instruction that child needs and write the name in the appropriate column of the "What Do We Need to Fill in" metacognitive instructional planner shown in Fig. 5.1. During the next week, you can place children into groups based on the types of literal and metacognitive processes that individuals need to be taught.

This boxed test format can be modified in many ways, as shown in the first- and second-grade classrooms in our study. Ms. Painter, a first-grade teacher, made one full sheet a single box in which students were to write the comprehension processes they used to deduce what the conclusion to the book would be (and to draw a picture of it.) Students drew what they thought the last picture in the book would be. Ms. Zinke, a second-grade teacher, asked students to use only four boxes to fill in pictures and/or text of what was needed at marked sections of the text to make the text fit together, and then she used the bottom portion of the boxed test as a single unit. Students were to take the full bottom half of the page to write the moral that the author was communicating in the story.

	Group 1	Group 2	Group 3	Group 4
1. Did not recognize that they did not comprehend	Robert Lance Paige			
2. Did not make connections between paragraphs		Suzette Margueretta		
3. Did not find main ideas				Paige Josh
4. Could not recall the sequence				
5. Did not infer				
6. Could not summarize			Robert Megan	
7. Did not image				
8. Did not determine author's writing pattern or till the text				
9. Could not draw a conclusion or summarize				

FIG. 5.1. What do we need to fill in metacognitive instructional planner.

Metacognitive Assessment 2: "What's the Problem?" Test

This test is designed to measure students' imagery and metacognition. To conduct this assessment, you can create two passages that children are to read aloud. In each passage, you substitute "Xs" (using the same number of "Xs" as there are letters in the missing word represented by the XXX's). The word that you select is one that could be visually imaged. You continue to make such substitutions in alternating sentences, so that one sentence would be left intact but it would be followed by a sentence that had an XXXX'd word typed in place of a word that is metacognitively rich because it has a high capacity for mental imagery. The words to be removed are vivid verbs and thick nouns.

For example, if you were to use sentences from *My Chinatown: One Year in Poems* (Mak, 2002), you would rewrite the underlined word into a nonsense word in the following two sentences: "I pass the cobbler everyday sitting and working on shoes. I stop and watch him cutting the leather in small curves, pulling the needle, tugging the thread tight" (Mak, 2002, p. 7). The reason that "thread" would be selected to be rewritten as "XXXXX" is because if students were imaging as they read, the visual image of "thread" must be present in their mental pictures. In addition, many context clues had been given so that students who are metacognitively processing text and imaging as they read would realize that thread would be the only word that could appear in that location in the text. Therefore, if students read this passage and do not recognize that "XXXXX" stood for thread, then you could deduce that these students needed instruction on how to metacognitively process and image as they read.

This assessment would not be based on only two sentences, however. New metacomprehension tests should use more than one page of text. The text a child reads should have at least 10 words removed from 20 sentences. Such a length will ensure that students have several opportunities to demonstrate their imagery abilities. However, if students miss the first three words, then you can stop the test. These students would not be able to score 80% proficiency even if they were to continue.

On a subsequent day, you can create a "What's the Problem" test with paragraphs in which a key detail sentence is removed. Select 10 paragraphs from the same text. Allow students to read these paragraphs. When they finish, ask them if they noticed anything that did not make sense in the text. According to Oakhill and Yuill (1999), "67% more skilled metacognitive readers will comment on problems than will less-skilled comprehenders (17%)" (p. 78). Then, in a second set of 10 paragraphs, tell the students in advance that there will be something wrong in every paragraph. Instruct them to stop reading and tell you if they find something that does not make sense.

According to Oakhill and Yuill's (1999) research, both skilled and nonskilled readers are equally able to detect problems in text when told to do so in advance. If students detect all errors in both testing experiences, they are independently engaging their metacomprehension processes with texts at that level of readability. If they scored higher on the second set of paragraphs than the first, the difference in these scores suggests that students may know that they are thinking metacognitively while reading, but are unable to initiate these processes. Similarly, if a student detects only a few problems in one or both sets of passages, these scores indicate that this student would profit from additional metacognitive, personalized teacher-scaffolded instruction.

Metacognitive Assessment 3: "Did You Till the Text?" Test

Tilling a text is defined as a students' metacognitive ability to deduce traits in an author's writing style that clue meaning. Tilling the text includes recognizing a text's organizational format, methods used to place emphases on key points, inferred meanings, and metacognitively falling in line with the pace and depth of an author's train of thought. According to research, a significant interaction occurs between students' abilities to till a text and retain literal information (Block, 2004; Oakhill & Yuill, 1999). Less skilled metacognitive comprehenders were more affected by the distance that existed between incongruent information than were skilled metacognitive readers.

The "Did You Till the Text?" test was created as a metacognitive assessment to identify whether or not students tilled a text and noticed inconsistencies separated by several sentences. To make this metacognitive test, identify a passage whereby a sentence is inserted on every other page that does not make sense. Then, ask children to read and decide if the passage does or does not make sense.

The statements individuals make will not only assess which children can till a text, but which ones can follow an authorial writing pattern. The error pattern on this test documents students' highest level of long-term memory and how much information can be retained. To deduce this information, it is important to know that short-term memory stores and integrates information, whereas long-term memory processes this information to make inferences. Poor readers are less able to monitor texts, detect anomalies, and make inferences if different parts of a text are inconsistent. Integration is especially difficult for this population if unusually large portions of their mental energy must be allocated to decoding (Oakhill & Yuill, 1998; Perfetti & Lesco, 1979; Stanovich, 1986; Tergeson & Wagner, 1987).

"Did You Till the Text?" tests can be conducted orally. When administered in this manner, stop students and ask them what they noticed or were thinking about a text feature (e.g., an author's subheading, character's dialogue, or descriptive passage) on a specific page. Metacognitive readers will include in their description statement indicators that they are using the information you highlighted to predict, or to create a connection between information. When conducted as a written assessment, this metacognitive test can become a self-assessment or a teacher-guided evaluation. To make this written version, you preview a text and list the features of the writing style that should be attended to by a reader. These features are listed on a sheet of paper. If the written test is to become a self-assessment, then students are to rank how often they paid attention to each of these features, as shown in the sample of such a test that appears in Fig. 5.2. Alternatively, students can write what they were thinking as they come to each of these features.

If the test is to become teacher guided, then ask a student to read a page silently or orally. The reader stops at a point. You ask the students what they are thinking as they read that authorial clue to meaning. If the student is processing the text metacognitively, write their answer and continue reading. If the student is not processing the text metacognitively, stop and perform a think-aloud, which can illuminate the metacognitive thinking that should be engaged at this point in this text (and at similar points in future text) to obtain a more complete and fulfilling meaning.

Name_____ Grade _____ Date _____

Write the numbers to describe your most self-initiated metacognition during a recent reading in the boxes below.

GUIDE MYSELF THROUGH TEXT	Always Do Without Teacher Prompting		Sometimes		Can't Do At All Without Teacher Prompting
	5	4	3	2	1
1. Set my purpose					
2. Make predictions					
3. Till the text					
4. Find Summaries					
5. Draw Inferences					
6. Ask Myself ?s					
7. Recognize Important Details					
8. Image					
9. Recall and Apply Information to Life					

FIG. 5.2.   Did you till the text metacognitive test.

Metacognitive Assessment 4: "Thinking to the End" Summary Test

This evaluation is administered after students have been taught to synthesize information at the end of paragraphs, stories, and pages. Students are to read a paragraph or page. Ask them what they did when they were inferred or imaged. When they describe what they did (whether they were putting single facts together, putting themselves in the text, or integrating new pieces of information in to the ongoing story), their answers provide clues as to what children can do metacognitively when reading large bodies of information, and what they can be taught to improve their self-initiated summarization/drawing conclusion processes.

Figure 5.3 is a prototype of the "Thinking to the End" metacognitive summary test. In this assessment, students write their answers to each query in the space that follows it. When an answer is incorrect, the student is not self-initiating this metacognitive step in the summary process. For younger students, instead of asking what they are thinking (which Pressley, 1976, determined to be a very difficult task), ask them to play school and teach someone else to read. You can also assess younger students' summative metacognitive processes by asking them to draw pictures to depict the end of a narrative or expository texts that you read to

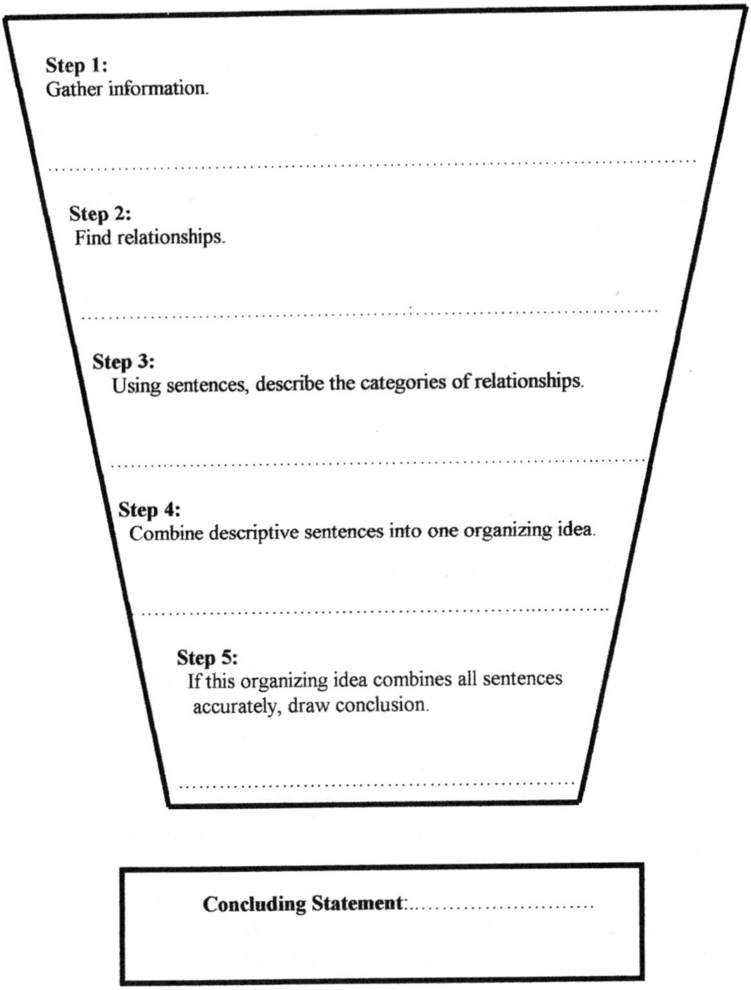

Step 1:
Gather information.

....

Step 2:
 Find relationships.

....

Step 3:
 Using sentences, describe the categories of relationships.

....

Step 4:
 Combine descriptive sentences into one organizing idea.

....

Step 5:
 If this organizing idea combines all sentences
 accurately, draw conclusion.

....

Concluding Statement:..........................

FIG. 5.3. Think to the end metacognitive summary test.

them. As the children draw, you can deduce what they are thinking and assess the quality of their independently generated summative thoughts.

Metacognitive Assessment 5: "What Were You Unable to Think About in the Harder Book?" Test

For children age 9 and older, metacognition can be assessed through this test by giving students two books. One book is at their grade level, and the second one is on a different topic above their grade level. Both books should be selected by the child to ensure that the affective domain is equal in both testing situations. Next, students read two consecutive pages from each book. Then, ask what they thought about while they read the more different book. Inquire as to what they were unable to think about as they read the more difficult book that they were able to think about while they read the easier book. Finally, ask what they thought about when they read the easier book and what they would like to learn to think more about so that in the future when they read difficult books comprehension will be easier.

You may receive answers like: "I want to remember more of the details"; "I want to think more about where the author's going. I can't follow what's being said"; or "I want to learn how to find the big ideas. I want to summarize what I read better." This assessment is based on the principle that children can determine (for themselves) how to become better comprehenders.

Metacognitive Assessment 6: Student-Selected Self-Assessments

These metacognitive evaluations enable students to measure their own comprehension and metacognition. Students can also select the type of metacognitive self-assessment format they like best. Such forms include a checklist in which they list the comprehension processes taught that week and give themselves a 5, 4, 3, 2, or 1 rating as to how well they learned each; an essay test in which they describe what they want to learn next; or work samples that they grade, stating the criteria they used to determine their own metacognitive grade on their reading of specific texts. Such metacognitive self-assessments as these have been demonstrated to increase students' motivation to think metacognitively as they read (Guthrie et al., 2000).

To become more effective, students use one metacognitive self-assessment form every 6 weeks (at the beginning of the year). They should not be used more frequently than once every 3 weeks in the second half of the year. Children store these self-assessments in their portfolios or reading folders, and share them with you during one-on-one conferences.

Metacognitive Assessment 7: Color-Coded Metacomprehension Process Portfolios

In this assessment, students choose the metacomprehension process for which they want to be evaluated. Students insert examples of text that demonstrate that they used a process correctly in a color-coded folder. For example, when students want to demonstrate how they let main ideas emerge as they read, they use a yellow highlighter to mark each paper that demonstrated their independent use of that metacognitive process. Or, when they are reading magazines or computer pages that can be printed and stored in folders, students mark a yellow strip across the top when they found the main idea independently. All papers with yellow highlights are stored together, or these papers can be placed in a yellow folder. When you teach another process, you highlight the papers to be used for pupils' independent practice with a different color. In like manner, when students independently initiated other metacognitive processes, such as imaging, inferring, or drawing conclusions, the different colored highlighter that you specified during that instructional period would mark them.

Then, when you are ready to assess students' independent ability to discern main ideas (or any other metacognitive ability), you can reference that folder and ask them to describe how the main ideas in one of the highlighted passages were found. The benefits of color-coded comprehension folders is that students learn metacognitive processes fast because color serves as a reference tool. Also, this evaluation enables students to be assessed using passages for which they know they have achieved a mastery of a specific metacomprehension process. In so doing, you increase their motivation, self-efficacy, and abilities to choose books wisely (Block, 2004). Moreover, color-coded metacognitive assessments enable students to set higher expectations than is possible through other forms of paper-and-pencil assessments, such as multiple-choice tests.

Metacognitive Assessment 8: "Telling What Metacomprehension Processes I'm Using" Test

This assessment is to be used after several metacognitive processes are taught. During the instructional period, students are taught to move their hands to depict a specific mental process that occurs when they complete a specific metacognitive process. For example, as depicted in the sample "Telling What Metacomprehension Processes I'm Using" test in Fig. 5.4, students would have been taught how to make the Comprehension Process Motions that are displayed from top left to right and bottom left to right: Inference, Using Context Clues, Clarifying a Confusion, Predicting, and Drawing a Conclusion. After these processes are taught, you distribute a copy of Fig. 5.4. To administer, stop student's reading at strategic points in a text in which a particular metacognitive process, depicted on the assessment, should be used. Say a number, using one for the first time you stop, and ask students to write the number you say below the thinking process they are using at that point in the text and to write that number on one of the lines in the center of the test. If they are not using any of the comprehension processes depicted on the "Telling What Metacomprehension Processes I'm Using" test at that moment, instruct students to write the number on one of the lines in the middle of the page. Next, ask students to describe what they are thinking after the number you said on the lines in the center of the test. You are to pause stu-

FIG. 5.4.   Tell what metacomprehension process I'm using test.

dents' reading for this assessment twice for kindergarten students, three times for first graders, and four times for second and third graders. After the written portion of the test is complete, collect the papers to grade individually and place them in groups for re-teaching using a form similar to Fig. 5.1.

Metacognitive Assessment 9: Long-Term Memory Test

To assess pupils' long-term memory, ask students to recall and list all the books that they have read (or all of the stories that have been taught within the past 2 weeks from the literature anthology). When you review this list, you can identify gaps in each student's long-term memory (e.g., the title of a story you know the child has read during the past 2 weeks that is not listed). Then you can ask the child to tell you about that story, noting specific facts and gaps between information recalled during this prompted retelling assessment. You then ask students to tell you (or write) about the most memorable book that they have read. When finished, ask them to tell you the differences they discern concerning how much was remembered from each reading experience. Next, have them deduce why those differences existed. These thoughts can be used to guide the metacognitive instruction provided in coming weeks so that students' self-initiated metacognitive thinking, without prompting, can be strengthened.

Metacognitive Assessment 10: Teaching Students the Process of Assessing Their Own Comprehension Processes When They Select Books

This test assists students to become more active participants in increasing their own metacognitive abilities. It also enables you to determine how well students assume the responsibility of assessing their own metacomprehension when they select a book.

Step 1. Metacognitive readers know that they can read more advanced books in topics about which they have read extensively in the past. Therefore, students identify the topic about which they want to read based on how much and what they want to learn in this particular reading experience. Do they want to learn, relax, review, or escape into another person's world? As students approach a set of books, their purpose for reading will determine the thickness of the book they select. For example, if they want to relax, they may choose a shorter book than if they want to learn very specific information about a topic.

Step 2. Metacognitive readers select books written by authors that they enjoy. Students are taught, and are then assessed as to how well they survey specific author writing styles. If a favorite author or captivating title attracts the attention of highly skilled metacognitive readers, they examine that book, till the text, and scan the authorial writing pattern before deciding to read it.

Step 3. Students are taught, and then assessed, to thumb through a book to determine the density of the text and the amount of effort that they will have to exert to enjoy this author's writing. Then, they are to select a single page near the middle of the book to read to determine whether or not they know the majority of words. As they read that page, students can press one finger down on the opposite page for every word that they do not know. If the student presses down all five fingers on one hand before a single page has been read, this student could deduce that this book may cause so much frustration in decoding, that the comprehension and enjoyment of it may be compromised. In such cases, students are taught and metacognitively evaluated as to whether or not they returned to Step 1 to repeat the prior steps in this book selection process.

DIRECTIONS FOR FUTURE RESEARCH

Much research must be completed before we can determine how many of the metacognitive tests in this chapter are needed in a single year. We must also identify which types of metacognitive evaluations can become standardized and norm referenced. Our body of knowledge has not yet proven which tests in this chapter should be administered first. Can an evaluation hierarchy be built? Are certain tests better indicators of young children's metacognition than others? The tests in this chapter are an initial effort to present research-based tests of metacognition. Many other metacognitive tests need to be created and validated.

CONCLUSIONS

It is important that our profession move ahead to expand our capacity to document students' self-initiated metacognitive processing before, during, and after reading. The assessments in this chapter have demonstrated significantly important ways to do so. This chapter was designed to describe several of the newly developed metacomprehension assessment instruments. Each is intended to demonstrate comprehension processes in action. Many are performance based, such as "What Do We Need to Fill in" tests, "What's the Problem" tests, and "Did You Till the Text" tests. Others assess students' abilities to reflect on their own metacomprehension processes, such as the "Thinking to the End Metacognitive Summary" test, the "What Were You Unable to Think About in the Harder Book" test, the "Tell Me What I Should Do and I'll Do It" test, and the long-term memory test. Many involve students' self-assessment or participation through written forms, folders, and multiple work samples (e.g., self-assessment systems, color-coded comprehension portfolios, and the selecting book test). By using these evaluations, educators provide valuable, metacomprehension instructional and evaluative experiences for students. Through them, students and teachers come closer than ever before in identifying specific meaning-making problems that have limited the pleasure and profitability of past reading experiences. Through them, our profession comes closer than ever before in determining the specific metacognitive processes that can be developed to create optimal enjoyment and information for all readers in the future.

METACONNECTION FOR CHAPTER 5

Part I provided us with a sound theoretical base for understanding metacognition. As we move into the assessment section, chapter 5 by Block defines metacognitive assessments and presents a variety of informal assessment strategies for the classroom teacher. In chapter 6, Schmitt guides us as we learn more about assessing student awareness and control of metacognitive strategies.

REFERENCES

Block, C. C. (2004). *Teaching comprehension: The comprehension process approach.* Boston: Allyn & Bacon.

Block, C. C., Gambrell, L., & Pressley, M. (2003). *Improving comprehension instruction: Rethinking research, theory, and practice.* San Francisco, CA: Jossey-Bass.

Block, C. C., & Israel, S. (2004). The ABC's of Effective Think Alouds. *The Reading Teacher, 47*(2), 117–130.

Block, C. C., & Mangieri, J. (1996). *Reason to read: Thinking strategies for life through literature.* Boston: Dale Seymour.

Brown, A. L., & Palincsar, A. S. (1985). *Reciprocal teaching of comprehension strategies: A natural history of one program to enhance learning* (Tech. Rep. No. 334). Urbana, IL: University of Illinois, Center for the Study of Reading.

Durkin, D. (1976/1977). The teaching of reading comprehension in elementary classrooms. *Reading Research Quarterly, 11*(1), 17–39.

Garner, R. (1987). *Metacognition and reading comprehension.* Norwood, NJ: Ablex.

Guthrie, J. T., Cox, K. E., Knowles, K. T., Buehl, M., Mazzoni, S. A., & Fasulo, L. (2000). Building toward coherent instruction. In L. Baker, M. J. Breher, & J. T. Guthrie (Eds.), *Engaging your readers: Promoting achievement and motivation* (pp. 209–236). New York: Guilford.

Harris, T. L., & Hodges, R. E. (1995). *The Literacy dictionary: The vocabulary of reading and writing.* Newark, DE: International Reading Association.

Mak, K. (2002). *My Chinatown.* New York: Harper Collins.

Mangieri, J. (2004). *Best practices in comprehension. Report 312.* Charlotte, NC: Institute for Literacy Enhancement.

National Institute of Child Health & Human Development (NICHHD). (2000, April). *Teaching children to read: An evidence-based assessment of the scientific research literature on reading: Report of the subgroup on vocabulary* (NIH Publication No. 00-4-4769, pp. 1–269).

National Reading Research Panel (NRP). (1999). *National Reading Research Panel Progress Report to the NICHD.* Washington, DC: NICHD.

Oakhill, J., & Yuill, N. (1999). Higher order factors in comprehension disability: Processes and remediation. In L. Cornoldi & J. Oakhill (Eds.), *Models of effective educational assessment* (pp. 111–135). Hillsdale, NJ: Lawrence Erlbaum Associates.

Pearson, P. D., Roehler, L. R., Dole, J. A., & Duffy, G. G. (1992). Developing expertise in reading comprehension. In J. Samuels & A. Farstrup (Eds.), *What research has to say about reading instruction* (pp. 145–199). Newark, DE: International Reading Association.

Perfetti, C. A., & Lesco, R. (1979). Sentences, individual differences, and multiple texts: Three issues in text comprehension. *Discourse Processes, 23,* 337–355.

Pressley, M. (1976). Mental imagery helps eight-year olds remember what they read. *Journal of Educational Psychology, 68,* 355–359.

Pressley, M., & Afflerbach, P. (1995). *Verbal protocols of reading: The nature of constructively responsive reading.* Hillsdale, NJ: Lawrence Erlbaum Associates.

Reznitskaya, A., & Anderson, R. C. (2001).The argument schema and learning to reason. In C. C. Block & M. Pressley (Eds.), *Comprehension instruction: Research-based best practices* (pp. 319–334). New York: Guilford.

Ryland, C. (1998). *Scarecrow.* New York: Scholastic Inc.

Stanovich, K. E. (1986). The Matthew effects in reading: Some consequences for individual differences in the acquisition of literacy. *Reading Research Quarterly, 21,* 360–407.

Stewart, M., Cummins, C., Block, C. C., & Lewis, S. (2004, December). *The international and transfer of comprehension process.* Symposium conducted at the National Reading Conference, San Antonio, TX.

Sweet, A., & Snow, C. (2002). The RAND Corporation: New perspectives on comprehension. In C. C. Block, L. Gambrell, & M. Pressley (Eds.), *Improving comprehension instruction: Rethinking research, theory, and practice* (pp. 7–23). San Francisco: Jossey-Bass.

Tergeson, J. K., & Wagner, J. (1987). What it means to learn to read. *Child Development, 56*(5), 1134–1144.

Tierney, R. (1998). A new look at reading assessment. *The Reading Teacher, 41*(3), 301–318.

Vygotsky, L. S. (1978). *Mind in society.* Cambridge, MA: MIT Press.

6

Measuring Students' Awareness and Control of Strategic Processes

Maribeth Cassidy Schmitt
Purdue University

I understand how important metacognition is to successful literacy learning. It is very evident in my classroom which students are demonstrating their metacognitive awareness. These students are aware of many skills to assist in their reading, they know how to employ those skills, and they are able to successfully use the skills during their reading. In self-selected reading, my students are in charge of monitoring their reading. I teach them many strategies, but they must choose the appropriate strategy. I can teach them the strategies, but they must decide to employ them. They must also decide which strategy to employ. If metacognition does not come naturally, what can I do to help?

—Melinda Young, First Grade, Illinois

Melinda recognizes the importance of awareness and control of metacognition in literacy learning. This chapter provides her with tools for measuring student awareness and control so that she can help her students who do not naturally develop this ability.

INTRODUCTION, OVERVIEW, BACKGROUND INFORMATION, AND STATEMENT OF PURPOSE

In *Handbook of Reading Research*, Baker and Brown (1984) introduced reading researchers to the relation between metacognitive skills and effective reading by explaining what they described as an influential trend in developmental cognitive psychology to study "the knowledge and control a child has over his or her

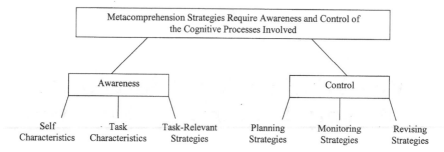

FIG. 6.1. Metacognitive theory and reading comprehension.

own thinking and learning activities, including reading" (p. 353). Although it was Flavell (1978, p.) who had earlier defined metacognition as "one's knowledge concerning one's own cognitive processes and products" (p. 232), Baker and Brown (1984) and Brown (1980) explicated the interrelated concepts of *awareness* and *control* in the definition as being critical to understanding the influence on reading theory and instruction (see Fig. 6.1).

As these concepts and the relations between them have been investigated since then, interesting theoretical and instructional implications have emerged (e.g., Baker & Brown, 1984; Brown, 1980; Cox, 1994; Palinscar & Brown, 1984; Schmitt, 1988; Paris, Wasik, & Turner, 1991). This chapter briefly explains these important components of metacognition (awareness and control) and their interrelations and presents two informal measurement instruments I designed to assess them.

HISTORICAL PERSPECTIVE AND RESEARCH OF METACOMPREHENSION: AWARENESS AND CONTROL OF STRATEGIC COMPREHENSION PROCESSES

To comprehend, learners need to use a variety of strategies deliberately and independently. To use them, put simply, they have to be knowledgeable about them, but as explicated in Fig. 6.2, there are three types of knowledge relevant to the complex relation between a reader and the task (Paris, Lipson, & Wixson, 1983). Declarative knowledge refers to knowing *what* or knowing *that*. One must have declarative knowledge about self characteristics (e.g., I like that topic; I have trouble with long words), task characteristics (e.g., reading is a left-to-right process; story characters usually have a problem to solve), and task-relevant strategies (I can use the picture to give me a clue; I can reread the sentence to help me figure out the word). In addition, procedural knowledge is important because one must know *how* to perform the various strategies involved to be successful, a part of the control aspect of processing. However, according to Paris et al. (1983):

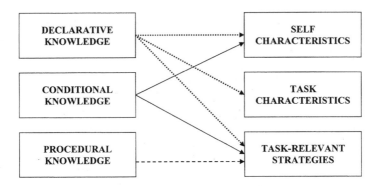

FIG. 6.2. Relationship of types of metacognitive knowledge to self, task, and strategy variables.

declarative and procedural knowledge alone are not sufficient to ensure that children read strategically. They only emphasize the knowledge and skills required for performance and do not address the conditions under which one might wish to select or execute actions. Because strategic behavior involves intentionality and self-control, any analysis that ignores learner's motivations is incomplete. We want to introduce a new term, *conditional* knowledge, to capture this dimension of learning to be strategic. Conditional knowledge includes knowing *when* and *why* to apply various actions. (p. 797)

This conditional awareness refers to knowing *when* or *why* strategies are relevant to the particular comprehension task or problem. In other words, there are several strategies appropriate for preparing to read (e.g., previewing the pictures or making predictions), different ones for problem solving a difficult word while you are reading (e.g., rereading to recapture the meaning and structure), and others appropriate for after reading (e.g., summarizing). Being a self-controlled, strategic reader involves not only knowing about the characteristics of the task, but also about online monitoring and choosing of the strategies to be successful relative to personal cognitive resources (i.e., knowledge about self). Often equated with executive control (Brown, 1980; Cox, 1994; Garner, 1994), this regulatory action is evidence of internal cognitive processing and presupposes awareness or knowledge as already described.

Figure 6.3 represents the flow of strategic comprehension processing based on the theoretical explanations of Baker and Brown (1984) and outlined in one of my instructional studies of metacomprehension (Schmitt, 1988). It reflects the processing system of a self-controlled learner building a meaningful interpretation of text, using task-relevant strategies in a recursive nature (Schmitt, 1988). For a simple description, consider this example: A reader turns the page and looks at the picture as a means of *planning* to understand; perhaps during that preview, she predicts the content, wonders what will happen, and compares it to what she

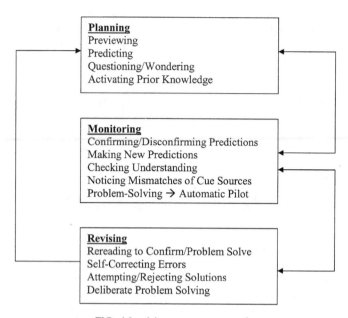

FIG. 6.3.   Metacognitive control.

knows. As she reads the page, she is *monitoring* her comprehension by confirming what she thought might happen and perhaps has to make new predictions. She is going along fine until she notices something is not making sense and has to do some deliberate problem solving in a *revising* mode, working at the problem until all sources match and she is back to *monitoring* or *planning*, being a self-controlled strategic processor throughout.

NEW IDEAS AND HOW WE CAN MOVE THE FIELD FORWARD: MEASUREMENT OF AWARENESS AND CONTROL OF METACOMPREHENSION

It is important to measure both awareness and control because of the plausible reciprocal relations and the effects on successful comprehension through independent strategic processing. Each allows for instructional decision making. It is "knowing about" and "doing" or "acting," if you will. The next two sections describe two informal measurement instruments I designed for specific reasons, that is, to measure metacomprehension awareness of task-relevant strategies and to measure growth in strategic processing during Reading Recovery lessons, both in empirical projects. I provide information on completing the tests and analyzing and interpreting the results for working with students. Without knowledge of students' levels of awareness and actual control of strategic comprehension processes, how does a teacher plan for instruction that is on the cutting edge of their understandings in order to foster independent, strategic processing?

Measuring Awareness: Metacomprehension Strategy Index (MSI)

Background Information on the Metacomprehension Strategy Index. To discover students' awareness of a variety of strategic reading processes that are appropriate for before, during, and after reading a text, the Metacomprehension Strategy Index (MSI) is a valuable measurement tool. The multiple-choice questionnaire (see the Appendix) was originally developed to measure strategic awareness of students who participated in a project to develop their metacomprehension, specifically, to become more actively engaged in their own comprehension by taking responsibility for strategies (Schmitt, 1988, 1990). This included declarative and conditional awareness of a variety of metacomprehension behaviors that comprised six broad categories: predicting and verifying, previewing, purpose setting, self-questioning, drawing from background knowledge, and summarizing and applying fix-up strategies. These categories derive from the early interest in metacognition where researchers were operationalizing the knowledge and control aspects of cognition (Baker & Brown, 1984; Brown, 1980) and the strategies are consistent with those taught in several metacomprehension instructional studies (e.g., Palinscar & Brown, 1984; Paris, Cross, & Lipson, 1984). The individual MSI items are correlated to the six categories in Table 6.1.

TABLE 6.1
Strategies Measured by the Metacomprehension Strategy Index

Predicting and verifying: Items numbered 1, 4, 13, 15, 16, 18, 23
Predicting the content of a story promotes active comprehension by giving readers a purpose for reading (i.e., to verify predictions). Evaluating predictions and generating new ones as necessary enhances the constructive nature of the reading process.
Previewing: Items numbered 2, 3
Previewing the text facilitates comprehension by activating background knowledge and providing information for making predictions.
Purpose setting: Items numbered 5, 7, 21
Reading with a purpose promotes active, strategic reading.
Self-Questioning: Items numbered 6, 14, 17
Generating questions to be answered promotes active comprehension by giving readers a purpose for reading (i.e., to answer the questions).
Drawing from background knowledge: Items numbered 8, 9, 10, 19, 24, 25
Activating and incorporating information from background knowledge contributes to comprehension by helping readers make inferences and generate predictions.
Summarizing and applying fix-up strategies: Items numbered 11, 12, 20, 22
Summarizing the content at various points in the story serves as a form of comprehension monitoring. Rereading or suspending judgment and reading on when comprehension breaks down represents strategic reading.

Paris and his colleagues developed the Index of Reading Awareness (Paris et al., 1984; Paris & Jacobs, 1984), which is a self-report measure of awareness of the need to evaluate, plan, and regulate reading processes; it correlated positively to the MSI given to the students in my instructional study (Schmitt, 1988). The MSI also has been reprinted in several literacy instruction textbooks as a valid means for measuring learners' metacognition or metacomprehension for the purpose of designing instructional programs (e.g., Barrentine, 1999; Cameron & Reynolds, 1999; Huber, 1993; Wood & Algozzine, 1995) and has been used in current research for measuring strategy awareness (e.g., Schmitt, 2003).

Students can complete the MSI as a group if they read well enough or teachers may read the items and the choices for them as a group, depending on the judgment of the teacher and the reading level of the students. It should also be noted that the questionnaire is designed to measure awareness of strategies specific to narrative text comprehension, however, it is easily adapted for expository text comprehension because previewing, predicting, summarizing, and so on, are relative to both types of text (Schmitt, 1990).

Interpreting the Metacomprehension Strategy Index. The results of the Metacomprehension Strategy Index can be used to consider students' individual strengths and weaknesses in metacognitive awareness or general patterns of an entire class (see, e.g., Schmitt, 1990). First, a teacher may wish to consider how the class performed with respect to types of strategies and conditional knowledge. The following questions could be considered:

1. Which strategies were the most well known? That is, which strategies had the highest percentage of recognition? Figure the percentages of correct responses for each category. For example, "predicting and verifying" has 7 items, so 5 correct would be 71%. Strengths and weak areas could be discerned.

2. Are there differences among the before, during, and after stages that might signal strengths or weaknesses? For example, were the scores particularly low in strategies for *after* reading, indicating a need for instruction in summarizing, etc.?

3. Are there patterns indicating difficulty with conditional knowledge for items that have distracters that are relevant for a different stage of reading? For example, Item 10 lists "Check to see if I am understanding the story so far" as a possible prereading strategy. This would be inappropriate because individuals cannot check understanding if they have not begun the reading yet.

Measuring Control: Strategic Processing Analysis (SPA)

Background Information on the Strategic Processing Analysis. Because no one can see what is taking place "inside the head" where strategies are initiated and carried out, inferences must be taken from outward behaviors (evidence, if you will) produced by the children as they generate meaningful interpretations of text. These behaviors presuppose knowledge of the tactic as relevant to the situation. Running Records of text reading (Clay, 1993a), or the types of coding used with text reading in informal reading inventories or miscue analysis (Goodman, 1969), can be useful for analyzing children's strategic processing and making hypotheses about their awareness of relevant problem-solving tactics. The strategies involved in the analysis of strategic processing included searching for information using various cue sources, self-monitoring, self-correcting, rereading for problem solving and confirming, and appealing for help. The processing is not unlike that described by Clay (1979) in *Reading: The Patterning of Complex Behaviour*:

> The competent children resourcefully cast around all their experience to find cues, strategies, and solutions.
>
> At the moment of making an error a child reading for meaning will notice the error; it will become self-evident. This is a monitoring activity. The reader takes some action. At this moment he is observing his own behavior very closely because he will have to decide which response is the best fit, which to retain and which to discard.
>
> As he searches and selects he must carry out two further types of self-regulatory action. He observes his own behavior and he assesses his own behavior. Has he solved it? Has he got it right? Do all the angles of this piece of the jigsaw fit in that particular slot? (pp. 252–253)

The Strategic Processing Analysis (SPA), developed as a research tool for measuring growth in independent strategic processing (Schmitt, 2001; Schmitt & Fang, 1995), is useful for evaluating children's problem-solving efforts on difficult words and their detection and correction of errors. This section includes instructions for using the SPA chart (see the Appendix) to analyze children's oral reading and provides examples of possible interpretations of children's control of strategic comprehension processes. In addition to the use of the SPA in research, I have taught Reading Recovery teachers across the country to use it to evaluate children's processing by analyzing their "reading work" (Clay, 1991, 1993b).

Instructions for Recording on the Strategic Processing Analysis Chart. The following outlines the instructions for completing the analysis sheet:

1. Select a coded sample of the child's oral reading. For an appropriate amount of problem solving or "reading work" (Clay, 1991, 1993b) to be evident in children's oral reading, there must be sufficient amounts of accurate responding. For this reason, the text samples should include text reading with 90%–94% accuracy. See the two text examples in Tables 6.2 and 6.3 for illustrations.

2. Go through the text and analyze every *attempt* on a *target word* on the SPA chart separately by hypothesizing the strategic processes used and by making an

TABLE 6.2
Running Record of Text Sample for David's Reading

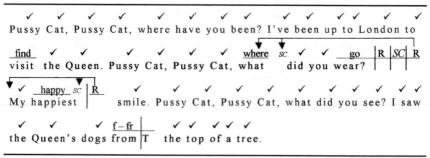

TABLE 6.3
Running Record of Text Sample for Michael's Reading

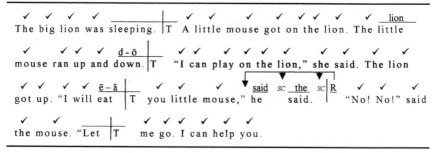

assumption about the information sources used (i.e., meaning, structure, and visual information). "Attempts" are characterized by obvious work to get at the target word, even if the work involved a meaningful substitution or even resulted in the child's being told the word by the teacher (the only allowable intervention by a teacher in a Running Record or miscue analysis). The process is as follows:

a) Record the target word on the chart in capital letters to distinguish it (see Fig. 6.4 for example of target word "VISIT").

b) On a separate line for each attempt, record what the child *did* to problem solve the word. For example, the child in Fig. 6.4 said "find" for "visit." There may be multiple attempts for each target word, but it is important to record each one on a separate line to clarify the *process* of the effort.

c) If the teacher tells the child the word, that is recorded on the Teacher Intervention section of the chart to the far right on the same line as the target word because the child made no outward attempts.

d) Using the descriptions of the following possible strategies, place a check mark under the strategy that you predict or hypothesize the child used, based on the evidence provided in the text sample.

Strategic Processing Analysis

Child: David

Target Word And Attempts	Searching for Info	Self-monitoring	Cross-checking	Rereading to Problem Solve	Rereading to Confirm	Self-correcting	Appealing for Help	Info Used	Told to	Encouraged to Try
VISIT										
find	✓							ms		
WHAT										
where	✓							msv		
→ R/SC	✓	✓	✓	✓		✓		msv		
WEAR										
go	✓	✓			✓			ms		
R	✓	✓	✓							
SC	✓	✓	✓			✓		msv		
HAPPIEST										
happy	✓							msv		
→ R/SC	✓	✓	✓	✓		✓		msv		
FROM										
/f-fr/	✓							msv		✓

FIG. 6.4. Analysis of David's strategic processing.

- *Searching for Information*
  When children make a meaningful substitution for a word, they have searched possible information sources to arrive at a prediction. An attempt to decode a word from letter to sound is also evidence of searching for information, using visual information sources in this case. The fact that the reader did something indicates a search effort.

- *Self-Monitoring*
  This is evidence of children's realization that something is wrong. It involves such things as repeating a word, rereading, self-correcting, trying another word, appealing for help, and so forth. In other words, children are self-monitoring if they are aware of a mistake or problem and not self-monitoring when a mistake is ignored.

- *Cross-Checking*
  This means that children are cross-checking one source of information against another to self-monitor or problem solve. Evidence of this would include instances where the children self-corrected, tried another word, repeated a word or phrase after a wrong response. It generally indicates they realize there is something wrong and try to resolve it by checking the source they used against another source (e.g., meaning cue against visual cue).

- *Self-Correcting*
  This is evident when children correct a wrong response. It may happen immediately (i.e., right after the response) or it may happen during a rereading (i.e., when children reread a phrase or sentence and correct the response at the same time).

- *Rereading to Confirm a Response*
  This involves children simply rereading in order to confirm that what they said made sense, looked right, and so forth. It often occurs after children have self-corrected or after the teacher has told them the word because it confirms the response by hearing it again in fluent reading.

- *Rereading to Problem Solve a Response*
  This involves children using the rereading or repetition of a word, phrase, sentence, or page as a means toward problem solving a word. It is evidence children are continuing to work.

- *Appealing to the Teacher for Help*
  This is when children appeal for help with the word. It reflects awareness on the part of children that they do not know the word and expect the teacher to assist.

- *Information Sources Used*
  This involves the evaluator's hypothesis regarding which information sources children used when making an attempt or self-correcting an error. It could be any of the following: meaning (M), syntactical structure (S), and/ or visual information (V), separately or in combination.

Interpreting the Strategic Processing Analysis Chart.   When the chart is completed, it is possible to analyze the hypotheses about strategy use and to interpret the control a child has on strategic processing. A comparison of the charts of David (Fig. 6.4) and Michael (Fig. 6.5), who were both successful in accuracy and self-correction rates on comparable texts, were qualitatively very different in terms of independent, strategic problem solving. A quick look at the SPA charts makes this visually obvious if you note the difference in the number of check marks under the "Child's Strategic Processing" section of the chart, although this changes over time for a child as processing goes underground.

David's profile suggests he was taking charge of his own problem solving: searching for information and making predictions, monitoring his choices, cross-checking information sources, and rereading as a problem-solving tactic and for confirming responses. David was, in fact, being strategic in his processing.

Although this is only a partial sample, a close inspection of his attempts on a complete text indicates that in general he would approach unknown words by making language predictions (e.g., find for visit), about half of which were visually similar at the initial letter (e.g., where for what). He often caught the dissonance between language (which provided phonological information) and visual cues, and often self-corrected immediately or upon rereading to problem solve.

When he attempted to solve words using visual analysis only, which was not as often, he was not as successful. These times generally ended in an appeal and an intervention by the teacher. These patterns of problem solving suggest that he generally engaged in strategic processing, using language quite successfully, and could detect error consistently. When his problem solving focused at the visual level, he was not as productive, and suggested that at these points he was not bringing meaning to the process effectively. However, once he was given the word by the teacher, he would usually reread to hear the language again to establish the meaning.

Michael searched for information primarily using visual information. In this partial sample, when his work resulted in a language prediction (word substitution), the words were visually similar (e.g., lion for little) and when he detected and corrected an error (e.g., said the phrase for he said phrase), it was likely the visual effort of noticing a known word mismatch that caused the dissonance. Explicit evidence of problem solving involved attempts to decode the words from letter to sound (e.g., /d-ō/ for down and /ē-ă/ for eat). Michael's most often used strategy was to wait for the teacher to intervene and provide the word for him.

Michael's problem-solving strategies and ability to detect and correct error indicate a lesser degree of independent, strategic processing than David, although he was achieving the same level of accuracy because of sufficient correct processing. He was not using rereading as a means of problem solving consistently nor effectively and this is problematic because such a strategy provides additional attention to meaning and structure to contribute to the problem solving. It seems that Michael developed moderately successful strategies for detecting and cor

Strategic Processing Analysis

Child: *Michael*

	Child's Strategic Processing								Teacher Intervention	
Target Word And Attempts	Searching for Info	Self-monitoring	Cross-checking	Rereading to Problem Solve	Rereading to Confirm	Self-correcting	Appealing for Help	Info Used	Told to	Encouraged to Try
SLEEPING									✓	
LITTLE										
lion	✓							msv		
DOWN										
/ d - ō /	✓							v	✓	
EAT										
/ ē - ă /	✓							v	✓	
HE										
said	✓							ms		
SAID										
the	✓	✓						ms		
R/SC	✓	✓	✓	✓		✓		msv		
LET									✓	

FIG. 6.5. Analysis of Michael's strategic processing.

recting error, but he was not yet skilled in problem solving unknown words using a balanced approach of attending to all information sources.

DIRECTIONS FOR FUTURE RESEARCH: WHAT ELSE DO WE NEED TO KNOW?

Metacognition in literacy is an important topic for research and instruction and I am pleased that it has reemerged as a topic of discussion because there are still issues of interest to be studied. For one, the reciprocal nature of awareness and control leads to questions regarding the instructional importance of each, such as: Is it necessary to teach both? Will teaching related to control alone simply lead to awareness, perhaps just for some and not others? Another interesting topic is the question of the level of consciousness of the awareness. Does one need to be able to verbalize the awareness for it to be categorized as metacognitive? Does the control need to be brought to the conscious level to be classified as metacognitive? Does the consciousness question really matter if we simply think of it as "independent, strategic comprehension processes?" In addition, I am interested in exploring the operationalization of strategic processing and children's paths of progress toward independence.

CONCLUSIONS

This chapter focused on two informal instruments for measuring awareness and control of strategic comprehension processes. The first was the Metacomprehension Strategy Index (MSI), a multiple-choice questionnaire that evaluates learners' awareness of strategies for before, during, and after reading (Schmitt, 1988, 1990). This included awareness of a variety of metacomprehension behaviors that comprised six broad categories: predicting and verifying, previewing, purpose setting, self-questioning, drawing from background knowledge, and summarizing and applying fix-up strategies. The second instrument, the Strategic Processing Analysis (SPA), is useful for evaluating children's problem-solving efforts on difficult words and their detection and correction of errors (Schmitt, 2001). It basically allows hypothesizing of strategic control based on evidence of processing on text, such as searching for information using various cue sources, self-monitoring, self-correcting, rereading for problem solving and confirming, and appealing for help. For each of the two measurement instruments, suggestions for analysis and interpretation were offered.

Prior to the presentation of the MSI and the SPA, a brief review of the theoretical explanations of the various types of knowledge of self, task, and task-relevant strategies that are necessary for metacognitive regulation was provided: that is, declarative, procedural, and conditional knowledge. It was hypothesized that conditional knowledge, or knowing when and why a strategy is appropriate to use, represents the heart of metacognitive knowledge because it allows strategic processing. And, finally, a suggestion for further research regarding the reciprocal relation of metacognitive awareness and control was made, along with a call for settling the issue of conscious awareness.

METACONNECTION FOR CHAPTER 6

In chapter 5, Block helped us understand the purpose and value of metacognitive assessments. Now, in chapter 6, Schmitt extends our thinking and helps us focus on two important aspects of metacognition. She provides two case studies to guide our understanding of how to assess a student's awareness and control of metacognitive strategies. As we progress, Paris and Flukes will show us how to assess strategies in chapter 7.

APPENDIX

METACOMPREHENSION STRATEGY INDEX

DIRECTIONS

Think about what kinds of things you can do to help you understand a story better before, during, and after you read it. Read each of the lists of four statements and decide which one of them would help *you* the most. *There are no right answers.* It is just what *you* think would help the most. Circle the letter of the statement you choose.

QUESTIONNAIRE ITEMS

In each set of four, choose the one statement that tells a good thing to do to help you understand a story better *before you read it.*

1. *Before* I begin reading, it's a good idea to:
   A. See how many pages are in the story.
   B. Look up all of the big words in the dictionary.
   C. Make some guesses about what I think will happen in the story.
   D. Think about what has happened so far in the story.
2. *Before* I begin reading, it's a good idea to:
   A. Look at the pictures to see what the story is about.
   B. Decide how long it will take me to read the story.
   C. Sound out the words I don't know.
   D. Check to see if the story is making sense.

3. *Before* I begin reading, it's a good idea to:
   A. Ask someone to read the story to me.
   B. Read the title to see what the story is about.
   C. Check to see if most of words have long or short vowels in them.
   D. Check to see if the pictures are in order and make sense.

4. *Before* I begin reading, it's a good idea to:
   A. Check to see that no pages are missing.
   B. Make a list of the words I'm not sure about.
   C. Use the title and pictures to help me make guesses about what will happen in the story.
   D. Read the last sentence so I will know how the story ends.

5. *Before* I begin reading, it's a good idea to:
   A. Decide on why I am going to read the story.
   B. Use the difficult words to help me make guesses about what will happen in the story.
   C. Reread some parts to see if I can figure out what is happening if things aren't making sense.
   D. Ask for help with the difficult words.

6. *Before* I begin reading, it's a good idea to:
   A. Retell all of the main points that have happened so far.
   B. Ask myself questions that I would like to have answered in the story.
   C. Think about the meanings of the words which have more than one meaning.
   D. Look through the story to find all of the words with three or more syllables.

7. *Before* I begin reading, it's a good idea to:
   A. Check to see if I have read this story *before*.
   B. Use my questions and guesses as a reason for reading the story.
   C. Make sure I can pronounce all of the words *before* I start.
   D. Think of a better title for the story.

8. *Before* I begin reading, it's a good idea to:
   A. Think of what I already know about the things I see in the pictures.
   B. See how many pages are in the story.
   C. Choose the best part of the story to read again.
   D. Read the story aloud to someone.

9. *Before* I begin reading, it's a good idea to:
   A. Practice reading the story aloud.
   B. Retell all of the main points to make sure I can remember the story.
   C. Think of what the people in the story might be like.
   D. Decide if I have enough time to read the story.

10. *Before* I begin reading, it's a good idea to:
    A. Check to see if I am understanding the story so far.

B. Check to see if the words have more than one meaning.
C. Think about where the story might be taking place.
D. List all of the important details.

In each set of four, choose the one statement that tells a good thing to do to help you understand a story better *while you are reading it.*

11. *While* I'm reading, it's a good idea to:
    A. Read the story very slowly so that I will not miss any important parts.
    B. Read the title to see what the story is about.
    C. Check to see if the pictures have anything missing.
    D. Check to see if the story is making sense by seeing if I can tell what's happened so far.

12. *While* I'm reading, it's a good idea to:
    A. Stop to retell the main points to see if I am understanding what has happened so far.
    B. Read the story quickly so that I can find out what happened.
    C. Read only the beginning and the end of the story to find out what it is about.
    D. Skip the parts that are too difficult for me.

13. *While* I'm reading, it's a good idea to:
    A. Look all of the big words up in the dictionary.
    B. Put the book away and find another one if things aren't making sense.
    C. Keep thinking about the title and the pictures to help me decide what is going to happen next.
    D. Keep track of how many pages I have left to read.

14. *While* I'm reading, it's a good idea to:
    A. Keep track of how long it is taking me to read the story.
    B. Check to see if I can answer any of the questions I asked *before* I started reading.
    C. Read the title to see what the story is going to be about.
    D. Add the missing details to the pictures.

15. *While* I'm reading, it's a good idea to:
    A. Have someone read the story aloud to me.
    B. Keep track of how many pages I have read.
    C. List the story's main character.
    D. Check to see if my guesses are right or wrong.

16. *While* I'm reading, it's a good idea to:
    A. Check to see that the characters are real.
    B. Make a lot of guesses about what is going to happen next.
    C. Not look at the pictures because they might confuse me.
    D. Read the story aloud to someone.

17. *While* I'm reading, it's a good idea to:
   A. Try to answer the questions I asked myself.
   B. Try not to confuse what I already know with what I'm reading about.
   C. Read the story silently.
   D. Check to see if I am saying the new vocabulary words correctly.

18. *While* I'm reading, it's a good idea to:
   A. Try to see if my guesses are going to be right or wrong.
   B. Reread to be sure I haven't missed any of the words.
   C. Decide on why I am reading the story.
   D. List what happened first, second, third, and so on.

19. *While* I'm reading, it's a good idea to:
   A. See if I can recognize the new vocabulary words.
   B. Be careful not to skip any parts of the story.
   C. Check to see how many of the words I already know.
   D. Keep thinking of what I already know about the things and ideas in the story to help me decide what is going to happen.

20. *While* I'm reading, it's a good idea to:
   A. Reread some parts or read ahead to see if I can figure out what is happening if things aren't making sense.
   B. Take my time reading so that I can be sure I understand what is happening.
   C. Change the ending so that it makes sense.
   D. Check to see if there are enough pictures to help make the story ideas clear.

In each set of four, choose the one statement that tells a good thing to do to help you understand the story better *after you have read it*.

21. *After* I've read a story, it's a good idea to:
   A. Count how many pages I read with no mistakes.
   B. Check to see if there were enough pictures to go with the story to make it interesting.
   C. Check to see if I met my purpose for reading the story.
   D. Underline the causes and effects.

22. *After* I've read a story, it's a good idea to:
   A. Underline the main idea.
   B. Retell the main points of the whole story so that I can check to see if I understood it.
   C. Read the story again to be sure I said all of the words right.
   D. Practice reading the story aloud.

23. *After* I've read a story, it's a good idea to:
   A. Read the title and look over the story to see what it is about.

    B. Check to see if I skipped any of the vocabulary words.

    C. Think about what made me make good or bad predictions.

    D. Make a guess about what will happen next in the story.

24. *After* I've read a story, it's a good idea to:

    A. Look up all of the big words in the dictionary.

    B. Read the best parts aloud.

    C. Have someone read the story aloud to me.

    D. Think about how the story was like things I already knew about *before* I started reading.

25. *After* I've read a story, it's a good idea to:

    A. Think about how I would have acted if I were the main character in the story.

    B. Practice reading the story silently for practice of good reading.

    C. Look over the story title and pictures to see what will happen.

    D. Make a list of the things I understood the most.

Answers: 1: C, 2: A, 3: B, 4: C, 5: A, 6: B, 7: B, 8: A, 9: C, 10: C, 11: D, 12: A, 13: C, 14: B, 15: D, 16: B, 17: A, 18: A, 19: D, 20: A, 21: C, 22: B, 23: C, 24: D, 25: A

Note. From "A Questionnaire to Measure Children's Awareness of Strategic Reading Processes" by M. C. Schmitt, 1990, *The Reading Teacher, 43*, pp. 454–461.

REFERENCES

Baker, L., & Brown, A. L. (1984). Metacognitive skills and reading. In P. D. Pearson, R. Barr, M. L. Kamil, & P. Mosenthal (Eds.), *The handbook of reading research* (pp. 353–394). New York: Longman.

Barrentine, S. J. (Ed.). (1999). *Reading assessment: Principles and practices for elementary teachers.* Newark, DE: International Reading Association.

Brown, A. L. (1980). Metacognitive development and reading. In R. J. Spiro, B. C. Bruce, & W. F. Brewer (Eds.), *Theoretical issues in reading comprehension* (pp. 453–481). Hillsdale, NJ: Lawrence Erlbaum Associates.

Cameron, R. J., & Reynolds, A. R. (Eds.). (1999). *Psychology in education portfolio: Learning style and metacognition.* Berkshire, United Kingdom: NFER-NELSON.

Clay, M. M. (1979). *Reading: The patterning of complex behavior.* Portsmouth, NH: Heinemann.

Clay, M. M. (1991). *Becoming literate: The construction of inner control.* Portsmouth, NH: Heinemann.

Clay, M. M. (1993a). *Observation survey of early literacy achievement.* Portsmouth, NH: Heinemann.

Clay, M. M. (1993b). *Reading Recovery: A guidebook for teachers in training.* Portsmouth, NH: Heinemann.

Cox, B. E. (1994). Young children's regulatory talk: Evidence of emerging metacognitive control over literary products and processes. In R. B. Ruddell, M. R. Ruddell, & H. Singer (Eds.), *Theoretical models and processes of reading* (pp. 733–756). Newark, DE: International Reading Association.

Flavell, J. H. (1976). Metacognitive aspects of problem solving. In L. B. Resnick (Ed.), *The nature of intelligence* (pp. 231–235). Hillsdale, NJ: Lawrence Erlbaum Associates.

Garner, R. (1994). Metacognition and executive control. In R. B. Ruddell, M. R. Ruddell, & H. Singer (Eds.), *Theoretical models and processes of reading* (pp. 715–732). Newark, DE: International Reading Association.

Goodman, K. S. (1969). Analysis of oral reading miscues: Applied psycholinguistics. *Reading Research Quarterly, 5,* 9–30.

Huber, M. M. (1993). *Literacy disorders: Holistic diagnosis and remediation.* Orlando, FL: Harcourt Brace Jovanovich.

Palinscar, A. S., & Brown, A. L. (1984). Reciprocal teaching of comprehension fostering and monitoring activities. *Cognition and Instruction, 1,* 117–175.

Paris, S. G., Cross, D. R., & Lipson, M. Y. (1984). Informed strategies for learning: A program to improve children's reading awareness and comprehension. *Journal of Educational Psychology, 76,* 1239–1252.

Paris, S. G., & Jacobs, J. E. (1984). The benefits of informed instruction for children's reading awareness and comprehension skills. *Child Development, 55,* 2083–2093.

Paris, S. G., Lipson, M. Y., & Wixson, K. K. (1983). Becoming a strategic reader. *Contemporary Educational Psychology, 8,* 293–316.

Paris, S. G., Wasik, B. A., & Turner, J. C. (1991). The development of strategic readers. In R. Barr, M. L. Kamil, P. Mosenthal, & P. D. Pearson (Eds.), *Handbook of reading research* (Vol. 2, pp. 609–640). New York: Longman.

Schmitt, M. C. (1988). The effects of an elaborated directed reading activity on the metacomprehension skills of third graders. In J. E. Readence & R. S. Baldwin (Eds.), *Dialogues in literacy research* (pp. 167–189). Chicago: National Reading Conference.

Schmitt, M. C. (1990). A questionnaire to measure children's awareness of strategic reading processes. *The Reading Teacher, 43,* 454–461.

Schmitt, M. C. (2001). The development of children's strategic processing in Reading Recovery. *Reading Psychology, 22,* 129–151.

Schmitt, M. C. (2003). Metacognitive strategy knowledge: Comparison of former Reading Recovery children and their current classmates. *Literacy Teaching and Learning: An International Journal of Early Reading and Writing, 7,* 57–76.

Schmitt, M. C., & Fang, Z. (1995, December). *Becoming a strategic reader: The Reading Recovery experience.* Paper presented at the National Reading Conference, New Orleans, LA.

Wood, K. D., & Algozzine, B. (1995). *Teaching reading to high-risk learners.* Boston: Allyn & Bacon.

7

Assessing Children's Metacognition About Strategic Reading

Scott G. Paris
Jonathan Flukes
University of Michigan

> *To become proficient readers it is critical for students to understand what they are thinking as they read. Most teachers assume that students will pick up the strategies naturally without direct instruction. Why wait until the student is in trouble? Checking the student's comprehension often, addressing problems immediately, and teaching comprehension strategies directly would help all students regardless of their reading levels. To allow a poor reader to continue practicing poor strategies is poor teaching!*
> —Pat Unger, Special Education, Grades 9–12, Indiana

We agree with Pat. Teachers should assess strategic reading in their students so that appropriate instruction can be delivered. This chapter describes ways to connect assessment and instruction for strategic reading.

As children learn to read, they gain knowledge about text characteristics, reading processes, and their own emerging abilities (Adams, 1990). These metacognitive insights help them acquire control of the skills involved in decoding, comprehending, and analyzing text (S. G. Paris, Wasik, & Turner, 1991). The content, as well as the depth of these insights, increases as a function of advances in children's cognitive development and reading proficiency because both develop rapidly from 5 to 10 years of age. Teachers and parents help children gain insights into their own reading and thinking with explicit information and indirect help while reading together. Metacognitive tutelage is important for students to become text users and text critics (Luke, 2000). Because children's emerging metacognition about reading is embedded in broader changes in children's academic achievement and self-regulated learning, metacognition can be both an outcome and a cause of different aspects of children's reading development (Snow, Burns, & Griffin, 1998).

Metacognition may be especially important for beginning and struggling readers who may have naïve or vague understanding about strategies they can use while reading. For example, beginning readers may not understand that they can skip unfamiliar words and use sentence context to figure out their meaning, and they may not pause to monitor their comprehension of sentences and text (Blachowicz & Ogle, 2001). Better understanding of what reading strategies are, how they facilitate reading, and when and why they should be applied can help children overcome reading difficulties. These types of metacognition about reading strategies have been designated as declarative, procedural, and conditional knowledge (S. G. Paris, Lipson, & Wixson, 1983), and they are necessary knowledge for children to use strategies deliberately and selectively. For example, a third grader should know that skimming text and scanning text headings and illustrations are appropriate strategies, readers can skim/scan some of the text and make reasonable hypotheses about the meaning, and skimming and scanning can be used before reading to identify the topic and difficulty of text or after reading to reinforce the key ideas. Learning what, how, why, and when to use a variety of reading strategies are hallmarks of metacognitive and self-regulated readers. Strategic reading stands in sharp contrast to reading that is passive, compliant, or unwavering for different purposes and texts (Almasi, 2003). That is why teachers need to emphasize metacognition about strategic reading in both instruction and assessment.

HISTORICAL PERSPECTIVE AND RESEARCH REVIEW

Since the pioneering research on metacognitive aspects of reading in the 1980s (cf. Garner, 1987), researchers have emphasized two main aspects of children's metacognition about reading. The first aspect includes insights that children acquire about text features, the different task demands of reading, and their own reading skills. S. G. Paris and Winograd (1990) referred to these kinds of metacognition as vital elements of cognitive *self-appraisal* and contrasted them with the second aspect of metacognition, *self-management* of thinking. Children who can plan their reading for different purposes, who can monitor their understanding as they read, and who can repair and regulate their comprehension are demonstrating metacognitive understanding and control over their cognitive processing of text. In plainer language, good readers understand and apply appropriate strategies in specific reading situations. Teachers today understand that children in grades K–3 need instruction on comprehension strategies in order to build a foundation for strategic reading (Stahl, 2004). Assessment that reinforces strategy instruction is therefore crucial to evaluate instructional effectiveness of interventions and developmental progress of students. The next section reviews briefly the main findings of research on assessments of children's metacognition about strategic reading.

ASSESSING STUDENTS' STRATEGIC READING

Teachers can observe students using some reading strategies such as following text with their fingers, looking forward or backward across pages or text segments, underlining important parts of text, and taking notes. Such external manifestations of strategic reading are less frequent than internal thinking during reading, however, which is why measurements of strategic reading are usually inferred from what readers say about their own mental actions. Self-reports are metacognitive because they involve reflecting, evaluating, and reporting various aspects of readers' thinking. There are three general methods that have been used by researchers to assess strategic reading. The first is through self-reports during reading, such as prompts to think aloud or periodic questions about what readers were thinking at various points in text. The second method is to interview readers about specific features of their strategic reading, usually after the reading has been completed. The first two methods are both administered individually. The third method is surveys of readers' thinking that can be administered in groups, and they are often not tied to a specific reading task. The three assessment methods can be used with readers of various ages and proficiency across a wide range of content and genre. The following sections provide representative examples of each method.

Self-Reports of Strategic Reading

One popular method to assess metacognitive aspects of strategic reading is to ask readers to think aloud during reading (Pressley & Afflerbach, 1995). The self-reports of thinking can reveal how students make plans, monitor their understanding, and resolve difficulties they may encounter. However, verbal reports of cognitive processes are not always accurate. The frequency and quality of the self-reports can be highly variable if the prompts are vague, such as "Just tell me what you are thinking as you read this text," because students may interpret the prompts differently. Alternatively, self-reports can be quite specific if the prompt queries a specific action, such as, "What were you looking for when you looked back on the previous page?" Both kinds of self-reports assume that readers' thinking when prompted is similar to their ordinary thinking while reading without prompting. Introspective reports may also be distorted to include more intelligent strategies than the reader actually used, perhaps to please the examiner or to appear smart. Self-reported thinking depends on the readers' abilities to introspect accurately and to use appropriate language to communicate their own thinking. These threats to validity may be more evident among young, unskilled, or beginning readers. Nevertheless, asking readers to explain their thinking provides insights about their strategic reading that can be diagnostically important for teachers' future instruction.

Assessing strategic reading is important when evaluating the impact of instructional interventions. For example, R. Brown, Pressley, Van Meter, and Schuder (1996) used a think-aloud task to evaluate whether children had become more strategic readers following Transactional Strategies Instruction (TSI) with second graders. In a pre–post intervention design, these researchers stopped children at various points as they read a passage and asked, "What are you thinking?" A child's use of appropriate strategies was an indication that the classroom intervention had been successful. Children's responses were analyzed and coded for evidence of strategy use. Comparisons between the intervention and control groups revealed that children in the TSI program applied reading strategies on their own significantly more often than children in the control classes.

Self-reports of thinking have also been gathered during writing activities. For example, Garner (1982) asked college students to remember what they were thinking while reading and summarizing an expository text passage. Garner also investigated the influence of the length of time between the self-report and the reading and summarizing activities. Twenty undergraduate participants read and summarized an expository text while being observed. Ten subjects described their thoughts and actions immediately and the other 10 reported their thoughts and actions 2 days later. The self-reported "cognitive events" were compared to the actions noted by observers. Adults who gave self-reports immediately reported more cognitive events, and the reports corresponded more closely to observations than for the group who gave self-reports 2 days later.

Interviews About Strategic Reading

Reading interviews may include open-ended questions about various aspects of reading. For example, Myers and S. Paris (1978) conducted the first metacognitive study about reading and asked second and sixth graders questions about how task, strategy, and person variables influence reading. They found developmental improvement in children's awareness of the strategies and variables that make reading easy or difficult. For example, second graders were less aware than sixth graders about how to skim, reread, or resolve comprehension difficulties. R. Brown et al. (1996) adapted the following five questions from Myers and S. Paris (1978) to evaluate TSI:

1. What do good readers do? What makes someone a good reader?
2. What things do you do before you start to read a story?
3. What do you think about before you read a new story?
4. What do you do when you come to a word you don't know?
5. What do you do when you read something that does not make sense?

The researchers found that children answered the questions with more meta-cognitive knowledge after the direct instructional intervention about reading strategies. Thus, interviews can be used to assess knowledge gains following classroom instruction.

S. Paris and Jacobs (1984) created an interview to assess the strategy knowledge of children who participated in a classroom intervention called Informed Strategies for Learning (ISL). Third and fifth graders were given whole group lessons for 2 months about a variety of reading strategies, how to use them, and why they are useful (S. G. Paris, Cross, & Lipson, 1984). The interviews about reading strategies revealed greater awareness among fifth graders and, overall, children who participated in ISL gained greater awareness about strategies than children in control classrooms. Two subsequent studies are worth mentioning. First, Cross and S. G. Paris (1988) used cluster analyses at four time points to show that the gains in metacognition following ISL were not limited to just some readers. All children, except the very lowest readers, made gains in awareness and performance. Indeed, children's reading awareness and performance became more congruent with increasing age and skill. Second, the open-ended interview questions reported by S. Paris and Jacobs (1984) were transformed into a multiple-choice survey using children's actual responses to determine correct choices and foils that was the basis for the Index of Reading Awareness (IRA) (described later).

S. G. Paris and Myers (1981) created a different type of interview that asked children to judge the value of different reading strategies and the frequency with which children used each one. The 20 strategies included internal strategies, such as paraphrasing, and external strategies, such as underlining important information. The list also included strategies that are generally useful, such as using context, and tactics that are not useful, such as saying a sentence over and over. The interview was given to fourth graders who were either successful or struggling readers. Both groups judged positive strategies as useful, but struggling readers reported that some of the negative strategies, such as "saying every word over and over," were beneficial. Moreover, struggling readers used harmful strategies more often than successful readers. These kinds of interviews can be used diagnostically because they reveal children's awareness of reading strategies, as well as the relative value of different strategies and the frequency of using them.

Craig and Yore (1996) explored strategy awareness and use in the context of science reading among students in grades 4–8. Although a systematic and uniform assessment was not the goal of these researchers, they sought to discover more about the approaches students use when experiencing difficulty in reading science texts. The researchers identified characteristics of good science readers and asked students such questions as, "What could you do to check to see if you understand what you are reading? Would that be useful? When should you look back and ahead in your science text? Why?" Twenty-four items were created that assessed declarative, procedural, and conditional aspects of being a good science reader. The qualitative analysis focused on the variables that the students reported using to resolve difficulties while reading science texts. Craig and Yore concluded that students were aware of a variety of strategies. However, they tended to adopt a "text-driven, bottom-up" approach to reading in which they viewed the goal of science reading as meaning getting instead of an active construction of understanding. They also concluded that students showed a lack of awareness that their prior knowledge can help resolve comprehension difficulties. The authors suggested that further instruction should be developed to enhance self-awareness and management, highlight important features of science texts, and make the interactive-constructive nature of science texts more salient. These kinds of instruction can help students develop deeper, more complex understanding of science texts and science reading strategies.

The previous examples of interview methods asked children to respond to general reading processes abstractly and hypothetically rather than from any specific experiences while reading text. This method may be used widely with readers of different ages, cultures, and languages to reveal how children reason about reading strategies and the causes of successful reading (cf. Wagner, Spratt, Gal, & S. G. Paris, 1989). However, the method poses problems for young children who cannot reason easily about hypothetical events so interviews can be organized around specific reading occasions. For example, S. G. Paris (1991) designed a think-along passage (TAP) as a way of interviewing children simultaneously about their comprehension and metacognition. After children are asked a comprehension question, they are asked, "How did you know that?" or "What could you do to find out the answer?" The TAP procedure adds a metacognitive layer of questions to the usual comprehension questions asked during guided reading. Thus, it provides a situated analysis of the strategies that children use or could use while reading a specific text.

Another method that provides a context and text basis for strategy assessment is a retrospective interview. Juliebo, Malicky, and Norman (1998) examined how five first graders, involved in an early intervention program, understood the book reading lessons they had just completed. The researchers observed and videotaped the children as they read and later conducted a retrospective interview about their reading. Instances of metacognition (mostly at the word decoding level as opposed to the comprehension level) demonstrated the wide range of strategic behaviors used by children. The retrospective recall sessions permitted more informative metacognitive assessments than observations alone.

Surveys and Inventories About Strategic Reading

Although interviews provide a rich source of highly personal data in a child's own words, interviews require intensive time to administer to individuals. Therefore, many researchers prefer metacognitive surveys that can be administered to groups of children at the same time. Jacobs and S. Paris (1987) used the open-ended interviews in S. Paris and Jacobs (1984) to create the Index of Reading Awareness (IRA), a 20-item assessment of children's knowledge about reading strategies. The items were grouped conceptually into four subscales of evaluation, planning, regulation, and conditional knowledge, but the factor analyses did not support these four factors as discrete subscales. So, only total IRA scores were used in data analyses. The multiple-choice questions are based on questions such as, "Why do you go back and read things over again?" Each of the three multiple-choice alternatives was judged to be worth 0, 1, or 2 points, so the IRA yielded total scores that ranged from 0–40. Jacobs and S. Paris (1987) reported that fifth graders knew more about reading strategies than second graders on the IRA, girls knew more than boys, and children who had participated in ISL knew more than children in control classrooms.

The IRA was also used in Australia in a longitudinal study to assess children's emerging reading proficiency and awareness (S. G. Paris & van Kraayenoord, 1998). Students in Years 1–4 were assessed with the IRA as part of a large reading battery and then 2 years later, they were assessed again. The IRA was correlated significantly with children's age, standardized reading scores, and TAP scores for students initially in Year 3 and 4 classes. Two years later, the IRA was correlated with teachers' ratings of younger children's reading comprehension and motivation. The IRA for older children was correlated significantly with their standardized reading scores, teachers' ratings, and their IRA scores from 2 years earlier. Clearly, children who are more aware of the dimensions of reading strategies achieve at higher levels than children who are less aware.

Schmitt (1990) created the Metacomprehension Strategy Index (MSI) as a variation of the IRA. The questions are not specific to particular strategies (e.g., "Before I begin reading, it's a good idea to . . ."), so the assessment is decontextualized like the IRA. Students choose an answer from a list of four possible strategies with one of the four options representing the most appropriate metacomprehension strategy. The MSI is a 25-item, multiple-choice survey designed to measure middle and upper elementary school students' strategic awareness. It focuses on the strategies that students can engage in before, during, and after reading narrative texts. Specific strategies addressed in the measure include predicting and verifying, previewing, purpose setting, self-questioning, drawing from background knowledge, summarizing, and applying fix-up strategies. Each of the 25 items begins with one of the following statements, followed by four multiple-choice options:

Before I begin reading, it's a good idea to . . .

While I'm reading, it's a good idea to . . .

After I've read a story, it's a good idea to . . .

Schmitt (1990) reported good internal reliability and the measure was correlated (r = .48) with the IRA, suggesting that the two instruments are measuring similar constructs. The MSI also correlated with other comprehension measures, an error detection task (r = .49) and a cloze task (r = .50). Furthermore, the measure was sensitive to the treatment effects of the intervention study with the experimental group scoring significantly higher than the control group.

Mokhtari and Reichard (2002) created the metacognitive awareness and use of reading strategies (MARSI), a 30-item Likert survey, to assess adolescent and adult readers' metacognition. The MARSI was designed to assess strategy use by students in grades 6–12 while reading academic texts. Items were created based on 15 reading strategies identified by Pressley and Afflerbach (1995, p. 105). Students are instructed to read each of the strategy statements (e.g., "I take notes while reading to help me understand") and then indicate how often they engage in this activity by selecting the number that applies to them on a 5-point scale (1 = I never or almost never do this, and 5 = I always or almost always do this). Three factors emerged from the factor analysis: global reading strategies, problem-solving reading strategies, and support reading strategies. These factors became the three subscales of the MARSI instrument. The authors suggested calculating average scores and using both overall and subscale means to assess the levels of strategy use. The overall internal reliability ratings, by grade, ranged from .86 to .93 (Cronbach's alpha). Although the study was primarily a means to discuss the development and validation of the instrument, the authors gathered data from more than 400 students and correlated the MARSI with students' self-reports of their own reading ability. Global strategy and problem-solving strategy subscores were related to self-reports of reading ability; readers who rated their reading ability as excellent reported significantly more use of global and problem-solving reading strategies than those who indicated their reading abilities were average or below average.

Moore, Zabrucky, and Commander (1997) created a metacomprehension scale (MCS) for adults based on research in metamemory and discourse comprehension. The 22-item scale is divided into seven components: regulation (methods of resolving comprehension failures), strategy (techniques to improve comprehension), task (knowledge of basic comprehension processes), capacity (perception of comprehension abilities), anxiety (stress related to comprehension abilities), achievement (importance of good comprehension skills), and locus (control of reading skills). Participants are asked their agreement on each of the 22 statements using a 5-point scale (1 = disagree strongly to 5 = agree strongly). Moore et al. (1997) tested more than 200 adult participants and compared the MCS to two other measures of metacognition to predict comprehension performance on brief passages. The MCS accounted for 19% of the variance in reading comprehension scores and 15% in a regression analysis after entering the other metacognitive measures. That was two to three times more unique variance than the Metamemory in Adulthood (MIA) Instrument (Dixon & Hultsch, 1984) and the Personality in Intellectual-Aging Contexts (PIC) inventory (Lachman, 1986). The MCS was also a better predictor of comprehension performance than the MIA but not the PIC. The authors suggested that the MCS is a valid and reliable measure of metacognition about comprehension. It is worth noting that the measure of reading comprehension was not a standardized test and the correlations between the MCS subscales and comprehension were low. The evidence for the validity of the MCS was mostly in contrast to other self-reported measures of metamemory and intellectual functioning, and it is not surprising that adults' metacognition about reading was a better predictor of reading comprehension than metacognition about other cognitive domains. Whether or not the MCS has any predictive or concurrent validity with standard measures of reading, especially for poor comprehenders or children, remains to be demonstrated.

DESIGN PRINCIPLES FOR ASSESSING CHILDREN'S STRATEGIC READING

The brief review of research on assessments of strategic reading reveals three main types: self-reports of thinking, interviews, and surveys. Each type tries to assess readers' mental processes used to construct meaning from words and text. We recognize that these three types can be combined and adapted in many ways so that assessments are text specific or general, immediate or delayed, and prompted or unprompted. In order to create effective assessments, it is necessary to identify the fundamental principles that guide metacognitive assessments of strategic reading. We describe five design principles in this section that can be applied to all assessments of metacognition about reading strategies (Table 7.1).

Assessments of Metacognition Should Focus on Important Reading Strategies That Can Be Used Widely and Frequently

Although there are many different reading strategies that proficient readers can use, some are more important than others, especially for beginning readers in grades K–5. For example, understanding punctuation influences reading fluency and comprehension, but it seems less important than identifying main ideas. Teachers are often overwhelmed trying to teach long lists of reading skills in commercial reading programs, and children can be confused as they try to learn skills that appear unrelated. We think that strategic reading can be taught and assessed more sensibly when a small group of key strategies is emphasized. Strategies in the following categories were identified by the National Reading Panel (2000) as crucial, and they make a sound foundation for assessment:

1. *Analyze text features*. Readers need to understand how titles, headings, and illustrations aid comprehension. They need to understand the structural elements and relations of narrative and expository text that can help organize comprehension and recall of text information. In general, children should gain progressively more insights about text features that signal key information in different types of text.

TABLE 7.1
Five Design Principles for Assessments of Strategic Reading

1. Assessments of metacognition should focus on important reading strategies that can be used widely and frequently.
2. Assessments should measure children's personal conceptions and perceived values of various reading strategies.
3. Assessments should be developmentally sensitive to children's progressive reading knowledge and proficiency.
4. Assessments should supplement and complement existing measures of reading fluency and comprehension.
5. Assessments should be aligned with instruction so they provide diagnostic and prescriptive information about specific reading strategies.

2. *Use inferences and imagery.* Perhaps the most essential feature of reading comprehension is going beyond the explicit information to create a situation model of the text that connects the text to prior knowledge, world knowledge, and other texts (Kintsch, 1998). Inferential strategies include understanding of temporal sequences, cause and effect, drawing conclusions, inferring psychological motives and emotions, and much more. Creating multisensory images while reading also helps to elaborate and personalize the text meaning.

3. *Monitor and clarify.* Readers must learn how to check their ongoing comprehension periodically by pausing, paraphrasing, rereading, and searching text selectively to clarify their understanding. Learning to ask and answer questions about text helps to internalize monitoring strategies.

4. *Summarize important information.* Summarizing is more than retelling; it is a condensed and organized version of the key text information. Good summaries include main ideas, concepts, or themes, as well as inferred information that renders the text coherent. Children need to learn strategies for identifying key information, organizing the ideas, and omitting irrelevant and redundant information (A. Brown & Day, 1983).

5. *Evaluate the text.* Readers must learn to analyze the text in order to identify the author's purpose, bias, style, and voice. Evaluative strategies help readers determine the genre of text, the evidential bases for claims, and the personal reactions to text by connecting the text to other knowledge and texts.

Assessments Should Measure Children's Personal Conceptions and Perceived Values of Various Reading Strategies

One of the persistent criticisms about assessments of children's metacognition is that children will report rote answers in order to look smart. This may occur in assessments that are not anchored to specific texts or that involve hypothetical reasoning such as, "What do you do when you come to a word that you do not understand?" Young readers may shrug their shoulders or reply, "Skip it," but older children may learn that teachers want to hear something like, "I try to sound it out or I skip it and figure it out after I read the rest of the sentence." In order to avoid such self-serving and virtuous responses that may not correspond to actual behaviors, assessments can query children's reactions to specific reading experiences, especially their personal reactions. For example, children can be asked as they read text how often they use strategy X in situations like this, or they can be asked how useful strategy X is in this situation. Another format might ask children to compare the relative frequency or usefulness of several alternative strategies in the same situation. Another option is to ask children to compare and evaluate alternative strategies that could be used before, during, or after reading. The purpose of each format is to assess the child's personal evaluation of the strategy in terms of frequency of use or perceived usefulness in particular and actual reading situations.

Assessments Should Be Developmentally Sensitive to Children's Progressive Reading Knowledge and Proficiency

Although each of the five categories of reading strategies identified earlier can be important for readers of any age, we expect children to display greater knowledge and control of strategic reading with age. However, it is difficult to identify a simple measurement scale that reflects developmental improvement so researchers have used scales that involve accuracy, frequency, or effectiveness of specific strategies. Each of these may be valid for quantitative scales because older, better readers are usually more accurate in their metacognitive appraisals and use strategies more often and more effectively. In addition, explanations about how, why, and when specific strategies can be applied should become more complex and detailed with increasing age and skill. For example, a second grader might report that stopping at the end of a page is a good strategy to monitor comprehension, but a fourth grader can explain in more detail how to clarify comprehension through paraphrasing or summarizing and why the actions are useful. Thoroughness of metacognition about strategic reading is expected to increase with reading skill, so it should be assessed.

Assessments Should Supplement and Complement Existing Measures of Reading Fluency and Comprehension

Teachers are currently inundated with reading assessments, so they need economical methods to assess multiple aspects of children's reading. Economy involves time and resources, so methods that are brief, easily integrated into guided or group reading time, and readily combined with other assessments may be the most useful. For example, many teachers collect data on children's oral reading fluency with running records or miscue analyses, so any assessment of strategic reading that can be embedded in them will save teachers time and provide additional diagnostic information using the same texts. We believe that teachers can use informal reading inventories to assess children's comprehension, recall, summarizing, writing, and strategic reading as well as the originally intended oral reading fluency. The information can be formal or informal and diagnostic or summative. Another promising method is to "piggyback" metacognitive assessments on traditional comprehension assessments. Self-reports, interviews, and surveys that can be appended to unit tests, content area reading, or high stakes tests are additional examples of ways that teachers can add value to current reading assessments.

Assessments Should Be Aligned With Instruction So They Provide Diagnostic and Prescriptive Information About Specific Reading Strategies

Strategy assessments have more value as diagnostic than outcome measures because comprehension is a more important outcome than the reported knowledge or use of strategies. However, teachers can use information from strategy assessments to improve comprehension when they provide appropriate instruction to individuals. Teachers generally prefer and value reading assessments that are internal rather than external, in other words, under their own control for when they are given and how they are used (S. G. Paris, A. H. Paris, & Carpenter, 2002). Therefore, strategy assessments should yield information that is immediately available, tied to specific reading experiences and texts, similar to classroom tasks, and readily integrated into daily instruction (S. G. Paris, 2002). An ideal strategy assessment could be embedded in a small group reading lesson, guided reading activity, or a parent–child dialogic reading activity. It would be a "point of use" assessment that can provide a teachable moment of instruction if required. The ideal strategic reading activity seamlessly includes both assessment and instruction in a manner similar to coaching athletic or musical strategies.

SUGGESTIONS FOR PRACTICE

Teachers can weave metacognitive assessments about strategic reading into their regular classroom activities. Consider some assessments that could be used at three different grade levels. Each method reflects the five design principles.

First Grade

Beginning readers focus most of their energy on decoding words on the page, but they still need to create meaning from text. Strategy assessments can support each instructional objective. For example, decoding by analogy is an important strategy that children learn in grades 1–2 in order to pronounce and identify unfamiliar words. The strategy is to find familiar phonemes and morphemes in the unfamiliar words, such as breaking apart "outstanding" into "out," "stand," and "ing." Similarly, children in primary grades learn strategies for identifying the key information in text, both narrative and expository. Consider strategy assessments for attacking words and text.

Teachers can assess decoding by analogy as children encounter unfamiliar words in their daily reading. When students stop reading orally at unknown words, teachers can ask questions such as "What can you do to figure out that word? Can you break it apart? Are there any words or sounds inside that word that you recognize? Can you say the parts and then say them altogether?" Teachers can record children's responses and strategic attempts in notes or a journal. Additional questions about other strategies, such as looking forward and backward in text to use context, can be asked to assess other strategies that children use. These kinds of assessments of decoding strategies can be used during small group reading or guided reading. The assessment is informal, immediate, and readily tied to instruction, which are all hallmarks of authentic and student-centered assessment (S. G. Paris & Ayres, 1994). For a more formal assessment, teachers can use prepared texts or a list of unfamiliar words to assess how children approach and recognize them. For example, teachers might make up a five-sentence text with five new words to assess their word attack strategies. Teachers can record children's responses on the page and use it to mark progress or share with parents at conferences.

Interviews about reading can be used with beginning readers too. Clay's (1993) Observation Survey provides a standard format for asking young children questions about their understanding of basic concepts of print such as directionality of reading and the meaning of punctuation marks. Clay's work is perhaps the earliest metacognitive assessment of beginning readers, and it shows the value of assessing how beginning readers approach text. Teachers can create interviews about the specific strategies they instruct too. For example, a first-grade teacher who is teaching children to retell important ideas in text can assess children's strategies in a retrospective interview. Imagine that a first grader has read and retold a brief text. Now the teacher can ask questions such as, "What was the most important information in your retelling? How do you know? Why did you say X? Did you leave out any information? Why?" In this manner, teachers can determine if children are focusing on important information in their retellings, omitting irrelevant information, and organizing their retelling—all good features of a retelling. Again, the results may be recorded informally and anecdotally.

If first graders cannot decode adequately to assess their reading strategies, then teachers can use wordless picture books to assess comprehension. For example, A. H. Paris and S. G. Paris (2003) created a narrative comprehension assessment of wordless picture books that includes retelling and comprehension measures.

The comprehension questions addressed the elements of story structure, including setting, characters, initiating event, problem, and solution, as well as implied relations such as characters' intentions and feelings. Teachers can assess strategies that children use to construct meaning from picture books by adding interview questions about why each narrative element or relation is important to include in a retelling, how readers knew the information was important, and why their retelling should include this information. Whether assessment occurs with wordless picture books, word lists, or actual text, the important part is teachers' questions about the strategies that children use to attack words and text. For beginning readers, it is usually more important to embed the assessments in daily instructional activities than to provide formal records of the assessments.

Fourth Grade

By fourth grade, children should have acquired many strategies to use while reading and writing. More specifically, they should be using various strategies before, during, and after reading to check and enhance comprehension. They should also have more metacognitive insights into reading than beginning readers and more articulate vocabularies to describe their thinking. For these reasons, self-reports of strategic reading can be used effectively by fourth-grade children. Perhaps the easiest method is to ask children to read aloud but to stop periodically to say what they are thinking. (The reflective think-aloud should occur about once per 100 words.) Teachers can record students' self-reports by audio recording, in anecdotal notes, or with a rubric depending on their purpose.

Teachers can assess the strategies that students use to answer questions following reading by asking them to think aloud while they answer questions or to interview students after they answer them. For example, a think-aloud as students consider multiple-choice options might reveal that some students answer impulsively or others are fooled by long answers. If teachers have taught students question–answer relation strategies, then asking students how they searched through text to find answers is appropriate. If they search text looking for answers, then it can be useful to examine how they search, where they start, and if they are looking for word matches or conceptual answers. Strategy assessments like this can be connected to instruction on study skills or test preparation so teachers can determine if students are using effective strategies for monitoring and inferring meaning.

The think-along passage (TAP) method works well with fourth-grade students because it connects metacognitive and comprehension assessments. After children answer comprehension questions, teachers can assess what strategies were used or could have been used. For example, after a student answers the question "What is the main idea in this paragraph?", teachers might ask students to describe how they knew that or what they could do to check their answer. The accuracy, complexity, and details of students' metacognitive explanations are indicators of strategy knowledge and use. It would be easy to add an assessment of specific strategies after reading. Teachers might make a list of 10 strategies, both useful and not useful, that could be used in the task, present the list to students, and ask them to rate the frequency with which they used each one and the perceived benefits they had for comprehending this text. Students' responses, both qualitative explanations and quantitative ratings, can provide teachers with valuable information about the students' strategic reading.

Seventh Grade

Reading and thinking aloud are less common practices in middle school and beyond, partly because adolescents may be embarrassed to do either one and partly because teachers have little time for individual reading assessments. Surveys of strategic reading, therefore, work well in middle school because they can be given to groups of students who can answer them silently. The data can be scored and the results can be displayed and stored electronically on the Internet or computers—all economical methods. A survey of how students use reading strategies can augment a survey of reading interests and habits or a survey of writing and study skills. Students might be asked to rate frequency or value of specific strategies or they might be asked to choose the best prediction or summary from among four options in a multiple-choice format. They could even be given true–false questions. Teachers can obtain rich information quickly from surveys that show students' strategic reading in the context of their reading interests and academic motivation (Guthrie & Wigfield, 2005).

Self-reports about strategic reading might be appropriate for adolescent readers who are experiencing comprehension difficulties because teachers need more detailed information about the specific difficulties. Thinking aloud while reading can allow teachers to understand useful strategies as well as intrusive and unhelpful tactics. Surveys and self-reports of thinking may also help teachers to disentangle motivational obstacles from reading comprehension strategy problems among older readers. Writing about one's own learning and reading strategies is also appropriate for middle and high school students. They can reflect and analyze their own strategies, describe their goals, and monitor their progress to assess their own reading development.

DIRECTIONS FOR FUTURE RESEARCH
AND DEVELOPMENT OF ASSESSMENTS

Teachers need assessments of strategic reading in order to gauge how well their students understand and apply strategies across tasks in the curriculum. Researchers need similar assessments so that they can evaluate the benefits of classroom interventions aimed at promoting strategic reading. Students can use the information from strategy assessments to gain understanding and to monitor their own reading accomplishments. All of these assessment purposes are formative rather than summative, so the key feature of strategic reading assessments is diagnostic utility as opposed to sorting students by abilities. Diagnostic assessments of strategic reading can be created within academic curricula (e.g., basal reading series, science and social studies curricula), as well as produced as stand-alone assessments for teachers. Commercial publishers should be involved in both enterprises to save teachers time and to create uniform assessments.

Future assessments of strategic reading can make better use of technology. Imagine strategy assessments administered via computers, hand-held PDAs, or multimedia platforms like LeapFrog pads. Students might undergo these assessments on their own time without supervision, which would be a huge savings of teachers' time. They might also take the assessments repeatedly for their own information in order to master the strategies and improve their comprehension. Technology-based assessments permit rapid scoring of the data, multiple displays of data and students' progress, and ready access to the data by multiple users. The economical assessments of strategic reading through technology might increase their diagnostic use too because teachers do not have to spend inordinate amounts of time scoring and interpreting assessment results.

Researchers need to design and create assessments of strategic reading, but more importantly, they need to conduct basic research on the reliability and validity of the tools. Such research should be rigorous yet innovative because the usual criteria may not be appropriate. For example, reliability of strategy use, calculated as test–retest reliability, is difficult to evaluate because rereading the same text should result in better strategy use and comprehension the second time. Moreover, strategic reading assessments may not correlate highly with all standardized tests of reading because the knowledge required for strategic reading is highly situated and specific, whereas standardized tests reflect individual differences in vocabulary, decoding, intelligence, experience, and a wide variety of factors. Thus, the usual calculations of concurrent and predictive validity may not be appropriate. Imagine a school where teachers provide extra instruction to struggling readers so that they can gain control over specific reading strategies. These readers might improve their reading comprehension, gain metacognition, and increase confidence in their reading, yet they may still score poorly on high stakes tests if those strategies are not applicable on the tests or if the tests require many additional skills besides strategic reading. It would be inappropriate to judge the strategy instruction as ineffective if the outcome measures are not sensitive to the actual cognitive and behavioral gains made by students (Cross & S. G. Paris, 1987).

CONCLUSIONS

Strategic reading is important because it is a foundation for self-regulated reading. Strategic reading allows flexible approaches for reading different texts for different purposes. Thus, it is important to instruct students about what, how, when, and why to use various reading strategies, and it is equally important to assess whether or not students understand and apply reading strategies effectively. The meta-cognitive aspects of self-appraisal and self-management during reading can be assessed with self-reports of thinking, interviews during or after reading, and surveys of the frequency and value of different strategies. Teachers need to become familiar with these methods, as well as the underlying knowledge about strategic reading development, in order to diagnose students' strengths and weaknesses and to provide appropriate instruction in the classroom. Instruction and assessment of strategic reading can be intertwined in daily reading activities so that they provide reciprocal support for each other. Future research should create uniform and useful methods for assessing strategic reading across grades K–12. If future strategic reading assessments are authentic, embedded in the curricula, and based on sound technology, they will be enormously helpful for teachers and students.

METACONNECTION FOR CHAPTER 7

Schmitt provided us with two case studies to improve our skills in assessing awareness and control of metacognitive strategies. In chapter 7, Paris and Flukes offer a guide for us to assess a reader's strategy use as text is read, with the ultimate goal of comprehension. Concrete examples are presented for students in grades 1, 4, and 7. We will continue through middle school with self-assessment strategies discussed by Afflerbach and Meuwissen in chapter 8.

REFERENCES

Adams, M. J. (1990). *Beginning to read: Thinking and learning about print.* Cambridge, MA: MIT Press.

Almasi, J. F. (2003). *Teaching strategic processes in reading.* New York: Guilford.

Blachowicz, C., & Ogle, D. (2001). *Reading comprehension.* New York: Guilford.

Brown, A., & Day, J. (1983). Macrorules for summarizing text: The development of expertise. *Journal of Verbal Learning and Verbal Behavior, 22,* 1–14.

Brown, R., Pressley, M., Van Meter, P., & Schuder, T. (1996). A quasi-experimental validation of transactional strategies instruction with low-achieving second-grade readers. *Journal of Educational Psychology, 88,* 18–37.

Clay, M. M. (1993). *An observation survey of early literacy achievement.* Portsmouth, NH: Heinemann.

Craig, M., & Yore, L. (1996). Middle school students awareness of strategies for resolving comprehension difficulties in science reading. *Journal of Research and Development in Education, 29,* 226–238.

Cross, D. R., & Paris, S. G. (1987). Assessment of reading comprehension: Matching test purposes and test properties. *Educational Psychologist, 22,* 313–332.

Cross, D. R., & Paris, S. G. (1988). Developmental and instructional analyses of children's metacognition and comprehension. *Journal of Educational Psychology, 80,* 131–142.

Dixon, R., & Hultsch, D. (1984). The metamemory in adulthood (MIA) instrument. *Psychological Documents, 14*, 3.

Garner, R. (1982). Verbal-report data on reading strategies. *Journal of Reading Behavior, 14*, 159–167.

Garner, R. (1987). *Metacognition and reading comprehension.* Norwood, NJ: Ablex.

Guthrie, J. T., & Wigfield, A. (2005). Roles of motivation and engagement in reading comprehension assessment. In S. G. Paris & S. A. Stahl (Eds.), *Current issues in reading comprehension and assessment.* Mahwah, NJ: Lawrence Erlbaum Associates.

Jacobs, J., & Paris, S. (1987). Children's metacognition about reading: Issues in definition, measurement, and instruction. *Educational Psychologist, 22*, 255–278.

Juliebo, M., Malicky, G., & Norman, C. (1998). Metacognition of young readers in an early intervention programme. *Journal of Research in Reading, 21*, 24–35.

Kintsch, W. (1998). *Comprehension: A paradigm for cognition.* New York: Cambridge University Press.

Lachman, M. (1986). Locus of control in aging research: A case for multidimensional and domain specific assessment. *Psychology and Aging, 1*, 34–40.

Luke, A. (2000). Critical literacy in Australia: A matter of context and standpoint. *Journal of Adolescent and Adult Literacy, 42*, 448–461.

Mokhtari, K., & Reichard, C. (2002). Assessing metacognitive awareness of reading strategies. *Journal of Educational Psychology, 94*, 249–259.

Moore, D., Zabrucky, K., & Commander, N. (1997). Validation of the metacomprehension scale. *Contemporary Educational Psychology, 22*, 457–471.

Myers, M., & Paris, S. (1978). Children's metacognitive knowledge about reading. *Journal of Educational Psychology, 70*, 680–690.

National Reading Panel (2000). *Teaching children to read: An evidence-based assessment of the scientific research literature on reading and its implications for reading instruction.* Washington, DC: National Institute on Child and Human Development.

Paris, A. H., & Paris, S. G. (2003). Assessing narrative comprehension in young children. *Reading Research Quarterly, 38*(1), 36–76.

Paris, S. G. (1991). Assessment and remediation of metacognitive aspects of reading comprehension. *Topics in Language Disorders, 12*, 32–50.

Paris, S. G. (2002). Linking reading assessment and instruction in elementary grades. In C. Roller (Ed.), *Comprehensive reading instruction across the grade levels* (pp. 55–69). Newark, DE: International Reading Association.

Paris, S. G., & Ayres, L. J. (1994). *Becoming reflective students and teachers with portfolios and authentic assessment.* Washington, DC: American Psychological Association.

Paris, S. G., Cross, D. R., & Lipson, M. Y. (1984). Informed strategies for learning: A program to improve children's reading awareness and comprehension. *Journal of Educational Psychology, 76*, 1239–1252.

Paris, S. G., Lipson, M. Y., & Wixson, K. (1983). Becoming a strategic reader. *Contemporary Educational Psychology, 8*, 293–316.

Paris, S. G., & Myers, M. (1981). Comprehension monitoring, memory, and study strategies of good and poor readers. *Journal of Reading Behavior, 23*, 5–22.

Paris, S. G., Paris, A. H., & Carpenter, R. D. (2002). Effective practices for assessing young readers. In B. Taylor & P. D. Pearson (Eds.), *Teaching reading: Effective schools, accomplished teachers* (pp. 141–160). Mahwah, NJ: Lawrence Erlbaum Associates.

Paris, S. G., & van Kraayenoord, C. E. (1998). Assessing young children's literacy strategies and development. In S. Paris & H. Wellman (Eds.), *Global prospects for education: Development, culture, and schooling* (pp. 193–227). Washington, DC: American Psychological Association.

Paris, S. G., Wasik, B. A., & Turner, J. C. (1991). The development of strategic readers. In R. Barr, M. Kamil, P. Mosenthal, & P. D. Pearson (Eds.), *Handbook of reading research* (2nd ed., pp. 609–640). New York: Longman.

Paris, S. G., & Winograd, P. W. (1990). How metacognition can promote academic learning and instruction. In B. J. Jones & L. Idol (Eds.), *Dimensions of thinking and cognitive instruction* (pp. 15–51). Hillsdale, NJ: Lawrence Erlbaum Associates.

Paris, S., & Jacobs, J. (1984). The benefits of informed instruction for children's reading awareness and comprehension skills. *Child Development, 55*, 2083–2093.

Pressley, M., & Afflerbach, P. (1995). *Verbal protocols of reading: The nature of constructively responsive reading.* Mahwah, NJ: Lawrence Erlbaum Associates.

Schmitt, M. (1990). A questionnaire to measure children's awareness of strategic reading processes. *Reading Teacher*, 454–461.

Snow, C. E., Burns, M. S., & Griffin, P. (1998). *Preventing reading difficulties in young children.* Washington, DC: National Academy Press.

Stahl, K.A.D. (2004). Proof, practice, and promise: Comprehension strategy instruction in the primary grades. *Reading Teacher, 57*(7), 598–609.

Wagner, D. A., Spratt, J. E., Gal, I., & Paris, S. G. (1989). Reading and believing: Beliefs, attributions, and reading achievement in Moroccan schoolchildren. *Journal of Educational Psychology, 81*(3), 283–293.

8

Teaching and Learning Self-Assessment Strategies in Middle School

Peter Afflerbach
Kevin Meuwissen
University of Maryland

My reading students use self-assessment checklists a lot in my class. I believe that it makes them aware of their thought process while they are engaged in the reading process. It not only forces them to be aware of their learning, but the checklists also remind them of other reading strategies that they may have forgotten. What are some other forms of self-assessments that middle school students can do besides checklists?

—Andrea Evans, Reading, Grades 6–8, Indiana

This chapter should give Andrea many ideas about how to teach and encourage self-assessment with her middle school reading students.

TEACHING AND LEARNING SELF-ASSESSMENT STRATEGIES IN MIDDLE SCHOOL

The ability to self-assess is central to middle school students' success in school. To read well, students must be able to plan, use, and coordinate different reading strategies. Students must be able to set goals, monitor near and far progress to these goals, and determine that goals have been met. They must call on relevant prior knowledge and determine that it is appropriate. Students must do so in relation to increasingly complex reading materials and content area curricula. The ability to self-assess facilitates students' growth and achievement in reading as it contributes to independence and success in school. This chapter intends to describe how teachers can help middle school students learn to self-assess in reading. Self-assessment is a collection of metacognitive knowledge, strategies, and mind-sets that middle school students use in the pursuit of learning (Baker, 2002). Self-assessment allows student readers to independently undertake, monitor, and complete the reading and reading-related tasks that they encounter in middle school (Paris, Wasik, & Turner, 1991).

The Importance of Self-Assessment

It is well established that human learning is more efficient when that learning is assisted by metacognition (Flavell, 1978; Markman, 1977). When students are in control of the act of reading and learning, they can provide their own guidance to increase their success. Students' learning and use of middle school course content attained through reading is enhanced by metacognitive routines, but many students lack self-assessment ability. There is clear need to help students develop such ability as they strive for attainment of proficient and advanced levels of reading (Grigg, Daane, Jin, & Campbell, 2003). Student self-assessment is requisite for success in middle school, and this proposal is made in relation to three areas of research: the expert reader (Pressley & Afflerbach, 1995), engaged reading (Guthrie & Wigfield, 1997), and students' relation to assessment (Black & William, 1998). Combined, this research describes the nature of metacognition in reading and the benefits of being a self-assessing middle school reader. The detail of this research allows us to characterize self-assessment in a manner that can inform instruction and learning.

Expert reader research portrays the extraordinary accomplishment of reading well. Using think-aloud protocol data, Pressley and Afflerbach (1995) determined that expert readers have extensive and well-practiced skills and strategies that are used to construct meaning from text. Expert readers regularly self-assess. They set goals and plan paths to meet these goals *a priori*. They monitor reading in service of identifying and remembering important information and evaluating what is read. Expert readers' use fix-it strategies when difficulties arise during reading and they evaluate their reading in relation to goals. Table 8.1 contains a list of typical self-assessment strategies that expert readers use.

Successful middle school readers must be increasingly focused on self-assessment. Planning strategies that help students set goals and the means to achieving these goals for both self-selected and teacher-assigned work are needed. Using these strategies, students may choose a purposeful path towards their goals, as opposed to a random path. As they plan, students use their knowledge of self in relation to the task, including their sense of prior knowledge for the subject, the familiarity of text type and their reading ability. They appraise the situation and reach one of two conclusions. Either they determine that they are in a good position to continue with their self-assessed knowledge and capabilities in relation to the task demands, or they identify areas that will need attention.

Consider the middle school student who reads well but finds the going extremely difficult when beginning a new textbook chapter in earth science, one

TABLE 8.1
Self-Assessment Strategies for Middle School Student Readers

Planning strategies
  Determining goals
  Determining means to achieve goals
  Determining path to achieve goals
Monitoring strategies
  Question asking while reading
    Does that make sense?
    How do I know?
    Do I understand this?
    Do I understand this well enough to use in the required task?
  Checking understanding in relation to the task at hand
Fix-it strategies
  Rereading text
  Slowing the rate of reading text
  Seeking help from an expert
Evaluating strategies
  Questions
    Does my work meet the task demands?
    Is my progress to this point aligned with my plan and standards?
    What evidence can I use to make this determination?
    How do I use this evidence?
    Can I use a rubric to estimate the grade I will get from my performance?
    Can I use the rubric to provide formative feedback during task performance and summative
      feedback upon the completion of the performance?

Note. (Adapted from Pressley & Afflerbach, 1995)

focusing on earthquakes. The student reads with the goal of preparing for the chapter test, which will include multiple-choice questions and prompts for extended written responses. Unfamiliar content, including vocabulary and related concepts, presents a challenge requiring the student to call on the appropriate reading strategies to help construct meaning. The reader determines that the meanings of *tectonic plates, fault zones,* and their relation to earthquakes must be learned. The student also notes that the lengthy text is marked by complex sentence structures and that it is peppered with visual displays: aerial photographs of the fault zones, charts with seismographic readings and a graphic representation of the Richter scale. The student reads to identify and remember important information in text. The reader's attention to progress signals that the amount of new content area information is substantial. As a result of this self-assessment, the student varies the reading rate as needed, going more slowly to better comprehend the text as it introduces the new concept of tectonic plate movement. The student also re-reads when necessary.

Monitoring of the construction of meaning is taking place. The reader regularly asks questions like, "Does that make sense?" and "Do I understand this well enough to answer the upcoming test questions?" A positive response to the question allows the reader to continue apace, while a response indicating a lack of understanding signals the need for rereading. The road to understanding may have bumps and potholes, so it is critical for students to learn strategic and effortful approaches to problematic school tasks is required. For readers of difficult and unfamiliar text, rereading and slowing the rate of reading are important behaviors that allow the application of specific meaning-building strategies as needed. As well, knowing that they have exhausted their own array of strategies may lead students to seek help from an expert, such as the classroom teacher. Knowing when to do this, by reason and not reflex, is one characteristic of the mindful, self-assessing student.

As student work and effort in reading continue, self-assessment strategies remain important. These strategies follow logically from a student's planning ability. If planning strategies are efficient, they help the middle school student establish parameters for their work. Students can anticipate the work that is needed to stay on task, while the determination that one is outside the parameters suggests to students that they are off task. Here, self-assessment can operate in relation to a series of questions that successful student readers ask and answer. We expect that students are asking questions like, "How does this relate to my goals?" (Why am I reading?) and "Do I understand this vocabulary word well enough to use it in the required task?" This is no idle questioning. Rather, the student is led to clear understanding of the nature of the effort by asking and seeking answers to these monitoring questions. Such questions promote an efficient toggling back and forth between micro- and macro-levels of self-assessment. Self-assessment strategies operate at the edge of consciousness when readers are practiced and experienced, but they must be taught and learned before they can be used as such.

Using metacognitive strategies has several obvious benefits for middle school students who are becoming better readers. First, the ability to set goals for reading and to calibrate reading performance to those goals makes reading efficient. Students can look ahead, estimate task difficulty, and then apportion their attention and resources as needed. Second, the strategies make manageable the more taxing reading and reading-related work in school. The middle school reader who carefully monitors the construction of meaning can divide the complex process of reading into manageable sections, creating a series of sub goals. For example, when an unfamiliar vocabulary word, *seismic*, is encountered, it is noted as such. The student sets about determining the meaning of this word, relying especially on the rich context of the paragraph that contains it. Once the word is "figured out," the student can proceed with further reading. If the process of constructing meaning breaks down, the student can apply appropriate fix-it strategies. The fully developed and ubiquitous self-assessment strategies of the expert reader are a work in progress for most middle school students. Thus, an immediate challenge is to help students develop expertise with self-assessment strategies as they develop an awareness of the importance of self-assessment.

A second construct that informs the conceptualization of self-assessment is engaged reading (Guthrie & Wigfield, 1997). Central to the idea of engaged reading are readers' strategies, prior knowledge and motivation, all working in concert to create meaning. A key contribution of engagement theory is the idea that strategic reading may enhance both the process of constructing meaning from text and the student's sense of self as a reader. Knowing it is possible to read about the complex relations between the movement of tectonic plates and fault lines, encounter obstacles and difficulties while reading, and then overcome them is affirming knowledge for developing readers. School accomplishments in reading help demonstrate the value of self-assessment and help students appreciate the metacognitive things they do. And metacognition, as a means of knowing the self, can help students build positive self-images as readers and increase their self-esteem. Succeeding and attributing success to self-assessment helps student readers understand that they are agents in the act of reading.

Picture the student who reads the challenging earth science text and manages to identify and successfully address difficulties in constructing meaning. The student progresses through the chapter by using self-assessment strategies. The student's ongoing accomplishment is immediately apparent in the comprehension that occurs. An accurate mental model of tectonic plates and fault lines is constructed. In addition, the student is experiencing success in managing the reading act. This experience can provide knowledge that is ultimately motivating: The student believes that comprehension is possible and success is within reach, even when reading challenging text. Students who are successful in using self-assessment strategies not only understand text, they better understand themselves as readers. They know that their ability and effort yield comprehension. The affirmation provided to students by such positive experiences in reading may contribute to the Matthew effect identified by Stanovich (1986). Students who are successful in middle school reading understand the connection between their success and their self-assessment ability. These students may seek out further reading experiences that, in turn, contribute to increased metacognition and comprehension. In summary, engaged readers use self-assessment strategies that contribute to their reading achievement. Engaged readers also may experience increased motivation to read and self-esteem as a reader, and they may develop an inclination to read as a result of their self-assessment ability. These outcomes further contribute to growth in reading.

Despite the benefits of self-assessment and its importance in the classroom, middle school curricula are not often characterized by consistent attention to students' self-assessment. Metacognitive ability in middle school students will not thrive unless students are expected to be participating members in the culture of assessment. Students must become familiar with assessment materials and procedures and their appropriate uses. Yet, Black and William (1998) likened the majority of assessment done in school to a black box in which the processes of assessment and evaluation remain distant and intangible for students. When teachers do not share the ways and means of reading assessment with students or when the curriculum is spare in relation to quality classroom based assessments, this creates an inappropriate distance between students and assessment. There may be few opportunities for students to develop their understanding of the manner of assessment. Applied to middle school, the black box model suggests that a student's typical experience with reading assessment involves undertaking and completing a reading task, handing in work (e.g., a paper or test) and after the passage of some time receiving the work back, with a grade and a teacher's pronouncement or some short written comments attached to it. Between handing in work and having it returned, students are at a loss to account for what assessment and evaluation are, and how they work. The opacity of assessment also is evident in teachers' questioning routines when student answers are elicited, but the means for evaluating and responding to student answers are not explained. More important to this chapter, there are lost opportunities to demystify acts of assessment and to connect them with students' nascent or developing self-assessment routines. For example, teachers can uncover their assessment processes by thinking out loud as they respond to students' contributions to a comprehension discussion. Capitalizing on these opportunities can lead to classroom assessment practice that serves as a model of how to do assessment for middle school students. Our work related to self-assessment in reading must be focused, in part, on uncovering the black box. Students must learn how assessment works, and opportunities must be provided for students to learn and use assessment for themselves.

Over the course of an instructional unit, a school year, or a student's experience in a particular school or school district, we believe that an optimal experience is one where students encounter a continuous series of opportunities to understand, practice and learn self-assessment. Students who are guided to utilize these opportunities will be building a working knowledge of self-assessment. In contrast, students whose awareness of assessment rises and falls only in relation to preparing for tests and quizzes and who have virtually no other opportunities to learn about assessment will remain needy in terms of the evaluation of their own work. The student who equates assessment with tests and quizzes is rarely the successful self-assessor.

The research on expert readers and engaged reading describes informed strategy use and the cognitive and affective outcomes of self-assessment. Further, Black & William (1998) described the importance of helping students become familiar with the culture of assessment. A combination of these perspectives suggests that curriculum in middle schools must be geared to teaching students how to take increasing responsibility for doing assessment themselves. Accomplished readers regularly deploy self-assessment strategies when they are involved in different reading tasks. These abilities and this mindfulness have attendant results: Success in reading and accurate student attributions to the role that self-assessment plays in success can foster continued, motivated reading.

Characteristics of Instruction That Support Middle School Students' Self-Assessments

Middle school student readers must self-assess (Pressley & Afflerbach, 1995; Snow, 2002), yet reading is rarely an instructional focus in middle school curricula. Reading instruction that focuses on self-assessment is rarer still, in spite of the fact that the reading challenges faced in middle school are continual. These students are faced with an increasing volume of reading and reading-related coursework. Texts increase in length and their structures become more complex. Vocabulary and the concepts they represent diversify and multiply. Middle school readers must assess themselves as they read, using metacognitive knowledge to optimize their reading experiences. Metacognitive ability, realized in self-assessment strategies, allows student readers to deal successfully with the increasing challenge of middle school work.

Self-assessment must be emphasized in the middle school curriculum. Yet, this is a difficult challenge because there is an over-focus on a single type of assessment, high-stakes testing, in almost all middle school classrooms. The devotion of school time and resources to prepare students to take tests in the hope that they will score high warps the curriculum. Test-like items and tasks offer little opportunity for students to learn self-assessment routines that are valuable in the daily conduct of the classroom. The prevalence of high stakes testing helps to maintain the idea that assessment is essentially external to the student and only indirectly associated with learning. It prevents the application of the very school resources that are needed to promote sustained and effective self-assessment instruction. The emphasis on testing produces students who remain outsiders to the culture of classroom assessment. This creates a dependency for students; if they want to know how they are doing in reading, they must rely on someone else to do the assessment. In contrast, self-assessment represents insights into one's own work and the rendering of judgments, and the appraisal of progress and ongoing challenge, each dependent on a shift of assessment responsibility and ability to the student.

To help students meet the increased work demands of middle school, to help them envision themselves as agents in their work, and to help them develop strong, positive attributions for their performance, strategy instruction should focus on self-assessment. We are optimistic that such strategy instruction will have positive impact on student reading. Based on previous efforts to teach comprehension strategies (e.g., Palincsar & Brown, 1984; Block & Pressley, 2002), we believe carefully modeled self-assessment strategies, detailed explanations of strategy use and demonstrations of assessment routines using think-aloud procedures should help students develop self-assessment ability. We suggest that metacognitive, self-assessment instruction concentrate on three types of knowledge. This knowledge relates to the self-assessment strategies themselves, the purposes of the strategies and the contexts in which the strategies prove most fruitful.

Although instruction is advocated in self-assessment strategies, knowledge of how to apply a strategy does not, by itself, guarantee student success. Knowing the mechanical steps of strategy use does not equate with successful self-assessment. A second and related type of knowledge focuses on why individuals use different strategies. Self-assessment strategies serve the purpose of making learning more efficient. These strategies may direct middle school students to regular successes in the classroom. They may help learners understand that the task at hand is quite manageable, or that a seemingly distant goal is attainable through careful work and good effort. Knowledge of the purpose and uses of strategies helps students select the strategies that are most useful to the task at hand. For instance, the strategies students use when evaluating their comprehension of science laboratory directions (in preparation of working with potentially volatile chemicals) may well differ from those used to evaluate the construction of meaning of a poem.

A third and closely related knowledge set is that which helps the student accurately identify the manner in which the learning context influences their use of particular strategies. Middle school curricula present students with diverse tasks that demand particular levels of attention and metacognition. For example, successful students reading a series of paragraphs and answering related comprehension questions will gauge the use of self-assessment strategies to the task at hand. A consistent question might be, "Am I reading with sufficient comprehension to answer the questions?" Later, the same students will bring to bear metacognitive strategies that help them gather and organize information about history in a manner that suits the overall goal of developing a historical sketch, complete with dialog and setting, for their classmates and teacher. With the different task and context, students monitor and self-assess accordingly. In each case, what students must do in relation to learning processes and products influences the choice of self-assessment strategies.

We advocate for middle school students needing to know how specific strategies work, the purposes of the strategies and the contexts in which they are useful. Prior successes in strategy instruction have been provided as an example of how students can learn new and useful strategies. Yet, the concern is that middle school teachers will now have the added burden of self-assessment strategy instruction. Such suggestions to teach self-assessment strategies within an already full middle school content area curriculum will most likely be met with a notable lack of enthusiasm. As an alternative, instruction could focus on building students' self-assessment strategies through the use of existing classroom assessments. The idea here is that existing classroom assessments provide opportunities for teachers to both carry on the work of classroom assessment for their evaluation needs and to teach students how to do assessment themselves. Existing classroom assessments, including performance assessments, portfolio assessments, self-assessment strategy inventories, teacher questioning, and content area tests can serve as models for students. Repeated experiences with the materials, procedures, and purposes of particular assessments can promote student development in self-assessment. This use of assessment is contextualized in the meaningful work of classroom lessons and other learning opportunities. Thus, learning self-assessment emanates from existing classroom learning and assessment practice. Teachers' assessment practices in the classroom can serve as a means of helping students learn the work of self-assessment.

Teaching Students Self-Assessment in the Classroom: Three Scenarios

Self-assessment helps middle school students become fully active participants in their reading. Becoming a skillful and strategic reader is an ongoing and long-term developmental process, and it is important for teachers to implement formative assessments that allow students to monitor their own progress. That way, students and teachers, in cooperation, can read and best understand their areas of strength and need in reading. One goal of the teacher must be the use of methods that foster self-assessment. This practice can lead to the shift of the accounting and analysis of reading strengths, needs, and solutions to students. This section includes examples of how students can learn and use self-assessment within three representative middle school contexts, focusing on instruction in the content areas of English language arts, social studies and mathematics. The purpose is to demonstrate how the teaching and learning of self-assessment strategies can be integrated into middle school classrooms. In each case, the focus is on the nature of the curriculum, the nature of the assessment that helps describe the breadth and depth of student learning, and the aspects of assessment that can be used to help middle school students learn to self-assess.

Portfolio Assessment in the English Language Arts Classroom. One important purpose of the middle school English Language Arts (ELA) curriculum is to help students develop full understanding of how authors construct and communicate messages with text. Such important student work and understanding rely on the use of analytical reading strategies. These strategies help students analyze and determine an author's point of view, the author's facility with literary devices like persuasion, irony, and satire, and the relation of a text's literary form to its content. Thus, within the middle school ELA classroom, students might be learning to critically examine texts and make assertions to classmates and teachers, based on their critiques of the texts. The curriculum reinforces these expectations with thematic framing questions like, "How does figurative language convey an author's intent or impact the meanings of a text?" and "How do poetry and fictional narratives help us to understand our experiences and the experiences of others?" In other words, the middle school curriculum extends beyond more typical abilities like summarizing main ideas and building vocabulary to explore how language is used to make meaning in different ways.

A key goal of assessment within the ELA curriculum is to describe changes in students' analytic reading strategies over time. To do this, assessment must be structured to provide specific pieces of evidence that demonstrate knowledge growth in a longitudinal manner (Moss et al., 1992). Portfolio assessment promotes the observation and description of student progress over time, and serves as a means of collecting student work. As well, portfolio assessment provides a forum for examining and evaluating this work. Portfolios encourage self-assessment in a number of ways. By implementing a portfolio and effectively modeling its application, teachers can help students appraise and demonstrate their progress with selected, tangible evidence. Portfolios can help students develop criteria for judging their own work (Afflerbach, 2002; Nitko, 2001), and this requires that students learn to critically and judiciously select examples that demonstrate growth and achievement. In the ELA classroom, students need to build a case, and in building the case, an understanding, of how their analytic reading has changed.

Nicole is a seventh-grade ELA teacher whose goals include teaching her students about different functions of reading using a range of literature, helping students build analytical reading strategies, and facilitating connections among texts and between texts and personal experiences. These goals are closely aligned the assorted middle school ELA learning standards developed by the school district, and state standards and those created by the National Council of Teachers of English and the International Reading Association (NCTE/IRA, 1996). These standards prioritize the comprehension and interpretation of text content and composition and the communication of textual understandings to others in critical and creative ways.

Nicole is interested in using portfolios for two primary reasons: to document and describe student learning of analytic reading strategies within the ELA curriculum, and to promote the development of students' self-assessment ability. This approach compels Nicole to conceptualize students' literal comprehension of text as a requisite building block and to scaffold for students the means to think critically about what they read. In Nicole's classroom, the portfolio is structured to contain drafts of student writing in response to prompts and an inventory of analytic reading strategies, which students are asked to use each time they read texts. An example of such an inventory is provided in Table 8.2.

Nicole supports the use of this inventory by discussing with students their perceptions of good reading and the consequences of using different reading strategies. For example, while reading Lois Lowry's *The Giver*, Nicole helps her students to develop questions about the society in which the characters live, to consider the author's impressions of such a society and to compare that society to their own as a means of evaluating both. In doing this, she scaffolds the use of analytic reading criteria. The intent is that over time and through repeated experiences with the portfolio elements, students assimilate and make these criteria

TABLE 8.2

Analytic Reading Strategy Inventory

Stage	Step	My Questions and Ideas
Previewing the Text	_____ I read the title, author, and date of publication	
	_____ I scanned the text for clues, including its length and format, information about the author and any passages or illustrations that stand out	
	_____ I used the information from the previous steps to make predictions about the text, including the author's purpose and intended audience, key ideas within the text, the context in which it was written and its reading level	
Capturing the Text	_____ While reading, I marked or wrote down main ideas and unfamiliar terms	
	_____ While reading, I wrote down my questions about and reactions to the text for future thought and discussion	
	_____ While reading, I considered the reasons why the author wrote what s/he wrote and the sources of his/her ideas	
Rereading the Text	_____ I reread sections of the text that I found confusing or difficult and sought answers to the questions that I had about them	
	_____ I reread my questions and comments about the text and searched for passages and other sources of information that would help me address them	
Evaluating the Text	_____ I summarized the points of view, arguments, or themes that the author presented in my own words and in writing	
	_____ I wrote down whether or not I enjoyed or agreed with the text and marked sections of the text that support my position	
	_____ I thought about and described my own experiences, beliefs, and prior knowledge that affected my understand of and feelings about the text	
Responding to the Text	_____ I assembled all of my notes, questions, and ideas into a written response to the text	
	AND/OR	
	_____ I discussed my knowledge of and reactions to the text with my classmates and supported my ideas with evidence from the text and prior knowledge and experiences	

their own. The support provided by the portfolio to the task of developing analytic reading strategies helps students understand the importance of self-assessment. Tools like the reading strategy inventory promote self-awareness in the
process of reading and serve Nicole's students as they set reading goals. Nicole
uses the portfolio to make the development and monitoring of analytic reading
strategies accessible within the context of reading course texts like *The Giver*
(Baker, 2002).

As a means of monitoring portfolio utilization and making the continual and
explicit connections of self-assessment to classroom learning goals, Nicole conferences regularly with her students in small groups and individually. First and
foremost, these discussions allow Nicole to observe how well and how often her
students draw on the section of the portfolio that contains the strategy inventory.
This allows Nicole to gauge students' progress. Before reading *The Giver*, for example, she models a series of in-depth previewing questions with a group of students. Asking, "What do the title and illustration on the front cover suggest?"
and "How do the teaser on the back cover and the first line of the text set a
mood?" she indicates that such questions should be asked by her students of
themselves during the previewing stage.

Nicole presents the portfolio to her students as a comprehensive means for
thinking about assessment, or a space in which different assessment tasks come
together to paint a detailed picture of a learner. Students are prompted to think
about the consequences and usefulness of portfolio components and the roles and
responsibilities of both student and teacher in attending to and interpreting their
results (Leipzig & Afflerbach, 2000). Moreover, Nicole demonstrates, using her
own classroom learning objectives, how to set reading goals that are outcome-
based and process-oriented, and she discusses with students the different means
by which they can determine whether or not those objectives have been met.
She describes her intention to use the analytic reading strategy inventory to assess her instructional goals, just as students use the inventory as a model in learning self-assessment. Also, she explains how to develop appropriate questions in
order to check for comprehension and establish a purpose for reading, and she
demonstrates, using a sample portfolio assignment, how she evaluates reading
strengths and weaknesses based on the questions that students might ask. The
portfolio changes from a teacher-structured assessment method to one for which
learners assume increasing responsibility, across the school year. Table 8.3 provides a basic demonstration of the process by which the portfolio permeates assessment in Nicole's classroom. In summary, the portfolio provides the tools for
Nicole's students to set goals and monitor the use of different reading strategies to
construct meaning and critically analyze texts. The portfolio is a continuous
source of information for Nicole and her students, as well as a continuous support
for the students. It provides the means to assess students' ELA learning while it
helps them learn assessment.

TABLE 8.3
Portfolio Tasks Used to Encourage Student Self-Assessment

Self-Assessment Objective	Portfolio Tool	Projected Student Output
Goal setting	A table in which students document their own and their teacher's objectives	Students use Nicole's learning objectives as models for their own; students develop goals that are outcome-based and process-oriented
Checking for comprehension and integrating prior knowledge	A series of open-ended questions on literary form (genre, plot, characters, perspective, etc.), vocabulary in context, key ideas and themes, and related personal experiences	Students build meaningful literal knowledge and address their own personal influences on which to base analyses and evaluations of texts and discussions with classmates and the teacher
Building analytic reading strategies	An analytic reading inventory that traces the process of previewing, interpreting, rereading, evaluating, and responding to texts	Students' self-awareness in reading is aided by a more transparent process for reading texts critically; students think more deeply and carefully about the messages presented by texts
Contemplating growth, motivation, and interest	A Likert-type interest inventory and journal writing process	Students develop a broader understanding of their purposes for reading and begin to pursue their own reading goals more independently

Performance Assessment in the Social Studies Classroom. At the middle-school level, most social studies curricula are organized around specific content areas, such as United States history or government. These curricula also draw from related content disciplines like geography, economics and anthropology to fortify students' content knowledge and concept development. The National Council for the Social Studies Standards (1994), for example, notes that building historical and civic knowledge requires students to work in an interdisciplinary manner. So prepared and challenged, students can identify such themes as the relationships of people to the environment and social changes brought on by technological advancement to the historical development of different political structures. As a means of promoting civic engagement in and outside of the classroom, the social studies curriculum engages students in using geographic, political and economic perspectives to examine and interpret social and historical phenomena. This is a process that encourages students to draw upon background knowledge and multiple sources of information to develop and defend their interpretations of history texts. Like the ELA curriculum, the social studies require that students have effective tools and procedures for obtaining information through texts and drawing inferences about that information.

Performance assessments have great potential to foster student self-assessment within the middle school social studies classroom. We should expect that most middle school students are capable of literal text comprehension and that middle school social studies curricula demand such comprehension as a prelude to critical reading and thinking. For example, history-focused assessment questions like "Why was the Jamestown colony founded?" and "With what groups of people did American colonists first interact?" are important preliminary questions that tap students' literal understanding of what they read. These can and should be expanded in the middle school social studies curriculum with questions like, "How am I weighing the validity and reliability of information sources that combine to tell the story of Jamestown?" and "What evidence do I select from the texts that I read and how do I select it to support the claims that I make?" In formulating answers to these questions, students will need to critically appraise the sources they read, related to the primary or secondary source status of the text, and the apparent trustworthiness of the author. In doing so, students will determine that they are reading excerpts from a colonist's diary from 1608, and a history textbook chapter created by a team of authors using many different sources almost 400 years after the fact. They will consider the consequences of how both texts were written and the authors' purposes for writing.

The effective self-assessor questions the criteria that he or she uses to make assertions about historical phenomena and attempts to understand the contexts in which documentary evidence, both primary and secondary, is situated. A history-based performance task that incorporates self-assessment can promote the application of critical literacy strategies, including the corroboration of sources and prior knowledge. In a social studies course that focuses on early American history, for example, the task could address an event or phenomenon that is laden with ambiguity, such as the establishment and decline of the Jamestown colony and its relative historical impact. Historical accounts of Jamestown, differing as we should expect when written from the perspectives of governor, colonist, Native American or British investor, present the middle school reader with competing accounts. Thus, a performance assessment might require that students assess their own capacities to understand and reconcile conflicting narratives and widely varied stances or positions. This assumes that the task is designed to place the interpretation and evaluation of textual evidence at the forefront.

Performance tasks must be kept manageable in terms of the time and energy required to make use of them. Teachers must plan opportunities to model historical reading strategies, such as challenging the claims of one document using information from another document and dealing with archaic or problematic vocabulary (Afflerbach & VanSledright, 2001). As well, teachers must be prepared for divergent conclusions when asking students to interpret and evaluate historical phenomena. Wineburg (1997) asserts that effective social studies assessments ought to focus on students' capacities to navigate the rocky terrain of weighing evidence and constructing accounts of history based on this evidence. This happens, in part, when assessments target students' abilities to deal with diverse accounts and positions using authentic, complex problems and communicate their interpretations through classroom discourse (VanSledright & Afflerbach, in press). Rhonda is an eighth-grade social studies teacher who uses a performance assessment to measure the critical thinking strategies that are essential to investigating the Boston Massacre. Students read both primary and secondary source texts that present conflicting accounts of the event. Rhonda asks her students to reconstruct the incident, discuss the factors that contributed to the event and posit its impacts. At each point in the process, Rhonda makes self-assessment an explicit component of students' investigations and models appropriate strategies. She addresses student self-assessment at the beginning of the project by distributing to students the performance assessment rubric that she will use to judge their work. Using the rubric, her students are able to identify the elements of the performance task that Rhonda has prioritized and consider the work to be done in relation to each. This rubric is detailed in Table 8.4 (VanSledright & Afflerbach, in press; VanSledright et al., 2002).

The rubric is an effective means of demonstrating to Rhonda's students that she is looking specifically for them to judge the reliability and significance of text information, corroborate that information across documents and support their own arguments using citations of evidence from particular texts. In other words, the rubric helps her students ask themselves, "Of the information that I read, how can I decide what will help me develop an argument for what happened and why?" and more specifically "What does the word 'massacre' mean to me, and is it appropriate in this case?" Thus, although Rhonda uses the rubric as a means of assessing student performance, her pupils also use it to inform their reading and problem solving.

Under the umbrella of the performance assessment, Rhonda uses the think-aloud procedure, whereby she reads a passage and stops periodically to make assertions about the text, compare it to others that she has read and ask herself questions about it. As she proceeds through a representative history document in this fashion, she writes down important ideas with regard to her reading and the content of the documents, such as potential author biases, her thoughts on the terminology used in the documents and the effects of when and where the documents were written. Thus, the strategies that students need to use (as informed by the rubric) are made visible through Rhonda's thinking aloud. She is helping her students monitor their perceptions while reading, their capacities to make meaning from the text, the problems and revelations that they encounter and their ability to determine source text status as they develop interpretations of the Boston Massacre.

Rhonda provides scaffolds to improve self-assessment in the reading and evaluation of documents. For example, her students are asked to consider complex in-

TABLE 8.4
Social Studies Performance Assessment Rubric

Category	Substandard (1)	Developing (2)	Proficient (3)	Exemplary (4)
Sorting and Analyzing Data	No method for sorting and analyzing information and it is not clear that given texts are read and understood	Uses vocabulary resources and context clues to determine word meanings and reads texts multiple times as a means of forming mental images of events or ideas	Meets developing level criteria; Also summarizes the texts and their key similarities and differences in writing or by underlining or highlighting them	Meets proficient level criteria; Also uses think-aloud process and note-taking to document analytical thinking and develop themes from texts
Building a Response	Fails to use texts to create an original response to the performance task or does not adequately address the given questions	Focuses primarily on the comprehension of factual information and the description of a main idea and ignores sources or perspectives that pose difficulties	Recognizes uncertainties and different degrees of relevance among sources to go beyond comprehension and discuss perspective	Meets proficient level criteria; Also comes up with critical questions about the complexities of the texts and the connections to prior knowledge and draws conclusions based on those questions
Content of the Response	Interpretations are not related to the given questions or contents of the texts	Interpretations address only some of the given questions and texts and/or may be based on key misconceptions or ignore crucial information	Interpretations address the given questions and texts in general detail and any inaccuracies have little impact on the strength of the response	Interpretations thoroughly address the given questions and texts and precisely argue a valid point of view that is explicitly tied to given evidence and prior knowledge
Using Evidence in the Response	Makes no mention of or reference to information contained within the text at all	Does not mention sources of evidence specifically, but reflects awareness and consideration of given texts in the response	Refers generally to the sources of evidence that support the response and/or cites one or two examples to defend the response	Refers consistently and by name to multiple sources of evidence and compares and contrasts them to justify interpretations
Assessing Source Reliability in the Response	Makes no attempt to consider and determine the reliability of given sources	Makes no mention of source reliability, but chooses a response or interpretation to which a majority of the sources point	Makes an attempt to assess source reliability using a single simplistic criterion	Uses several sophisticated criteria in assessing source reliability and clearly explains that assessment in the response

fluences on primary and secondary source accounts, such as authors' loyalties and motivations. Moreover, Rhonda asks her students to contemplate, using textual evidence and prior knowledge, how the differences between their own historical contexts and that of colonial America impact their interpretations of the text. These approaches to using critical reasoning to look deeply into the texts that students read are reflected in the performance assessment rubric that Rhonda provides for her students. It is her hope that such open-ended queries, asked across the school year, will provide a strong and consistent model of the types of important questions to ask when assessing one's own understanding of historical texts. These questions may, through repeated use, become helpful schemas that assist students in knowing what to ask, why one asks, and under what conditions asking questions is called for.

As a consequence of Rhonda's use of a performance assessment that requires students to be active, critical readers within the context of an historical investigation, her students develop more consistent and deeper inquiries into their own work. They reflect upon the positions that they advocate and evaluate their bases for supporting those positions, using both the assessment rubric and their critical thinking questions to do so. As well, they are more conscious of the subtexts behind what they read (e.g., how does the author's status as a Tory or colonial taxpayer influence the writing and perspective?) and they integrate their critical reading and historical analysis strategies into the formal debate that Rhonda uses to bring the performance assessment to a close. The debate provides the students with additional assessment information. Rhonda evaluates their arguments and how well they are grounded in evidence, students use a checklist, designed and provided by the teacher, to keep track of their objectives. Students are also given the opportunity to evaluate their classmates' arguments through rebuttals, the students assess each other's citations of supporting evidence, claims about source reliability, and interpretations of the Boston Massacre using the same checklist with which they assess themselves.

Shared Design of Traditional Assessment in the Mathematics Classroom. Mathematics curricula typically focus on students' conceptual and operational understandings and the capacity to apply that knowledge to a variety of problems. By the time students reach middle school, it is assumed that they have developed a working comprehension of numbers and an understanding of the relations that manifest through fundamental computational processes, such as addition, subtraction, multiplication and division. The middle school math curriculum is designed to build on that knowledge by introducing multistep equations, consolidating students' conceptions of functions, and building fluency in the development of mathematical language and the management of problems that require them to choose among different computational tools and approaches to solutions. Curricular goals include student understanding of geometric properties and relations, drawing conclusions with probabilities, analyzing data using histograms, and working smoothly within verbal, graphic and algebraic representations of equations. Given these goals, reading within the mathematics curriculum becomes increasingly important as students encounter math word problems that require students to use reading and math strategies simultaneously.

The role that traditional paper–pencil tests play in policy, curricular decision making and instruction in math is a hotly debated topic. As noted previously, traditional assessment is something that is done to students rather than for or with them (Black & William, 1998). In math, for example, quizzes and tests are given at the end of a unit or course of study, and students are expected to answer series of questions that focus solely on the use of computations to arrive at the correct answers. Thus, they come to see assessment as a purely summative process involving a set of instruments that teachers and other decision-makers use to measure content knowledge. For most students, the reliability of assessment is only obliquely encountered, as when all effort is invested to keep students from viewing tests in advance. The consequences of assessment are understood simply as passing and failing. As a result, students' understandings of assessment are relatively undeveloped and they perceive their assessment roles and responsibilities as preparing for tests and performing as competently as possible.

To promote self-assessment in mathematics, educators must help their students ask important questions about their math learning, such as "How effectively do I translate word problems into solvable equations?" and "What types of problems intimidate me the most?" before implementing summative measures. Teachers can examine traditional forms of math assessment, including tests, with their students to provide those students with the means to understand how assessment maps back to classroom learning. Such analysis may also help students better understand what tests can and cannot reveal (Afflerbach, 2002). It is our belief that students should be encouraged to consider the uses, strengths, and weaknesses of paper and pencil tests. Moreover, investing in the analysis and design of tests as a process to be shared by teachers and students has implications for motivation, test anxiety, and comprehension of the functions of assessment.

Current content standards at the middle school level suggest that specific mathematics operations should be contextually grounded. In addition, students should analyze mathematical problems individually and collaboratively, and assessment should be an instructional tool rather than a means of simply checking for procedural memorization (Heaton, 2000). Efforts to promote the act of self-assessment should focus on a student's capacity to conceptualize mathematical abstractions, understand which calculations are appropriate for which contexts, and answer the question, "How do I know my answer is correct?" This monitoring of mathematical literacy mirrors, to some extent, that of reading in the literature and social studies classrooms, as students develop mathematical arguments based on their comprehension of a problem or piece of text and the application of specific analytical tools for addressing it.

Blake is a sixth-grade math teacher who is teaching his students about manipulating fractions using various real-world measurement applications and probabilities as a foundation for doing so. Summative assessment of what the students have learned is planned for the conclusion of the unit that focuses on conceptual foundations and applications of fractions in equations. Throughout his professional career, Blake has been challenged by the pressure to prepare students for large-scale tests. He believes that such pressure leads to math instruction that focuses primarily on the sorts of decontextualized operations and graphic representations that often appear on standardized assessment forms. Knowing that traditional paper–pencil tests are widely used within his district, he develops an assessment approach that strikes a balance between the pervasiveness of high stakes testing and the promise of self-assessment. He explains to his students, several weeks prior to the conclusion of the unit, that they will aid him in designing an assessment tool that represents what they learned about fractions in his math class.

The shared design of math assessment by the teacher and students is, in itself, a performance task. Blake communicates through a precise set of expectations that the assessment items should be situated in a common, everyday context, include both visual and textual information, be mathematically sound and map back to course content. The examination is used, in conjunction with its design process, to assess students' content and procedural knowledge. In taking part in such a project, students build deeper understandings of key products of math instruction and a more active conceptualization of assessment as a whole, and they recognize that the design of an assessment task requires a complex understanding of the content being tested. Students must be metacognitive in their front-end planning and analysis, considering and attempting to avoid fallacies in their questioning and ensuring that their textual and visual representations included as items in the assessment communicate the intended meanings (Schoenfeld, 1988). In other words, designing an assessment item requires the student to not only ask, "What is the correct answer?" and "Is the prompt as directive as it can be?" but also "How does one figure it out, and how well do I understand the mathematical process?" This experience immerses students in the culture of assessment.

Social interaction is an important component of Blake's assessment design project. He employs two-student teams as a means of checking understandings and promoting collaborative growth in math knowledge, and he serves as an expert in clarifying content and process outcomes and simplifying the concepts of validity and reliability for the students so they understand how to make their test items effective (Baker, 1994). For example, as a means of checking for congruency between course content and the skills and strategies targeted in the assessment items, Blake asks, "Where in this particular unit are the procedures that you are testing with your problem?" His students then go through the process of tying their items to specific unit objectives and lessons, just as Blake ties his lessons to curricular standards. Blake models the item design process by demonstrating and critiquing with his students several examples of effective and problematic test items, and he subsequently asks each pair to use the same process to analyze its own question. Thoughtful written responses to queries like, "What does our item measure?" and "What are the possible reasons why someone might answer it incorrectly?" help in this regard. This process attests to thorough understandings of math content within the students' questions and makes more transparent the process of understanding and completing written test items.

Each student pair develops an answer key and rationale that Blake uses to score the resultant summative assessment tool, the items are combined into a traditional paper-pencil instrument for his students to complete. The final self-assessment component comes after the examination is finished, when the students come together to analyze the test items and provide feedback to each author pair. Through whole-class discussion, each team is provided time to discuss the process of developing the item, their rationale for it and the solution. Blake then indicates the percentage of students who answered correctly and incorrectly and the implications of this, and he invites other students to critique the strengths and weaknesses of each item from their perspectives. This allows the students to reflect upon others' interpretations and methods of solving their test items, giving them an opportunity to justify their work and note any critiques that are particularly challenging or clarifying.

Together, the work of Nicole, Rhonda and Blake suggests that students can learn self-assessment strategies within the different content areas of middle school. Teachers can help teach self-assessment within the routines of assessment that are already in place in their classrooms. Each teacher does the important work of determining how we take existing assessments and have them serve double duty: reading assessments that inform our teaching while informing students' self-assessment development.

FUTURE RESEARCH DIRECTIONS
IN SELF-ASSESSMENT AND READING

A rich and evolving knowledge base continues to inform our understanding of self-assessment and reading strategies. This knowledge should inform ongoing inquiry. We need to examine the influence of instruction in self-assessment on the development of students' metacognition and reading achievement. While metacognition is clearly present and operating in expert readers' performances, we have not examined how the development of students' metacognition and self-assessment influences reading achievement and school success. Further, we do not know how (or when) students might generalize the self-assessment knowledge they possess to different school tasks and contexts. We also need to identify the particular types of assessment that present the most consistent and strong models for self-assessment strategy development. Using diverse assessment materials and procedures, such as the performance assessments, portfolio assessments, inventories and teacher questioning discussed in this chapter, we must determine how we can provide students with the tools they need to immediately meet content course requirements while they build competence in self-assessment for success in future reading.

Research on classroom and school-wide programs that seek to bring consistent assessment materials and procedures to students is needed. The previous section contained three scenarios in which teaching and curriculum supported students' development of self-assessment strategies. A most fruitful approach to supporting mindful, self-assessing learners is to model and present consistent self-assessment opportunities in different content areas. For example, a school-wide or district-wide initiative to develop performance assessments for use in the different content areas would allow for students to develop familiarity and competence in relation to the general characteristics of the performance assessment across the content domains. Commonality in the types of rubrics used and in the manner in which rubric use is introduced, taught and reinforced might increase students' opportunities for learning and application of self-assessment routines. Further, referencing performance assessment samples that are clearly tied to rubrics and explicitly discussing the characteristics and intended results of performance assessments among students and teachers can build assessment commonality across grades and content areas.

Research is also needed on the issue of teachers' professional development as it focuses on teaching self-assessment strategies. Strategy instruction is demanding work that requires an accomplished teacher who models and explains the nature of the strategies. Teachers must also teach and model the purposes for using self-assessment and the influence of the reading and learning situation on self-assessment strategy selection and use. There is a long tradition of reading instruction not being a specific focus in content area classrooms. As well, self-assessment is not always an instructional focus within reading instruction. Thus, there is a double challenge: to encourage curriculum development that focuses on reading within content areas and metacognition and self-assessment within reading. Professional development must be present to support teachers who are working towards these goals.

CONCLUSIONS

The ability to self-assess resides at the intersection of middle school students' learning, metacognition, and progress. As described in the three classroom scenarios, students' growth in self-assessment must be supported through curriculum that presents important content area material and allows for the modeling, explanation, and learning of self-assessment. Learning to self-assess depends on a combination of effective strategy instruction and student comprehension of: the reasons why self-assessment is important, and the relationship between the reading context and strategy use. The success of prior efforts to teach reading strategies bodes well for an explicit focus on self-assessment strategy instruction. Priority must be given to those quality assessment materials and procedures that are already in use in classrooms. Self-assessment is learned through modeling, detailed explanation and frequent practice, and existing classroom assessments present the immediate and familiar ground on which to begin. These assessments must also serve their intended purpose of informing our understanding of students' content area learning.

Becoming a self-assessing reader clearly contributes to the development of expertise in reading. With the means to self-assess, middle school students may independently select and engage in reading tasks. The benefits of self-assessment show themselves as metacognitive routines in which readers plan, undertake, and successfully complete reading in and out of school. Yet, the potential benefits of self-assessment are hardly limited to the improvement of cognitive processing. Middle school students, like most readers, need to be engaged in the work they are assigned and in the work they choose. When readers use self-assessment strategies, use them successfully, and understand the relationship of outcome to strategy use, critical learning occurs. These students learn that their work and effort in using these strategies makes a difference. They learn that they have increasing control and agency in acts of reading. This can promote middle students' self-esteem, motivation, and ongoing use of self-assessment while reading.

METACONNECTION FOR CHAPTER 8

In the Paris and Flukes chapter, we learned that as children grow older, assessing their metacognitive strategy usage progresses from oral to written format. Chapter 8, by Afflerbach and Meuwissen, extends our thinking and helps us understand that if children have seen skills modeled, then they should have the skills to self-assess. It also looks at how assessment for all ages can inform the developmental levels of skills needed to begin instruction. In chapter 9, Bauserman presents an instrument that can be used to assess our understanding of the developmental nature of the metacognitive processes for children of all ages.

REFERENCES

Afflerbach, P. (2002). Teaching reading self-assessment strategies. In C. Block & M. Pressley (Eds.), *Comprehension instruction: Research-based best practices* (pp. 96–111). New York: Guilford Press.

Afflerbach, P., & VanSledright, B. (2001). Hath! Doth! What? Middle graders reading innovative history text. *Journal of Adolescent and Adult Literacy, 44,* 698–709.

Baker, E. (1994). Learning-based assessments of history understanding. *Educational Psychologist*, 29, 97–106.

Baker, L. (2002). Metacognition in comprehension instruction. In C. Block & M. Pressley (Eds.), *Comprehension instruction: Research-based best practices* (pp. 77–95). New York: Guilford Press.

Black, P., & William, D. (1998). Inside the black box. *Phi Delta Kappan, 79*, 139–148.

Block, C., & Pressley, M. (Eds.). (2002). *Comprehension instruction: Research-based best practices.* New York: Guilford Press.

Flavell, J. (1978). Metacognitive aspects of problem-solving. In L. Resnick (Ed.), *The nature of intelligence* (pp. 231–255). Hillsdale, NJ: Lawrence Erlbaum Associates.

Guthrie, J., & Wigfield, A. (1997). *Reading engagement: Motivating readers through integrated instruction.* Newark, DE: International Reading Association.

Grigg, W., Daane, M., Jin, Y., & Campbell, J. (2003). *The Nation's Report Card: Reading 2002.* Washington, DC: National Center for Educational Statistics.

Heaton, R. (2000). *Teaching mathematics to the new standards: Relearning the dance.* New York: Teachers College Press.

Leipzig, D., & Afflerbach, P. (2000). Determining the suitability of assessments: Using the CURRV framework. In L. Baker, M. Dreher, & J. Guthrie (Eds.), *Engaging young readers* (pp. 159–187). New York: Guilford Press.

Markman, E. (1977). Realizing that you don't understand: A preliminary investigation. *Child Development, 50*, 643–655.

Moss, P., Beck, J., Ebbs, C., Matson, B., Muchmore, J., Steele, D., & Taylor, C. (1992). Portfolios, accountability, and an interpretive approach to validity. *Educational Measurement: Issues and Practice, 11*, 12–21.

National Council for the Social Studies. (1994). *Expectations of excellence: Curriculum standards for social studies.* Silver Spring, MD: National Council for the Social Studies.

National Council of Teachers of English/International Reading Association. (1996). *Standards for the English language arts.* Urbana, IL: National Council of Teachers of English.

Nitko, A. J. (2001). *Educational assessment of students* (3rd ed.). Upper Saddle River, NJ: Merrill Prentice Hall.

Palincsar, A., & Brown, A. (1984). Reciprocal teaching of comprehension-fostering and monitoring activities. *Cognition and Instruction, 1*, 117–175.

Paris, S., Wasik, B., & Turner, J. (1991). The development of strategic readers. In R. Barr, M. Kamil, P. Mosenthal, & P. Pearson (Eds.), *Handbook of reading research* (Vol. 2, pp. 609–640). Hillsdale, NJ: Lawrence Erlbaum Associates.

Pressley, M., & Afflerbach, P. (1995). *Verbal reports of reading: The nature of constructively responsive reading.* Hillsdale, NJ: Lawrence Erlbaum Associates.

Schoenfeld, A. H. (1987). What's all the fuss about metacognition? In A. H. Schoenfeld (Ed.), *Cognitive sciences and mathematics education* (pp. 189–215). Hillsdale, NJ: Lawrence Erlbaum Associates.

Snow, C. (2002). *Reading for understanding: Toward an R&D program in reading comprehension.* Washington, DC: Rand.

Stanovich, K. (1986). Matthew effects in reading: Some consequences of individual differences in the acquisition of literacy. *Reading Research Quarterly, 21*, 360–407.

Tierney, R., Carter, M., & Desai, L. (1991). *Portfolio assessment in the reading–writing classroom.* Norwood, MA: Christopher-Gordon Publishers.

VanSledright, B. A., & Afflerbach, P. (in press). Assessing the status of historical sources: An exploratory study of eight elementary students reading documents. In P. Lee (Ed.), *Children and teachers' ideas about history: International research in history education* (Vol. 4). London: Woburn Press.

VanSledright, B., Alexander, P, Maggioni, L., & Kelly, T. (2002). *The Historical Knowledge Teaching Assessment Battery*. College Park, MD: University of Maryland.

Wineburg, S. (1997). Beyond "breadth and depth": Subject matter knowledge and assessment. *Theory Into Practice, 36,* 255–263.

9

Metacognitive Processes Inventory: An Informal Instrument to Assess a Student's Developmental Level of Metacognition

Kathryn L. Bauserman
Indiana State University

I am an elementary education teacher who spends most of her school day teaching literacy concepts. One of the strategies I use is the KWL chart which strongly represents the practice of Metacognition because students must think about what they already know about a topic, what they want to know about it, and then must connect their new-found knowledge to what they knew before. However, just because I guide this thinking process with my young students does not mean they will do it on their own. How can we know if they are using this thinking process?
—Molly Mendenhall, Kindergarten, Illinois

Molly asks a very good question about assessing metacognition. This chapter provides an informal instrument that can be used as an authentic assessment tool.

Erin performed very poorly on the Qualitative Reading Inventory-3 (3rd edition) (QRI–3; Leslie & Caldwell, 2000). She is in the fifth grade and barely scored at third grade for her instructional level. She has decoding difficulties (22 total miscues), fluency issues, and comprehension failures. Her major decoding difficulties were vowels, especially vowel digraphs and r-controlled vowels, as well as poor basic sight word knowledge. Erin's fluency issues were a result of her decoding breakdowns. She could answer all of the explicit questions from the text, "Where Do People Live?" but could only answer one implicit question. These results are useful to place Erin at her correct reading level, but do they provide a complete picture of Erin's strategy usage and instructional needs? What will provide a more in-depth look at Erin? How can her ability to express her thoughts about how she is learning be assessed? What assessment instrument can be used to help provide insights into Erin's metacognitive processes as they relate to her comprehension ability?

Flavell (Flavell & Wellman, 1977) coined the term *metamemory* (later changed to *metacognition*) to help individuals understand that they can recall the thinking processes they go through to perform cognitive activities such as comprehension. Jacobs and Paris (1987) further delineated the concept of metacognition as the ability to verbally report those thinking processes because of an internal awareness that they are present. Brown (2002) clarified the definition of metacognition as the awareness of a reader in three specific areas: what the reader is thinking while reading, reader responses to reading challenges, and reader selection of processes to overcome challenges.

This chapter provides a tool, a Metacognitive Processes Inventory (MPI), for teachers to use with their students as a means of gathering assessment data on student implementation of metacognitive processes for literacy learning. This chapter proposes to answer the following questions:

1. Why do we need to do a Metacognitive Processes Inventory?
2. How do we effectively administer a Metacognitive Processes Inventory?
3. What do we do with the results of the Metacognitive Processes Inventory?

HISTORICAL PERSPECTIVE AND RESEARCH REVIEW

Giving inventories, questionnaires, and conducting interviews have long been hallmarks of literacy assessment. For example, numerous informal reading inventories have been developed and made available through the years to provide an assessment of a student's reading level. Clay (1972) interviewed emergent readers to determine their understanding of concepts about print. She later created an informal inventory (Clay, 1979) to measure concepts about print in young children. Interviews helped Wixson, Bosky, Yochum, and Alverman (1984) learn young children's thoughts about reading: Young children described reading as saying the words correctly and recalling only literal information from the text.

Some early studies in the area of metacognition have also used interview techniques and inventories. Myers and Paris (1978) created a metacognitive interview for older readers. It was based on Flavell and Wellman's (1977) categories: person, task, and strategy. They produced a structured interview format, but allowed students to respond freely to the open-ended questions. They found that 12-year-olds were more able to think metacognitively than the 8-year-olds they interviewed, implying a developmental nature to the acquisition of metacognitive processes.

Likewise, Paris and Jacobs (1984) used the interview technique to analyze 8-year-old and 10-year-old students' strategic use of metacognition and found that metacognitive strategies could be successfully measured and taught. They used a modification of the Myers and Paris (1978) instrument. Their instrument contained 15 open-ended questions revolving around three categories: evaluation, planning, and regulation. Evaluation questions referred to the appraisal of the task and one's abilities to handle the task. The planning questions pertained to choices of actions to reach reading goals. Finally, regulation questions concerned monitoring and "fix-it" strategies to keep reading comprehension on track. These interview questions were general in nature and could apply to any reading situation.

Because one-on-one interviewing was tedious and time consuming, Jacobs and Paris (1987) adapted their metacognitive interview assessment to a written version with a total of 20 questions and a new category: *conditional knowledge*. Conditional knowledge was defined as an awareness of the conditions that dictated choices, such as what strategies to use and when it was appropriate to use them. This written version was called the "Index of Reading Awareness Items." Each question had four possible answer choices. At least two answer choices for each question were considered effective strategies. At least one answer choice for each question was considered an ineffective strategy. The fourth answer choice was either effective or ineffective. Students completing the questionnaire could respond with more than one answer to each question. Higher scores indicated a greater awareness of metacognitive strategies used during reading.

Miholic (1994) used the Jacobs and Paris (1987) questionnaire as a basis for creating an abbreviated inventory to measure metacognitive activity of young students. He called his inventory the "Metacognitive Reading Awareness Inventory." It was composed of 10 questions that asked students to select (from four choices) all choices that they would or could use when they encountered difficulties in reading. Like the Paris and Jacobs format, each question had 4 choices: 2 or 3 possible choices that were effective and 1 or 2 possible choices that were ineffective. Readers with the highest level of metacognitive awareness would select all or most of the effective strategies.

Hill (2000) used interviews to ask children to explain their thinking on multiple-choice tests. Frequently, children chose wrong answers, that is, distractors. These children were asked to elaborate on their thinking about the choices they made. Hill found that children could substantiate their choices of distractors with logical interpretations. Some modern teaching practices have taught children the value of original, authentic interpretations of text, rather than focusing on one right answer to a multiple-choice test. Unfortunately, creative thinking is penalized on most standardized testing instruments.

Another method of assessing metacognitive ability is think-alouds and verbal protocols (Pressley & Afflerbach, 1995). To instruct students in think-alouds and verbal protocols, teachers model their own thinking processes when they are reading a passage with their class. For instance, in *Where the Wild Things Are* (Sendak, 1963/1988), the teacher could model how she figured out the meaning of "mischief" by looking at the pictures of Max doing some activities of dubious value. After repeated examples of teachers modeling a variety of strategies, students are then able to transfer the examples to their own metacognitive processes and apply them to difficult or challenging reading situations. Students can demonstrate their metacognitive thinking processes for teachers through think-alouds and verbal protocols.

Teachers can learn much about student behavior and metacognitive processes by observing and taking anecdotal records from observations. Goodman (1985) reported the value of taking and keeping anecdotal records of observable behaviors. Many observable behaviors in readers can be interpreted to determine what strategies readers are using when reading (see Schmitt, chap. 6, this volume). For instance, astute teachers can observe a reader who rereads a passage. Interviewing students about why they reread the passage may reveal the students' metacognitive awareness that rereading is a strategy to use when understanding fails.

Teachers can also use student self-assessments (Afflerbach & Meuwissen, chap. 8, this volume) to gain insight into metacognitive processes students are aware they use. The ability to self-assess is a metacognitive process (Cooper & Kiger, 2001), and interviews can enhance the information gained through the self-assessment process by providing further metacognitive insights. Cooper and Kiger (2001) warned teachers not to overuse self-assessments, making them a chore for students instead of providing a means of growth. Students also need a safe environment that allows risk-taking to provide honest answers to self-assessment questions. Without this honesty, self-assessments have little value.

NEW IDEAS AND HOW WE CAN
MOVE THE FIELD FORWARD

"One way to assess whether a reader is using the strategies we have discussed is to ask the reader to describe what he or she did while reading" (Cooper & Kiger, 2001, p. 377). This chapter focuses on using a Metacognitive Processes Inventory to gain insight into a student's metacognitive processes usage in literacy learning during an authentic reading exercise. What are the metacognitive processes students use and how are they used to enhance student learning and reading comprehension?

Since Durkin's (1978) landmark research, exposing the dearth of comprehension instruction in elementary classrooms, many researchers have focused on comprehension instruction. Durkin's research sparked a plethora of comprehension strategies instruction. Recent research has indicated that Durkin's results may still be replicated: Teachers assess reading comprehension more often than they teach it (Pressley, Wharton-McDonald, Mistretta-Hampton, & Echevarria, 1998). At the same time as this focus on comprehension began, researchers were also developing metacognitive theory. A natural bond formed connecting the two research paths.

Modern research has identified the importance of metacognitive processes for readers to comprehend text (Baker, 2001; Block & Pressley, 2002). Block (2002, 2004) identified the following 11 metacognitive processes that readers use:

1. **Semantic Processes:** As readers read, word meanings are understood or deduced from the context.
2. **Syntactic Processes:** The grammatical structure of the text is processed and understood by readers.
3. **Fusion of Semantic and Syntactic Features:** Readers are able to use meaning and grammar to identify and compare authors' viewpoints.
4. **Internal Consistencies:** Readers are able to determine that the author's ideas are logical and the text is consistent throughout.
5. **External Consistencies:** The facts in the text or story match the life experiences of readers.
6. **Propositional Cohesiveness:** Readers understand each paragraph's proposition and its consistency to the whole text.
7. **Structural Cohesiveness:** Readers can identify the author's theme and author's writing style: cause–effect, description, compare–contrast, sequence of events, and problem–solution.
8. **Informational Processes:** The text or story is understood by readers, and the main idea is identified.
9. **Character's Personality Development:** (for narrative text) Readers analyze and predict the thoughts and actions of the characters as described by the author.
10. **Personal Reflections:** Readers make personal connections to the text as they read.
11. **Metacognitive Coherence:** Readers can tie life experiences with text information.

Flavell (1979) stated, "I also think that increasing the quantity and quality of children's metacognitive knowledge and monitoring skills through systematic training may be feasible as well as desirable" (p. 910). Flavell believed in the desirability of teaching children metacognitive processes. The latest research agrees with Flavell's statement. Block (2004) had many practical instructional strategies for teaching the 11 metacognitive processes to aid in comprehension during reading.

But how can we inform metacognitive instruction without an appropriate assessment instrument? (See Baker, chap. 4, this volume.) Therefore, the need for such an instrument was perceived to be critical to further the instruction of metacognitive processes. The Metacognitive Processes Inventory (MPI) was developed to provide an assessment tool for the 11 metacognitive processes identified by Block (2004). Unlike previous interviews and inventories that asked students to recall what they have done when reading multiple passages from their past, this inventory is more authentic in that it asks students to read an expository or narrative passage first, and then it assesses their natural responses to metacognitive questions specifically addressing the passage just read. In effect, it is situated within the context of real reading and is designed to assess student metacognitive processes using those authentic reading experiences. The purpose is to find out what children are thinking while reading, what metacognitive processes they have an awareness of using, and what processes they actually employ to aid their comprehension during the act of authentic reading.

This inventory is different from the previously described surveys and interviews in that it is situated within the context of reading, therefore it is text specific. It was designed to be used in a one-on-one setting between the teacher and student. The teacher systematically asks questions (prompts) that inventory the student's use of the 11 metacognitive processes to determine proficiency. It can also be used in conjunction with other informal assessments, such as IRIs or running records, thus saving administration time. The teacher applies the MPI questions to the passage the student has just read. The MPI gathers information from the student in the situated context of reading and immediately after the reading event takes place, thus increasing the likelihood of accuracy of reporting all metacognitive thoughts. Reports based on recall of previous reading experiences are not considered as complete or as accurate (Garner, 1987).

The art of asking metacognitive questions is paramount to the success of the MPI. Metacognitive-centered questions need to focus on the student's thoughts while reading. They are questions that do not have one correct response, and they require sophisticated thinking to answer. Consider sample questions that can identify student use of the metacognitive processes: How did you decide the meaning of that word? Explain why you think this story could (or could not) really happen. Can you describe what you were thinking when you read that passage? How did you figure out the character's personality or motives? Metacognitive-centered questions can be inserted in the daily routine of literacy discussions as well as being used for this inventory. Asking open-ended questions allows for students to clarify their thought processes during their responses. Using these general metacognitive-centered questions during grand conversations or small group discussions can help to encourage metacognition and higher level comprehension. Furthermore, one-on-one conferences are an ideal time to use these types of questions, especially in conjunction with the MPI.

The MPI was designed to incorporate metacognitive-centered questions. Likewise, it was designed to ask questions that reflect the four domains of metacognition (Jacobs & Paris, 1987): regulation (monitoring and redirecting efforts), knowledge of strategy application, awareness to plan for the cognitive event, and self-evaluation of one's metacognitive processes. Furthermore, questions reflect on all aspects of the reading process: decoding, fluency, vocabulary, and comprehension.

The MPI can be used with expository text passages, narrative text passages, or poetry on the student's instructional reading level. Teachers need to select a passage of about two pages in length or a poem composed of several stanzas. It can be administered in a one-on-one setting in less than 30 minutes. An example of the inventory is seen in Fig. 9.1.

In Fig. 9.1, the 11 metacognitive processes are identified and described in Column 1. Sample metacognitive-centered questions are given in Column 2. These questions consist of two parts. The first part identifies the skill, word meaning, or comprehension answer. The second part of the question identifies the student's metacognitive response, in other words, how the student figured out the answer to the first part. In Column 3, the teacher writes student responses. After administration, the teacher determines levels of proficiency based on student responses and the teacher's evaluation of the student's understanding and comprehension of the passage. For example, student responses would be considered proficient if students could answer the first part of the question and could explain their metacognitive process in arriving at a reasonable answer to the first question (part 2 of the question). The students' responses would show some evidence of proficiency if they could only answer part 1 of the question. Finally, students' responses would be considered as showing no evidence of proficiency if they could not give a reasonable answer to part 1 of the question or simply stated they did not know the answer.

For the pilot study, 20 classroom teachers and senior level elementary education preservice students used the inventory in a tutor–tutee setting with elementary and middle school students identified as at risk readers. Tutees ranged from grade K to grade 8. (See Table 9.1 for disaggregate data by grade level.) Tutors used a narrative reading passage or poem on each student's instructional level for the MPI. Results presented a very interesting pattern of developmental aspects. The majority of the students were proficient with the semantic processes, the syntactic processes, the external consistencies processes, the character's personality development processes, and the metacognitive coherence processes. Table 9.2 shows sample responses from students that were rated as proficient.

For an example of semantic processing, students were asked to give a meaning for a word that challenged the student during the reading phase (oral or silent). Tutors asked students questions such as, "What does the word _____ mean? How do you know?" Some typical responses to metacognitive-centered questions for the semantic processes level were as follows. A first-grade response for the meaning of "dive" was "jump in the water." When asked how she figured it out, the student responded that she "saw them jump in the water (picture clues)." A third grader said "approximately" means "almost." She "thought of the sentence" to figure it out. While reading A Corner of the Universe by Ann M. Martin, the tu-

Directions: Select an unfamiliar narrative or expository passage from the reader's instructional level. For narrative text, the passage should be several paragraphs long. The first few paragraphs of a story or book are usually effective selections. For expository text, select an entire section (between two sub-headings). Be sure to ask the student to clarify their thinking while they were reading.

Metacognitive Process Being Monitored:	Question Prompts (Reflective: After Oral Reading)	Student Answers and Comments	Proficient	Some Evidence of Proficiency	No Evidence of Proficiency
Semantic Processes: word meanings understood or deduced from context	Teacher: select a word that offered a challenge. Ask: What does ___ mean? How did you figure it out?				
Syntactic Processes: grammatical structure is processed & understood	Select a pronoun. What does this pronoun refer to? How do you know? Does (noun) make sense?				
Fusion of Semantic and Syntactic Features: reader identifies different viewpoints	What is the viewpoint of this story or text? What is the author's purpose in writing? Explain.				
Internal Consistencies: author's ideas are logical, text is consistent throughout	How is each paragraph organized? What does this tell you about the author's style?				
External Consistencies: facts in text or story match life experiences of reader	What are some text facts that you know are true from your life experiences? Any not true? Why?				
Propositional Cohesiveness: paragraphs consistent with whole text	What words does the author use to identify relationships? (causal, comparison, sequence, main idea)				
Structural Cohesiveness: identify style; cause, describe, compare, sequence, problem	What do you think is the author's writing style? What elements from the text helped you decide?				
Informational Processes: text or story is understood by reader, main idea identified	Is there anything in the text that confused you? Explain. What is the main idea? How do you know?				
Character's Personality Development: thoughts and actions are analyzed	Narrative Text: What kind of person do you think the main character is? Why?				
Personal Reflections: reader makes personal connections to text	What did the text make you think about? Explain why the text made you think of those things.				
Metacognitive Coherence: tying life experiences with text information	How does your life compare to the characters or events in the text? How is it different?				

FIG. 9.1. Metacognitive Reflective Inventory: Identifying reader strengths and weaknesses.

TABLE 9.1
Grade Levels of Students in Pilot Study for Administration of MPI

Grade Level	Number of Students
Kindergarten	1
First Grade	7
Second Grade	5
Third Grade	2
Fourth Grade	1
Sixth Grade	1
Eighth Grade	2
Ninth Grade	1

TABLE 9.2
Samples of Proficient Student Responses
for Metacognitive Processes Inventory

Metacognitive Process Being Monitored	Question Prompts (Reflective: After Oral Reading)	Samples of Proficient Student Answers
Semantic Processes: word meanings understood or deduced from context	Teacher: select a word that offered a challenge. Ask: What does ____ mean? How did you figure it out?	A first grader responded to the meaning of the word dive as "jump in the water." She knew because she "saw them jump in the water (picture clue)."
Syntactic Processes: grammatical structure is processed & understood	Select a pronoun. What does this pronoun refer to? How do you know? Does (noun) make sense?	A third grader said, " 'It' refers to the brain" because "it talked about the brain right before."
Fusion of Semantic and Syntactic Features: reader identifies different viewpoints	What is the viewpoint of this story or text? What is the author's purpose in writing? Explain.	A sixth-grade student identified the author's purpose: "entertainment." The author's viewpoint was to "tell a story."
Internal Consistencies: author's ideas are logical, text is consistent throughout	How is each paragraph organized? What does this tell you about the author's style?	An eighth grader noted that "Each paragraph tells a different story that has passed in the last year. The author is a storyteller."
External Consistencies: facts in text or story match life experiences of reader	What are some text facts that you know are true from your life experiences? Any not true? Why?	A sixth grader stated that the story she read could not be true because "Kangaroos can't do human actions."
Propositional Cohesiveness: paragraphs consistent with whole text	What words does the author use to identify relationships? (causal, comparison, sequence, main idea)	An eighth-grade student identified the author's use of sequence words: "first," "after that."

(Continued)

TABLE 9.2
(Continued)

Metacognitive Process Being Monitored	Question Prompts (Reflective: After Oral Reading)	Samples of Proficient Student Answers
Structural Cohesiveness: identify style; cause, describe, compare, sequence, problem	What do you think is the author's writing style? What elements from the text helped you decide?	An eighth grader identified the author's writing style as follows: "(It is) a sequence of events because she is telling past events that were videotaped, and she tells them in order."
Informational Processes: text or story is understood by reader, main idea identified	Is there anything in the text that confused you? Explain. What is the main idea? How do you know?	An eighth grader identified the main idea of her story as, ". . . telling about how her life changed."
Character's Personality Development: thoughts and actions are analyzed	Narrative Text: What kind of person do you think the main character is? Why?	A third grader said, "He is a bully because he is mean."
Personal Reflections: reader makes personal connections to text	What did the text make you think about? Explain why the text made you think of those things.	No student was proficient. Some evidence of proficiency was evidenced by an eighth grader who said the "Barbie Doll" poem made her think about why society emphasizes good looks, but she could not state why the poem made her think so.
Metacognitive Coherence: tying life experiences with text information	How does your life compare to the characters or events in the text? How is it different?	A first grader said, "My baby brother isn't a bear."

tor asked an eighth-grade girl, "What does 'regime' mean?" The girl responded that from the text she determined it was "a routine, something done every night." Almost all of the students could figure out a word meaning in the context of the passage using semantic metacognitive processes. The primary strategies identified in this process were the use of picture clues or context (word) clues.

Most students were proficient using syntactic metacognitive processes. For example, the inventory asked the teacher to select a pronoun from the reading and ask the student to determine its referent. A first grader stated the pronoun referred to "monkeys" because "there are monkeys there (picture clue)." An example of a proficient response from a third grader was: "It refers to the brain" because "it talked about the brain right before." A sixth grader stated that the pronoun referred to "principal" because it "says it in the sentence." Students were giving evidence of paying attention to the context and meaning of the story to determine the pronoun referents, thus demonstrating proficiency using syntactic processes.

A majority of students demonstrated proficiency with the external consistencies processes. For example, a first-grade student reported that the story she read could not be true, because she knew that "real elephants don't ride bikes." "You get in trouble from fighting at school," was a response from a third grader that demonstrated her match of life experiences to the story she read. A sixth-grade student stated that the story she read was not true because "Kangaroos can't do human actions."

Students showed proficiency in the character's personality development processes. They were able to analyze the thoughts and actions of the characters and explain motives for those actions. Student responses that demonstrated proficiency were: "Baby bear is fun and good (first grader)." "He is a bully because he is mean (third grader)." "She has low self-esteem. (Why?) Because she hates her body and her face (eighth grader reading the poem, 'Barbie Doll')."

Finally, students demonstrated proficiency with the metacognitive coherence processes. Students were able to tie life experiences with text information. Some examples of proficient responses included: "My baby brother isn't a bear (first grader)." After reading a story about visiting a zoo, the student responded, "Mom said she might take me to the zoo (first grader)." "I'm different from the kangaroo in the story because I don't act out. I know better than that (sixth grader)."

The only area where the majority of students demonstrated some evidence of proficiency was the personal reflections processes. This metacognitive process requires the reader to make personal connections to the text. Some examples are: An eighth grader responded that the "Barbie Doll" poem made her think about "why people think looks are so important," but she could not explain why the poem made her think of that thought. A first grader responded that the story made him think about "my baby brother when he was born," but he could not explain why he had those thoughts. Students had accurate interpretations of the text, but could not explain their reasoning (part 2 questions).

Most students did not show any evidence of proficiency for fusion of semantic and syntactic features processes, internal consistencies processes, propositional cohesiveness processes, structural cohesiveness processes, or informational processes. When readers can fuse semantic and syntactic features, they are able to determine the author's viewpoint. A sixth grader was able to identify that the purpose of the story was for "entertainment" and the author's viewpoint, "to tell a story." Internal consistencies are evident when the reader has recognized that the author's ideas are logical and consistent throughout the text/story. An eighth grader noted that "Each paragraph tells a different story that has passed in the last year. The author is a storyteller." The student was able to recognize the author's consistency with format throughout the story. Evidence of proficiency for propositional cohesiveness, that each paragraph is consistent with the whole text/story, was demonstrated by an eighth grader who identified the author's use of sequence with such words as "first," "after that," and so on. An eighth grader (reading A Corner of the Universe) was the only student who identified an example of structural cohesiveness through the author's writing style as follows: "(It is) a sequence of events because she is telling past events that were videotaped, and she tells them in order." Informational processes are when the reader has comprehended the story and identified the main idea. The same eighth grader was one of three students who identified the main idea of her story as, "telling about how her life changed."

One of the teachers who participated in the pilot study made some reflective comments that were perceptive. She used the poem, "Barbie Doll," with an eighth-grade female. She commented:

> This lesson gave me insight into the student's strengths and weaknesses. It also provided a framework to analyze text on a deeper level. I found the set-up to be very helpful and useful. I would use this inventory again to evaluate a student's reading and comprehension. I was able to find out significant information that will help me guide my student's learning as our sessions continue. My student was able to give me answers to almost all questions (part 1 questions), but was not always able to provide me with why she felt this way (part 2 questions). Many times she could answer the first part of a question, but not the second, more reflective part. For example, she was able to tell me the viewpoint of this story, but unable to tell me the author's purpose in writing it. With nudges and guidance, my student could answer these questions. The questioning really made my student think about what she was saying. She commented to me later that her "brain hurt." This activity really made her stretch her thinking and consider why she was feeling that way. This was difficult for her and something we'll need to practice more. Even after some guiding, my student was unable to provide an answer for internal and external consistencies.

Statistical analyses were not performed on the results of the pilot study because there were so few participants ($n = 20$). However, several general observations can be drawn from the results: Even the very youngest readers (first graders) were able to do some of the 11 processes, primarily semantic processes, syntactic processes, character's personality development processes, and personal connections via external consistencies processes and metacognitive coherence processes. Young readers could only identify simple metacognitive processes in two areas. These were related to making literal meaning of the passage and making personal connections with the passage. Only very advanced readers were able to do the metacognitive processes that related to the author's writing style: fusion of semantic and syntactic features (author's viewpoint), internal consistencies (logical text), prepositional cohesiveness (paragraph construction), structural cohesiveness (author's writing style), and informational processes (identify main idea). These generalizations suggest the possibility of a developmental aspect to the acquisition of metacognitive processes.

Classroom teachers and teachers of reading need to be aware of the 11 metacognitive processes (Block, 2004) readers use to enhance their comprehension. Classroom teachers also need to have an awareness of the metacognitive-centered questioning technique as a means of gathering data to identify student usage of metacognitive processes. Once teachers have a strong knowledge base of the 11 metacognitive processes and metacognitive-centered questions, they can use the MPI to gather data about their students for instructional purposes. For example, more could be learned about Erin, the student in the opening scenario, through the use of this assessment inventory. Results from the QRI–3 provide information about Erin's decoding abilities, fluency, and literal comprehension of the text that she read. Erin does not appear to have the ability to answer higher level comprehension questions. Also, there is no information concerning her ability to perform any of Block's (2004) metacognitive processes. While giving the IRI, Erin's teacher could also have administered the MPI over the same reading passage. She could have asked metacognitive-centered questions as described in the MPI to determine Erin's metacognitive abilities and described her metacognitive strengths and weaknesses. Then the teacher could have designed a program of instruction based on the MPI assessment results to help Erin learn about and apply metacognitive processes as a reader. There are many methods for incorporating metacognitive processes instruction into daily instruction for students like Erin. (See part III of this volume.)

The Metacognitive Processes Inventory should be used twice a year as a pre–post assessment instrument. It can provide great insight into each student's metacognitive ability. Teachers who know their students' metacognitive abilities are able to reinforce and teach the processes as needed to benefit their comprehension of text.

DIRECTIONS FOR FUTURE RESEARCH

Metacognition and understanding of metacognitive processes are paramount to understanding how good readers monitor their comprehension. Scientifically based research is needed to measure the effectiveness of teaching metacognitive processes to students. Several specific areas of research interest have emerged from this pilot study.

One of the research themes that emerged relates to the following questions: Are metacognitive processes developmental in nature? If so, do all students learn metacognitive processes in the same order? Are older students more articulate in describing their metacognitive processes? Further research needs to be conducted to determine if there is a developmental nature to the acquisition of metacognitive processes.

Another area for further research is determining best practice in teaching metacognitive processes. Block (2004) developed several instructional strategies for teaching metacognitive processes, but questions still remain. What strategies work best for what processes? Do different age groups need to be taught using different methods? What instructional methods work best? Do different genres require different teaching strategies?

Research needs to focus on helping children transfer instruction in metacognitive processes to practice. When children can articulate what metacognitive processes are, does that mean they use them? Do teachers see the value in metacognitive process instruction? Do students see the value in metacognitive process use?

The MPI has been designed to determine metacognitive processes as they apply to reading. What about writing? Do these metacognitive processes apply to writing? Are there different processes that apply to writing? What are the similarities and differences in the metacognitive processes as they apply to reading and writing?

Finally, are the 11 metacognitive processes discrete? Do some of the processes overlap and need to be collapsed into one process? Can they be measured accurately using the MPI? A SBRR investigation with a large sample of student responses from all age groups (kindergarten through high school) needs to be conducted to determine if the metacognitive processes can be assessed as discrete.

CONCLUSIONS

This chapter has proposed to answer three questions: Why is a Metacognitive Processes Inventory necessary? How can an MPI be effectively administered? What can be done with the results of the MPI? Conducting a Metacognitive Processes Inventory is helpful to determine student strengths and weaknesses in their metacognitive thinking processes, which in turn affects their comprehension of text, especially higher order comprehension of text. Using an authentic reading passage (narrative, expository, or poetry), the teacher can administer the Metacognitive Processes Inventory in 30 minutes or less. The MPI can be done using any authentic passage or in conjunction with another informal assessment such as an IRI or a running record. This inventory examines all 11 of the metacognitive processes (as defined by Block, 2004) and how they are used by readers of all ages. As a result, metacognitive strengths and weaknesses can be determined. Teachers can design lessons to strengthen weak areas, and students can gain metacognitive skills and improve their comprehension of text. If teachers know that Erin, in the opening scenario, is weak in 9 of the 11 metacognitive processes, then they have more specific knowledge about what to teach to strengthen her areas of metacognitive weakness. They can help her learn how to do what they know good readers do to comprehend text efficiently.

METACONNECTION FOR CHAPTER 9

Afflerbach and Meuwissen (chap. 8) challenged us to think of assessment, especially self-assessment, as it informs instruction. Chapter 9, by Bauserman concludes our assessment section by offering an informal assessment of metacognitive processes based on Block's work. The primary purpose of the assessment is to inform instructional needs for individual students. Part III will follow with emphasis on metacognitive instructional strategies.

REFERENCES

Baker, L. (2001). Metacognition in comprehension instruction. In C. Block & M. Pressley (Eds.), *Comprehension instruction: Research based best practices* (pp. 274–289). New York: Guilford.

Block, C. C. (2002). *Literacy difficulties: Diagnosis and instruction for reading specialists and classroom teachers* (2nd ed.). Boston: Allyn & Bacon.

Block, C. C. (2004). *Teaching comprehension: The comprehension process approach.* Boston: Pearson Education.

Block, C. C., & Pressley, M. (2002). *Comprehension instruction: Research based practices.* New York: Guilford.

Brown, R. (2002). Straddling two worlds: Self-directed comprehension instruction for middle schoolers. In C. Block & M. Pressley (Eds.), *Comprehension instruction: Research based practices* (pp. 337–350). New York: Guilford.

Clay, M. (1972). *Sands—the Concepts about Print Test.* Portsmouth, NH: Heinemann.

Clay, M. (1979). *Observation survey.* Portsmouth, NH: Heinemann.

Cooper, J. D., & Kiger, N. D. (2001). *Literacy assessment: Helping teachers plan instruction.* Boston: Houghton Mifflin.

Durkin, D. (1978). What classroom observation reveals about reading comprehension instruction. *Reading Research Quarterly, 14,* 481–533.

Flavell, J. H. (1979). Metacognition and cognitive monitoring: A new area of cognitive developmental inquiry. *American Psychologist, 34*(10), 906–911.

Flavell, J. H., & Wellman, H. M. (1977). Metamemory. In R. Kail, Jr. & J. W. Hagen (Eds.), *Perspectives on the development of memory and cognition* (pp. 3–33). Hillsdale, NJ: Lawrence Erlbaum Associates.

Garner, R. (1987). *Metacognition and reading comprehension.* Norwood, NJ: Ablex.

Goodman, Y. (1985). Kidwatching: Observing children in the classroom. In A. Jaggar & M. T. Smith-Burke (Eds.), *Observing the language learner* (pp. 9–18). Newark, DE: International Reading Association.

Hill, C., & Gates, A. (2000). Creative reading: Oral and literate circles, Keynote Presentation, Seventh Annual Conference on Language and Literature Teaching, Makere University, Kampala, Uganda. Retrieved on November 24, 2004.

Jacobs, J. E., & Paris, S. G. (1987). Children's metacognition about reading: Issues in definition, measurement, and instruction. *Educational Psychologist, 22,* 255–278.

Leslie, L., & Caldwell, J. (2000). *Qualitative Reading Inventory 3.* Boston: Allyn & Bacon.

Martin, A. M. (2002). *A corner of the universe.* Danbury, CT: Scholastic.

Miholic, V. (1994). An inventory to pique students' metacognitive awareness of reading strategies. *Journal of Reading, 38*(2), 84–86.

Myers, M., & Paris, S. (1978). Children's metacognitive knowledge about reading. *Journal of Educational Psychology, 70,* 680–690.

Paris, S. G., & Jacobs, S. E. (1984). The benefits of informed instruction for children's reading awareness and comprehension skills. *Child Development, 55,* 2083–2093.

Pressley, M., & Afflerbach, P. (1995). *Verbal reports of reading: The nature of constructively responsive reading.* Hillsdale, NJ: Lawrence Erlbaum Associates.

Pressley, M., Wharton-McDonald, R., Mistretta-Hampton, J., & Echevarria, M. (1998). The nature of literacy instruction in ten grade 4/5 classrooms in upstate New York. *Scientific Studies of Reading, 2,* 159–194.

Sendak, M. (1988). *Where the wild things are*. New York: Harper Collins. (Originally published in 1963)

Wixson, K. K., Bosky, A. B., Yochum, M. N., & Alverman, D. E. (1984). An interview for assessing students' perceptions of classroom reading tasks. *The Reading Teacher, 37*(4), 346–352.

III

Metacognition and Literacy Instruction

As promised for the section opener of part II, once practitioners have understood the rationale, assessment, and analysis of the results that were obtained prior to instruction, they can begin to contextualize metacognitive research in instructional classroom practices. The purpose of part III is to help infuse metacognitive best practices into reading programs. This section begins in an order not typically found in edited research books. Chapter 10, by Israel and Massey, describes two important instructional strategies for middle school students. It begins at the middle school level because, at present, most metacognitive instruction in literacy occurs with young adolescence. This chapter is distinctive in that it not only teaches educators how to provide a gradual release from teacher directed to student initiation in metacognition, but it includes an intact description of how to implement this model. Teachers will receive a list of books that can be used in content areas in which metacognitive literacy strategies can be applied. In addition, readers will find a list of more than 10 think-alouds that can be delivered in the teacher-directed portion of these lessons. Equally important, this chapter presents an important link between teacher instruction and student awareness of their own self-initiation of their own strategies when they are motivated and highly engaged with text.

Knowledge of these strategies makes it easier for the readers to move to chap. 11, which describes the role of self-monitoring and literacy instruction at the elementary level. Joseph provides extremely valuable information and methods for helping 16 students to set goals before they read. His discussion further documents that when students formulate a plan, and self-monitor their implementation of that plan, their results provide significant qualitative and quantitative growth in cognition, literacy behavior, and meta-cognition. Once Joseph describes each of these processes for building student self-monitoring skills, he provides an innovative lesson for incorporating each of these instructional reproaches into a classroom instructional program that extends beyond the reading classroom. This chapter is unique in that it unifies more than 7 lessons that can be used to build student self-monitoring behavior.

Chapter 12 provides a unique metacognitive experience for readers. Schreiber develops an innovative and comprehensive 24-day lesson plan of integrating metacognition and self-regulation into a literacy reading program. He does so in such a way that you can contrast his ideas to those of Joseph, Israel, and Massey from chapters 10 and 11. Schreiber's chapter is also innovative in the perspective that it demonstrates how metacognitive instruction can occur for some of our youngest students.

After contrasting the three models presented in chapters 10, 11, and 12, Donndelinger (in chap. 13) pulls readers through a metacognitive lesson in action. He not only integrates comprehension and metacognitive reading strate-gies, but does so in a manner that has not been possible prior to his research work with children. As you read his classroom strategies and the highly significant ef-fects they have on his children, you may be able to actually visualize the lesson in your classroom. Through his in-depth and vivid descriptions of the work he has done, you will be empowered to enact these same processes and strategies with your children.

We close this section by looking inside two other single classroom lessons. The first classroom is distinct in a multifaceted number of ways. Smith appropri-ately entitled her chapter "Window into a Thinking Classroom." She not only generates metacognition, self-regulation, and higher level thinking into a read-ing lesson, but she describes how she's able to do this through media in which children are engaged. Similarly, in chapter 15, Cummins, Stewart, and Block de-scribe other lesson formats in which multiple metacognitive abilities can be built. Among the exceptionally high quality features of both chapters is the description of newly award-winning children's literature and how it can be used to enhance students' metacognition. Samples of students' work and pictures of metacognitive lessons in action in the curriculum through reading, art, nonfiction tradebooks, science, social studies, and multicultural studies. After finishing these chapters, you will not only feel empowered that you can provide such high level teaching for your students, but you will be sparked to think about many other creative di-rections in which you can develop lessons that we have been unable to present in part III of this book. When this occurs, our goal will have been met as editors.

10

Metacognitive Think-Alouds: Using a Gradual Release Model With Middle School Students

Susan E. Israel
University of Dayton

Dixie Massey
North Carolina A&T State University

> *My knowledge on metacognition is limited. I know only a little about the informa-*
> *tion in most of the chapters. Using think-alouds is something I am familiar with and*
> *use often in my classroom. Thinking aloud is very important when teaching primary*
> *grades. Students have limited knowledge on strategies needed to understand nonfic-*
> *tion texts. Talking through the pictures and making predictions shows students how*
> *to do it on their own. Thinking aloud as you reread and find important parts of a*
> *passage is essential in showing students the correct way to do it on their own.*
> —Julie Kimpel, Fourth-Grade Teacher,
> Englewood Hills, Northmont City Schools

Think-aloud is a metacognitive process that students use in which their thoughts are verbalized while reading a selection of text, thus modeling the process of comprehension (Block & Israel, 2004). According to Baker (2002), metacognition is a reflective process in which think-aloud strategies provide a method for students to become cognitively engaged in reading. In addition, Massey (2003) suggested think-aloud can be used as instructional tools to scaffold comprehension awareness. This chapter examines the theory, research, and practices that relate to think-aloud strategy instruction and their effects on metacognition. By chapter's end, you will have answers to the following questions: How are think-alouds related to improved student achievement and motivation? Why is nonfiction important when using think-alouds? How can think-alouds be used before, during, and after reading to improve comprehension? And, how can think-alouds be assessed?

HISTORICAL PERSPECTIVE
AND RESEARCH IN REVIEW

This chapter investigates how the think-aloud strategy is used with middle school readers when reading nonfiction text. Research in the following areas of meta-cognition, think-aloud, and nonfiction text with middle school readers is summarized to explain the importance of understanding features of nonfictional text selections: changing instructional strategies to realize excellence, understanding how think-aloud strategies can be used to advance middle school readers' achievements, motivation and the adolescent reader, and the role of instruction using nonfiction text with middle school readers.

Awareness of one's thinking is necessary for students to be able to monitor their comprehension (Pressley, 2002). Good readers recognize when they do not understand a text. Poor readers may fail to recognize that the reading no longer makes sense to them, or they may not know what to do when they do recognize a comprehension breakdown.

This thoughtfulness is the essence of metacognition—knowledge about one's thinking processes. But, in order to help students be metacognitive, teachers must first become more aware of their own thinking. They can help students learn to be thoughtful and purposeful readers through thinking aloud about their own comprehension strategies when reading a text and then allowing students to practice using the strategies and thinking aloud (Duffy, 2003). As Pressley (2002) pointed out, "It seems especially helpful if such practice provides opportunities to explain one's strategies and reflect on the use of strategies" (p. 292).

The content of the material used to model thinking aloud is also important for teachers to consider. The use of nonfiction provides an excellent point for middle school teachers to practice using think-alouds. First, many middle schoolers are already familiar with fiction story elements and find comprehension easier with this genre, whereas nonfiction text is less familiar, provides more of a challenge, and makes up the bulk of their academic reading. Further, using nonfiction text with middle school readers satisfies their curiosity, expands their vocabulary, builds content knowledge, creates background knowledge to supplement and support the material in textbooks, and familiarizes readers with expository text structures commonly found in technical manuals, textbooks, and standardized tests.

Understanding How Think-Aloud Strategies Can Be
Used to Advance Middle School Readers' Achievements

Traditionally, from early childhood throughout middle childhood, exposure to fiction texts tends to increase, whereas knowledge about nonfiction text structures takes place in content areas. Paris and colleagues (e.g., Myers & Paris, 1978; Paris & Jacobs, 1984) found that knowledge about the purpose of reading and knowledge about the information provided by conventional features of text is related to both and reading comprehension. Older readers and better comprehenders are more successful at explaining information gained in the introduction and ending of a text. Children with comprehension impairments struggle with explaining story structures of nonfiction text.

Equally important is the effect of interestingness of nonfiction text on comprehensibility (Chambliss, 2000). When nonfiction texts are optimally informative, well structured, coherent, highlight the structure of the text, reveal the author's voice, and provide vivid details that can be "pictured," students become more eager to read. When these features are missing, they too often judge nonfictional texts to be uninteresting.

Another variable in comprehensibility is the accuracy of clarity of textual features, such as subheadings, graphics, and charts. Donovan and Smolkin (2002a, 2002b) recommended an evaluation of content and the accuracy of information. Books with misinformation reinforce children's misconceptions and impair accurate comprehension. Moreover, when the visual features (e.g., the size, the shape, the cover, appearance of the pages, and the font) are reader friendly, they serve the important comprehension function of helping readers link information-containing portions of the text together.

The organization of nonfiction text also impacts reading comprehension. Poorly written textbooks play a role in the comprehension difficulties of poor readers (Dickson, Simmons, & Kameenui, 2002). Well-presented physical text facilitates reading comprehension, as does student awareness of these text structures. Thus, instruction in the physical presentation of nonfiction text and the structure of the text should be explicit.

Motivation and the Adolescent Reader

Motivation is a crucial factor influencing comprehension and metacognition (Baker, 2002). Struggling readers often have poor comprehension and lack the awareness of fix-up strategies to repair their own comprehension. Poor comprehension, in turn, can decrease a student's motivation to read. Cast in a positive light, readers who successfully comprehend text are more likely to be engaged readers and are more likely to become lifelong readers and learners (M. F. Graves, Juel, & B. B. Graves, 2001).

It is important to make a distinction between engagement and motivation. P. Cunningham and J. Cunningham (2001) described engagement as learners working in a motivated way—"that is, they employ whatever skills and strategies they have with effort, persistence, and an expectation of success" (p. 89). Defined in this manner, motivation is part of engaged reading. Guthrie et al. (1996) defined engaged readers as readers who are strategic, motivated, and intentional. Further, engaged readers make choices about what strategies they will use. A salient conclusion revolves around these researchers' observation of strategic reading as linked to engaged reading. Guthrie and Wigfield (2000) proposed that "engaged readers in the classroom or elsewhere coordinate their strategies and knowledge (cognition) within a community of literacy (social) in order to fulfill their personal goals, desires, and intentions (motivation)" (p. 404). Guthrie et al. (1996) found that students who increased in intrinsic motivation also increased in reading strategy use.

Unfortunately, engaged reading, and the motivation to read, often decreases as children move into middle and secondary school (Guthrie & Wigfield, 2000). Initial research suggests that nonfiction, informational tasks can be particularly motivating for middle school students (Ivey & Broaddus, 2001; Moss, 2003), especially when students' comprehension is supported through teacher instruction and modeling.

How do think-alouds impact student motivation? First, teacher think-alouds can be enjoyable for students. Ivey and Broaddus (2001) surveyed 1,765 middle schoolers, following up with interviews in those settings students designated as engaging. Students consistently reported that they enjoyed and were motivated by listening to the teacher reading and thinking aloud, and that such interaction provided "scaffolds to understanding." Second, teacher think-alouds help students understand what to focus on in particular types of text. Hennings (1993) described using think-alouds with nonfiction history texts, modeling for students what is important to pay attention to when reading. Through strategy instruction in how to handle specific text structures, students are able to attend to the important information and not become lost and disengaged by focusing on confusing details. Third, the read-aloud/think-aloud process can allow struggling readers to participate in common classroom experience and thereby become more engaged (Ivey, 2002).

The Role of Instruction Using Nonfiction Text
With Middle School Readers

According to Block (2002), using nonfiction text requires a change in instructional strategies. Using nonfiction text helps increase students' knowledge of a variety of disciplines, specifically textual features and genre-relevant writing patterns, while at the same time providing opportunities to increase comprehension. Without the tools or knowledge of how to go about navigating nonfiction text, struggling readers' frustrations only increase. Teachers should evaluate readability of nonfiction text to ensure comprehension effectiveness. Nonfiction text traditionally is written using vocabulary that is more difficult.

As proof in point, Afflerbach and VanSledright (2001) investigated 7 fifth graders who first read chapters in innovative history textbooks and then excerpts from a traditional history textbook in order to gain a better understanding of whether or not a historical stance and position was assumed during verbalization. After individual training sessions on think-aloud methodology, students provided think-alouds. Reports were analyzed to determine the challenges faced and reading strategies used by students. Findings indicated that students responded to different challenges posed by history texts with different strategies that led to meaning construction.

Coté, Goldman, and Saul (1998) investigated how fourth- and sixth-grade students construct mental representations and how these processing activities during reading relate to what they understand and remember. In addition, they investigated differences when students were asked to think-aloud, or when asked to read silently when reading easier and harder informational passages. The findings indicated that the types of processing observed using informational texts were similar to those observed using narrative texts but were different in the relevant proportions of processing activities. For informational text, more emphasis on monitoring positive instances of comprehension and identification of problems occurred than during narrative text. With regard to children's processing and construction of mental representations, for older readers, thinking aloud improved the quality of their recall performance and encouraged active processing strategies that resulted in the integration of prior knowledge and the formation of more coherent representations.

Israel (2002) analyzed metacognitive strategies of above average, average, and weaker middle school readers using nonfiction, fiction, and poetry. Israel documented that best readers make strategic decisions, employ numerous reading strategies, and adapt their thinking to an author's intention within the constraints of a particular genre and reading objective. Before all readers can become good readers who are opportunistic, vary their reading goals according to their level of prior knowledge, clearly state and follow their intentions throughout a passage, monitor their comprehension, and become self-motivated, many will need a teacher who is an expert in the use of think-aloud methods.

SUGGESTIONS FOR INSTRUCTION AND PRACTICE

To conduct think-alouds, teachers must be aware of their own reading strategies (Duffy, 2003; Maria & Hathaway, 1993). If think-alouds are to be effective with students, then teacher educators need to think about explicit ways of teaching teachers how to think aloud in our teacher education programs. Following are some specific considerations for the teacher when modeling think-alouds:

Understand What It Means to Think Aloud

For the gradual release process to be effective, it is important that teachers understand what it means to think aloud. Thinking aloud is a strategy used to verbalize as much as possible of what you are thinking.

Selecting a Nonfiction Text

It is crucial that the teacher selects nonfiction texts that are interesting to the students. Research demonstrates a direct correlation between interest in text and motivation to read. Table 10.1 summarizes how teachers can use nonfiction text with themes. In addition, Table 10.1 helps teachers select nonfiction texts that correspond with content being read in fictional books. Linking nonfiction to fiction within a thematic unit demonstrates to students' the relevancy and importance of reading nonfiction and how it helps increase comprehensibility.

After using think-alouds with his struggling readers, Mr. Parsons, a seventh-grade language arts teacher, noticed a change in students' enthusiasm for reading. He described one particular student going to the library and checking out several books with "enthusiasm and joy. It is apparent that her eagerness in the library had come from learning a new and useful skill."

TABLE 10.1
Think-Aloud Text Selections for Middle School Readers Based on Theme

Theme	Nonfiction Selections	Fiction Selections
Achievement	As Long as the River Flows by Paula Allen Girls Who Rocked the World by Amelie Welden J.R.R. Tolkien: The Man Who Created The Lord of the Rings by Michael Coren Lives of Extraordinary Women by Kathleen Krull Tiger Woods by Nicholas Edwards	Bright Shadow by Avi The Contender by Robert Lipsyte Crash by Jerry Spinelli Jazzimagination by Sharon Draper The Mozart Season by Virginia Wolff
Freedom	Anthony Burns: The Defeat and Triumph of a Fugitive Slave by Virginia Hamilton Freedom Train by Dorothy Sterling From Slave Ship to Freedom Road by Julius Lester Kids at Work by Russell Freedman To Be a Slave by Julius Lester	Adaline Falling Star by Mary Pope Osborn Bluish by Virginia Hamilton Bright Freedom's Song by Gloria Houston The Captive by Joyce Hansen Kidnapped by Robert Louis Stevenson
Inspiration	Indian Chiefs by Russell Freedman Taste Berries for Teens by Bettie and Jennifer Youngs Gutsy Girls by Tina Schwager and Michele Schuerger To Love This Live by Helen Keller	Any Small Goodness by Toni Johnston Arilla Sun Down by Virginia Hamilton Carolina Crow Girl by Valerie Hobbs
Survival	I Am Fifteen—and I Don't Want to Die by Christine Arnothy Long Journey Home by Julius Lester Memories of Anne Frank by Alison Leslie Gold	Bat 6 by Virginia Euwer Wolff Brian's Winter by Gary Paulson Call of the Wild by Jack London Miles' Song by Alice McGill

Practice With Students Until They Feel Comfortable With the Think-Aloud Procedures

To help increase students' motivation to use the think-aloud strategy during reading nonfiction text, it is important to model thinking aloud and then practice thinking aloud with the students. This can be done in small group settings. Students can read a practice passage from their nonfiction text and think aloud at strategic points. Teachers can help students by thinking aloud about the same sections and comparing the think-alouds as a way to provide a scaffold for reluctant readers.

Activate Comprehension Strategies While Thinking Aloud

Nonfiction text can be very difficult for students to comprehend. Once students feel confident in using the think-aloud strategies, teachers can model specific strategies that will help increase reading comprehension. Israel (2002) identified six strategies utilized by successful readers to improve comprehension when reading nonfiction text. These six strategies are summarized here and can be activated when utilizing think-alouds. These strategies can be separated into before-, during-, and after-reading strategies:

Before Reading:
  • Activate prior knowledge

During Reading:
  • Relate text to text
  • Relate text to prior knowledge
  • Infer

After Reading:
  • Utilize strategies such as summarize, predict, question
  • Reflect

Crucial to moving the field forward is the idea that teachers allow students some control. This has typically been an area of difficulty for middle and secondary teachers (Alvermann, O'Brien, & Dillon, 1990; O'Brien, Stewart, & Moje, 1995). Often, content teachers like to

> control the content and pace of classroom interaction because the control provides an efficient way to respond to organizational and time constraints they face within the institutionalized curriculum. A consequence of the pedagogy of control for content literacy is that secondary teachers often substitute their explanations of texts

for students' reading. Indeed secondary students often depend on teacher talk rather than texts as their primary source of information. (O'Brien et al., 1995, p. 451)

The following section describes, in greater detail, each of the six comprehension strategies and how students used each strategy with nonfiction texts.

STUDENTS THINKING METACOGNITIVELY ABOUT THINK-ALOUDS

It is important to recognize that it is not just the teacher's place to think aloud. Thinking aloud should involve the gradual re-release of responsibility back to the students. This then becomes a valuable assessment to evaluate the effectiveness of a particular modeled strategy (Afflerbach & VanSledright, 2001). To help teachers with the gradual release of responsibility of using think-alouds during reading, it is important for middle school students to understand think-aloud procedures and how the procedures can be integrated during the reading process, especially when reading challenging text (like nonfiction). Just as with the teachers, there are several general principles students must know and understand when thinking aloud.

Procedures for Eliciting Think-Alouds Using Nonfiction Text

There are three basic steps in eliciting think-alouds in middle school classrooms.

Understand What It Means to Think Aloud. Students need to speak freely about what they are thinking. Thinking aloud does not have to be well-structured or perfectly sequenced. It is important for students to accurately reflect thoughts or even bits and pieces of their thoughts. Almost everything a student says is important information.

Practice. To help increase students' motivation to use the think-aloud strategy during reading nonfiction text, it is important to have students practice thinking aloud. This can be done in small group settings or one-on-one. Students can read a practice passage from their nonfiction text and think aloud at strategic points.

Activate Comprehension Strategies While Thinking Aloud. Using comprehension strategies to aid and even correct comprehension is an important follow-up for thinking aloud. Thinking aloud can help students identify when their comprehension is lacking and what strategy they might need to use to correct their comprehension. Specific examples of students' comprehension before, during, and after reading provide valuable exemplars of the symbiotic relation between think-alouds and comprehension strategies. These procedures can be followed each time think-alouds are elicited in middle schools, regardless of whether the think-aloud is a before-, during-, or after-reading strategy.

Before-Reading Strategies

Activation of Prior Knowledge.   The strategy of activation of prior knowledge is evident in responses when readers activate or report information related to their prior knowledge to interpret text. In some cases, this might be evident when the reader in the verbal report generated a hypothesis about the text being read, or might have made a prediction about the text content. In some cases, prior knowledge occurred automatically, and it might have been difficult to detect if the prior knowledge was being activated. However, the richer the prior knowledge the more automatic the activation, and, therefore, the richer the verbal report. Therefore, verbal reports were examined carefully, looking for evidence of existing schemas being activated during meaning construction. As an example, consider the nonfiction text excerpt that teachers can use to ask students to demonstrate the activation of prior knowledge:

> Students read: *Gandhi felt different from other people and was a weak student. He barely graduated from high school and failed classes in college. Gandhi went to London to study law.*

> *Example of a student's think-aloud response.* Now it is starting to say he wasn't a great student or anything and he barely graduated from high school. He went to London to study law so it's showing that he's like going places to learn about new things, so even though he is not doing well in school he will probably still succeed. Because he believes in good things and plus he is learning about new customs.

The excerpt helped improve the reader's prior knowledge of lawyers and how he perceived them as being successful. Even though Gandhi was a poor student, the good reader made a prediction that Gandhi would do well in law school despite his prior performance in school. When the good reader was reading about the czar, his prior knowledge about empires and emperors was activated, therefore aiding in the increased comprehensibility of the text.

During-Reading Strategies

Three strategies during reading think-alouds can increase students' use of comprehension strategies while they read.

Relating Text to Text.   The strategy *relating text to text* includes responses that relate important points in text to one another in order to understand the text as a whole. The integration of text structures—such as story grammar elements, cause–effect, or compare and contrast—helps explain how the parts contribute to the overall meaning of the text. An example follows:

> Nonfiction Text Excerpt. *When Gandhi was thirteen years old, he was married according to Jain tradition. His wife was Kasturbi Makanji, a beautiful thirteen-year-old girl who possessed qualities of patience, strength, and courage.*
>
> *Example of Think-aloud.* He was married at the age of thirteen. I think that is kind of different, and it has something to do with his religion. I think that helps me learn about like . . . most of his life and his culture because they have different things and they believe in different things. Over here we don't get married at the age of thirteen. So I guess that helps me understand his culture and everything and that might be influential in why he became the person he was.

The preceding response demonstrates that the participant focused on using part of the text and relating it to other parts of the text previously read. This relation demonstrated how this piece of text relates further to his religion and cultural beliefs. By using the text to make connections between other parts of the text, the good reader was able to construct the meaning related to how Gandhi was an influential person. Using portions of the text and relating them to other parts of the text allows the reader to construct meaning.

Relating Text to Prior Knowledge.   The strategy *relating text to prior knowledge* can be indicated when responses include information showing a student relating text content to prior knowledge, especially as part of constructing interpretations of text. It is demonstrated when students relate new material to what they already knew. Evidence of this strategy can be demonstrated when a reader's verbal response indicated relating information encountered in text to prior knowledge, or from associations to holistic themes of the entire text to focused associations to very specific points made in the text, for example:

> Nonfiction Text Excerpt. *Gandhi grew up believing in karma—the idea that to keep a soul clean, one should pray, be disciplined, honest, have few possessions, and harm no one.*
>
> *Participant's Response.* This is telling about what they believed in and it tells how they grew up following karma. It is pretty much the same as any religion in that you shouldn't harm anyone or hurt them in any way.

Relating text to prior knowledge is characterized by the verbal reports that identified part of the text (content) and then made the connection to prior knowledge. In the nonfiction excerpt, the student used the information from the text about karma and related it to his understanding of other religions. His prior knowledge about other religions was important in helping him understand the meaning of karma.

Infer. The strategy *infer* can be reflected by responses that attempt to infer information not explicitly stated in the text when the information is critical to comprehension of text. This also might be evident if a student uses internal and external clues to infer the meaning of a word. Further evidence of this strategy can be evident when a student elaborates, or speculates, ideas about the author's purpose or goals. Oftentimes, the reader uses inferences to fill in the gap between the text and interpretation, for example:

> *Nonfiction Text Excerpt. Gandhi's brother knew of a law firm in South Africa that needed a lawyer, and so, in 1893, Gandhi and his wife left India.*
>
> *Participant's Response.* Now it says that he is going thousands of miles away because they need a lawyer. It shows that he is willing to make sacrifices to help people because the law firm needs him and he is just leaving his family and everything going far away to help.

In this think-aloud example, inferences help construct meaning from the text. In the nonfiction text, the reader infers that Gandhi sacrifices himself to pursue a job in South Africa. The reader does not know whether or not that is true, but he makes a speculation about Gandhi.

After-Reading Strategies

Two after-reading think-alouds assist students to initiate comprehension processes after they read.

Using Summarizing, Predicting, and Questioning Strategies. Readers use many strategies when comprehending nonfiction. These strategies are best reflected by reports that summarize, visualize, paraphrase, and repeat the text being processed. Evidence of using strategies might be demonstrated in a verbal report when a reader paraphrases parts of the text into more familiar terms. In addition, they might visualize a portion of the text in their mind and report such visualizations, for example:

> *Nonfiction Text Excerpt. Gandhi felt different from other people and was a weak student. He barely graduated from high school and failed classes in college. In 1888, at his uncle's urging, Gandhi left his wife at home and went to London to study law.*

Participant's Response. Gandhi grew up with very few learning so he didn't get a good education. Then he went to study law and learn more.

In most cases, using strategies occurs early on in a verbal report after reading a text excerpt. When reading the nonfiction text, the reader uses strategies to help construct meaning by paraphrasing the text.

Reflect.   The strategy *reflect* can be characterized as when a reader indicates they reflected on and processed text additionally after a part of text has been read or after a reading is completed. For example, a reflection might indicate an acceptance or rejection of one's understanding of text. One tactic for dealing with difficult text is to pause and to reflect on the meaning. In addition, reflection can be demonstrated in a verbal report when a reader attempts to fit pieces of information together, for example:

> **Nonfiction Text Excerpt.** *When Gandhi was thirteen years old, he was married according to Jain tradition.*
>
> *Participant's Response.* He wasn't very good in school. It says he left home. I am not sure if he got a divorce or moved away. So I guess he came back.

In this response, the student reflects on the understanding of why Ghandi wasn't a good student in school.

ASSESSING THINK-ALOUDS

Using think-alouds in the classroom is not only a valuable motivational and cognitive tool to improve middle school students' comprehension, it is also a valuable assessment tool for evaluating comprehension (Afflerbach & VanSledright, 2001). All too often, teachers view assessment as something that takes place after the reading. Information about a student's comprehension before and during reading can alert the teacher to the need for intervening instruction.

But how should these think-alouds be assessed? Very little literature exists that suggests specific assessment means for think-alouds, leading to the need for research in this area. Suggestions are based on our experience and on the experience of other teachers who have used think-alouds successfully. When considering student think-alouds as assessment, almost everything a student says is important information. Thinking aloud does not have to be well-structured or perfectly sequenced. It is important that students accurately reflect thoughts or even bits and pieces of their thoughts. In order to keep track of student thinking, it is helpful to create a file or portfolio of transcribed student think-alouds. Teachers should review the file regularly and evaluate the complexity of responses over time. Teachers may tailor their own assessment scheme to their fit their individual models, but a system should be set to track numbers of strategies used, flexibility of strategy use, and of course, appropriate comprehension of the text.

DIRECTIONS FOR FUTURE RESEARCH

Although this chapter highlights the implementation of think-aloud strategies of middle school readers while reading nonfiction text, there is considerable work to be done, and many unanswered questions remain. Consider three questions on think-alouds and metacognition where future research is warranted:

1. *How do reluctant readers use think-aloud strategies when approaching increasingly difficult informational text and remain motivated to continue reading?* The place of think-alouds in motivation of reluctant readers offers an area of little research. Whereas the potential of nonfiction texts for contributing to students' motivation to read and learn has been noted (e.g., Dreher, 2002), the role that think-alouds may play in contributing to students' motivation to continue reading difficult text is less understood. Self-talk has long been a part of motivational theory (Brophy, 1997)—that is, the internal dialogue a person conducts to guide themselves through a difficult problem. High achievers may already know how to use self-talk to guide themselves through problems, such as poor comprehension, and maintain motivation; low achievers have difficulty breaking down the task and often abandon the task. Think-alouds specific to reading comprehension strategies may provide a critical link between teacher modeling and students' ability to use self-talk to maintain motivation and achievement.

2. *Can think-aloud strategies become more frequently used as metacognitive diagnostic assessment tools to increase self-regulation of the reading comprehension process?* Several syntheses of the research suggest using think-alouds as assessment tools. Caldwell and Leslie (2003/2004) suggested that application of a strategy such as thinking aloud is influenced by such factors as the difficulty of text and the presence of knowledge underlying text content. Although think-aloud strategies are used to obtain data, for example, with the Qualitative Reading Inventory–3, it has not been used effectively as a diagnostic strategy for students to use.

3. *What can be done to prepare teachers to use think-alouds in the classroom?* Palmer (1998) suggested that good teaching is closely connected to knowing who we are as people and that "knowing myself is as crucial to good teaching as knowing my students and my subject" (p. 2). Thus, although the first step is helping teachers understand their own thinking when reading, teachers must move beyond their own experiences. Often, reading has been an easy process for teachers. Think-alouds must be purposeful and must model a variety of comprehension strategies for students. Effective ways of helping teachers think about their own thinking and add new reading strategies to their own repertoire will prove to be important as we examine the impact of think-alouds on teaching.

SUMMARY OF THINK-ALOUDS
AS MOTIVATIONAL TOOLS

The purpose of this chapter was to investigate think-aloud strategies for middle school readers using nonfiction text, providing a review of the rationale for using nonfiction texts, as well as using think-alouds with adolescent readers. The intention throughout was to encourage the integration of think-alouds and comprehension strategies in instruction, as well as the release of teacher-centered strategy application to student-centered strategy application, which were posed as four central questions. Answering those questions emphasized the important link between teacher think-alouds and students' increased awareness of comprehension strategies and motivation and engagement with texts. Further, the central role of nonfiction was explained to be both as a genre that requires explicit modeling when working toward comprehension and a way to motivate middle school readers. Through modeling and practice, the teacher first provides the scaffolds of reading at all three points of reading (before, during, and after), and then gradually removes the supports as students are able to monitor their own comprehension. The teacher also monitors students' use of the think-alouds through assessment at all three points of reading. Always, the ultimate goal is to help students become independent readers and lifelong learners.

METACONNECTION FOR CHAPTER 10

In chapter 10, you increased your ability to describe to students the metacognitive thoughts that you engaged when you read. In addition, you learned the speed at which students can begin to initiate these metacognitive thought processes themselves, as well as several teaching aids that you can apply at the middle school level and for students above and beyond that level. You should be able to talk about metacognitive thought processes in language that students can readily understand. Once students readily understand the metacognitive thought processes, they can move to becoming more self-regulated. Chapter 11 discusses the role of self-regulation in literacy learning.

REFERENCES

Afflerbach, P., & VanSledright, B. (2001). Hath! Doth! What? Middle graders reading innovative history text. *Journal of Adolescent & Adult Literacy, 44*(8), 696–707.

Alvermann, D. E., O'Brien, D. G., & Dillon, D. R. (1990). What teachers do when they say they're having discussions of content area reading assignments: A qualitative analysis. *Reading Research Quarterly, 25,* 296–322.

Baker, L. (2002). Metacognition in comprehension instruction. In C. C. Block & M. Pressley (Eds.), *Comprehension instruction: Research based best practices* (pp. 77–95). New York: Guilford.

Block, C. C. (2002). Helping children comprehend nonfiction text: What we know, what we can do, and what we still need to learn. *California Reader.*

Block, C. C., & Israel, S. E. (2004). The ABC's of performing think-alouds. *The Reading Teacher, 58*(2), 148–167.

Brophy, J. E. (1997). *Motivating students to learn.* New York: McGraw-Hill.

Caldwell, J., & Leslie, L. (2003/2004). Does proficiency in middle school reading assure proficiency in high school reading? The possible role of think-alouds. *Journal of Adolescent & Adult Literacy, 47*(4), 324–335.

Coté, N., Goldman, S., & Saul. (1998). Students making sense of informational text: Relations between processing and representation. *Discourse Processes, 25*(1), 1–53.

Cunningham, P., & Cunningham, J. (2001). What we know about how to teach phonics. In A. Farstrup & S. J. Samuels (Eds.), *What research has to say about reading instruction* (3rd ed., pp. 87–109). Newark, DE: International Reading Association.

Dickson, S. V., Simmons, D., & Kameenui, E. (2002). *Text organization and its relation to reading comprehension: A synthesis of the research.* Document prepared by the National Center to Improve the Tools of Educators. Available at http://idea.uoregon.edu:16080/~ncite/documents/techrep/tech17.html

Donovan, C. A., & Smolkin, L. B. (2002a). Children's genre knowledge: An examination of K–5 students' performance on multiple tasks providing differing levels of scaffolding. *Reading Research Quarterly, 37*(4), 428–465.

Donovan, C. A., & Smolkin, L. B. (2002b). Considering genre, content, and visual features in the selection of trade books for science instruction. *The Reading Teacher, 55*(6), 502–520.

Dreher, M. J. (2002). Children searching and using information text: A critical part of comprehension. In C. C. Block & M. Pressley (Eds.), *Comprehension instruction: Research based best practices* (pp. 289–304). New York: Guilford.

Fournier, D. N., & Graves, M. F. (2002). Scaffolding adolescents' comprehension of short stories. *Journal of Adolescent & Adult Literacy, 46*(1), 30–39.

Graves, M. F., Juel, C., & Graves, B. B. (2001). *Teaching reading in the 21st century.* Boston: Allyn & Bacon.

Guthrie, J. T., Van Meter, P., McCann, A. D., Wigfield, A., Bennett, L., Poundstone, C. C., Rice, M. E., Faibisch, F. M., Hunt, B., & Mitchell, A. M. (1996). Growth of literacy engagement: Changes in motivations and strategies during concept-oriented reading instruction. *Reading Research Quarterly, 31*, 306–332.

Guthrie, J. T., & Wigfield, A. (2000). Engagement and motivation in reading. In M. L. Kamil, P. B. Mosenthal, P. D. Pearson, & R. Barr (Eds.), *Handbook of reading research* (Vol. 3, pp. 403–422). Mahwah, NJ: Lawrence Erlbaum Associates.

Hennings, D. G. (1993). On knowing and reading history. *Journal of Reading, 36*(5), 362–370.

Israel, S. E. (2002). *Understanding strategy utilization during reading comprehension: Relations between text type and reading levels using verbal protocols.* Unpublished doctoral dissertation, Ball State University, Muncie, IN.

Ivey, G. (2002). Building comprehension when they're still learning to read words. In C. C. Block & M. Pressley (Eds.), *Comprehension instruction: Research based best practices* (pp. 234–246). New York: Guilford.

Ivey, G., & Broaddus, K. (2001). "Just plain reading": A survey of what makes students want to read in middle school classrooms. *Reading Research Quarterly, 36*, 350–377.

Maria, K., & Hathaway, K. (1993). Using think alouds with teachers to develop awareness of reading strategies. *Journal of Reading, 37*(1), 12–18.

Massey, D. D. (2003). A comprehension checklist: What if it doesn't make sense? *The Reading Teacher, 57*(1), 81–84.

Moniuszko, L. K. (1992). Motivation: Reaching reluctant readers age 14–17. *Journal of Reading, 16*(1), 32–34.

Moss, B. (2003). An exploration of eight sixth graders' engagement with nonfiction trade books. In C. Fairbanks, J. Worthy, B. Maloch, J. Hoffman, & D. Schallert (Eds.), *52nd yearbook of the National Reading Conference* (pp. 321–331). Oak Creek, WI: National Reading Conference.

Moss, B., & Hendershot, J. (2002). Exploring sixth graders' selection of nonfiction trade books. *The Reading Teacher, 56*(1), 6–17.

Myers, M., & Paris, S. G. (1978). Children's metacognitive knowledge about reading. *Journal of Educational Psychology, 70,* 680–690.

National Institute of Child Health and Human Development. (2000a). *Report of the National Reading Panel: Teaching children to read: An evidence based assessment of the scientific research literature on reading and its implications for reading instruction* (NIH Publication No. 00-4769). Washington, DC: U.S. Government Printing Office.

National Institute of Child Health and Human Development. (2000b). *Teaching children to read—Summary report of the National Reading Panel.* Washington, DC: U.S. Government Printing Office.

O'Brien, D. G., Stewart, R. A., & Moje, E. B. (1995). Why content literacy is difficult to infuse into the secondary school: Complexities of curriculum pedagogy, and school culture. *Reading Research Quarterly, 30,* 442–463.

Palmer, P. (1998). *The courage to teach: Exploring the inner landscape of a teacher's life.* San Francisco: Jossey-Bass.

Paris, S. G., & Jacobs, J. E. (1984). The benefits of informed instruction for children's reading awareness and comprehension skills. *Child Development, 55,* 2083–2093.

Pressley, M. (2002). Metacognition and self-regulated comprehension. In A. Farstrup & S. J. Samuels (Eds.), *What research has to say about reading instruction* (3rd ed., pp. 291–309). Newark, DE: International Reading Association.

Pressley, M., & Afflerbach, P. (1995). *Verbal protocols of reading: The nature of constructively responsive reading.* Hillsdale, NJ: Lawrence Erlbaum Associates.

RAND Reading Study Group. (2001). *Reading for understanding: Toward an R & D program in reading comprehension.* Technical report for the Office of Educational Research and Improvement.

Vacca, R. T. (1998). Let's not marginalize adolescent literacy. *Journal of Adolescent and Adult Literacy, 41,* 604–609.

11

The Role of Self-Monitoring in Literacy Learning

Laurice M. Joseph
Ohio State University

Reading is Thinking is posted on a bulletin board. It is the first mini-lesson to start off our class reader's workshop for the year. I want my third graders to realize that if you are not thinking you are not really reading. This is eye-opening for some of my students. The exciting part is that, through all the strategy instruction, my students are beginning to internalize this view. I just received a card from a student yesterday. The inside message was "Reading is thinking." My sincere desire is to deepen and strengthen my students' abilities to think critically.
—Beth Bernlohr, Third-Grade Teacher

It is impossible to discuss metacognitive activities without discussing the role self-monitoring plays in cognition about cognition. In fact, metacognition, in part, is defined as knowing how, when, and where to apply strategies to complete tasks successfully (Garner, 1994). One of the activities involved in knowing how, when, and where to apply strategies is referred to as *monitoring* (Pressley, 1999). Flavell (1979) indicated that monitoring occurred throughout various phases of metacognitive processes, including knowledge, experiences, planning, and application of strategies. Examples of monitoring activities are checking for understanding and evaluating the effectiveness of one's efforts or strategy use. *Self-monitoring* is defined as attending to an aspect of one's behavior through data-recording procedures (Mace & Kratochwill, 1988). Self-monitoring is a term often used interchangeably with *self-regulation*. Although these terms are used synonymously, they are distinct. Self-regulation is a broader term referring to the control of emotions, feelings, thoughts, and actions associated with attaining a goal (Zimmerman, 1994). One of the activities used to regulate emotions, thoughts, feelings, and actions for the purpose of achieving goals is to monitor one's behavior using data-recording methods (Schunk, 1996).

In regard to literacy behaviors, self-monitoring essentially refers to exercising inner control to check, record, and correct reading behaviors (Clay, 1991). Research shows that good readers monitor their reading behaviors, particularly their understanding of text material, in contrast to poor readers, who do not monitor their comprehension of text material and do not realize when they fail to understand information so they can exert more efforts toward comprehending the material (Garner, 1980). Moreover, poor readers' lack of monitoring behaviors also prevents them from knowing to change strategies when the text material becomes increasingly more difficult to comprehend (Phillips, 1988). This chapter presents the importance of goal setting and planning, various recording methods of self-monitoring literacy behaviors, connections between self-monitoring, motivation, and self-efficacy, a discussion about various evidence-based literacy instruction techniques and instruction strategies that incorporate self-monitoring methods, followed by suggestions for furthering the research in relation to self-monitoring and literacy learning.

GOAL SETTING

Before monitoring behaviors should occur, goals should be established. Establishing achievement goals has been found to be related to self-regulatory behaviors and academic performance (see Urdan, 1997, for a review). Goal setting makes monitoring activities meaningful as well as process to product oriented. In regard to literacy activities, goals may consist of the completion of reading or writing a story, reading a specified number of words read or written correctly within a certain time period, segmenting a number of sounds in words or blending sounds accurately, or answering a specified number of literal and inferential comprehension questions correctly. Goals can be stated in general and specific terms. However, it is easier to determine appropriate type or types of self-monitoring methods to use if goals were stated in observable and measurable terms.

FORMULATING A PLAN

Once a goal or goals are established, a plan for achieving those goals should be developed. Plans often involve the application of strategies. The effectiveness of the plan or strategy for achieving a goal can be measured through self-monitoring procedures. If the goal is to answer literal and inferential comprehension questions, then note taking and review strategies might be implemented followed by answering literal and inferential questions. The effectiveness of the note taking and review strategy can be determined through the implementation of a self-monitoring method. A self-monitoring method, in this case, may include recording the number of questions answered correctly. Sometimes, the most efficient and appropriate strategy is implementing a recording method of self-monitoring performance. For instance, if the goal is to increase the amount of time one spends silently reading a book, then the strategy might be to implement a self-monitoring recording procedure to ensure approximation of this goal. In the former instance, the effectiveness of the plan or strategies for achieving the goal was measured through a self-monitoring method and, in the later instance, the strategy and the monitoring procedures were one in the same.

SELF-MONITORING RECORDING METHODS

Similar to the various methods used to record the behaviors of others are methods used to record behaviors of the self. Several of the same recording methods that teachers use to evaluate student progress and to evaluate the effectiveness of an instructional strategy can be used by students to evaluate their own progress and to evaluate the effectiveness of a strategy they implement. Schunk (1996) provided a discussion about various types of self-monitoring recording methods that may be used in general for monitoring academic and social behaviors. This section also provides a discussion of several of these recording methods as they are applied to developing and maintaining literacy skills. These methods include various types of qualitative data recording and quantitative data recording procedures. Depending on the literacy behavior, one type of method may be better suited for checking progress than another type, and in some cases, multiple methods may be applied. These methods can help individuals check their progress and alter their strategy if they are not working toward meeting their goals or according to their plans. These methods provide a mechanism of ongoing recording or charting so that visual inspection of performance data over time can be analyzed and evaluated. Based on the results from self-monitoring records, students may wish to revise their goals or set new ones. For example, a student may find that by examining self-recorded data, 20 minutes of thinking and planning time have elapsed before he begins writing anything on paper. This particular student may set a goal of reducing this time period to 10 minutes of thinking and planning followed by writing a topical outline before he begins writing his first draft. The process of setting goals, devising plans, and monitoring performance is cyclical. Continuous improvement and advancement can be emphasized as a result of responding to data, revising or generating new goals and plans (strategies), and selecting and implementing monitoring methods again, and so forth.

Qualitative Recording Procedures

A common type of qualitative recording method is narration. *Narration* consists of written connected text of self-behaviors in a particular context. For instance, narration might be used to record retellings of a story read. The degree of accuracy and details conveyed in the retellings will allow individuals to assess their level of understanding of the reading material. Narration could also involve written accounts of individuals' reflections and evaluation of their understanding of text and their perception of their progress as a reader. Reflections have shown how readers plan, strategize, monitor, and evaluate their understanding of the content (Wade, Trathen, & Schraw, 1990). Open-ended narratives are usually written as if one were recording events in a diary or personal journal. More structured narratives that are composed from specified prompts provided by an instructor may also be recorded in a journal. Narratives can also be presented orally and tape-recorded and transcribed later. This may allow more immediate thoughts to be recorded while an individual is engaged in the literacy activity rather than reflections about past literacy events that occurred. Themes that are reflective of various comprehension levels may emerge from tape recordings that have been transcribed over time. For instance, individuals may be able to detect their advancement in describing the main ideas, discussing details about events and characters, making inferences about metaphors, and predicting outcomes.

Portfolio self-assessment is another qualitative form by which individuals can monitor their progress over time (Winograd & Arrington, 1999). Students can select written work samples that they completed at the beginning, the middle, and the end of the school year. They can evaluate the quality of their written products at different times during the school year using a rubric or a checklist. Conferences with their teacher can occur, and students can compare their evaluations and reflections with their teacher's evaluation of their written work.

Quantitative Recording Procedures

There are various quantitative methods of self-recording academic behaviors and they include frequency counts, latency measures, duration measures, time-sampling measures, behavior ratings, and behavioral traces or archival records (Schunk, 1996). In relation to literacy activities frequency counts can be used, for example, during silent reading activities when the goal is to increase engaged reading time. Students may record how many times they are off task during the daily silent reading class time period or during the creative writing time. Students can accomplish this by recording tally marks on a chart that is taped to their desks each time they are off task during a given time period. Latency measures can be used to record how much time it takes individuals to begin engaging in a literacy activity. For instance, they can keep track of how much time has elapsed before they begin to write a passage or read a chapter from a book. This can be accomplished by self-recording the amount of time it takes them to begin writing from the time the direction to write was given by the instructor. Duration measures could consist of self-recording the amount of time it takes to read and write a story or report (e.g., the number of minutes, hours, etc., it took to read a story).

Time-sampling or interval recording procedures can be used to divide a relatively long period of time into smaller segments or time intervals to facilitate manageable self-recording behaviors. For instance, a 30-minute silent reading time can be divided into six 5-minute interval time periods. A timer can be set to beep every 5 minutes. Each time a beep is heard, individuals can record whether they are engaged in reading or off task in some manner. This is an example of a fixed interval recording schedule of silent reading behavior, but they can also set the timer to beep on a variable interval recording schedule to prevent themselves from exhibiting engaged silent reading behaviors only during the 5-minute intervals.

Behavioral rating scales or inventories may also be used to monitor one's perception about their reading and writing behaviors. Behavioral rating scales or inventories are more subjective in nature because the ratings of behavior are completed on an ordinal scale requiring estimates of how often behaviors occur. For instance, certain reading and writing behaviors may be rated on a scale ranging from *always, sometimes, very infrequent,* and *never occurring.* These descriptors are accompanied by a quantitative value (e.g., 5 = *always* to 1 = *never occurring*). Self-recordings about literacy skills on behavioral rating scales are probably used periodically rather than on a daily or weekly basis. They are also completed after substantial time of performing the literacy behavior has elapsed. For instance, writing behaviors may be rated after a series of writing assignments were completed. Thus, behavior rating scales or inventories are not a direct measurement of literacy behaviors, but rather an indirect measurement of perceptions about literacy behaviors.

There have been several metacognitive awareness inventories containing items related to reading behaviors, such as the Index of Reading Awareness (Jacobs & Paris, 1987), Reading Strategy Use (Pereira-Laird & Deane, 1997), Schmitt's (1990) questionnaire, and Miholic's (1994) inventory. In attempts to improve these metacognitive awareness inventories from a psychometric and theoretical perspective, Mokhtari and Reichard (2002) developed and tested the Metacognitive Awareness of Reading Strategies Inventory (MARSI). The items on this inventory consist of statements reflecting thoughts, actions, and strategies associated with comprehending text material. The student is to respond to each item by circling a quantitative value that represents 1 = *never do this* to 5 = *always do this.*

SELF-MONITORING, MOTIVATION, AND SELF-EFFICACY

An awareness of how the self is thinking and performing while engaged in an academic endeavor such as reading facilitates motivation (Paris & Winograd, 1990). Self-monitoring can serve as a mechanism for helping children to become aware of their thinking and their performance while engaged in a reading task. When children learn to self-monitor their behaviors toward achieving a literacy goal, the act of recording data can serve as a motivator. When children chart progress on the number of words they read accurately during a minute, for instance, they typically wish to beat their previous score the next time they read a passage so they could record a higher score or shade more of the bar graph in, and so on. In other words, keeping score serves as a motivator. It also helps children develop self-efficacy. Once children see they are making progress on their reading or writing skills, they are likely to believe they are capable of making further progress. Thus, perception of progress contributes to self-efficacy (Schunk, 1996). Through self-monitoring, children can evaluate their efforts and the strategies they use to complete tasks, which helps them attribute progress to their efforts and the strategies used rather than external influences that are beyond their control.

INCORPORATING SELF-MONITORING IN LITERACY STRATEGY INSTRUCTION APPROACHES

Learning strategy instruction models, such as those described by Pressley and Woloshyn (1995), include self-monitoring of strategy use and evaluating strategy effectiveness for achieving learning goals. These models can be applied across various types of academic areas. They have certainly proven to be effective for helping children develop and advance in reading skills (Pressley & Woloshyn, 1995). There are several reading and writing strategy/techniques that also incorporate self-monitoring within the technique itself. The following provides a description about some of these techniques at both the word reading and spelling level and the comprehension level. The strategies described are not exhaustive of all possible strategies and so the reader of this chapter is encouraged to consult the literature for additional strategies that incorporate self-monitoring.

Word Level Strategies That Embed Self-Monitoring

Word Sorts. *Word sorting techniques* are often referred to as word study approaches for teaching reading and spelling because they involve the examination of spelling and sound patterns of words for the purposes of classifying common characteristics and making distinctions among sound and spelling patterns of words (Bear, Invernizzi, Templeton, & Jonston, 1996). Word sorts have been used within comprehensive literacy programs such as Early Steps (Santa & Hoien, 1999), Howard Tutoring Program (Morris, Shaw, & Perney, 1990), and the Four Blocks Program (Cunningham, 1999). Word sorts involve categorizing words according to either shared sound, spelling, or morphemic patterns (Bear et al., 1996). Categories are predetermined by an instructor, and category names are printed on index cards and placed across children's desks or tables in the class-room. Words are printed on a shuffled stack of index cards and are provided to the children so they may examine and sort them by placing them below desig-nated category cards. Word sorts are also considered to be a spelling-based pho-nics technique. For example, this technique can be used when teaching word family or phonogram words that share similar sound and spelling patterns. Words may also be sorted according to morphemic patterns or sorted based on shared meaning (Zutell, 1998). For instance, words ending in "ian" (e.g., pediatrician, magician, musician) may be sorted below a category called "people" and words ending in "ion" (e.g., institution, education, constitution) may be sorted below a category called "things."

Self-monitoring is involved as children examine and place words in catego-ries. The designated category words serve as cues and/or prompts for the children. Therefore, children can check their sorts by examining the category words so they can make self-corrections if they place a word below the wrong category (Zutell, 1998). Children can keep a running record of how many types of sorts they completed by keeping a portfolio or notebook of completed sorts. In several rather recent investigations exploring the usefulness of word sorts with samples of first graders and samples of children with disabilities, children were observed to monitor performance by checking their sorts against the designated categories and making self-corrections if words were placed incorrectly (e.g., Joseph, 2000; Joseph & McCachran, 2003). Preschool children were also observed to make self-corrections after receiving demonstrations and corrective feedback on sort-ing pictures that depicted words into categories according to same beginning sound (Maslanka & Joseph, 2002).

Copy, Cover, and Check.   This technique is designed to help children self-monitor their spellings of words. Children who have difficulty learning weekly spelling words and who do not automatically engage in self-monitoring may ben-efit from the use of this technique. Children are asked to copy one of their spell-ing words. They are asked to cover up the copied version of the word and attempt to spell the word on their own. The students uncover the copied version to allow them to check if their spelling of the word matches the copied version, and they make corrections if they spelled the word incorrectly. This procedure is repeated until children's spellings match the spellings of the covered words. Children can record on a graph or on a chart the number of trials it takes to spell each word correctly.

Another version of this technique is called "Add-A-Word Spelling Practice." This procedure has been found to be most helpful for helping children who con-sistently obtain a score below 70% on their weekly spelling tests. Students copy 10 spelling words to practice on a copy column of their worksheet. Students cover the words and tell them to write the words from memory on a different column on their worksheets. Next, students uncover the copied words and compare their responses with the correct spelling list of words. This process should be repeated at least two times per day for children who have difficulty. After two trials, students may drop the words spelled correctly from the list, retain those spelled incorrectly, and add a new word for every word that is dropped. Students can record their progress on a chart. This procedure has been found to be effective for helping children improve their spelling performance (Pratt-Struthers, Struthers, & Williams, 1983).

Word sorts have also been compared with copy, cover, check and traditional spelling instruction (Dangel, 1989). Findings from this study revealed that participants who were taught a combination of word sorts and copy, cover, check outperformed participants who either were provided with word sorts alone or traditional spelling instruction. Participants who prepared with word sorts alone performed better than participants who used traditional spelling instruction. The results indicated that methods that explicitly incorporated self-monitoring procedures were especially powerful for helping children spell words accurately.

Response Cards. The strategy allows every student in a classroom to practice spelling words and allows the students to monitor their performance by observing others' responses and receiving immediate feedback from the instructor. Students are provided with dry erase boards, small chalkboards, or small poster boards. The teacher says a word, and the children are required to write the word on their response cards and hold them up. Children are encouraged to observe their classmates' responses and compare them with their responses. After students are given the opportunity to display their responses, the teacher may display the correct response so students can record if their response matches the teacher's response. Students can also use preprinted response cards with multiple responses on it, and students can use a clothespin to pinch the correct spelling of the word on the card. The correct answers can be provided on a score sheet or on the back of the preprinted card for the students to self-monitor their responses. Heward et al. (1996) provided a summary of studies and variety of uses of response cards for learning academic skills.

Incremental Rehearsal. Incremental rehearsal is a drill rehearsal technique designed to teach unknown items using a ratio of 90% known and 10% unknown items (Tucker, 1989). This technique can be used to teach word recognition and spelling skills using ratio of known words to unknown words. The procedures inherent in this technique may also help students and instructor monitor word recognition progress by assessing the number of unknown words that become known words to the reader. Nine known words and one unknown word are written on 3 × 5 index cards. Then, the first unknown item is visually presented to the student while the instructor provides the verbal pronunciation. The first unknown is interspersed with the known words nine times throughout the process. The child is asked to verbally state the word each time it is presented. After completing this sequence, the first unknown word will be treated as the first known, the previous ninth known will be removed, and a new unknown word will be rehearsed. Therefore, the number of cards used will always remain at 10. Children can self-monitor their progress by recording the number of unknown words that become known during instructional sessions.

MacQuarrie, Tucker, Burns, and Hartman (2002) compared Tucker's (1989) Incremental Rehearsal (IR) drill model, which involves rehearsing one unknown word with nine known, to more challenging ratios of known to unknown, including a traditional condition that utilized all unknown words. Results found significantly better retention for IR than the other conditions. Recently, a comparison of less and more challenging ratios of known to unknown words used to teach spelling words was investigated and findings reported that more words were learned in a shorter amount of time using more challenging ratios of known to unknown words (Cates et al., 2003).

Repeated Readings. Reading text repeatedly is highly related to reading comprehension and building whole word recognition fluency (Rasinski, 1990). During repeated reading exercises, children read a passage for a minute several times until mastery of the passage has been achieved. Mastery usually means reading the passage fluently, which means reading all of the words accurately and quickly. Reading fluency is highly correlated with reading comprehension. Children are considered to be reading within grade level if they are reading between 75 and 100 words per minute correct on a grade level passage with 3 to 5 errors (Shinn, 1989). Self-monitoring can be involved when children are engaged in repeated reading exercises by having them record the number of words read correctly within a minute and the number of times a passage was repeatedly read before reaching mastery criterion levels.

Phonological and Strategy Training (PHAST) Program. A reading program that incorporates self-monitoring along with other metacognitive strategies is called the PHAST program (Lovett, Lacerenza, & Borden, 2000). It involves five strategies that are presented in a metacognitive organizational structure called the "Game Plan": sounding-out strategy, rhyming strategy, peeling off strategy, vowel alert strategy, and the I spy strategy.

The *sounding-out strategy* involves systematic training in letter–sound correspondences, phonological remediation of sound segmentation and sound blending difficulties, and phonologically based teaching of word identification skills. This phase includes many of the components and lessons contained in the Direct Instruction Reading Mastery program. The *rhyming strategy* teaches children words that share common spelling patterns or word family words (sometimes referred to as phonograms). Children learn that many of these words serve as keywords for learning more complex words. For example, recognizing the word "cat" may one day help them pronounce the word "catastrophe." Children are guided toward making word analogies through explicit dialogue with their instructor. The *peeling off strategy* is used to teach students prefixes and suffixes by segmenting affixes at the beginning (e.g., "re") and end of a word (e.g., "ing"). The students "peel off" the affixes to identify the root word. The *vowel alert strategy* involves having students attempt different vowel pronunciations in an unknown word until they say the word correctly. Single short or long vowel sounds are taught initially using this strategy and then vowel combinations, such as "ou" and "ea," are taught. The *I spy strategy* involves looking for small familiar parts of a longer unknown word. This strategy is mostly used when teaching compound words. For the word "handshake," the children would say: "I spy" the word "hand" so I will put a box around the word "hand" and then "I spy" the word "shake" so I will put a box around the word "shake."

Children are taught when to use the various strategies (i.e., depending on the types of words they are learning) through a "game plan." The game plan might consist of planning to use the rhyming strategy and then the I spy strategy. The children are encouraged to monitor their strategy use by checking to see if they are using the strategy appropriately and by determining if the strategy is helping them identify words. Children record correct responses by giving themselves a score and not giving themselves a score if the strategy did not yield successful results. If a strategy did not yield desirable results, then the students are encouraged to choose another strategy in the program. In a recent investigation, Lovett, Lacerenza, Borden, Frijters, et al. (2000) found that positive outcomes were observed in word identification, passage comprehension, and nonword reading for a sample of children who received the PHAST program in contrast to children who only received either phonological or strategy training.

Reading Comprehension and Written Expression Strategies That Embed Self-Monitoring

K-W-L.   A comprehension strategy for teaching children self-monitoring skills is called *K-W-L* (Ogle, 1986). K-W-L is an acronym for what you already KNOW about a topic, what you WANT to know, and what you have LEARNED. Before reading a book, a story in a basal reader, or a chapter in a content area textbook, the students are asked to divide a sheet of paper into three columns. In the first column, students are instructed to list the things they already know about the topic of the book or topical contents of the textbook chapter. Students are asked to list the things they want to know in the second column. The students then are instructed to read the book or chapter from a textbook. After reading the book or chapter from a textbook, the students list the things they learned in the third column. The students can examine the contents of their lists in the three columns to determine if they have learned what they wanted to know and if they learned more than what they already knew. They also compare the length of their lists to determine which lists contain the most items. Jennings (1991) and McAllister (1994) found the K-W-L procedure to be useful as an instructional and assessment tool.

Product-Oriented Semantic Mapping. Monitoring understanding of text can be accomplished through applying semantic mapping. After students read a chapter from an expository text, they can arrange the concepts discussed in that chapter by creating a map of the connections between concepts and ideas presented in the chapter. Some students need more structure and assistance with selecting concepts and ideas to be mapped. In this case, the teacher may place concepts and ideas on index cards and have the students arrange and categorize them in a meaningful way (McCormick, 1999). Students can monitor their understandings by examining their product maps and determining if they categorized and drew appropriate relations between concepts and ideas.

Reciprocal Teaching. Reciprocal teaching is a reading comprehension approach that usually occurs within the context of a small group of students. This approach places heavy emphasis on teacher–student interactions in a rather cognitive apprenticeship fashion. After students and teacher read from common text, they dialogue with each other about the reading material. Initially, the teacher leads the dialogue by modeling strategies of predicting, question generating, summarizing, and clarifying text. Each student takes a turn and leads the discussions and applies the strategies that were demonstrated by the teacher. Guided practice is provided until students can use the strategies effectively. The goal of these reciprocal teaching interactions is to construct meaning from texts. This approach has helped delayed readers catch up and even exceed typically developing readers (Palinscar & Brown, 1984).

Monitoring occurs at various levels. When students play a leadership role, they need to engage in the process of engaging deeply in reading material and creating plans for leading the discussion. As they prepare, they need to continually monitor their understanding of text so they will be able to question, summarize, and clarify concepts and ideas when they meet in their small group. On another level, the students who are required to answer the questions and discuss the reading material also need to monitor their understanding of the reading material. Finally, the student leader, as well as the other students in the group, need to monitor their process and behaviors as group members so the goals of their interactions are achieved. In order to systematically monitor a reciprocal teaching group process, one student may be the designated recorder of responses.

Plan, Draft, Compose, Edit, Publish. Directly teaching students the writing process can be very effective for helping them develop self-regulatory writing behaviors (Harris & Graham, 1996) and produce adequate written products, especially if students are given opportunities and time for writing (Routman, 1996;

Shanahan, 1997). The writing process entails planning, drafting, composing, editing, and publishing. Self-monitoring may be involved throughout all steps in the process. Plans as well as the written product can be assessed and revised. In the planning phase, this can be accomplished by having the students create graphic organizers or outlines of the main ideas, topics, events, and sections that will be included in their written reports or stories (Bromley, Irwin-DeVitis, & Modlo, 1995). In the drafting and composition phases, students may record whether or not they have adhered to their plans depicted on a graphic organizer or an outline. Those who need to increase the number of words they write on a page can record this data on a chart or graph until they reach their goal. Students can also keep a running record of the number of grammatical and spelling errors they make by graphing these figures to see if they are decreasing their number of errors. There are various versions of the writing process. For example, Englett and Mariage (1992) taught students the writing process using a mnemonic, POWER, which refers to plan, organize, write, edit, and revise. This strategy consists of the teacher scaffolding each stage of the process by modeling through "think-alouds." The students gradually implement the process independently. At more advanced levels, students need to monitor their writing style and conventions to produce products in different genres such as narrative versus expository (Englett & Mariage, 1992; Gersten & Baker, 2001).

DIRECTIONS FOR FUTURE RESEARCH

Self-regulation of literacy behaviors has been discussed more in the literature than self-monitoring of literacy behaviors. Self-monitoring has been discussed more in the literature in relation to general behavior issues rather than academic performance issues. Therefore, there is a definite need for more research in this area. It would be interesting to further discover the unique role self-monitoring plays in the metacognitive processes associated with literacy. This may be accomplished through correlation analyses exploring the relation between self-monitoring and other metacognitive variables associated with literacy learning. Research investigations are needed to explore the differential effectiveness of various self-monitoring recording methods (e.g., narration, time-sampling, behavior rating scales) on cognitive awareness, student motivation, self-efficacy, and various types of literacy performance (e.g., spelling, reading fluency, comprehension of narrative text, comprehension of expository text, written compositions). For instance, does completing portfolios produce better awareness of processes involved in learning literacy skills, provide a useful tool in self-assessment of performance, provide a mechanism for responding to feedback and making improvements, contribute to self-efficacy by changing beliefs about capability of obtaining literacy skills, and help with setting goals, adhering to plans, and regulating performance? It would also be interesting to explore the quality and quantity of literacy instruction strategies or approaches that incorporate a self-monitoring component. It would be interesting to explore differences in self-monitoring characteristics between children with disabilities, children with gifted characteristics, and children who are not identified with exceptionalities. It would be interesting to examine differential effects of explicit instruction on using self-monitoring methods in contrast to implicit instruction on using self-monitoring methods.

CONCLUSIONS

Self-monitoring is a key behavior that should be executed while engaged in metacognitive processes of literacy learning. Goals and plans of achieving particular literacy goals will help students choose a self-recording method that will best assess whether or not they achieved their goals and adhered to their plans. In several instances, multiple methods may be used for achieving different aspects of their goals and plans as well as providing multiple lenses from which to evaluate their progress. Self-monitoring is related to motivation and self-efficacy about literacy performance. Various literacy strategies, some covered in this chapter, incorporate self-monitoring. The reader is encouraged to consult the extant literature for additional strategies that may best meet the needs of the particular students with whom they are working. More research is needed in exploring the effectiveness of self-monitoring on the literacy learning process and outcomes. Additionally, further research is needed in exploring the relations between self-monitoring and other behavioral, cognitive, metacognitive, and affective variables.

METACONNECTION FOR CHAPTER 11

Chapter 11 is among the first in the body of knowledge to have provided the instructional steps that are necessary for students to self-monitor their own literacy learning as it relates to their metacognitions. The chapter also summarizes methods that have been used in the past as teacher-directed methods to develop students' self-regulation. The reader will likely enjoy the contrast between the different methods that have been used in the past and those that Dr. Joseph projects for the future. Like Israel and Massey, Joseph also provides additional guidelines for future research and instruction that we can begin in the future.

REFERENCES

Bear, D. R., Invernizzi, M. A., Templeton, S., & Johnston, F. (1996). *Words their way: Word study for phonics, vocabulary, and spelling.* Englewood Cliffs, NJ: Prentice-Hall.

Bromley, K., Irwin-DeVitis, L., & Modlo, M. (1995). *Graphic organizers*. New York: Scholastic.

Cates, G. L., Skinner, C. H., Watson, S., Meadows, T. J., Weaver, A., & Jackson, B. (2003). Instructional effectiveness and instructional efficiency as considerations for data-based decision making: An evaluation of interspersing procedures. *School Psychology Review, 31*(4), 601–616.

Clay, M. M. (1991). *Becoming literate: The construction of inner control*. Portsmouth, NH: Heinemann.

Cunningham, P. (1999). What should we do about phonics? In L. B. Gambrell, L. M. Morrow, S. B. Neuman, & M. Pressley (Eds.), *Best practices in literacy instruction* (pp. 68–89). New York: Guilford.

Dangel, H. L. (1989). The use of student directed spelling strategies. *Academic Therapy, 25*, 43–51.

Englett, C. S., & Mariage, T. V. (1992). Shared understandings: Structuring the writing experience through dialogue. In D. Carnine & E. Kameenui (Eds.), *Higher order thinking* (pp. 107–136). Austin, TX: PRO-ED.

Flavell, J. H. (1979). Metacognition and cognitive monitoring: A new area of cognitive-developmental inquiry. *American Psychologist, 34*, 906–911.

Garner, R. (1980). Monitoring of understanding: An investigation of good and poor readers' awareness of induced miscomprehension of text. *Journal of Reading Behavior, 12*, 55–64.

Garner, R. (1994). Metacognition and executive control. In R. B. Ruddell, M. R. Ruddell, & H. Singer (Eds.), *Theoretical models and processes of reading* (4th ed., pp. 143–158). Newark, DE: International Reading Association.

Gersten, R., & Baker, S. (2001). Teaching expressive writing to students with learning disabilities: A meta-analysis. *The Elementary School Journal, 101*, 251–272.

Harris, K., & Graham, S. (1996). *Making the wiring process work: Strategies for composition and self-regulation* (2nd ed.). Cambridge, MA: Brookline.

Heward, W. L., Gardner, R., III, Cavanaugh, S. S., Courson, F. H., Grossi, T. A., & Barbetta, P. M. (1996). Everyone participates in this class: Using response cards to increase active student response. *Teaching Exceptional Children*, 4–10.

Jacobs, J. E., & Paris, S. G. (1987). Children's metacognition about reading: Issues in definition, measurement, and instruction. *Educational Psychologist, 22*, 255–278.

Jennings, J. H. (1991). A comparison of summary and journal writing as components of an interactive comprehension model. In J. Zutell & S. McCormick (Eds.), *Learner factors/teacher factors: Issues in literacy research and instruction* (pp. 67–82). Chicago: National Reading Conference.

Joseph, L. M. (2000). Developing first-graders' phonemic awareness, word identification, and spelling: A comparison of two contemporary phonic approaches. *Reading Research and Instruction, 39*(2), 160–169.

Joseph, L. M. (2002). Facilitating word recognition and spelling using word boxes and word sort phonic procedures. *School Psychology Review, 31*, 122–129.

Joseph, L. M., & McCachran, M. (2003). Comparison of a word study phonics technique between students with moderate to mild mental retardation and struggling readers without disabilities. *Education and Training in Developmental Disabilities, 38*(2), 192–199.

Lovett, M. W., Lacerenza, L., & Borden, S. L. (2000). Putting struggling readers on the PHAST track: A program to integrate phonological and strategy-based remedial reading instruction and maximize outcomes. *Journal of Learning Disabilities, 33*(5), 458–476.

Lovett, M. W., Lacerenza, L., Borden, S. L., Frijters, J. C., Steinbach, K. A., & De Palma, M. (2000). Components of effective remediation for developmental reading disability: Combining phonological and strategy-based instruction to improve outcomes. *Journal of Educational Psychology, 92*(2), 263–283.

Mace, F. C., & Kratochwill, T. R. (1988). Self-monitoring: Applications and issues. In J. Witt, S. Elliot, & F. Gresham (Eds.), *Handbook of behavior therapy in education* (pp. 489–502). New York: Pergamon.

MacQuarrie, L. L., Tucker, J. A., Burns, M. K., & Hartman, B. (2002). Comparison of retention rates using traditional, drill sandwich, and incremental rehearsal flash card methods. *School Psychology Review, 31*(4), 584–595.

Maslanka, P., & Joseph, L. M. (2002). A comparison of two phonological awareness techniques between samples of preschool children. *Reading Psychology: An International Quarterly, 23,* 271–288.

McAllister, P. (1994). Using K-W-L for informal assessment. *The Reading Teacher, 47,* 510–511.

McCormick, S. (1999). *Instructing students who have literacy problems* (3rd ed.). Englewood Cliffs, NJ: Prentice-Hall.

Miholic, V. (1994). An inventory to pique students' metacognitive awareness of reading strategies. *Journal of Reading, 38,* 84–86.

Mokhtari, K., & Reichard, C. A. (2002). Assessing students' metacognitive awareness of reading strategies. *Journal of Educational Psychology, 94*(2), 249–259.

Morris, D., Shaw, B., & Perney, J. (1990). Helping low readers in grades 2 and 3: An after school volunteer tutoring program. *The Elementary School Journal, 91,* 133–150.

Ogle, D. M. (1986). K-W-L: A teaching model that develops active reading of expository text. *The Reading Teacher, 39,* 564–570.

Palinscar, A. S., & Brown, A. L. (1984). Reciprocal teaching of comprehension-fostering and comprehension-monitoring activities. *Cognition and Instruction, 1,* 117–175.

Paris, S. G., & Winograd, P. (1990). How metacognition can promote academic learning and instruction. In B. F. Jones & L. Idol (Eds.), *Handbook of reading research* (Vol. 3, pp. 545–561). Hillsdale, NJ: Lawrence Erlbaum Associates.

Pereira-Laird, J. A., & Deane, F. P. (1997). Development and validation of a self-report measure of reading strategy use. *Reading Psychology: An International Journal, 18,* 185–235.

Phillips, L. M. (1988). Young readers' inference strategies in reading comprehension. *Cognition and Instruction, 5,* 193–222.

Pratt-Struthers, J., Struthers, J., & Williams, R. (1983). The effects of the add-a-word spelling program on spelling accuracy during creative writing. *Education and Treatment of Children, 6,* 277–283.

Pressley, M. (1999). Self-regulated comprehension processing and its development through instruction. In L. B. Gambrell, L. M. Morrow, S. Neuman, & M. Pressley (Eds.), *Best practices in literacy instruction* (pp. 90–97). New York: Guilford.

Pressley, M., Woloshyn, V., & Associates. (1995). *Cognitive strategy instruction that really works with children* (2nd ed.). Cambridge, MA: Brookline.

Rasinski, T. (1990). Effects of repeated reading and listening while reading on reading fluency. *Journal of Educational Research, 83,* 147–150.

Routman, R. (1996). *Literacy at the crossroads: Crucial talk about reading, writing, and other teaching dilemmas.* Portsmouth, NH: Heinemann.

Santa, C. M., & Hoien, T. (1999). An assessment of Early Steps: A program for early intervention of reading problems. *Reading Research Quarterly, 34,* 54–79.

Schunk, D. H. (1996). *Learning theories.* Englewood Cliffs, NJ: Prentice-Hall.

Schmitt, M. C. (1990). A questionnaire to measure children's awareness of strategic reading processes. *The Reading Teacher, 43,* 454–461.

Shanahan, T. (1997). Reading–writing relationships, thematic units, inquiry learning. In pursuit of effective integrated literacy instruction. *The Reading Teacher, 51*(1), 12–19.

Shinn, M. R. (Ed.). (1989). *Curriculum-based measurement: Assessing special children.* New York: Guilford.

Tucker, J. A. (1988). *Basic flashcard technique when vocabulary is the goal.* Unpublished teaching material, Andrews University, Berrien Springs, MI.

Urdan, T. (1997). Achievement goal theory: Past results, future directions. In M. Maehr & P. Pintrich (Eds.), *Advances in motivation and achievement* (Vol. 10, pp. 99–141). Greenwich, CT: JAI Press.

Wade, W., Trathen, W., & Schraw, G. (1990). An analysis of spontaneous study strategies. *Reading Research Quarterly, 25,* 147–166.

Winograd, P., & Arrington, H. J. (1999). Best practices in literacy assessment. In L. B. Gambrell, L. M. Morrow, S. Neuman, & M. Pressley (Eds.), *Best practices in literacy instruction* (pp. 210–241). New York: Guilford.

Zimmerman, B. J. (1994). Dimensions of academic self-regulation: A conceptual framework for education. In D. H. Schunk & B. J. Zimmerman (Eds.), *Self-regulation of learning and performance: Issues and educational applications* (pp. 3–21). Hillsdale, NJ: Lawrence Erlbaum Associates.

Zutell, J. (1998). Word sorting: A developmental spelling approach to word study for delayed readers. *Reading and Writing Quarterly: Overcoming Learning Difficulties, 14,* 219–238.

12

Metacognition and Self-Regulation in Literacy

Fredric J. Schreiber
Haskins Laboratories
Yale University

The role of metacognition in education cannot be overstated. For children to be able to reason, they must be aware of the thought processes that occur while they are learning. This is especially significant for children who do not live in environments that challenge them to question the way they think. I have seen this with ESL students who experience great difficulty in literacy. Their challenge is that they are unaware of why they have such difficulty despite great efforts. During effective assessment and instruction, students can become aware of the thought processes that interfere with literacy success. It is my hope that effective teaching strategies that involve metacognition can be developed to help students reach their full literacy potential.

—Lori Wardrup

To suggest that reading is not an activity that relies on a host of interacting cognitive, affective, social, and perceptual capacities would be a difficult argument to uphold. When reading is functional and automatic, it seems to draw on everything we have ever said, seen, heard, tasted, smelled, touched, felt, or imagined. When reading comprehension skills are highly developed, we turn phrases and propositions over in our minds so effortlessly that we forget we are even doing so, and knowledge is easily evidenced in our ability to articulate it. It is through a cycle of integration and reintegration of language and text that literacy emerges, and continues to do so for our entire lives. To some, it may even be like watching a movie in their head. Sometimes we cannot help ourselves from doing so . . .

However, if we are stumped by something, if something does not seem to make sense, if something seems out of place, then we pause, we reread, we reflect, and we reconsider. Alternatives in meaning and structure are examined. Surrounding words are considered for clues as to the nature of our upset and its resolution. We might reread a sentence or paragraph, or flip back a page or two to check if we missed something. We may even read the passage out loud. What is the origin of our uncertainty and the methods we invoke to resolve it? More interesting perhaps is how we came to be aware that something was amiss in the first place.

Whether we are reading without hitches, or if we stumble, at least one thing is common to both situations: We are monitoring, at some level of consciousness, our comprehension of the material we are engaged with. At some level we are using what we know about what reading is, and about how to do *it*. You are doing it now. Conversely, it is likely that we are also aware (again, at some level) about what reading is not, and how not to do *it*. These skills and abilities have taken a significant time and effort to develop, both on our part and with the guidance of others. However, whereas it is true that there are many methods and instructional techniques that help us along the way, the reality is that we each do so in our own way, in our own time, and to the extent to which we are able, because it is something no one can do for us. We can be read to, but no one can read for us. No one can take a poem and transfer its images and meanings directly into our consciousness. We are required to construct meaning for ourselves based on all of our skills, abilities, and experiences.

Although a broad interpretation of literacy includes the subject of writing as well as reading, this chapter focuses on the relations between two theoretical constructs in the cognitive domain (metacognition and self-regulation) and the process of reading, more specifically, the development and promotion of reading comprehension. The two constructs are examined from a historical and conceptual development perspective, and then consideration is given to how they have come to be associated with reading and the emergence of literacy. This is not to suggest that metacognition and self-regulation are the only things that "explain" reading or literacy. On the contrary, an entire body of literature exists that instantiates the relation between the affective domain and reading. It is beyond the scope of this chapter to thoroughly explore these relations. However, research shows it is tenable to assume that metacognition, as both knowledge and regulation of cognition, is related to the process of developing proficiency in reading. Moreover, its significance increases with the emergence of literacy, with this transition characterized by an alteration of emphasis in both reading and instruction from "learning to read" to "reading to learn," a process that may continue throughout our lives.

In addition, the development of reading comprehension and metacognition in the context of reading instruction and instructional programs is considered and a few classroom examples are examined. Finally, consideration is given to what the future may hold in store, and how our children's children may benefit from the application of research findings based on new technologies and emerging research methods and analytic techniques.

ORIGINS OF METACOGNITION AND SELF-REGULATION: THE COGNITIVE DOMAIN

Over the course of several decades, the field of cognitive developmental psychology has produced a large corpus of literature theorizing about and examining the nature of reading ability, achievement, and development, essentially attempting to address how reading manifests in human beings (e.g., Stanovich, 2000). However, the picture is far from clear as the cognitive, behavioral, and environmental dimensions associated with the development of reading and comprehension are myriad, varied, and richly interactive (Mosenthal, Walmsley, & Allington, 1978). What is relatively clear is that individual developmental paths, although sharing fundamental characteristics, are quite dissimilar in both vector and magnitude. This diversity is broadly attributed in the literature to social and asocial environmental factors (Cunningham & Stanovich, 1998; Vaughn, Klingner, & Bryant, 2001; Vygotsky, 1978), biological propensities, and predispositions (Grigorenko, 1999; Piaget, 1971; Riccio & Hynd, 2000; Schwartz, 1988; Stanovich, 1990). It is also apparent that the distinction often made in reading instruction between *learning to read* and *reading to learn* signals a partitioning of both the process and intent of reading instruction that is necessitated by a student's transition from mere reading to literacy—with comprehension heralding the advent of literacy (Cox, 1983).

Flavell's and Wellmann's introduction of the term *metacognition* in the literature on memory and comprehension in reference to individuals' knowledge of their own cognitive processes (Flavell, 1976) and Brown's link of metacognition and self-regulation to reading (Baker & A. L. Brown, 1984; Reeve & A. L. Brown, 1987) began a literature that sought to examine the cognitive structures foundational to the development of literacy.

During the intervening years, cognitive and metacognitive skills have come to be distinguished from one another in that cognitive skills assist an individual in performing a task, whereas metacognitive skills function to facilitate understanding and the *regulation* of performance (Slife & Weaver, 1992). In turn, metacognition has been implicated in both learning and performance (Paris & Jacobs, 1984; Winne & Hadwin, 1998; Zimmerman & Kitsantas, 1997). Specifically, metacognition refers to "one's knowledge concerning one's own cognitive processes" (Flavell, 1976, p. 232) and consists of two primary components, knowledge about cognition and regulation of cognition (Jacobs & Paris, 1987; Palincsar & D. A. Brown, 1987; Paris & Jacobs, 1984; Schraw & Dennison, 1994). Schraw and Dennison (1994), in their assessment of metacognitive awareness, suggested (as did Artzt & Armour, 1992) that knowledge about cognition is composed of "three subprocesses that facilitate the reflective aspect of metacognition" (p. 460): declarative knowledge, or the knowledge one has about one's self and about strategies, or "knowing-that"; procedural knowledge, or the knowledge one has regarding how to use reflective strategies, or "knowing-how"; and conditional knowledge, or "knowing-when or why" to apply procedural or declarative knowledge. These two elements, knowledge of cognition and regulation of cognition, constitute the metacognitive self-regulated aspects of student learning.

Likewise, self-regulation has been described in terms of a multitiered, although cyclical, three-way process: a forethought or planning phase that precedes performance, a performance control or monitoring phase occurring during an activity, and a self-reflective or evaluative phase that occurs after performance (Zimmerman, 1998).

In a reading environment, the expected outcome would be the gradual emergence of comprehension and literacy from simple decoding and word recognition. From a cognitive perspective, there should be an accompanying development and sophistication in the use of and ability to explicate specific aspects of metacognition in the form of knowledge of cognition and regulation of cognition.

METACOGNITION, SELF-REGULATION, AND READING

Myers and Paris (1978) were among the first researchers to discuss metacognition with regard to reading competencies, although the first mention in the literature is by Mosenthal (1977). Myers and Paris investigated sixth graders' perceptions of their personal abilities, cognitive strategies, and task parameters. Baker and Brown (1984) found that metacognition, as comprehension monitoring, was imperative in the acquisition of the capability of reading for meaning and reading for remembering. Remembering required readers to be able to identify important ideas, test their mastery of material, develop effective study strategies, and affectively allocate study time. Other researchers (e.g., Armbruster, Echols, & A. L. Brown, 1982; Borkowski, Ryan, Kurtz, & Reid, 1983; Forrest-Pressley, Waller, & Pressley, 1989; Garner, 1987a; Guthrie, 1982) followed this line of research with similar findings.

This research suggests that the emergence of reading fluency and comprehension, the hallmark of literacy, requires the successful development and integration of several interactive processes: phonological, orthographic, morphological, semantic, and lexical (Cunningham, Perry, & Stanovich, 2001; Seidenberg & McClelland, 1989; Swanson & Alexander, 1997), as well as metacognitive and self-regulatory strategies (Cooper, 1998; Lederer, 1997; Tregaskes & Daines, 1989). The resultant of this grand integration is a high degree of automaticity in the act of reading. Therefore, the emergence of literacy, although based on alphabetic and phonological processing skills that result in decoding accuracy, is necessary but not sufficient. Reading instruction requires a move beyond accuracy to automaticity, to the development of strategies that facilitate an individual's metacognitive awareness and self-regulation in the service of finding meaning in text. Metacognition, as both awareness and regulation of strategic skills, orchestrates the construction of meaning in the expert reader.

However, reading is more than a collection of strategies; rather, it is a process wherein an individual interacts with text for the purpose of constructing meaning. As such, a reader is, as Anderson put it, a motivated "active agent" (as cited in Garner, 1988, p. 1) engaged in his or her own learning; this manner of engagement is characterized as metacognitive self-regulation (Zimmerman, 1989). Research points out that accomplished learners exhibit the capacity to use a variety of metacognitive skills in both the construction of new knowledge and in the process of improving their ability to learn (Artelt, Schiefele, & Schneider, 2001; Borkowski, Schneider, & Pressley, 1989; A. L. Brown, 1981; R. Brown, Pressley, Van Meter, & Schuder, 1996; Forrest-Pressley et al., 1989; Garner, 1987b; Pressley, Johnson, Symons, & McGoldrick, 1989). In this manner, the proficient reader enters into a self-initiated and self-regulated iterative learning cycle reminiscent in structure to the one suggested by Nelson and Narens (1990).

Dickson and colleagues (Dickson, Collins, Simmons, & Kame'enui, 1998) further supported the relation between metacognition and its role in the facilitation of reading comprehension in a thorough review and synthesis of the literature. Regarding this association, they found several areas of convergence: metacognitive knowledge and self-regulation facilitate reading comprehension; metacognitive instruction facilitates reading comprehension; and "motivational beliefs may mediate students' use and benefit from metacognitive knowledge and self-regulation strategies" (p. 305). This lends credibility and support not only to the notion that metacognition as a multilevel construct is strongly associated with successful reading development and the emergence of literacy, but also to the claim that it is teachable.

Consequently, the essential nature of metacognition and self regulation in reading literacy exists in the ability of an individual to detect and correct errors in comprehension. This may require the introduction, deletion, or modification of information associated with existing schema for the purpose of extending or redefining the depth and/or complexity they represent. These modifications are accomplished using existing or novel strategies. Moreover, comprehension failures are tolerated to the extent that they are attributed to a failed strategy that can be corrected rather than to an intrinsic self-deficiency. This is a position Zimmerman and Schunk (2001) presented in a commentary on naïve learners and self-regulated learning as a cyclically interactive process.

READING COMPREHENSION: METACOGNITIVE INSTRUCTION IN THE CLASSROOM

The previous section illustrated the strong association between reading comprehension and metacognition. Additionally, metacognition was described in terms of two constructs: knowledge of cognition and regulation of cognition. The discussion next concentrates on ways in which metacognition and comprehension are linked in the classroom.

In a very simplistic sense, reading instruction consists of two things. There is the "what" should be taught and the "how" to teach it. It is important for teachers to remain aware (metacognitively?) that this framework exists and within it exist alternatives in pedagogical technique and content. Ultimately, it is a matter of emphasis based on student need. Personal philosophy and choice are certainly issues for consideration; however, this consideration should not override evidenced-based methods and their applicability to specific developmental levels and needs. Regardless, the intent of reading instruction is to produce effective readers. In terms of comprehension, this begs the question of what characterizes effective readers, and what constitutes exceptionally effective instruction?

Characteristics of Strategic Readers

Pearson, Roehler, Dole, and Duffy (1992) suggested several characteristics of effective readers that echo within metacognitive literature. They are accomplished in (the use of): (a) prior knowledge, or linking existing knowledge with textual information for clarification or error correction; (b) predicting, proposition making, hypothesizing, or drawing inferences before, during, and after reading; (c) identifying main ideas and summarization, concurrent reading, and synthesis of textual information; (d) questioning to establish a purpose and/or access additional information; and (e) visualization, or the construction of real or mental pictures.

Pressley, El Dinary, Wharton McDonald, and R. Brown (1998), in a study employing a verbal protocol analysis of skilled readers for the purpose of examining "consciously controllable comprehension processes" (p. 43), identified very similar attributes (for a thorough explication, see Pressley & Afflerbach, 1995). One insight that summarizes their findings is: "These readers are constructively responsive in their reading" (p. 43). They went on to itemize indicators in the verbal protocol of this constructive responsivity, most of which are applicable prior to, during, and after reading. This flexibility in the application and adaptation of strategies is the hallmark of the exceptionally effective reader. Interestingly, they found the application of these strategies to be more typical of mature readers. This is made all the more intriguing as comprehension skills have been found to be eminently teachable (e.g., Baumann, 1984; Bruce, 1991; Decker & Sullivan, 1990; Dickson et al., 1998; NRP, 2000; Silven & Vauras, 1992) across grade and ability levels, using a variety of instructional models.

Metacognition and Comprehension Strategy Instruction

The educational environment may best be described as a complex dynamical system. As such, it is multidimensional, nonlinear in nature, and may well display hysteresis effects. Therefore, any reading instructional model that facilitates the development of metacognition, however promising as an evidence-based methodology, must be considered in context and with an eye for adaptation at a fine grain level. What may well work in one situation may be less effective in another depending on the interaction of instructional model itself, students' needs across grade and ability level, and a myriad of internal and external affective and social factors. However, research has shown that certain general categories and characteristics of instruction may be applied effectively and efficiently across a wide spectrum of grade and ability levels in service of developing strategic readers.

As pertains to instructional models in general, a continuum exists between two extremes across two dimensions. In the most general terms, these dimensions address questions relating to how a person learns to read, and how text comprehension occurs. The two are inextricably interrelated and so need to be considered in relation to one another when considering methods of instruction that favor the development of metacognition and self-regulation in reading literacy. The two extremes across these dimensions relate to instructional focus.

On the topic of learning to read, the spectrum is defined by teacher- or student-directed instructional activities. In the case of how a reader interacts with text to extract meaning, there are reader-based and text-based explanations. For each topic, an alternative, interactive explanation accommodates the explanatory power of each of the contrasting positions. First, take a brief look at differing views about how readers extract information from text (reading comprehension). Then consider alternative instructional frameworks and their relation with metacognition and the development of reading literacy. Together, instructional theory and practice in both areas contribute toward an understanding of a dynamical classroom environment that facilitates the development of metacognitive self-regulation and reading literacy.

Reading Instruction Models That Support Metacognitive Development

At the program level, it is a daunting task to select an exemplary instructional model or models that facilitate metacognitive development considering that a recent review of research-based reading and literacy programs (St. John, Loescher, & Bardzell, 2003) identified 17 major reading programs. The job is made less complex if instruction is considered at the framework level. Therefore, consider next three broad categories of instructional programs. Keep in mind our considerations regarding text comprehension when examining three specific examples of classroom teaching that apply what appear to represent best practices.

Holistic reading instructional programs, such as Whole Language, represent an implicit approach to reading instruction that is primarily student centered and based on a sociopsycholinguistic theory of the language learning process (Goodman, 1994; Harste & Burke, 1978; Watson et al., 1984). As pertains to learning, they are characterized as "constructivist" in nature, with an emphasis placed on the development of literacy. As such, they maintain that human beings develop concepts through their own intellectual interactions with and actions on their world. In this view, learners are not passive, but active agents (Anderson, 1984) forming concepts in an inductive manner about what they read or hear by considering the whole, natural language in authentic contexts, not as fragments and pieces of language.

Specific skills instructional programs are teacher-directed and explicit in nature. These direct instruction approaches assign a central role to the teacher in explaining, modeling, and providing opportunities for practice with feedback. Characteristics of this methodology include classroom management styles that tend to minimize interruptive behavior; teachers maintain a strong academic focus using instructional time to intensively engage in learning activities; instructional activities are targeted to the group as a whole or in small groups; specific subject matter information is presented along with solution strategies; and procedural skills are presented as having specific sets of operations (Rosenshine, 1978; Simmons, Baker, L. Fuchs, & D. Fuchs, 1995).

Integrated instructional programs, as might be expected, seek to accommodate the strengths as well as the real or perceived deficiencies associated with the two previous programs. First, they avoid the restrictive nature of teacher-directed skills instruction, thus avoiding turning off some students to reading in general, while still providing the structure other students require. Second, they acknowledge the problems associated with placing much of the responsibility for reading development on the students themselves, yet provide opportunities for student choice and authentic reading experiences. In either case, the role of the teacher is more mercurial, providing direct instruction, or taking on the role of collaborator as required. Examples of this school of thought are the cooperative frameworks (e.g., Reciprocal Peer Teaching, Reciprocal Questioning, Transactional Strategies Instructions, and Socratic Discourse, or Dialogue).

What cooperative frameworks have in common is that as students progress in their ability to read with comprehension, as evidenced in part by their increasingly sophisticated ability to engage in metacognitive self-regulatory activities with the purpose of extracting meaning from text, the role of the teacher changes. Specifically, she may incrementally decrease the emphasis placed on explicit instruction with a concomitant increase in implicit instruction aimed at the development of higher order cognitive processes. At the same time, students assume more responsibility for their own learning and comprehension monitoring, they invoke metacognitive self-regulatory strategies with increasing degrees of automaticity, and they may begin to view both teachers and fellow students as collaborators and resources.

In short, this balanced instructional style is appealing in that it accommodates an interactive and compensatory account of the learning process (both teaching and learning) reminiscent of Stanovich's model of the reading process itself. As such, it acknowledges the value of strategic skills (e.g., activating prior knowledge) while validating the necessity of elemental skills (e.g., decoding), each contributing in kind, as required by students across the spectrum of skills and abilities in the process of comprehension.

Ultimately, the most satisfying aspect of evidence-based balanced approach to comprehension instruction in reading is that it places the student at the center of the learning equation and forgoes the ideological and political disputes of the past several decades. The next section examines several examples of this instructional style as it relates to facilitating metacognition and self-regulation with the intention of improving reading comprehension.

Integrated Instruction in the Classroom

The previous sections identified five characteristics of strategic readers and three reading instructional models and it was suggested that integrated instructional models possess many attributes that facilitate the development of metacognitive and self-regulatory skills. This position is supported by the National Reading Panel (2000), wherein they cited cooperative learning as being an effective, evidence-based instructional model that "produces reliable and replicable near-term transfer" (p. 4-45). In addition, of the seven "strategies" cited as "promising for classroom instruction" (p. 4-42), cooperative learning was the only instructional model mentioned. Moreover, it subsumes the other six (comprehension monitoring, graphic organizers, question generation and answering, and summarizing), all of which are specific metacognitive strategies. Two cooperative learning techniques are described and then several specific classroom examples are provided.

Reciprocal Peer Teaching. As described by A. L. Brown and Palincsar (1989), reciprocal peer teaching (RPT) is "a form of guided, cooperative learning featuring a collaborative learning environment of learning leaders and listeners; expert scaffolding by and adult teacher; and direct instruction, modeling, and practice in the use of four strategies that serve to prop up an emergent dialogue structure" (p. 443). Groups provide cognitive and motivational support in the form of rewards (intrinsic or extrinsic), yet each student is held individually accountable for their own learning. The teacher provides a model of expert behavior, identifies and maintains a clear instructional goal, and monitors the learning leaders. The four principal strategies are questioning, clarifying, summarizing, and predicting, all of which align with metacognitive and self-regulatory activities.

Transactional Strategies Instruction. The difference between RPT and transactional strategies instruction (TSI) is not so much found in instructional methodology as it is in the relation TSI supposes between the text and the reader. A transactional theory of reading, as explicated by Rosenblatt (1969, 1970), suggests that the relationship between reader and text is one of an iterative exchange that acts to define each in terms of the other. She spoke of this relationship in terms of continuum across intent and experience. On the one hand, a reader may assume an efferent stance wherein the engagement of the reader is moderated by the desire or need to extract information from text, perhaps for some purpose. In a sense, this supposes that text meaning is unambiguous, common, explicit, and accessible by deduction. Miscomprehensions and discrepancies in interpretations between parties may be resolved by uncovering the origin and nature of error(s) with the direct assistance and guidance of the teacher. Conversely, readers may arrive at text meaning assuming an aesthetic stance. Herein the reader engages more fully with the text, involving not only intellect but also emotion, recalling prior experiences and sensations as may be evoked during the engagement. Meaning is more ambiguous, highly personal, uncommon, and implicit in nature. Moreover, interpretive differences are not so much resolved as they are employed as a means to explore the nuance of meaning brought to the text by each reader. Ultimately, the most important role the student plays in this instructional process is to select a stance along the continuum; a primary role of the teacher is to open students to the interpretive possibilities inherent in the text. Consequently, the uniqueness of each student is acknowledged and accommodated (Rosenblatt, 1994). Probst (1987) suggested seven implicit principles of transactional instruction:

1. Invite response. Make clear to students that their responses, emotional and intellectual, are valid starting points for discussion and writing.
2. Give ideas time to crystallize. Encourage students to reflect on their responses, preferably before hearing others.
3. Find points of contact among students. Help them to see the potential for communication among their different points of view.
4. Open up the discussion to the topics of self, text, and others. The literary experience should be an opportunity to learn about all three.
5. Let the discussion build. Students should feel free to change their minds, seeking insight rather than victory.
6. Look back to other texts, other discussions, other experiences. Students should connect the reading with other experiences.
7. Look for the next step. What might they read next? About what might they write?

Seminal studies in the area of cooperative learning and reading, with their strong reliance on comprehension strategy instruction and use, were conducted by Slavin and Tanner (1979) and A. L. Brown and Palincsar (1989). It is beyond the scope of this chapter to present instances of all possible strategies, across grade and ability levels. However, the following section examines several examples that illustrate variants on the theme for the purpose of suggesting the applicability of interactive instructional techniques for the development of meta-cognitive self-regulatory strategies. The first presents a broad view of strategy instruction over time in an elementary setting; the second demonstrates an instructional technique in a specific metacognitive strategy at the third- and sixth-grade levels; and the third suggests a variety of ways strategies may be introduced and employed to encourage a more generalized metacognitive awareness across disciplines.

CLASSROOM EXAMPLE 1: WHOLE-CLASS TEXT COMPREHENSION INSTRUCTION

The first example is an intervention implemented by De Corte, Verschaffel, and Van De Ven (2001) intended to improve text comprehension strategies at the upper primary level (fifth grade), with the aim of the research being to explore the effects of learning environment on the development of those strategies. They identified five strategies, four of which they referred to as "comprehension" (activation of prior knowledge, clarification of difficult words, creating schematic text representations, and formulating main ideas), and one as "metacognitive" (self-regulation of the reading comprehension process), although all five are considered metacognitive or capable of inducing metacognitive awareness and activity in the literature (e.g., Pearson et al., 1992; Schraw, 1998). These strategies were taught in a normal class context in an additive-sequential manner over the course of twenty-four 50-minute lessons over 4 months (see Fig. 12.1), which allowed for integration of strategies over time and compensatory instruction as required. An assessment of student progress was made prior to the introduction of a new strategy. A hybrid interactive instructional technique that borrowed aspects of reciprocal and transactional approaches was employed to accommodate teacher modeling, direct instruction, whole-class, and small group discussion, as well as "promote a positive attitude toward reading in general, and reading comprehension in particular" (De Corte, Verschaffel, & Van De Ven, 2001, p. 536).

The study made use of short expository texts (150–300 words) that were developmentally challenging and experientially appropriate. This optimized strategy instruction due to its inherent structure and ability to present marginally difficult content in a clear and concise manner. From a practical perspective, this manner of text is ubiquitous in real-world and classroom learning situations. It is pointed out that existing text was sometimes edited to achieve these standards.

The five text comprehension strategies included:

1. Activation of prior knowledge. This was introduced as a before-reading strategy that addressed the question of "What do I already know about this topic?" Practically, this strategy could be invoked at any point at which the reader encounters information that is either novel or familiar.

Lesson 1	Introduction

Lesson 2-5	Step 1: Activating prior knowledge
	Step 2: Clarifying difficult words
	    Lesson 2: Modeling and whole-class discussion
	    Lesson 3: Whole-class discussion
	    Lesson 4: Small group work
	    Lesson 5: Small group work

Lesson 6	Intermediate test

Lesson 7-13	Step 1: Activating prior knowledge
	Step 2: Clarifying difficult words
	Step 3: Making schematic representations
	    Lesson 7: Modeling and whole-class discussion
	    Lesson 8: Whole-class discussion
	    Lesson 9: Modeling and whole-class discussion
	    Lesson 10: Whole-class discussion
	    Lesson 11: Small group work
	    Lesson 12: Small group work
	    Lesson 13: Small group work

Lesson 14	Intermediate test

Lesson 15-18	Step 1: Activating prior knowledge
	Step 2: Clarifying difficult words
	Step 3: Making schematic representations
	Step 4: Formulating main ideas
	    Lesson 15: Modeling and whole-class discussion
	    Lesson 16: Small group work
	    Lesson 17: Small group work
	    Lesson 18: Small group work

Lesson 19	Intermediate test
Lesson 20-24	Regulating one's reading process
	Lesson 20-24: Individual work

FIG. 12.1. Lesson structure and sequence. Adapted from "Improving Text Comprehension Strategies in Upper Primary School Children: A Design Experiment," by E. De Corte, L. Verschaffel, and A. Van De Ven, 2001, *British Journal of Educational Psychology, 71*(4), p. 25. Adapted with permission from the authors.

2. Clarifying words. Unknown or unfamiliar words were underlined during the text's first reading. Contextual clues to meaning were explored and evaluated. Alternative sources were identified and consulted.

3. Creating schematic text representations. Emergent text themes were considered and mapped using signal words as cues. Four types of schema were available: (a) part–whole, (b) sequence, (c) compare, or (d) cause–effect.

4. Formulating main ideas. Single-sentence text summaries were based on text schemas.

5. Regulating one's own reading process. In this study, this represents the active, autonomous, and self-regulated application of the four comprehension strategies on specific text passages.

Instructional techniques included the following:

1. Teacher modeling, wherein think-aloud procedures externalized internal strategic metacognitive reading comprehension processes and activities. Researchers referred to this in terms of a direct instruction technique, although it is not nearly as constrained as some models make use.

2. Teachers and students next made use of text passages for the purpose of practicing the teacher-modeled strategy within the context of a whole-class discussion. This was primarily a teacher-directed and regulated session that gradually relinquished responsibility for strategy use to students as their confidence and competency developed.

3. Finally, small-group work that built on whole-class discussions was used. This employed reciprocal peer teaching and organizational strategies. The researchers point out that small-group work initially requires a high level of involvement on the part of the teacher as students begin to apply comprehension monitoring strategies. As a practical matter, with several groups engaging in these activities simultaneously, teachers could not be reasonably expected to provide the attention necessary. Consequently, a rotating sequence was established such that small groups not working directly with the teacher were assigned to studies in a different content area. To further facilitate this activity, small groups were made *moderately* (research author's italics) heterogeneous (high–average ability and average–low ability) based on participating teacher recommendation.

As the instruction and integration of strategies progressed, students assumed more responsibility for the application of those strategies. The culminating lessons (20–24) required students to work independently on specific texts, applying strategies as required to complete a worksheet. Students were initially provided with some assistance in the form of a card outlining the four strategies they had studied; a hint for their application was also provided. A fifth item requested students to reflect on their understanding of the text they had just read, and the process by which they arrived at this understanding. It is interesting to note that, from a transactional perspective, this opens an entire spectrum of interpretive responses. As these final lessons progress, the cards, and the scaffolding they provide, were progressively removed. Ultimately, this requires students to function metacognitively in a fully autonomous and self-regulatory manner.

CLASSROOM EXAMPLE 2:
SPECIFIC STRATEGY INSTRUCTION

Modeling is common to all metacognitive instructional techniques. It is useful in that it externalizes the otherwise private dialogue of the accomplished practitioner. This practice is also available to the novice as they develop the metacognitive skill of visualization. Rubman and Salatas Waters (2000) investigated constructive processes (visualizations) as a function of comprehension monitoring in third- and sixth-grade students. Their findings indicate that simple visualization techniques are capable of "enhance(ing) the integration of text propositions and increase(ing) inconsistency detection, particularly for less skilled readers" (p. 503). The particular constructive process they employed was storyboarding, but the effectiveness of the technique for text comprehension can be generalized to graphic organizers as a whole (e.g., Chang, Sung, & Chen, 2002). However, as a scaffolding technique, creating storyboards or cartoons (stereotypical representations) is useful for younger children who are beginning to engage in proposition making and text integration. These visual schemas, which represent the text narrative at the sentence level, externalize the process of reading comprehension extant in skilled, strategic readers, allowing the less skilled reader to move from decoder to meaning-maker. This transition corresponds nicely with moving from a state of learning to read to reading to learn, and marks the transition into literacy.

The practical significance of this visualizing technique is that it requires the use of a metacognitive skill for the purpose of integrating propositions that constitute the meaning of the text. Specifically, the figurative schemata found in a storyboard represent the time sequence of events and the causal relations that connect them. During their formation, missing or incorrect information, or out-of-sequence events, may be uncovered. This activity corresponds to a during-reading and/or after-reading comprehension monitoring procedure. Rubman and Waters, citing earlier research (August, Flavell, & Clift, 1984; Wiener & Cromer, 1967), also described "proficient decoders who demonstrate poor comprehension" (p. 10). These readers have the ability to recall specific propositions but do not integrate them within the context of the story in which they are found. Garner (1981, 1988) called this "piecemeal processing," a propensity among poor readers to "focus on lexical items and on intrasentence consistency, rather on intersentence consistency" (p. 46).

Rubman and Waters' work was conducted as a short-term intervention used to examine a series of specific research questions; consequently, it was not fully developed as a curriculum tool. Therefore, this discussion takes some liberties, in accordance with suggestions offered by the researchers in their discussion and in keeping with an interactive instructional model, in order to illustrate how it could be integrated into a program designed to facilitate the development of metacognitive self-regulatory activities.

Initially, teacher modeling sessions would be conducted to introduce the technique to students. During this time, students as a group would be familiarized with terminology and procedures via discussions about sentence and story meaning, visualization techniques, checking for comprehension errors, and ways to resolve these errors and misconceptions. It should be noted that a degree of skill in reading preexists at a level beyond simple decoding, as the technique assumes comprehension at the sentence level. Specifically, the teacher would have prepared several short stories consisting of approximately 12 lines and at a developmentally appropriate level. In addition, several critical propositions are identified that are fundamental to an understanding of the story and any inconsistencies it might contain. For demonstration and instructional purposes, some stories should contain inconsistencies of either an internal or an external nature.[1] An example of a story with an external inconsistency used by the researchers is titled *A Snowy Day*:

A Snowy Day (External Inconsistency)

It had been snowing all afternoon, but it was not yet cold enough for the pond at the bottom of the yard to freeze over with ice. Tiddles the cat sat by the front door patiently waiting for someone to let her back into the warm house. She had been outside all afternoon watching the children, Tim and Lisa, playing in the snow. The children had wanted to skate on the fish pond, but since it was not cold enough for the pond to freeze, they had built a snowman instead. They were delighted with their snowman that now stood beside the old pine tree. Having finished their snowman, the children were now skating happily across the fish pond, while the fish jumped in and out of the water. Tiddles looked at the fish and dreamed of dinner.

Critical Propositions
   1. Not cold enough for pond to freeze
   2. Children skating across pond
   3. As the children skated, fish jumped

After several teacher modelings have been accomplished, a story with inconsistencies is distributed to each student, who then performs an initial readthrough. Next, students are asked to read the story again and this time to construct a storyboard (a pictorial representation) of the text. To deemphasize individual differences in drawing ability and facilitate storyboard production, the researchers prepared and distributed cutouts of the story items for students to use. During and/or afterward, the teacher inquires if students have discovered any problems (inconsistencies) in the story. If students did not identify any problems in the story after the second reading and the production of the storyboard, then the teacher uses several general and story specific questions to probe for understanding:

---

[1]"An internal inconsistency contains information that is contradictory within the context of the story: however, each individual sentence makes sense in isolation. An external inconsistency occurs when a textual proposition conflicts with a potentially known fact" (Rubman & Salatas Waters, 2000, p. 503).

General Probe Questions:
 1. Did everything in the story make sense?
 2. Was there anything wrong with the story?

A Snowy Day: Story-Specific Probe Questions:
 1. What were the children in the story doing?
 2. Where were the children skating?
 3. What were the fish in the story doing?
 4. Do you think that children can skate while fish are jumping in and out of the water (restatement of the inconsistency the story in question form)?

In addition, students are asked to retell the story in their own words for a memory check of the story's propositions, regardless of whether or not they have identified the inconsistency.

This is a very simple, engaging, and effective technique that can easily be expanded on and woven into a more comprehensive metacognitive instructional program. As the authors pointed out, its strength lies in two specific areas: "It allows children to witness a process to which they may not have access by externalizing both proposition assembly and integration, and the storyboards provide children with an external memory aid" (p. 511).

CLASSROOM EXAMPLE 3: PROMOTING GENERAL KNOWLEDGE AND REGULATION OF COGNITION

The previous classroom examples examined the instruction of relatively specific metacognition and self-regulatory skills and abilities. However, in earlier sections, more general characteristics of metacognition were considered. Specifically, metacognition was described as consisting of two fundamental factors, knowledge of cognition and regulation of cognition, each of which influenced the operation of the other (recall the Nelson & Narens, 1990, model). Additionally, each of these two constructs were said to be composed of three distinct yet highly interactive components. Knowledge of cognition consisted of certain declarative, procedural, and conditional knowledge; regulation of cognition consisted of planning, monitoring, and evaluating.

Schraw published "Promoting General Metacognitive Awareness" (1998) outlining his thoughts on the nature of metacognition and several instructional strategies that would serve to "promote the construction and acquisition of metacognitive awareness" (p. 113). In much the same way as has been presented in the preceding sections, he argued that metacognition is fundamentally different from cognition, it is multidimensional and interactive, and it is domain-general in nature. However, it is his clear explication of specific activities associated with the different dimensions of metacognition that are related here.

These strategies may be included as elements across the spectrum of instructional techniques and subject area. They may be taught individually or as part of a more comprehensive review of the entire system he presented. Specifically, he addressed knowledge of cognition in the form of a strategy evaluation matrix (SEM), summarized in Fig. 12.2.

The SEM identifies five strategies, how they are used, the conditions where they would be best employed, and a consideration of why individuals would choose use them. Schraw offered some insights into the manner in which teachers could use this matrix in a classroom environment.

Strategy	How to Use (D)	When to Use (P)	Why to Use (C)
Skim	Search for headings, highlighted words, previews, summaries	Prior to reading an extended text	Provides conceptual overview, helps to focus one's attention
Slow Down	Stop, read, and think about information	When information seems especially important, or unfamiliar	Enhances focus of one's attention
Activate Prior Knowledge	Pause and think about what you already know. Ask what you don't know	Prior to reading or an unfamiliar task	Makes new information easier to learn and remember
Mental Integration	Relate main ideas. Use these to construct a theme or conclusion	When learning complex information of a deep understanding is needed	Reduces memory load. Promotes deeper level of understanding
Diagrams	Identify main ideas, connect them, list supporting details under main ideas, connect supporting details	When there is a lot of interrelated factual information	Helps identify main ideas, organize them into categories. Reduces memory load

FIG. 12.2.   Knowledge of cognition: Strategy evaluation matrix (SEM) (Schraw, 1998, p. 120).

There are a variety of ways that a teacher could use a SEM in the classroom. The basic idea is to ask students, either individually or in a group, to complete each row of the matrix over the course of the school year. As an illustration, imagine a fourth-grade teacher who introduces the SEM during the first week of school. He informs students that they will focus on one new strategy each month, and should practice four additional strategies throughout the year that can be included in the SEM. Students are given time each week to reflect individually and as a small group about strategy use. Reflection time might include exchanging thoughts with other students about when and where to use a strategy. Extra credit can be earned by interviewing other students in the same grade, or older students, about their strategy use. Students are expected to revise their SEMs as if a mini-portfolio. (pp. 119–120)

He continued with a consideration of regulation of cognition, introducing a regulatory checklist (RC). This checklist (see Fig. 12.3) is based on a problem-solving prompt card similar to one developed by King (1991). Schraw credited this checklist as being useful in "enabling novice learners to implement a systematic regulatory sequence that helps them control their performance" (p. 120).

The power of the SEM and RC is that individually and/or together they provide a framework on which to model the cognitive processes of experts. As these processes are considered to be domain general, it is an easy step to include them as part of instruction in any curricular area. I have found this transference across domains to be the case in an as-yet-to-be-published professional development study at the middle school level. This study, headed by Sheckley and Kehrhahn at the University of Connecticut, examined aspects of in-service professional development. One topic the study's teachers wished to learn more about was self-

---

Planning
1. What is the mature of the task?
2. What is my goal?
3. What kind of information and strategies do I need?
4. How much time and resources will in I need?

Monitoring
1. Do I have a clear understanding of what I am doing?
2. Does the task make sense?
3. Am I reaching my goals?
4. Do I need to make changes?

Evaluating
1. Have I reached my goal?
2. What worked?
3. What didn't work?
4. Would I do things differently next time?

FIG. 12.3.   Regulation of cognition: A regulatory checklist (RC) (Schraw, 1998, p. 121).

regulation strategies, and how these strategies could aid their students. The idea was for them to develop an expert level competency in these strategies, based on Schraw's model, allowing them to model and teach the same strategies to their students using the RC. Initially, the science teacher took the lead, with the expectation that the other subject area teachers would gradually learn and introduce the strategies into their own classrooms. As it turned out, after a short time, the science class students began to develop a degree of competency in the application of the strategies and spontaneously began to adapt and apply them to other situations.

A Word About Metacognitive Assessment

Metacognitive skills and abilities are useful to students in that they facilitate learning, and whereas their use may sometimes be overt and evident, it is more likely they will remain hidden as part of some internal dialogue. As such, ongoing assessment will likely be informal, punctuated by the use of specific measures and instrumentation. Informal evaluations may take place on several levels. A teacher may involve an entire class in a discussion of metacognition, not only offering their own notions but also eliciting responses from students on their learning styles and conceptions of metacognition and self-regulation. Individual conversations can follow on group discussions, allowing the teacher to explore and evaluate specific student abilities and needs that may be used to differentiate instruction as required. These one-on-one sessions also provide opportunities for the student to self-evaluate and solicit positive feedback from the teacher. Finally, keep in mind that the intent of assessment in this area should be focused on encouraging the positive development and application of these skills and abilities in the service of each individual student's learning.

DIRECTIONS FOR FUTURE RESEARCH

Two areas are considered for further investigation. The first is eminently practical and promises near-term application to real-world classroom environments. The second is more esoteric and distal in terms of applicability, although it has the capability to revolutionize reading comprehension instruction in particular and education in general.

The interaction of cognitive and metacognitive strategies and abilities are well represented in the literature of the cognitive domain; there is less representation in the affective domain. Still less is known about the range of interactions found across the cognitive and affective domains (Zeidner, Boekaerts, & Pintrich, 2000). One particular aspect of the affective is motivation and it has been closely associated with metacognition and self-regulation in social cognitive theory (Zimmerman, 1995). This theory suggests that strictly cognitive accounts of instances where students fail to successfully apply metacognitive strategies in naturalistic settings is deficient. This is primarily based on the fact that information theory makes no provision for personal agency within highly complex and interactive social environments.

Another perspective on motivation and metacognition is offered by Wolters (2003) in his consideration of metacognitive structure applied to motivation. He made the argument that it is useful to speak of the knowledge of motivation and the regulation of motivation. Moreover, he pointed out that "strategies for regulating motivation and strategies for regulating cognition are closely related and may be used in conjunction with one another" (p. 192). He went on to outline eight specific motivational strategies found in the literature: self-consequating, goal-oriented self-talk, interest enhancement, environmental structuring, self-handicapping, attribution control, efficacy management, and emotion regulation. The parallel is then extended to knowledge of motivation and its relation with self-regulation across the declarative, procedural, and conditional. This extension to metacognitive theory as it relates to reading comprehension instruction and the interactions it suggests is very exciting.

Although metacognition has been intensively studied for decades, research in the field is still in its infancy with many unresolved questions. Specifically, considering the relationship interplay between text comprehension and metacognitive activities, this chapter brushed on fundamental questions in the field of cognitive neuropsychology. For instance, one topic was how visual stimuli, once perceived, are parsed and utilized in the process of comprehension. One classroom example considered the use of schematic representations that assist in the process of integrating propositions across multiple sentences ("A Snowy Day") for the purpose of comprehension monitoring. What neuropsychological mechanism(s) facilitates this process? What processes constitute syntactic and semantic processing at the sentence level? How can ambiguity be accommodated? Why do these processes sometimes fail? These, and many other questions, are under investigation at research facilities. The question is, how do they translate into practice? The understanding of fundamental cognitive processes could inform instruction at several levels.

As a diagnostic, it might be possible to identify cognitive or perceptual problems as systemic in nature. A recent review of research on the neurobiological basis of reading (Sandak, Mencl, Frost, & Pugh, 2004) cites converging evidence from neuroimaging studies suggesting that skilled reading is associated with the development and integration of specific cortical systems. Some of these circuits are found to be dysfunctional in children with developmental dyslexia. They also note compensatory activity in other neural circuits and suggested that if this can be confirmed using imaging and behavioral measures, then associated reading deficits may be better understood, and a framework will be available for the interpretation of developmental changes and evaluating remediation measures. Perhaps it might also be possible to use this methodology to design and evaluate instructional methods that optimize existing developmental propensities. In a regular classroom instructional setting, this might translate into providing teachers with specialized knowledge and extending the range of instructional techniques and curricular material available to facilitate the development of students' understanding.

CONCLUSIONS

Metacognition is a relatively recent addition to educational theory and practice. However, it has proven to be an exceptionally potent concept on which to model reading comprehension instruction. Its strength and vitality stem from its deep roots within the field of developmental cognitive psychology and a growing body of evidence-based instructional models. It also appears robust in its ability to be incorporated into developmental theories across domains while adding explanatory power to the synthesis of ideas and practices in the service of promoting literacy.

METACONNECTION FOR CHAPTER 12

In chapter 12, Schreiber provides several lessons with step-by-step actions that address the development of metacognition and self-regulation through literacy instruction in a classroom setting. In support of these practices, the reader is introduced to the fundamental concepts in this area. In addition, both general and critical propositions are examined. The magic of this chapter is that Schreiber weaves past practices with innovative new methods in such a way that both are relevant and mutually reinforcing. Schreiber also reports on the benefits students can gain by the implementation of the instructional approaches reviewed. In conclusion, the direction of future research is considered. The goal of this chapter is to enable you to develop your own instructional program before you read chapter 13, which describes a day in a creative classroom where the methods you have just read about have been adapted and expanded upon.

REFERENCES

Anderson, G. S. (1984). *A whole language approach to reading.* Lanham, MD: University Press of America.

Armbruster, B. B., Echols, C. H., & Brown, A. L. (1982). The role of metacognition in reading to learn: A developmental perspective. *Volta Review, 84*(5), 45–56.

Artelt, C., Schiefele, U., & Schneider, W. (2001). Predictors of reading literacy. *European Journal of Psychology of Education, 16*(3), 363–383.

Artzt, A. F., & Armour-Thomas, E. (1992). Development of a cognitive-metacognitive framework for protocol analysis of mathematical problem solving in small groups. *Cognition and Instruction, 9*(2), 137–175.

August, D. L., Flavell, J. H., & Clift, R. (1984). Comparison of comprehension monitoring of skilled and less skilled readers. *Reading Research Quarterly, 20*(1), 39–53.

Baker, L., & Brown, A. L. (1984). Metacognitive skills and reading. In P. D. Pearson (Ed.), *Handbook of reading research* (pp. 353–394). New York: Longman.

Baumann, J. F. (1984). The effectiveness of a direct instruction paradigm for teaching main idea comprehension. *Reading Research Quarterly, 20*(1), 93–115.

Bawden, R., & Duffy, G. G. (1979, April). *Teacher conceptions of reading and the impact on instructional behavior.* Paper presented at the annual meeting of the International Reading Association, Atlanta, GA.

Borkowski, J. G., Ryan, E. B., Kurtz, B. E., & Reid, M. K. (1983). Metamemory and metalinguistic development: Correlates of children's intelligence and achievement. *Bulletin of the Psychonomic Society, 21*(5), 393–396.

Borkowski, J. G., Schneider, W., & Pressley, M. (1989). The challenges of teaching good information processing to learning disabled students. *International Journal of Disability, Development and Education, 36*(3), 169–185.

Brown, A. L. (1981). Learning to learn: On training students to learn from texts. *Educational Researcher, 10*(2), 14–21.

Brown, A. L., & Palincsar, A. S. (1989). Guided, cooperative learning and individual knowledge acquisition. In L. B. Resnick (Ed.), *Knowing, learning, and instruction: Essays in honor of Robert Glaser* (pp. 393–451). Hillsdale, NJ: Lawrence Erlbaum Associates.

Brown, R., Pressley, M., Van Meter, P., & Schuder, T. (1996). A quasi-experimental validation of transactional strategies instruction with low-achieving second-grade readers. *Journal of Educational Psychology, 88*(1), 18–37.

Bruce, M. E. (1991). Reciprocal teaching and transenvironmental programming: A program to facilitate the reading comprehension of students with reading difficulties. *RASE: Remedial and Special Education, 12*(5), 44–54.

Chang, K. E., Sung, Y. T., & Chen, I. D. (2002). The effect of concept mapping to enhance text comprehension and summarization. *Journal of Experimental Education, 71*(1), 5–23.

Cooper, J. M. (1998). An exploratory study of the metacognition of verbally gifted/learning disabled learners with and without reading disabilities. *Dissertation Abstracts International Section A: Humanities and Social Sciences, 58*(12-A), 4559.

Cox, C. (1983). Learning to read, reading to learn: An interview with Jeanne S. Chall. *Curriculum Review, 22*(5), 11–15.

Cunningham, A. E., Perry, K. E., & Stanovich, K. E. (2001). Converging evidence for the concept of orthographic processing. *Reading and Writing, 14*(5–6), 549–568.

Cunningham, A. E., & Stanovich, K. E. (1998). What reading does for the mind. *American Educator, 22*(1–2), 8–15.

De Corte, E., Verschaffel, L., & Van De Ven, A. (2001). Improving text comprehension strategies in upper primary school children: A design experiment. *British Journal of Educational Psychology, 71*(4), 531–559.

Decker, B. C., & Sullivan, B. W. (1990). Metacognitive reading strategies for diploma seeking special education students. *Journal of Instructional Psychology, 17*(3), 107–117.

Dickson, S. V., Collins, V. L., Simmons, D. C., & Kame'enui, E. J. (1998). Metacognitive strategies: Instructional and curricular bases and implications. In D. C. Simmons & E. J. Kame'enui (Eds.), *What reading research tells us about children with diverse learning needs: Bases and basics* (pp. 361–380). Mahwah, NJ: Lawrence Erlbaum Associates.

Flavell, J. H. (1976). Metacognitive aspects of problem solving. In L. B. Resnick (Ed.), *The nature of intelligence* (pp. 231–235). Hillsdale, NJ: Lawrence Erlbaum Associates.

Forrest-Pressley, D., Waller, T. G., & Pressley, M. (1989). Forrest-Pressley and Waller (1984) concluded that metacognition about reading is related to reading performance: A comment about Jacobs and Paris (1987). *Educational Psychologist, 24*(2), 207–210.

Garner, R. (1981). Monitoring of passage inconsistency among poor comprehenders: A preliminary test of the "Piecemeal Processing" explanation. *Journal of Educational Research, 74*(3), 159–162.

Garner, R. (1987a). *Metacognition and reading comprehension*. Norwood, NJ: Ablex.

Garner, R. (1987b). Strategies for reading and studying expository text. *Educational Psychologist, 23*(3–4), 299–312.

Garner, R. (1988). *Metacognition and reading comprehension* (2nd ed.). Norwood, NJ: Ablex.

Goodman, K. S. (1994). Reading, writing, and written texts: A transactional sociopsycholinguistic view. In R. B. Ruddell (Ed.), *Theoretical models and processes of reading* (4th ed., pp. 1093–1130). Newark, DE: International Reading Association.

Grigorenko, E. L. (1999). Heredity versus environment as the basis of cognitive ability. In R. J. Sternberg (Ed.), *The nature of cognition* (pp. 665–696). Cambridge, MA: MIT Press.

Guthrie, J. T. (1982). Research views: Metacognition: Up from flexibility. *Reading Teacher, 35*(4), 510–512.

Jacobs, J. E., & Paris, S. G. (1987). Children's metacognition about reading: Issues in definition, measurement, and instruction. *Educational Psychologist, 22*(3–4), 255–278.

King, A. (1991). Effects of training in strategic questioning on children's problem-solving performance. *Journal of Educational Psychology, 83*(3), 307–317.

Lederer, J. M. (1997). Reciprocal teaching of social studies in elementary classrooms. *Dissertation Abstracts International Section A: Humanities and Social Sciences, 58*(1-A), 0073.

Mosenthal, P. (1977). *Children's metacognitive reproductive and reconstructive comprehension in listening, reading silently, and reading aloud: A problem of psychosocial development*. Paper presented at the 27th annual meeting of the National Reading Conference, New Orleans, LA.

Mosenthal, P., Walmsley, S., & Allington, R. (1978). Word recognition reconsidered: Toward a multi-context model. *Visible Language, 12*(4), 448–468.

Myers, M., & Paris, S. G. (1978). Children's metacognitive knowledge about reading. *Journal of Educational Psychology, 70*(5), 680–690.

National Reading Panel (NRP). (2000). *Report of the National Reading Panel. Teaching children to read: An evidence-based assessment of the scientific research literature on reading and its implications for reading instruction: Reports of the subgroups*. Washington, DC: U.S. Government Printing Office.

Nelson, T. O., & Narens, L. (1990). Metamemory: A theoretical framework and new findings. In A. C. Graesser (Ed.), *The psychology of learning and motivation* (Vol. 26, pp. 125–173). New York: Academic Press.

Palincsar, A. S., & Brown, D. A. (1987). Enhancing instructional time through attention to metacognition. *Journal of Learning Disabilities, 20*(2), 66–75.

Paris, S. G., & Jacobs, J. E. (1984). The benefits of informed instruction for children's reading awareness and comprehension skills. *Child Development, 55*(6), 2083–2093.

Pearson, P. D., Roehler, L. R., Dole, J. A., & Duffy, G. G. (1992). Developing expertise in reading comprehension. In S. J. Samuels & A. E. Farstrup (Eds.), *What research has to say about reading instruction* (pp. 145–199). Newark, DE: International Reading Association.

Piaget, J. (1971). The epigenetic system and the development of cognitive functions. In M. H. Johnson (Ed.), *Brain development and cognition: A reader* (pp. 31–38). Malden, MA: Blackwell.

Pressley, M., & Afflerbach, P. (1995). *Verbal protocols of reading: The nature of constructively responsive reading.* Hillsdale, NJ: Lawrence Erlbaum Associates.

Pressley, M., El Dinary, P. B., Wharton McDonald, R., & Brown, R. (1998). Transactional instruction of comprehension strategies in the elementary grades. In D. H. Schunk & B. J. Zimmerman (Eds.), *Self regulated learning: From teaching to self reflective practice* (pp. 42–56). New York: Guilford.

Pressley, M., Johnson, C. J., Symons, S., & McGoldrick, J. A. (1989). Strategies that improve children's memory and comprehension of text. *Elementary School Journal, 90*(1), 3–32.

Probst, R. E. (1987). *Transactional theory in the teaching of literature. ERIC Digest.* Urbana, IL: ERIC Clearinghouse on Reading and Communication Skills.

Reeve, R. A., & Brown, A. L. (1987). Metacognition reconsidered: Implications for intervention research. *Journal of Abnormal Psychology, 13,* 343–356.

Riccio, C. A., & Hynd, G. W. (2000). Measurable biological substrates to verbal-performance differences in Wechsler scores. *School Psychology Quarterly, 15*(4), 386–399.

Rosenblatt, L. M. (1969). Towards a transactional theory of reading. *Journal of Reading Behavior, 1*(1), 31–49.

Rosenblatt, L. M. (1970). *Literature as exploration.* London: Heinemann.

Rosenblatt, L. M. (1994). The transactional theory of reading and writing. In R. B. Ruddell (Ed.), *Theoretical models and processes of reading* (4th ed., pp. 1057–1092). Newark, DE: International Reading Association.

Rosenshine, B. (1978, March). *Instructional principles in direct instruction.* Paper presented at the annual meeting, American Educational Research Association, Toronto, Canada.

Rubman, C. N., & Salatas Waters, H. (2000). A,B seeing: The role of constructive processes in children's comprehension monitoring. *Journal of Educational Psychology, 92*(3), 503–514.

Sandak, R., Mencl, W., Frost, S. J., & Pugh, K. R. (2004). The neurobiological basis of skilled and impaired reading: Recent findings and new directions. *Scientific Studies of Reading, 8*(3), 273–292.

Schraw, G. (1998). Promoting general metacognitive awareness. *Instructional Science, 26*(1–2), 113–125.

Schraw, G., & Dennison, R. S. (1994). Assessing metacognitive awareness. *Contemporary Educational Psychology, 19*(4), 460–475.

Schwartz, S. (1988). A comparison of componential and traditional approaches to training reading skills. *Applied Cognitive Psychology, 2*(3), 189–201.

Seidenberg, M. S., & McClelland, J. L. (1989). A distributed, developmental model of word recognition and naming. *Psychological Review, 96*(4), 523–568.

Silven, M., & Vauras, M. (1992). Improving reading through thinking aloud. *Learning and Instruction, 2*(2), 69–88.

Simmons, D. C., Baker, J., Fuchs, L., & Fuchs, D. (1995). Teacher-directed reading instruction in the mainstream: A call for instructional reform. *Reading and Writing Quarterly: Overcoming Learning Difficulties, 11*(1), 19–36.

Slavin, R. E., & Tanner, A. M. (1979). Effects of cooperative reward structures and individual accountability on productivity and learning. *Journal of Educational Research, 72*(5), 294–298.

Slife, B. D., & Weaver, C. A. (1992). Depression, cognitive skill, and metacognitive skill in problem solving. *Cognition and Emotion, 6*(1), 1–22.

St. John, E. P., Loescher, S. A., & Bardzell, J. S. (2003). *Improving reading and literacy in grades 1–5: A resource guide to research-based programs.* Thousand Oaks, CA: Sage.

Stanovich, K. E. (1990). Concepts in developmental theories of reading skill: Cognitive resources, automaticity, and modularity. *Developmental Review, 10*(1), 72–100.

Stanovich, K. E. (2000). Matthew effects in reading: Some consequences of individual differences in the acquisition of literacy. In *Progress in understanding reading: Scientific foundations and new frontiers.* New York: Guilford.

Swanson, H. L., & Alexander, J. E. (1997). Cognitive processes as predictors of word recognition and reading comprehension in learning-disabled and skilled readers: Revisiting the specificity hypothesis. *Journal of Educational Psychology, 89*(1), 128–158.

Tregaskes, M. R., & Daines, D. (1989). Effects of metacognitive strategies on reading comprehension. *Reading Research and Instruction, 29*(1), 52–60.

Vaughn, S., Klingner, J. K., & Bryant, D. P. (2001). Collaborative strategic reading as a means to enhance peer-mediated instruction for reading comprehension and content-area learning. *Remedial and Special Education, 22*(2), 66–74.

Vygotsky, L. S. (1978). *Mind in society: The development of higher psychological processes.* In M. J.-S. Cole, Vera; Scribner, Sylvia; Souberman, Ellen (Eds.), Cambridge, MA: Harvard University Press.

Wiener, M., & Cromer, W. (1967). Reading and reading difficulty: A conceptual analysis. *Harvard Educational Review, 37*(4), 620–643.

Winne, P. H., & Hadwin, A. F. (1998). Studying as self-regulated learning. In D. J. Hacker (Ed.), *Metacognition in educational theory and practice* (pp. 277–304). Mahwah, NJ: Lawrence Erlbaum Associates.

Wolters, C. A. (2003). Regulation of motivation: Evaluating an underemphasized aspect of self-regulated learning. *Educational Psychologist, 38*(4), 189–205.

Zeidner, M., Boekaerts, M., & Pintrich, P. R. (2000). Self-regulation: Directions and challenges for future research. In P. R. Pintrich (Ed.), *Handbook of self regulation* (pp. 749–768). San Diego, CA: Academic Press.

Zimmerman, B. J. (1989). A social cognitive view of self-regulated academic learning. *Journal of Educational Psychology, 81*(3), 329–339.

Zimmerman, B. J. (1995). Self-regulation involves more than metacognition: A social cognitive perspective. *Educational Psychologist, 30*(4), 217–221.

Zimmerman, B. J. (1998). Developing self-fulfilling cycles of academic regulation: An analysis of exemplary instructional models. In D. H. Schunk & B. J. Zimmerman (Eds.), *Self-regulated learning: From teaching to self-reflective practice* (pp. 1–19). New York: Guilford.

Zimmerman, B. J., & Kitsantas, A. (1997). Developmental phases in self-regulation: Shifting from process goals to outcome goals. *Journal of Educational Psychology, 89*(1), 29–36.

Zimmerman, B. J., & Schunk, D. H. (2001). Reflections on theories of self-regulated learning and academic achievement. In B. J. Zimmerman & D. H. Schunk (Eds.), *Self regulated learning and academic achievement: Theoretical perspectives* (2nd ed., pp. 289–307). Mahwah, NJ: Lawrence Erlbaum Associates.

13

Integrating Comprehension and Metacognitive Reading Strategies

Stephen J. Donndelinger
University of Notre Dame

I've taught third, fourth, and fifth grade for twelve years. I've known that many metacognitive processes germinated just below the surface in even my nine-year-old readers' minds. I've never known how to develop these metacognitive abilities. I want this chapter to describe how I, and my students, can recognize and assess the rich understandings that grow from and emerge through their broad and deep comprehension of text.

—Amelia McWilliams

One of the common themes in standard educational psychology is metacognition (Woolfolk, 2004). Those familiar with metacognition often describe it as "thinking about thinking." A skill, such as decoding words on a page, becomes automatic as the unconscious mind takes over the experience or performance of that task. The conscious is thus left to engage in a second degree of discursive processing. If musicians are technically proficient, for example, they can put the majority of their thought effort into the expression and delivery of the performance. The higher order of conscious thought in metacognition allows for deeper and greater control over one's mental activity.

More practically, metacognition has been applied to educational practice across all domains. For example, Polya's (1957) stages of problem solving—understand, plan, solve, and check—represent the beginnings of a consciously directed thought process that has begun to saturate mainstream instruction. The basis for using metacognition as the foundation for research-based instruction is that it counters the view that students passively absorb what they hear, see, and read. Constructivist theories demand that students be taught how to connect old ideas with new ones, how to think about what they learn and how they learn, how to value what they learn so that they are motivated to learn more of it, and ultimately how to build that knowledge into a schema that can synthesize progressively larger quantities of information (Woolfolk, 2004).

This chapter is about metacognitive reading. The background of the problem lies in the attempt to reconcile the tenets of constructivist and metacognitive theory with my day-to-day practice as a fourth-grade teacher. Granted, there is no shortage of research, techniques, or practitioners that are working on the task. I am in my own learning process, however, which demands that I construct my own best model for teaching. As I learn how to teach, I find that several decades of good research and ideas have indeed allowed me to add even more muscle to this paradigm, which may well become the 21st century's best practice for how to teach reading. This chapter, then, seeks answers to the following questions:

1. Can we name and describe the metacognitive processes used in expert reading?
2. How can these metacognitive processes be organized and taught so as to promote successful reading development in the elementary years?
3. What questions are left remaining with respect to this specific strategy and metacognitive reading comprehension?

HISTORICAL PERSPECTIVE AND RESEARCH

One of the first techniques to apply a metacognitive-like (since the term was not around at the time) strategy to the reading of nonfiction was SQ3R or PQ4R (Thomas & Robinson, 1972). Skills like previewing, questioning, reading, reflecting, reciting, and reviewing (PQ4R) at least began to approach what we have today. Concurrently, a procedure known as *reciprocal teaching* (Palincsar & Brown, 1984) helped take further steps from a basal-reader approach into a process-driven view of reading. The method involves modeling, guided practice, and cooperative implementation of a reading process that occurs sequentially: predicting, questioning, visualizing (a stage added in more recent versions), clarifying, and summarizing. It should be praised for its masterful use of scaffolding to get students thinking about underlying processes of reading.

Other research shows that rigid sequential models like PQ4R and reciprocal teaching are nevertheless inadequate. The metacognitive skills used in authentic reading seldom, if ever, occur in the step and sequence described. In fact, they are more complex than most 20th-century researchers imagined. This is where the work of Pressley and Afflerbach (1995) opened a new era in the understanding of the reading process. Their seminal work, *Verbal Protocols of Reading*, has become a nearly definitive description of how people read well. *Verbal protocols* is a technical term for the method whereby practitioners of a process verbalize their thoughts in order for the researcher to ascertain the thought processes being used to perform that skill.

Although many teachers (myself included, until recently) have not heard of verbal protocol analysis, the term *think-aloud* has become popular. The think-aloud is the equivalent to verbal protocol analysis, only for purposes of instruction, and usually with less rigor. Think-alouds (Israel & Massey, chap. 10, this volume) enable teachers to read aloud, and then stop to recite what they are thinking while reading. For example, this becomes useful when trying to demonstrate how to make an inference—a process not otherwise easy to explain.

Pressley and Afflerbach (1995) took strong adult readers and used think-aloud-type research to portray the inner workings of strong comprehension processing. It turns out to be a process largely organized by metacognition. They used their data to synthesize insights of previous reading process models, including reader response theory, metacognition (Baker & Brown, 1984), and constructivist schema theory. The result was something Pressley and Afflerbach (1995) called "constructively responsive reading." It takes into account that good readers approach text with a sense of purpose (or at least having to discover a purpose) and a massive amount of prior knowledge that will form the "standard" against which the text is previewed, read, interpreted, understood or misunderstood, and eventually evaluated. Reading is presented as a process of continually comparing and contrasting the known and the new, problem solving, and shifting strategies as the reader attempts to reconcile text with expectations.

According to constructively responsive reading, the metacognitive processes used to move beyond the automated processes of seeing, pronouncing, and recognizing words are vast and recursive, rather than sequential. Pressley and Afflerbach (1995) argued that constructively responsive reading is in fact expert reading, using the term *expert* against the backdrop of research in that area. In order for expertise to develop in any skill, Pressley and Afflerbach pointed to the importance of long-term (several years to a lifetime) engagement with that skill in authentic contexts. This is bad news for the analytical approach to reading, where every skill is broken down in isolation. Rather, Pressley and Afflerbach (1995) contended that early reading experiences must be rich, bringing a full variety of complete high quality reading materials. In addition, students must constantly be pushed into books that require demanding processing and problem solving, echoing Vygotsky's (1978) concept of the zone of proximal development.

Metacognition is a central part of the contemporary educational paradigm. Thus far, I have summarized early reading methods that began teaching with, if not explicitly building on, metacognitive skills. I have explained how *Verbal Protocols of Reading* (Pressley & Afflerbach, 1995) helped us understand that any approach to developing long-term success in students' reading must steer from the analytical and push into demanding authentic literature. Furthermore, the whole structure with which we teach metacognition in reading will need to be reformulated. The next section explains how I began to build my own strategy for teaching metacognition in reading.

NEW IDEAS AND HOW WE CAN MOVE
THE FIELD FORWARD

Consider a simple question: Is there a connection between the metacognitive reading skills that have been emerging in the literature and the more traditional or lower level comprehension skills? Is there an effective way to teach comprehension at both levels? Most mainstream comprehension instruction assumes that learning a collection of basic skills—cause–effect, main idea–details, sequence, inference, compare–contrast, fact–opinion, and so on—leads to successful reading. My reading as an educator, however, suggests that we need a system that allows students to develop comfort, ownership, and autonomy in the reading process to the extent that they can read and discuss literature without feeling restricted by artificial, separate comprehension skills. This is not to say that traditional comprehension tasks are irrelevant; rather, the way they have been taught does not meet the constructivist expectation of authentic, process-oriented learning. In response to the question, I was told that this is all new, and thus felt compelled to embark on my own preliminary investigation of the problem.

I surmised that students respond best to something they can easily internalize, which meant simplifying the vocabulary. I sought an acronym that would group the traditional text comprehension processes under the umbrella of commonly researched metacognitive processes. I started with predicting, inferring, overviewing, visualizing, asking questions, and summarizing. These represented a sampling of the terms borrowed from reciprocal teaching and other early models. I changed the order, sought out synonyms, and combined processes (an exploration period of nearly 2 weeks) until I created PROMISE—Prior knowledge, Reflection, (Organizational) Overview, Monitoring, Inquiry, Sensitivity, and Evaluation.

I reviewed *Verbal Protocols of Reading* (Pressley & Afflerbach, 1995) to reassure myself that each PROMISE process does constitute a relevant facet of the metacognitive reading experience. I took my cues from *Verbal Protocols*, but began defining the processes in my own words. Prior knowledge is the foundation of metacognitive reading. Maintaining awareness and constant reference back to one's prior knowledge enables every other process. Overviewing, based on prior knowledge and the anticipation of new knowledge, is critical for setting up a successful comprehension effort. It helps verify the reader's purpose while generating the questions that will drive inquiry. If the overview is a forward-looking process, reflection is its retrospective counterpart. Reflection drives the summary and synthesis of details into main ideas and themes from which further evaluations and inquiry may be made.

Monitoring stands firmly in the center of a reading experience. It helps readers determine if they are ready to move on to the next stage of reading and provides possible courses of action should some awareness of misunderstanding arise. Inquiry, or questioning, is both the result of and generator of the thoughts that occur during overview, reflection, and monitoring. Sensitivity embraces the reader's affective response to the images, descriptions, tone, figurative language, and literary devices of the text. Sensitivity also grows from the reader's empathy (again, prior knowledge) for the situations that characters and real people face. It is the stepping stone to evaluation in which the reader judges the elements within the text, the quality of the text itself, and the underlying success or motivations of the writer.

The point of this careful explanation of terms is to help those unfamiliar with metacognitive strategies begin to understand how the terms are defined; to show that whereas the terminology of metacognitive reading is to some degree a matter of semantics, the PROMISE instructional strategy does reflect those that our best research has named; and, most critical for the remainder of this chapter, it shows that it is impossible to separate and isolate these reading processes as in traditional methods, because each reaches into and across all the others. The PROMISE acronym is designed to help students learn and remember the metacognitive thought process, but—contrary to its predecessors—it should not be taught in discrete, sequenced steps. The PROMISE strategy constitutes a fluid web, which means that movement from one domain to the next is determined by the readers' needs and the characteristics of the text—not a prescribed cycle. As we look for ways to instruct students in the use of metacognition, it is essential to convey the weblike and recursive nature of the process. It will not be enough to teach or practice them one at a time (Block, 2004).

I will share an example that illustrates this last point. I recently conducted a lesson in which the objective was for students to compare "Gluskabe" (Gluskabi) stories (retold by Joseph Bruchac) as a way of studying the form and purpose of myth. I kept trying to help students decide whether each point of comparison represented one process or another until I realized that labeling and using one process at a time would be inadequate. Any legitimate point during a comparison of story types would involve—at least—*reflection* on the story currently being read, reference to *prior knowledge* about other stories like it, and finally, *inquiry* into the specific similarities and differences between the two stories. Combining elements of prior knowledge, reflection, and inquiry to produce one good observation about the nature of a Gluskabe myth was a testament to the sophistication of reading at its best.

As I looked at what I first created, I decided that I could not have conjured a more encouraging word to serve as the instructional vehicle for metacognitive reading. That is but a tribute to what young educators can do when they combine creativity, determination, patience, and a little luck. Once the simplistic marvel of my idea wore off, however, I was left with the task of validating its merits in a classroom with real students. The next section describes my efforts and their results.

SUGGESTIONS FOR INSTRUCTION
AND PRACTICE

The following three methods have been developed for teaching and practicing the PROMISE reading strategy.

The PROMISE Thought Web

There are two forms of the thought web, the "Literature" form and the "Non-fiction" form, which can be examined in Figs. 13.1 and 13.2, respectively. The web is fundamentally a graphic organizer. The metacognitive processes are organized according to how they are most effectively introduced during reading. This is not a sequential model; however, some metacognitive processes will most likely be activated earlier in reading than others and will carry different weight as reading proceeds.

Prior knowledge is necessary for all phases of reading, hence it is the central process on both PROMISE instructional charts. In addition to this, most readers activate overview and inquiry early in the reading process. The top left corner of the chart shows this priority. As focused reading begins, monitoring should become ongoing and constantly in reference to the products of prior knowledge, inquiry, and overviewing. Along with monitoring, the student will likely activate sensitivity, which includes most visual, emotional, and interpretive comprehension of the text.

Developing a healthy sensitivity to the subtleties of text is an important step for reflection and evaluation—the last metacognitive processes to become fully engaged. Do not misunderstand what I am saying: A good reader will begin reflecting and evaluating as reading begins, but these processes take on more significance as reading progresses. There is not much overview or inquiry taking place during the final chapters of a novel. Rather, readers are busy reflecting on and evaluating the decisions, results, and themes, all the while monitoring to see how well those episodes sit with their own experience in such situations. The thought web, therefore, is organized such that the reading process generally develops from top left to bottom right. Once all processes are introduced and in play, however, the two-way arrows are a reminder that numerous legitimate metacognitive thought paths could result from any given reading experience.

Inside each box or bubble of both thought webs are phrase beginnings that leave open pauses for elaboration, followed by a more defined series of choices. Students use these "leading phrases" to prompt metacognitive thinking. The

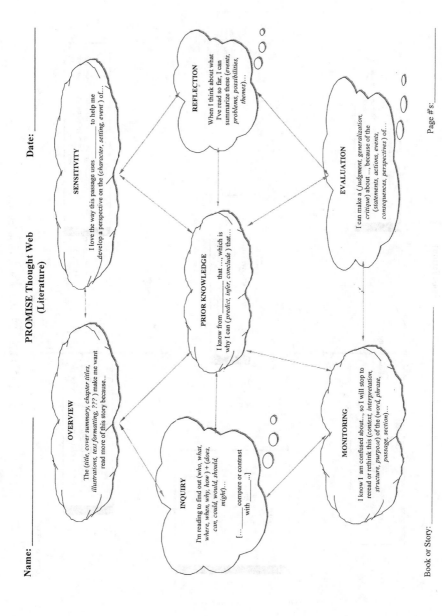

PROMISE Thought Web
(Literature)

Name: _____   Date: _____

SENSITIVITY

I love the way this passage uses _____ to help me develop a perspective on the *(character, setting, event)* of...

REFLECTION

When I think about what I've read so far, I can summarize these *(events, problems, possibilities, themes)*...

EVALUATION

I can make a *(judgment, generalization, critique)* about ... because of the *(statements, actions, events, consequences, perspectives)* of...

OVERVIEW

The *(title, cover summary, chapter titles, illustrations, text formatting, ???)* make me want read more of this story because...

PRIOR KNOWLEDGE

I know from _____ that ... which is why I can *(predict, infer, conclude)* that...

INQUIRY

I'm reading to find out *(who, what, where, when, why, how)* + *(does, can, could, would, should, might)*...

[... _____ compare or contrast with _____]

MONITORING

I know I am confused about... so I will stop to reread or rethink this *(context, interpretation, structure, purpose)* of the *(word, phrase, passage, section)*...

Book or Story: _____   Page #'s: _____

FIG. 13.1.   PROMISE web (literature).

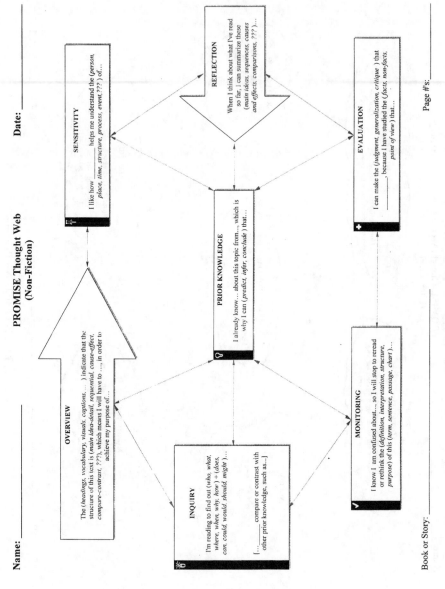

FIG. 13.2. PROMISE web (nonfiction).

phrases are designed to start the reader's mind thinking along certain lines, but then they leave significant gaps for filling in substance. The structure of each phrase helps define the skill for the student, and it builds awareness of the traditional text-level comprehension vocabulary (cause–effect, compare–contrast, generalization, etc.). By putting the common vocabulary of reading instruction under the umbrella of the PROMISE instructional strategy, I hope students will use those skills in a more natural and useful manner.

Close examination of the leading phrases on the literature and nonfiction charts reveals subtle distinctions in wording. This reflects how the reading of fiction and nonfiction requires a different application of the same metacognitive activities. Consider the overview, which plays a less salient role in fiction, where the norm is front to back reading. Taking time to review one's familiarity with the title, author, genre, and cover illustrations will help activate appropriate schema, while generating a whole series of predictions and questions to guide reading throughout the novel. If the overview is a convenience in reading fiction, it is indispensable for the successful reading of nonfiction. Nonfiction sources may or may not be designed for front to back reading, and useful information can be gleaned from careful reading of the table of contents, indexes, graphic aids, and even isolated segments of text. Similarly, the role of sensitivity must be redefined in nonfiction, where graphics, sidebars, and glossaries take the place of fiction's literary elements and devices. These adjustments are referred to particularly in light of content reading (i.e., science and social studies texts), where students should learn to read more independently, judiciously, and critically as they get older.

Another difference between literature and nonfiction webs includes the shapes. The clouds on the literature form are meant to represent thoughts—recorded thoughts, but those that would not always end up on paper. The solid lines and square boxes of the nonfiction form are meant to suggest a physical space for note-taking, where writing down thoughts is appropriate and often required. On both versions, students are encouraged to think between and among domains. Bubbles and boxes are minimized so that students must write between the process bubbles rather than in them. They are further encouraged to connect new thoughts to those in other domains by drawing their own lines or arrows.

There is no formal procedure for teaching students to use the PROMISE strategy and thought webs. Activities may be adapted based on what student work and other assessments indicate to be areas for continued practice. The only "rule" is that I want to avoid breaking down the web into a rigid, sequential series of lessons. So although using minilessons and specific titles or genres to define each process more clearly is suggested, all processes should still be named and practiced as the reading activity proceeds.

Modeling via reading and thinking-aloud constitutes the first phase of instruction for both literature and nonfiction forms. I choose literature that exceeds the fluency level of most students in the class, so their comprehension is challenged.

Recorded books are ideal for this purpose. These free me to put the thought web on an overhead and write ideas for students to observe while they listen, which reinforces the "thought" component of the metacognitive process. I will occasionally pause to describe how I am thinking through the web.

During think-aloud modeling, I encourage students to compose their own web based on my model. As they grow more comfortable, I encourage students to start developing ideas based on their own, rather than my, view of the text. I may turn the transparency on to record and reflect, but I turn it off during reading so students cannot copy verbatim. At this point, I do less thinking of my own, instead asking students to share their most recent metacognitive thought on their personal marker boards.

I encourage, but do not require, students to use the leading phrases when they think and share. The leading phrase becomes an important layer of scaffolding during guided and independent practice. Rather than spend several class periods trying to define and practice each individual skill, I expect that repeated exposure to the phrases will give students a natural sense of how and when to use each skill. As they feel more comfortable with the concept behind each process, I worry less about the phrases, because the best thoughts will not fit neatly into them. Moreover, the amount of time spent recording thoughts should be minimized relative to the time spent reading. Students need to be reminded that their written notes represent fragments of ideas that are more continuous and complex than writing can ever convey. Thinking, not writing, is the ultimate goal of the PROMISE strategy.

Modeling metacognitive thought with the nonfiction web is equally important for developing successful reading of content area texts. Here I open the text and preread by thinking aloud. I discuss why I am reading and what questions (inquiry) come to mind as I scan the assigned pages. I make notes about vocabulary, section headings, and possible organizational formats (overviewing) while pointing out information that I already know (prior knowledge) about this topic. Finally, I decide whether or not the chapter has the right structure and information to match my learning goals (overviewing again).

Eventually, I turn this task back over to the students, encouraging them to develop their own sense of prereading. (Figure 13.3 is a sample of student work from an Indiana history lesson.) Once the reading process commences, students are encouraged to make frequent use of monitoring, reflection, and sensitivity (to devices like illustrations, graphs, and sidebars)—frequently going back to answer previous questions and connect new ideas to their prior knowledge. Finally, they should begin evaluating the chapter's contents, which may include formulating judgments about persons, policies, or ethical dilemmas.

There is no hard and fast rule for when and how to lead students from modeling to guided practice, and then finally to independent use of the webs. These phases should overlap, and I try to use all three on a weekly basis. I model, I let students practice as I model, and then I put them to work in independent settings

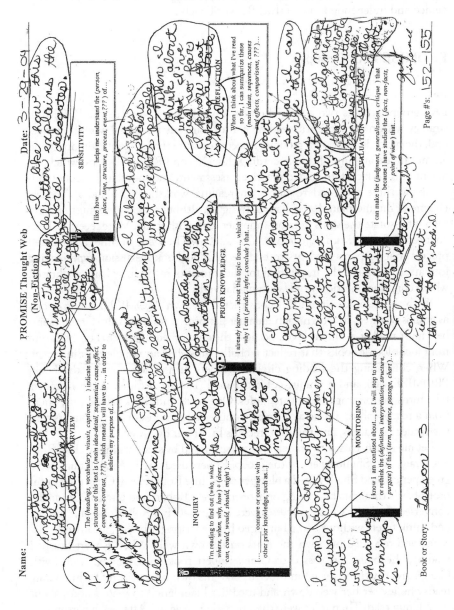

FIG. 13.3. PROMISE thought web (nonfiction).

such as cooperative groupings or through homework/note-taking assignments. The second new idea, PROMISE PAL groupings, is one method for promoting guided and independent use of the PROMISE webs.

PROMISE PAL Groups

PAL is my abbreviation for "peer assessment of learning." The development of PAL groups reflects two goals. The first was my desire to place the PROMISE strategy within an authentic reading context such as a readers' workshop. Second, the procedure for such groupings needs to assure that students will not spend an inordinate amount of time recording thoughts on PROMISE webs, which are meant only to facilitate guided practice, assessment, and individual accountability. Now there are good resources on reading workshops. *Mosaic of Thought* (Keene & Zimmerman, 1997) has its strengths, although, again, we must be careful not to isolate the skills from one another as its authors do. More recently, I encountered *Knee to Knee, Eye to Eye* (Cole, 2003). This book outlines a graduated process that prepares students to engage in adult book discussion-type reading formats. (It was also the inspiration for the format of my inquiry leading phrases, which combine question words with modal verbs.)

With these sources in mind, I constructed my own PROMISE reading circles as groups of three, in which each member performs a rotating role. Group members must read at a similar level, because they are asked to select their literature from a choice of books that reflect a challenging, but attainable, reading level. When composing the reading circle, members bring their copy of the book, PROMISE web, and a unique-colored pencil. During reading, group members take turns performing one of three roles. One reads and thinks aloud (anywhere from a paragraph to a page at a time), another takes notes on the thoughts that the reader verbalizes, and the third records his or her own web.

Let me clarify this with an example as performed by students in my class. Robert, Craig, and Shelley were in the group. Robert used a red pencil, Craig used a green pencil, and Shelley used a blue pencil. While Robert read, Craig took notes on Robert's thoughts by writing on Robert's web. Robert and Craig occasionally conversed to clarify which processes were being used, but Robert was able to read and think freely without being burdened by the writing. Shelley, meanwhile, listened and recorded her own thoughts on her own web. When Robert finished reading, the book was passed to Craig. Robert took back his own web (with Craig's green writing on it) in order to take his own notes (in red) while Craig read. Shelley set her web down and used her blue pencil to record notes about what Craig read. Then roles were then passed once again. After each person performed each role—reading, recording, and listening/self-recording—the group conducted a brief conversation to share and expand on points from the reading. These students borrowed ideas from notes they took and added to notes. In one case, they reread a portion to make sure they understood it correctly. Then the whole cycle repeated.

The PROMISE PAL group creates a reading process that balances reading and writing. Some students focus their metacognitive effort on the process of reading and thinking aloud, whereas the others use it for listening and recording thoughts. The teacher must look at the group product collectively when assessing the results, because students will have their own color of writing on at least two different webs. Even if one student has trouble dictating or summarizing another's thoughts, the combination of the three webs should provide a telling view of the metacognitive thoughts produced by the group and its individuals.

As students became accustomed to the PAL procedure, one group asked if they could stop using the PROMISE web in order to spend more time "just enjoying the book." I first had to assess whether or not these students had met the goals of the original PAL procedure—which they did. I then tried letting the three students pass a single web among them. Students continued using their own color pencil, so the product could be assessed both collectively and individually. One student read aloud. The second student listened or read along silently. The third student recorded his or her own thoughts, as well as any others that came up in conversation. They discussed their thoughts on an open and "as needed" basis. Then roles were exchanged as each reader finished. So far this has proven to be a reasonable compromise, which promotes a natural reading process while maintaining an artifact for student accountability and assessment.

Self-Evaluations

New ideas in education must be judged, in part, by how well they attract and motivate students. With this principle in mind, I decided to add a third leg to the teaching and assessment process—self-evaluation. Recent research has shown that students' evaluations of their own work can be an informative measure of their own learning and abilities (see Afflerbach & Meuwissen, chap. 8, this volume, for related research and applications of self-assessments). In my classroom, the self-evaluation helps me gauge the effectiveness of the PROMISE strategy and how students perceive its impact on their reading. I use the following format:

READING SELF-EVALUATION

Please read the beginning part of each question, then read and think about ALL the possible answers. Circle the answer that BEST DESCRIBES your attitude. There are NO right or wrong answers. The BEST answer is the one that describes your strongest present feelings.

1. When I consider FICTION BOOKS (historical, realistic, fantasy, science fiction, adventure, etc.) from the school or classroom library . . .

    A . . . *I pick books that I know will be easy or fun to read. I don't usually challenge myself because there are a lot of books I simply cannot read.*

    B . . . *I read mostly what challenges and excites me. With patience I could eventually read and understand any book in the library.*

    C . . . *I pick some books for challenge and easier books for fun. I do try to read harder books, but sometimes they frustrate me too much.*

2. When I choose NON-FICTION BOOKS (books about plants, animals, science, technology, games, magazines, newspapers, poetry, biographies) or read assigned TEXT BOOKS (science, math, social studies) . . .

    A . . . *I try to read both the words and pictures as long as I know the topic well enough.*

    B . . . *I like it better when they mostly have pictures, since the words are probably too hard for me to learn anything from.*

    C . . . *I choose books based on what I need or want to know. Even if there are fewer pictures, I know how to find the information I want.*

3. When I read NON-FICTION BOOKS or TEXT BOOKS . . .

    A . . . *I start reading from the beginning. I often get stuck unless I already know a lot about the topic.*

    B . . . *I use tools such as the table of contents, index, glossary, pictures, section and chapter headings. Sometimes these still aren't enough for me to understand all that I read.*

    C . . . *I am pretty good at studying the whole book then deciding the best way to read it. I know how to find the information I want, so that I don't have to read the whole thing so carefully.*

4. When I am reading any sort of book . . .

    A . . . *I think about a lot of things in my mind. Sometimes it's like I'm having conversations with myself, the author, or the people in the book.*

    B . . . *I mostly just read all the words from start to finish, because if I do I will probably understand it.*

    C . . . *I spend so much time trying to figure out the words that I don't always have time to think about what it all means.*

5. I think the PROMISE strategy . . .

    A . . . *is really neat. I now understand that I must think ideas to myself when I read. When I do this I find that I enjoy reading and learn more from it.*

    B . . . *makes sense, but it is not helpful to me. I'm already a good reader and I know how to make myself a better reader.*

    C . . . *is both helpful and confusing. I actually use some of those thought processes as I read, but there are certain ones that I just don't get.*

6. When we do reading in 4th grade I would most appreciate . . .

    A . . . *having more time to read on my own or to read and discuss with my classmates. I don't need so much extra help.*

B   . . . having the teacher there to read with me and to me more often. I want to read better, but I don't feel like I can do it all on my own.

C   . . . listening to stories read aloud using the PROMISE strategy more often. Sometimes I would still like to read on my own.

7. Now please look back at all the questions that you answered. Choose one that you think is **most interesting or important** to you. Write *three sentences* describing why you gave the answer you did. Give specific examples if possible.

The self-evaluation can be scored according to the chart below. A score of 1 suggests high reading confidence and active use of metacognitive processing; a score of 2 means developing reading confidence and use of metacognitive processing; and a score of 3 indicates low reading confidence and emerging use of metacognitive processing. Note that results of one part will not necessarily match those of the others. The point is to see how well they do match, and what can be learned if they don't:

Answer of	A =	B =	C =	
PART I: Questions about the student's general reading confidence				
1.	3	1	2	
2.	2	3	1	Average = _____
PART II: Questions about the student's use of metacognition in reading				
3.	3	2	1	
4.	1	2	3	Average = _____
PART III: Questions about the student's attitude toward metacognitive strategy instruction				
5.	2	1	3	
6.	1	3	2	Average = _____

Averaging the scores in each category allows the teacher to correlate students' perception of reading ability against their perceived use of metacognitive process, then against their perceived benefit from using the PROMISE strategy. This becomes an initial indicator as to whether or not there is in fact a connection between a reader's self-efficacy and the relative need for instruction through the PROMISE strategy.

The results of my own class's self-evaluation suggested that students with higher reading confidence and metacognitive awareness prefer to read on their own, bypassing what they see as redundancy in PROMISE strategy instruction. These students fell mostly in the high to average scoring range on reading achievement tests. Even while students rated themselves confidently with respect to fiction and metacognition, 60% of the students (including most of those in the average and low ranges of achievement testing) gave responses indicating they could benefit from additional support reading nonfiction with the help of the PROMISE strategy. Students whose reading confidence and reported use of metacognition were in the medium range (often correlating to lower achievement scores, but some in the average to high ranges) were the ones who showed the most interest in continuing to learn about their own metacognition and the PROMISE strategy through read-aloud modeling or reading with the teacher.

Responses to Question 7 were rich on all ranges of the achievement spectrum. Here are some samples (most referring to Question 4). Students' self-evaluation averages are ranked from highest confidence to lowest confidence:

Score avg.: 1 (high confidence)—"I like to wander in a book and just kind of relax. I love to ask myself questions and let myself answer them."

Score avg.: 1—"I really do find myself reasoning with characters and often asking them to make a certain choice."

Score avg.: 1.3 (high-medium confidence)—"I always question the author and I tell the characters what to do. Like if they are stuck I tell them to get out. But I tell the author where there is a typo."

Score avg.: 1.7—"I like to imagine what I would say if I were there. I pretend characters are talking to me. I try to see what characters are wearing."

Score avg.: 1.7—"I don't want to stop in the middle of my book and think if it doesn't help my reading. I'm already a good reader and it is a waste of time."

Score avg.: 2.5 (low confidence)—"I don't understand books that much . . . I would like to learn more about books. I need help with the words."

In summary, the self-evaluation responses did not fit as neatly with predetermined achievement categories as I predicted, but they taught me a lot about my students. High achievers have high confidence, but several lower achieving students showed higher confidence and stronger use of metacognitive processing than I expected. The last response reminds me that struggling readers need continued practice in word recognition and fluency for their metacognitive ability to grow. Results also showed widespread need for work in nonfiction reading strategies. This self-evaluation format should be used once or twice per semester. In this way, students' results can be compared for growth throughout the year, used as the basis for grouping decisions, and guide the type and intensity of reading support that individual students will receive. Ultimately, it empowers teachers to supplement standardized test results and meet the needs of all students.

DIRECTIONS FOR FUTURE RESEARCH

Numerous research questions remain unanswered. We must watch whether students' reliance on the PROMISE strategy or webs causes too narrow a perception of their own reading abilities. For example, if students only memorize and use the words and phrases on Figs. 13.1 and 13.2, they may never develop autonomous control of their reading. Moreover, given the most smoothly operating PROMISE PAL groups, is the process still too artificial in these settings? Even the best readers may remain ambivalent. They may not be willing to assimilate a process when they are already successful at reading on their own.

Equally as important, there is a need to develop more comprehensive and valid assessments of metacognition. We must examine how traditional and authentic assessments of metacognition can be balanced and made to inform one other. Instruments that rely on large quantities of writing are no longer realistic. Teachers need to have more context-based and individualized evaluations. One approach has been to tape-record students as they read aloud at a natural pace, allowing them to elaborate where they would normally pause to think during their reading. Only later does the teacher go back to the recording and assess the think-aloud process. This can be prohibitively time consuming to use on a regular basis, although Keene and Zimmerman's (1997) explanation of the Major Point Interview is a good example with which to begin and end the year. A middle-ground approach may be for the teacher to fill in a PROMISE web as the student verbalizes.

Introducing comprehension process motions (Block, Rodgers, & Johnson, 2004) in support of the PROMISE strategy may help bridge the assessment gap in two ways. First, ideas are more rapidly learned when tasks activate a combination of visual, auditory, tactile, and kinesthetic input systems. Second, simple gestures, rather than written artifacts, could help promote more authentic reading and metacognitive processing. Students indicate which mental, metacognitive process is being used by displaying a designated gesture. The teacher notes and records the event as such, asking students to elaborate on only some occasions.

Initially I think of using a hand over the brow—as though standing on top of a hill to take in the whole of a scene—to indicate making an overview. Conversely, hands cupped over the eyes like binoculars would signify monitoring—zeroing in to take a closer look at one particular piece of the puzzle. This goal will not be so hard to accomplish once I take more time to work on it. I leave it here for contemplation, however, because others may be able to take it further sooner for purposes of modeling, practice, and assessment.

Then there is the policy-oriented question of how well the PROMISE instructional strategy can support the vocabulary and expectations of traditional instruction, state standards, and standardized testing models. So far I have worked from the assumption that learning to read using metacognitive strategies should translate to strong standardized test results, but this hypothesis has not been proven. The hope would be that the tests' contents and formats, along with state standards, gradually account for present research on successful reading. Current tests and standards nevertheless continue to assess students using noncontextualized and artificial excerpts. Comprehension is still measured through the application of separate, mostly lower level reading skills.

Then, there are more adventurous questions. Research has shown many parallels between the process of reading and writing. The primary difference between the two is that the writer is the "sender" of communication and the reader is the "receiver." Good writers learn to shift roles as they write, so they can think like their audience in order to know whether or not their writing will be successful. On the flip side, *Verbal Protocols* (Pressley & Afflerbach, 1995) depicted the reading process as one requiring the reader to think more like the writer at times— outlining, constructing, and revising the meaning of the text until the reader's purpose agrees with the writer's goals.

Future research is needed to answer these questions: Will using the PROMISE strategy help students see the reading–writing connection more clearly? Although PROMISE is not meant to supplant the well-established *plan–draft–revise–edit–publish* writing model, could it substitute some of those terms in favor of a more authentic, recursive model? Additionally, given the current popularity of analytical writing assessments (e.g., Northwest Regional Educational Laboratory's *6 + 1 Traits*, 2001), could the elements of *idea, organization, voice, word choice, sentence fluency, conventions*, and *presentation* be added to the vocabulary of the PROMISE web, only now for writing purposes? Finally, can we make the more daring (or glaringly obvious!) leap into the problem-solving process in mathematics, where the ability to read well and process between prior skill knowledge and immediate task constraints would seem to be the perfect moment for a metacognitive strategy like PROMISE?

CONCLUSIONS

This chapter set out to explain the current state of metacognition with respect to reading instruction. Although numerous strategies and devices have been put forth in recent decades, research from the last 10 years has pointed us to a new generation of approaches. The best reading occurs for a variety of purposes, is used in genuine contexts, and challenges readers' abilities as they develop expertise in reading. Moreover, comprehension cannot be taught as a series of isolated skills. Real understanding and discussion of reading result from several thoughts being put together at once, with prior knowledge at the center of every point in the reading process.

Second, I outlined the definition and tools for a strategy of teaching reading metacognition called PROMISE. The following metacognitive thought processes are embedded in this model: building on prior knowledge; reflecting; making an overview of text organization; monitoring; making inquiries; developing sensitivity to person, place, and style; and evaluating. PROMISE thought webs are graphic organizers used to model, practice, and assess the strategy. The nonfiction form can be used for note taking in content areas. PROMISE PAL groupings and self-evaluations are methods for individualizing instruction and assessment. These empower students to develop autonomous metacognitive abilities while producing self-reported evidence of this growth.

Finally, I suggested several areas that pose significant research questions or areas of further development for the PROMISE strategy. I invite readers to build on the ideas presented in this chapter, because I will not be able to explore each on my own. I hope this chapter inspires practicing teachers to continue creating every day. It is we who must innovate and cooperate with those in research to achieve lasting educational success.

METACONNECTION FOR CHAPTER 13

When you read chapter 13, you saw a reflection from Amelia McWilliams. She stated so vividly what this chapter did to increase her abilities to teach metacognition. Like her, we anticipated that this chapter would challenge you and provide many answers for students who have special needs within your own classroom. In addition, you might receive a joy of feeling as if you are present in this classroom as instruction unfolds. The description of the PROMISE strategy was so explicit that you could implement this approach to metacognition instruction today.

REFERENCES

Baker, L., & Brown, A. L. (1984). Metacognitive skills and reading. In P. D. Pearson, R. Barr, M. Kamil, & P. Mosenthal (Eds.), *Handbook of reading research* (pp. 353–394). New York: Longman.

Block, C. C. (2004). *Teaching comprehension: The comprehension process approach.* Boston: Allyn & Bacon.

Block, C. C., Rodgers, L., & Johnson, R. (2004). *Teaching comprehension in kindergarten through grade 3: Bringing success to all students' reading.* New York: Guilford.

Cole, A. D. (2003). *Knee to knee, eye to eye: Circling in on comprehension.* Portsmouth, NH: Heinemann.

Keene, E. O., & Zimmerman, S. (1997). *Mosaic of thought: Teaching comprehension in a reader's workshop.* Portsmouth, NH: Heinemann.

Northwest Regional Educational Laboratory. (2001). *6+1 trait writing.* Retrieved April 5, 2004, from http://www.nwrel.org/assessment/department.asp?d=1

Palincsar, A. S., & Brown, A. L. (1984). The reciprocal teaching of comprehension-fostering and monitoring activities. *Cognition and Instruction, 1,* 117–175.

Polya, G. (1957). *How to solve it.* Garden City, NY: Doubleday.

Pressley, M., & Afflerbach, P. (1995). *Verbal protocols of reading: The nature of constructively responsive reading.* Hillsdale, NJ: Lawrence Erlbaum Associates.

Thomas, E. L., & Robinson, H. A. (1972). *Improving reading in every class: A sourcebook for teachers*. Boston: Allyn & Bacon.

Vygotsky, L. S. (1978). *Mind and society: The development of higher mental processes*. Cambridge, MA: Harvard University Press.

Woolfolk, A. (2004). *Educational psychology* (9th ed.). Boston: Allyn & Bacon.

14

A Window Into a Thinking Classroom

Paige A. Smith
University of Notre Dame

Reading is not an assignment but a daily way of looking at the world.
—Peck (2002)

I consider my classroom a thinking classroom. Students are engaged in meaningful reading, writing, science, social studies, and mathematics activities. On any given day in my classroom, my students are questioning, inferring, experimenting, and working cooperatively. These are only a few of the things happening. You may be wondering how I created this thinking classroom. It all started from day one where I began working on building classroom community. The first few weeks were devoted to sharing and working together to get to know one another. If there is an absence of classroom community, it is hard to create an atmosphere where students can feel comfortable enough to engage in learning activities that are beyond their usual activities. Once students began to feel comfortable in my classroom, they began to experiment with words, language, reading, science, and math. It is only then that my students truly become part of our thinking classroom. I ask myself, "Is it possible to have a thinking classroom without a shared sense of community?"
—Sara Berner, Third-Grade Teacher

This chapter answers Sara's question. It provides an in-depth view into a thinking classroom, like Sara's, and the steps taken to create it. This viewing includes photographs, projects, and products to document the thinking that exists there. The following questions are answered:

1. How can metacognition be promoted in classrooms of primary-age students?
2. How can educators view literacy in a way that supports metacognition?

3. How can curriculum be used to integrate a sense of community, self-identity, and critical thinking for students through classroom instruction?

4. How can teachers continue to improve instruction as it relates to meta-cognition and literacy?

FROM THE RENAISSANCE
TO POSTMODERNISM

Despite the deep challenge of guiding children toward genuine metacognition, the subjective bridge to link this level of discovery with our students' abilities lies within the students themselves. A child's experience of the world, full of imagination and wonder, gives way to a natural inclination toward metacognition that can be unlocked by looking through a lens of thought given to us historically in the Renaissance and presently in a postmodern world. As these windows are opened, it becomes clear that the children in our classrooms hold the power to broaden our conception of teaching from a literacy of words toward a literacy of being. In order for students to engage in sincere metacognitive thinking, students must first understand who they are. As both students and teachers simultaneously sojourn down a path of self-discovery, the reach for metacognition in instructional practice clearly reveals that we are in fact not just teachers, but stewards of spirit.

Many objective truths taught in school are learned through rote memory (i.e., two plus two equals four, there are seven continents, verbs are words that show action). The thinking, however, that students encounter when learning these truths is subjective, not objective. One student may imagine verbs as a list in the grammar book, one as letters with feet prancing across looseleaf paper, and another as words that inspire them to rise from their chair and dance. It is when the objective world meets the subjective world that students begin to grasp "a thinking about thinking," or metacognition. Metacognition then serves as subjective evidence of a student's individuality as a learner. The discovery of these different ways of learning or seeing a single truth should be received by educators as guideposts for instruction. The variability that inevitably surrounds students' individual metacognitive creations should be embraced. This reciprocal give-and-take between the teacher as knower and student as discoverer also can create a need to find strategies that make sense of the swirl of prior knowledge, new information, and subjective thinking that is formed in the students' individual intangible spaces between reception of information and mastery of knowledge.

HISTORICAL PERSPECTIVE AND RESEARCH

The striving to develop metacognition through literacy instruction offers a new perspective from traditional teaching. The latter has had a tendency to focus on lower order thinking and uniform rote memorization. Hart (2003) spoke to this view, commenting that "parents, teachers, and society as a whole are concerned with what our children know. However, *how* we know, not just *what* we know, is fundamental to the pursuit of wisdom" (p. 38). The shift of thought that is currently taking place in pedagogy and inside numerous thinking classrooms parallels the revolution that changed society in the dawning of the Renaissance between 1400 and 1600.

Prior to the Renaissance, there was a certain stagnation in people's encounter with the world. Discovery and rebirth was as stilled and quiet as the unexplored seas. Nothing was made new (Gelb, 1998). But then from somewhere in Italy came a breath of grace-filled inspiration nudging scholars, sculptors, and painters to rediscover the mind of ancient Greece and Rome. As Renaissance thinkers studied the culture of the Greeks and Romans, they gained inspiration and energy to see their current world with fresh eyes. This renewed perspective prompted people to study the world to see how it worked. In the process, they discovered how all aspects of philosophy, literature, science, architecture, and art were integrated to create a culture of thinking.

Renaissance thinkers beckon the world with curiosity and excitement. They remind me of the children who come running down the hall every morning with smiles on their faces, floating on air because they have a voice of discovery within them. With both of these populations, there is purity and honesty in their innovative thinking marked by surprise and creativity. When the natural disposition for exploration in students meets the world of the Renaissance, it creates a cognitive environment rich with possibility.

Despite this inherent richness and generosity of children, we must meet them where they are. We do not live in the 1500s in pursuit of the ideal, but in a postmodern world of subjective experience that brings a new twist to the hue in which our students view their learning, the classroom, and themselves as young human beings.

Following the Middle Ages, the Renaissance was a reinvention of ancient Greek and Roman ideas. In contrast, postmodernism has developed from a rejection of objective truths and deductive reasoning of earlier 20th-century thought (Winch, Johnston, Holliday, Ljundahl, & March, 2001). This has given way to a distrust of reason and reliance on experience and inductive, subjective morality. As a result, whereas modern thinkers progressed toward a goal, postmodern thinkers progress toward "whatever." Postmodern life is fragmented and unintegrated. The contemporary strategy of living is to compartmentalize the intellect, religion, politics, and science into separate caverns. In a way, this approach is circuitous rather than complete. (Interestingly, teachers tend to nobly swim against this society tide as they instruct toward connectedness through thematic units and a use of instructional statements that guide students to connect one body of knowledge to another.)

A concrete example of the postmodern paradigm is the shift taking place in children's literature. Wiesner's (2003) Caldecott winning book, *The Three Pigs*,

exhibited this with its nonlinear narrative and pictures that sometimes contra-
dict, rather than support, text. He also used irony and playful absurdity to carry
the plot. He invited readers to coauthor the story (Goldstone, 2004). This
postmodern bent illustrates the sense of ownership and power given to children
to create their own literary experience. Postmodern books "shatter readers' expectations, demand active coauthoring, and raise questions about what is real"
(Goldstone, 2004, p. 197).

The myriad-pieced postmodern world in which we find ourselves, informed by
a study of the Renaissance, sensitively directs the search for knowing and thinking. If we continue to understand "renaissance" as rebirth, then the gift of learning with children allows us to enter into personal renaissances daily. Encounters
with the academic content we are merging with our own human subjectivity and
individual experience pushes knowledge to meet metacognitive thinking. Lesson
Plan 4 of the unit that appears in Fig. 14.1 provides an example of this kind of development in that the closing of the lesson requires a reflective letter to Michelangelo to be written after students have shared in an emulation of painting the
Sistine Chapel ceiling. Through such activities, for both the students and ourselves, the information we teach is transformed into something unique and personal as it becomes not just an assignment but a constituent of our very being because of our awareness of epistemological activity. The next section gives an
example of how this interchange can be used in a classroom to create richer
metacognitive abilities in students.

TEACHING WITH LEONARDO
DA VINCI'S THOUGHT

Leonardo da Vinci is the quintessential Renaissance man. Today, society continues
to benefit from his contributions to the fields of science, writing, architecture, and
art. He did it all. Leonardo da Vinci, the patron saint of independent thinkers, is
the ideal role model for the integration of metacognition with literacy instruction
(Gelb, 1998). To teach with Leonardo's thought is to teach for metacognition.

Gelb's enlightening book, How to Think Like Leonardo da Vinci (1998), presented seven "da Vincian Principles" that create the structure for a language arts
study on how students can build their own deeper cognitive thinking to build
stronger supports in their everyday lives. The first principle taught in this study is
da Vincian curiosity: The importance of curiosity to increase metacognition
emerges through asking questions. Curiosity is something that inspires children
to think, learn, and seek out processes to allow them the journey of seeking the
hows of the world and their minds. Curiosity is a passport for the sojourn toward
truth. In a classroom setting, you teach this principle by bringing equivocal central questions about a subject to the students' attention so that they can work toward many possible answers. For example, in Lesson Plan 8 of Fig. 14.1, students
are asked, "How do you express beauty and virtue within yourself?"

2nd Grade

Unit Goal: Through exploration, creativity, and discovery, students will be able to recognize important figures (Leonardo da Vinci, Michelangelo, and Galileo) and concepts (curiosity, virtue, and perspective) of the Renaissance in Europe and identify their significance to this period of rebirth in history in relation to their own personal births or rebirths as independent thinkers.

Prior Knowledge: Students will be able to activate prior knowledge and utilize critical thinking skills including questioning, predicting, visualizing, and summarizing to work with new information. Students will be able to write in complete sentences.

Unit Evaluation—Authentic Assessment: Students will be able to classify and organize lesson assessments from the unit into a Renaissance Museum. Then, students will critique and evaluate some of the museum's artifacts by completing a written entrance and exit slip. In addition, after being presented with important figures and concepts of the Renaissance, students will be able to distinguish between these artifacts and ideas and write in complete sentences why they are significant to the period. Students will also be able to distinguish between our modern day life and the world of the Renaissance.

LP1—Our Renaissance Backpack (1 day): Students will be able to distinguish between items that can or cannot be used during the period of the European Renaissance, 1400–1600. In preparation for our imaginary journey, students bring in an important object for our "trip." We discuss if these objects can be taken back in time and used during the Renaissance.

LP2—Leonardo da Vinci, Renaissance Man (2 days): Students will be able to defend the characterization of Leonardo da Vinci as "Renaissance Man." On the first day of Lesson 2, we discuss the concept of "Renaissance Man" and da Vinci as an artist and scientist. On the next day, we create da Vinci Notebooks for students to use to record thoughts and ideas throughout the unit.

LP3—Cabinet of Curiosities (2 days): Students will be able to create "Cabinets of Curiosities." "Cabinets of Curiosities" are collections of items that imitate the interaction with the world that people of the Renaissance had during this period of rebirth and discovery. On the first day of Lesson 3, we review the concepts introduced in previous lessons including rebirth and the "Renaissance Man." We cover cereal boxes to make "Cabinets of Curiosities." On the next day, students complete their cabinets with decoration and discuss ideas for what to collect in the cabinets.

LP4—Michelangelo and the Sistine Ceiling (4 days): Students will be able to measure their drawing paper to be 1/6,000th of the size of the Sistine Ceiling and reproduce a version of their own "fresco" painting. Students will be able to write a letter to Michelangelo describing their drawing and the experience of creating it. On the first day of Lesson 4, we discuss the life and times of Michelangelo with photocopies of Michelangelo related pictures in envelopes. On the next day, we measure paper and sketch celestial themed pictures. On the third day, we color and paint the pictures. Paper is affixed to the undersides of students' desks, and they paint while bending backwards mimicking the posture of Michelangelo, as shown in the photo in this chapter. On the last day of Lesson 4, students write letters to Michelangelo to relate their personal experience imaginatively to a historical figure.

LP5—Perspective in "The Last Supper" (2 days): Students will be able to define perspective and identify examples and non-examples of perspective in different representations of "The Last Supper." On the first day of Lesson 5, we discuss and define perspective and what makes it work (vanishing point). We review the story of the Last Supper and compare and contrast paintings. On the next day, we create perspective drawings, share work, and discuss techniques for recreating three-dimensional perspective on flat surfaces.

FIG. 14.1. *(Continued)*

LP6—Writing With Quill Pens (1 day): Students will be able to write to practice cursive handwriting strokes using ink and feathers. Then they describe the difference of the experience compared to writing with pencils. In Lesson 6, students spend one day writing with ink and feathers and reflecting/discussing on the experience.

LP7—Galileo, The Pendulum and Leaning Tower of Pisa Experiments (2 days): Students will be able to identify scientific contributions of Galileo and hypothesize why his experiments exhibited scientific truths. On the first day of Lesson 7, students will be able to infer why the length of time of the pendulum swing is the same from different launch heights. On the next day, students will be able to infer why objects of different weights hit the ground at the same time when traveling equal distances.

LP8—Virtue and Beauty (2 days): Students will be able to develop an understanding of the beauty and virtue in themselves. On the first day of Lesson 8, we discuss the concepts of virtue and beauty as revealed in da Vinci's work and paintings. On the next day, we create doubled sided self-portraits based on da Vinci's Ginevra de'Benci.

FIG. 14.1.   The Renaissance unit: Exploring the Renaissance in Europe.

There was a unique purity to da Vinci's second principle: the quest for truth. This purity also exists within primary schoolchildren. Unlike other Renaissance geniuses, Leonardo had no ulterior motives for his work (Gelb, 1998). He sought the truth of the world with the altruistic notion that the truth was worth seeking. Similarly, most children are not yet tainted by passionate love, high school cliques, or a political agenda. They come to school because they love it; they come to school because their curiosity is urging them to learn. Therefore, my instruction of this Renaissance principle to the second grade began through a study of contributions of da Vinci. I've done so because I believe in the power of the image to act as the road map to students knowing who they are, which I see as a prerequisite to any hope of metacognition.

People know themselves through subjective experiences. People and children begin to know themselves as unique through a reflective gaze inward as they think and choose throughout their lives (Hogan & LeVoir, 1988). People experience the wonder of nature as a seagull pierces the burst of the sunset over a salty ocean, as rain taps out a rhythm on flushed cheeks, or as they realize the silent strength in a mountain range. In looking at nature, individuals not only see the sunset, rain, or mountain but see themselves in their experience of it. There is a self-aware metacognitive realization of the person as a thinking, choosing, unique individual (Hogan & LeVoir, 1988). When this objective world meets the subjective world of the person's experience, the ability to grasp "a thinking about thinking" develops. I create this important event within the four walls of my classroom by providing a variety of reading, writing, mathematical, and aesthetic experiences that may speak to a child's individuality as a learner.

The visual arts are also ideal for allowing objective–subjective connections to take place. The arts have this awesome power because they not only present a bridge for these connections to occur, but also provide material for students to create new ones. Eisner (2003) iterated that "even when treated imaginatively, the social value of an image or idea does not secure importance unless something else happens. . . . The contents of consciousness need to be made public; they need to be represented" (p. 342). When students experience great works of art, metacognition inevitably takes place but is also stirred to create something tangible of that experience, most often in ways that support literacy. I use the great works of art to help students' metacognition become public by using artwork as prompts for writing and thinking experiences.

In addition, I support a more expanded use of the arts in the classroom because it is less intimidating for many primary-age students than the "foreign appearing" code of print on a page. Such children can instantly experience an image from a very early age, before words and linguistic abilities demand a stake in their cognitive energy during the interaction with the world. For instance, babies come to recognize the face of their mother, a cherished animal, a favorite picture book, or simply a field of color before they can articulate the labeled connections they have made. Other artists' images can meet cognition before the written or spoken word can express the experience. This develops a nonlinguistic infrastructure in children; "children do not only think in written language but in visual image as well" (Piro, 2002, p. 128). As a result, I have found my students to be drawn to both the images of the Renaissance and contemporary art (particularly abstract expressionism) because they can understand an intricately complex message more readily when it is presented on a brush-stroked canvas than with syntax or text. However, as Eisner pointed out, the experience of the encounter with the image does not end with the cognitive experience of it, but that very cognitive experience elicits further metacognitive representation that promotes the literacy of the one who met the image. People come to know themselves more deeply because of the image. In this way, art most certainly promotes a literacy of being, a literacy of who we are. For instance, in my class, I present different versions of paintings of *The Last Supper* with which my students interact and come to define perspective and artistic techniques and use this knowledge to recreate their own perspective drawings. Using art, students are able to set their own purposes, play with new methods of using different types of artists' styles, and apply meaning to their own learning experience as a result of this lesson.

CABINETS OF CURIOSITIES, DA VINCI NOTEBOOKS, AND THE ABSTRACT

Painting is a state of being . . . self-discovery. Every good artist paints what he is. (Jackson Pollock; in Fineberg, 1995, p. 5)

Another project that I give to my students to promote curiosity is the creation of a "Cabinet of Curiosities." Constructed from a cereal box covered with butcher paper, my students have the freedom to decorate the exterior according to their personality and place within it items they find interesting and worthy of study. This sense of discovery reflects the lifestyle of Leonardo da Vinci, as well as the people of the Renaissance who sought to portray their world and the human mind. In like manner, my students bring favorite toys, rocks they find at recess, and cherished possessions (e.g., adorned deer hooves from Mexico). The Cabinets of Curiosities are an ongoing presence throughout the Renaissance unit and are ideal for inspiring discussion and reflection about our subjective experiences of the world.

The pictures on the following two pages are exhibits of discovery and exploration that the children experience in the context of our studies. Students peek into handmade monuments of curiosity, discover books that inform their thinking, and gaze at works of art as they come to know that in seeking not just content, but their cognitive process as well, they begin to understand who they are.

We also emulate the work of da Vinci by contributing regularly through students' creations of personal versions of a Leonardo da Vinci notebook. They record their daily metacognitive thoughts in these books through drawings, sketches, text, or scribbles much like da Vinci did. The reflection topics vary. Sometimes students may fill the page with whatever they are creatively led toward or are guided to by a particular prompt. To encourage an identity awareness, a metacognitive union with concrete knowledge, I sometimes give students a prompt to write, such as: "How does the world around me help me to understand myself?" (See Figs. 14.2 and 14.3.)

Another aspect of the ways we develop metacognition through the study of art is by comparing and contrasting the work of Renaissance artists and contemporary artists that express postmodern ideas. Abstract art brings into tangible view the metacognitive workings of the mind in its treatment of "both image and concepts as radically polyvalent. This permits a fluid reconfiguring of one's experience of the world" (Fineberg, 1995, p. 360). After we have described the similarities and differences as a class, students create their individual painting to portray their views of the way in which some dimension of their world works. A sample of abstract art created by one of my students appears in Fig. 14.4 and shows an expression of the student's own thinking. In this task, students are asked to create a visual representation of a feeling or experience without using recognizable images. The outcomes approach the work of renowned artists, including Pollock (after whom our class guinea pig is named), Stella, Frankenthaler, Rothko, and Oldenburg; as in Reynolds' The Dot (2003), children come to make their mark in our classroom world and realize they have an artistic voice.

Where do all of these aesthetic experiences take us? In the teaching of the Renaissance as a way to reach toward metacognition, my students develop the perspective and viewpoint that learning is not created by the accumulation of assignments, but through the accumulation of experience.

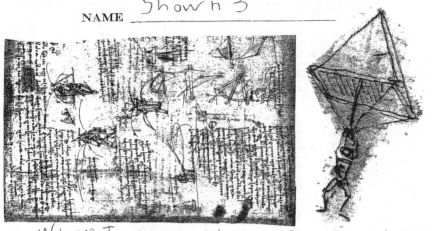

FIG. 14.2. Shawn's da Vinci notebook.

SUGGESTIONS FOR INSTRUCTION AND PRACTICE

Teachers can move instructional practice toward meaningful experience by creating opportunities for students to create personal experiences that promote a literacy of being. The goal of such experiences is to allow students to have a variety of learning experiences in the classroom while being supported with skills that allow them to discern their intellectual movements so that they become aware of their thinking and subjective tendencies. Each lesson or instructional attempt may not stir metacognition into action for each student, but the potential should always be present.

Earlier I stated that discoveries of these different ways of learning or seeing a single truth should be received by educators as guideposts for instruction, but how can this be done? How should student output be used to affect subsequent instruction that creates literacy experiences and builds metacognition?

In the case of the da Vinci journals used throughout the unit, students record reflections and original ideas stemming from studies of Renaissance art, thought, and scientific questions. Because the da Vinci notebooks provide continuity in the students' thinking during our study, they have the power to serve as road maps for my instruction. They are my navigating tool to informally assess how

MY LEONARDO DA VINCI NOTEBOOK

NAME __Juliana2__

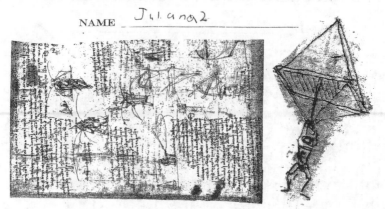

My fiands help me understand who I am. My Mom Hope help me understand who I am. Shool help me understand who I am. Agatha help me understand who I'm. God help me understand who I am. The End.

FIG. 14.3. Juliana's da Vinci notebook.

students are thinking and the level at which they are making connections between the material on a rote level and their personal integration of that knowledge into their own schemas.

The key to bringing this out in students' work is to communicate these expectations to them as they work on these written reflections that may be expressed in words, drawings, or color. A rubric for their musings can be helpful, but care should be taken to ensure that the rubric enhances creativity and subjective experience rather than stifle or inhibit it. In my experience, the da Vinci journal entries change and evolve in the course of the unit; there should be a certain freedom in allowing the journal rubric to do the same. The rubric can be used by students to help them identify ways to think about their thinking and increase responsibility and ownership in the evaluation of their work.

FIG. 14.4. Art abstraction by Shawn, *The playground*.

Classroom sharing and discussion in community is also an integral aspect of this unit. As iterated by Sara Berner at the beginning of this chapter, students need to feel comfortable in a classroom to experiment with words, language, reading, science, and math. This unit should come well into the year so that students are at a point where they are acclimated to each other and their teacher so that they can share the intimate movings of their mind in an unintimidating environment. They should be able to talk through their experiences in think-pair-share, small group, and large group settings. Teachers can support these interactions by modeling supportive statements to student responses and encouraging the welcoming of all ideas and subjective responses as contributions that add another important perspective to personal metacognition and learning experience. As members of one human family, we are reflected in each other and build up an understanding of ourselves as individuals most saliently in community.

DIRECTIONS FOR FUTURE RESEARCH

With the importance of learning in community, further research to support the way in which students learn about their individual thinking patterns in the context of a learning community would benefit teacher instruction. In the need of building community while also building the knowledge of the individual, questions arise, such as: How can instruction be differentiated when learning experiences are so subjective? What uniting factor can be presented to students to provide integration and understanding despite the myriad of methods of thought processes? How can subjective experiences best be assessed in a way that is meaningful to students, teachers, and parents? How should teachers communicate to parents a new emphasis on metacognition rather than rote ways of learning?

New qualities are becoming evident in the elementary classroom. Teachers must teach students to set their own meaningful purposes for learning, to identify new methods to tackle different types of writing styles, ways to connect pictures with text to gain meaning by applying it to their lives, and ways to draw conclusions and inferences better and more independently.

With these many concerns and focal points, educators need to look at ways to maintain the commitment to cross-curricular integration of all subjects so that metacognition garners a natural and omnipresent place in students' encounters with school experiences not only in the language arts, but in science, social studies, math, computers, and physical education as well. Metacognition should touch the whole child.

CONCLUSIONS

When we assume the role of steward of spirit in the education of students, then our teaching has cosmic effects. We can assist students to attain an individual identity, and the discovery of it becomes a treasure to be nurtured and protected. There is fragility and tenderness, yet also abiding strength, in the journey toward truth. As a result, what we learn as teachers and students becomes a constituent of our very being, not an accident, making it clear that to engage students in metacognition promotes not only a deeper understanding of the human person, but it promotes a literacy of being.

Classroom instruction that moves toward metacognitive activity can be unlocked by looking through a lens of thought given to us historically in the Renaissance and presently in a postmodern world. Exposing children to Renaissance art and scientific inquiry while simultaneously providing ways to explore postmodern art and literature creates the framework in which subjective learning experiences can take place. As young students are given strategies to express their own profound wisdom, they begin a pursuit of not just knowing information, but learning how to identify how they come to know. With the hope of future research exploring metacognition across the curriculum, this movement toward building a community of metacognitive thinkers is paramount for building a culture of genuine understanding. It is important for educators to promote metacognition to support the literacy of words, but even more important, educators must use their instruction of metacognition to help students to read the language of their being.

METACONNECTION FOR CHAPTER 14

Having read chapter 14, you may feel as if you have an arsenal of instruction tools at your disposal already. Dr. Smith provided that additional security and wonderful resources for you to gain that sense of security. To review a few of the gems that you discovered in this chapter, she promoted that reading and the visual arts are an ideal setting for allowing students' objective and subjective metacognitions to take place and her argument was very convincing. She not only provided methods of teaching metacognition through units of study, but she illustrated them with student work, photographs from her classroom, and deep student reflections of the assessments that they experience in their growth as metacognitive readers and viewers. Because of the richness of images contained in this chapter, Smith not only provided you with a "window," but her invitation to join her to bring this type of classroom to your students as well.

REFERENCES

Eisner, E. W. (2003). The arts and the creation of mind. *Language Arts, 80*(5), 340–344.

Fineberg, J. (1995). *Art since 1940: Strategies of being.* Upper Saddle River, NJ: Prentice-Hall.

Gelb, M. J. (1998). *How to think like Leonardo da Vinci: Seven steps to genius every day.* New York: Bantam Doubleday Dell.

Goldstone, B. P. (2004). The postmodern picture book: A new subgenre. *Language Arts, 81*(3), 196–204.

Hart, T. (2003). *The secret spiritual world of children.* Maui: Inner Ocean Publishing.

Hogan, R. M., & LeVoir, J. (1988). *Faith for today: Pope John Paul II's catechetical teachings.* New York: Bantam Doubleday Dell.

Peck, R. (2002). *Acceptance speech for Anne V. Zarrow Award*. Tulsa Library Trust Fund.

Piro, J. M. (2002). The picture of reading: Deriving meaning in literacy through image. *The Reading Teacher*, 56(2), 126–134.

Reynolds, P. H. (2003). *The dot*. Cambridge: Candlewick Press.

Wiesner, D. (2003). *The three pigs*. New York: Clarion Books.

Winch, G., Johnston, R., Holliday, M., Ljundahl, L., & March, P. (2001). *Literacy: Reading, writing, and children's literature*. Melbourne, Australia: Oxford University Press.

15

Teaching Several Metacognitive Strategies Together Increases Students' Independent Metacognition

Carrice Cummins
Louisiana Tech University

Margaret T. Stewart
Louisiana State University

Cathy Collins Block
Texas Christian University

Dr. Stewart, the children and I are absolutely loving this strategy. They continue to amaze me on a daily basis. The students did not want me to stop the lesson because the children were so interested in the learning. There is incredible participation and enthusiasm for learning. The children seem to love having their thoughts written on the chart. I heard one child say, "I got two answers up there today."
—Traci Solleau, Grade 1, Teacher Strategy Journal, Week 3

My students could really understand the bookmarks and the two-page main idea.
—Mrs. Cheryl Adams, Grade 3, Teacher Strategy Journal, Week 5, Day 2

The majority of my students communicated at levels of thought higher than my expectations. My students think this is helping their comprehension."
—Mrs. Cheryl Adams, Grade 3, Teacher Strategy Journal, Week 5, Day 4

Researchers have learned much about comprehension in the past 30 years (see Block & Pressley, 2002, for a review). This new knowledge has provided educators with many innovative strategies designed to improve comprehension instruction; however, there is still one area in which minimal research is available. For years, children have been taught to find main ideas, to preview a book, to ask questions, to think of the structure in which the book is written, and to attend to access features. Unfortunately, most of these strategies have been taught as stand-alone procedures, making it difficult for students to view them as a unified process of mental activity that flows back and forth as the reader tries to follow an author's train of thought.

The process of becoming a metacognitive reader is intensified in the reading of expository text. There are several reasons for this. First, elementary-grade students typically have not been overly exposed to nonfiction texts, especially for use in comprehension instruction, because fiction is frequently the primary source of instruction in the classroom (Duke, 2000). Second, teachers often do not know how to teach strategies for reading nonfiction texts; therefore, minimal explicit instruction is provided. Third, the access features found in informational texts (to help guide the readers' thinking while reading) are often ignored by both students and teachers.

This chapter describes a national research study that begins to fill the gap in research concerning instructional components of metacognition. Specifically, this chapter offers information concerning ways metacognition can increase when students are provided with a series of comprehension processes designed to help them "see" some of the thinking that should occur while reading nonfiction texts; the time it takes for students to begin the process of becoming fluent, metacognitive readers when they receive direct and explicit instruction in reading nonfiction texts; and the myriad activities involved in helping teachers better understand how to facilitate students' reading of nonfiction text.

THEORETICAL BACKGROUND

Views of the comprehension process have changed drastically over the past 30 years (see Block & Pressley, 2002, for a review of these changes). What was considered a passive–receptive process prior to 1970 slowly began to be viewed as a process in which the reader took on a more active–constructive role (Brown, Collins, & Duguid, 1989; National Reading Panel [NRP], 2000). This shift in thinking held strong implications for comprehension instruction as teachers began to realize that it involved more than just checking students' understanding of a text but actually included teaching them how to comprehend the text (Durkin, 1978–1979). Teachers not only had to know and consider the text itself (Pearson, 1985), but also had to understand and teach the many other facets involved in helping students become independent meaning-makers (e.g., activating prior knowledge, identifying text structure, using strategic thinking, etc.). For years, teachers have done just that—teach facets of the comprehension process in isolation, waiting for mastery of one to occur prior to moving to another.

We decided to study the effects of putting several processes together in a variety of formats because past research concerning teaching metacognitive comprehension processes as single lessons has not produced the transfer that was expected. For example, Baker (2001) found that adults could engage three processes simultaneously when given explicit instruction to check for propositional, structural, and informational completeness. When researchers taught young students to do so, both strong and weak comprehenders benefited equally from the instruction. This research also found that metacognition could be developed. Other researchers are also exploring ways of combining comprehension strategies instruction in the effort to maximize understanding (e.g., see review of this research in Duke & Pearson, 2002).

Because reading comprehension is not an isolated process that is activated only after reading, but is a network of in-the-head processes that work together before, during, and after reading, our goal was to teach metacognitive processes that would work together to bring about meaning at various times during a reading. To help students develop their thinking about text at these times, teachers used three approaches that utilized a repertoire of comprehension strategies. The first was a chart that tracked the class's *previewing; predicting; questioning; identifying vocabulary, text structure, access features, author's purpose; thinking critically;* and *creating graphic organizers/mindmaps* as they shared a book of expository text together. The second was teaching students to write their thoughts about three comprehension processes (setting purposes for reading, having inferences, and drawing conclusions) on post-it notes placed strategically on pages of a book in which those metacognitive processes would occur automatically for expert readers. This treatment, used only in Grades K–2 classrooms, was altered and expanded for Grades 3–5 students. It became our third treatment. Instead of writing on three post-it notes, upper grade students reflected, wrote, and discussed 15 comprehension processes identified on a tri-folded bookmark (Block & Israel, 2004). The first bookmark contained five thoughts that help students build meaning as they begin to read, the second contained four processes that expert readers use to enhance comprehension during reading, and the third contained three metacognitive strategies that expert readers report to increase the value of their reading as a text comes to a close. Examples of the post-it notes and bookmarks appear in Figs. 15.1 and 15.2.

We based our theoretical assumptions on the fact that students who truly become effective metacognitive readers construct in the text personalized "benchmarks" that serve to connect the textual events to their lives (Trimble, 1994). Thus, we developed a method by which students could make personal connections at each of these specific points. We asked the students to pause and reflect, then independently apply the metacognitive strategies as the ultimate goals of their lessons at every stage of instruction.

For years, researchers have known that it takes longer to develop automaticity in comprehension than in decoding (e.g., Fielding & Pearson, 1994; NRP, 2000; Samuels, 2002; Stewart, 2004); however, we have never known exactly how long it takes. Research suggests that students can transfer instruction and cognitive

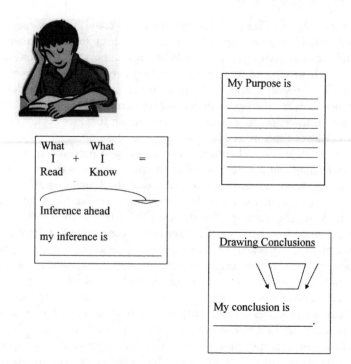

FIG. 15.1. Teach how to think about more than one metacomprehension
process while reading a book: Post-it-noting instructional strategy.

strategies to standardized tests if they have had instruction for 8 months (Anderson & Pearson, 1984; Block, 1993). Each of these researchers discusses the fact that extenuating factors prolonged the length of time required for transfer to occur. The most common reason identified was that students did not have a mechanism that would unite each of these processes, thus helping it to become a way of thinking. There has been even less research on the length of time that it takes for children to become metacognitive with nonfiction text. One might assume that an absence of familiarity with this type of textual structure would increase the amount of time it takes for students to become automatic readers; however, this assumption has not yet been tested.

METHOD

Data for this project were collected over a period of 8 months during the 2003–2004 school year. Following this treatment period, data were obtained from both norm-referenced and criterion-referenced assessments. Additional qualitative measures (e.g., teacher and student surveys, journals) were also included in data analysis.

First Few Pages	As You Read	After Reading For Awhile
1) Overviewing a Text: How to select a Book and Begin to Think about the Topic ____	1) Revising Prior Knowledge & Predicting ____	1) Noticing Novelties in the Text ____
2) Looking for Important Information: Find Repeated Ideas in the First Three Pages ____	2) Recognizing Author's Speed and Depth of Writing ____	2) Putting the Book In My Life: Summarizing, Evaluating, Reflecting and Paraphrasing ____
3) Connecting to Author's Big Idea: Tie Main Ideas to a Big Theme ____	3) Determining Word Meanings: Decode, Use Context & Learn New Words ____	3) Anticipating the Use of Knowledge in the Future: Rereading & Reading Ahead ____
4) Activating Relevant Knowledge ____	4) Questioning to Confirm or Disconfirm ____	
5) Putting Myself in the Book and Thinking about What I Know so Far ____		

FIG. 15.2.   Bookmarks: Teaching multiple metacomprehension processes in Grades 3–5.

Participants and Setting

The initial project sample included 1,278 students from six schools located in Louisiana and Texas. Of that original number, 420 students were excluded from final analysis due to exiting the school, lack of parental permission, and/or being absent for scheduled standardized testing. This resulted in a final sample size of 858 students. Classes were randomly selected for inclusion in the project, and teachers and their classes were randomly assigned as experimental or control groups. The participants within a class were not randomly selected but represented all students whose parents returned the parental consent forms. An additional group of three participants were selected from each classroom to serve as focal students. These students were selected based on previously identified reading achievement levels: above-, on-, or below-grade level.

The participants included students in kindergarten through Grade 5 from six schools in Louisiana and Texas. The Louisiana sites included one rural PK–1 school, one rural 2–5 school, and one suburban school located in the southern part of the state, as well as one rural school located in a northeast Louisiana community. The two urban schools chosen for the study were located in the area of greater Fort Worth, Texas. No formalized explicit instruction in the use of expository text was part of the reading curriculum in any of the research sites prior to the study. Teachers in the experimental groups were provided with 2 full days of training in the teaching of nonfiction and received explicit scripts to guide the daily instruction.

Design

The study employed a quasi-experimental design in which classrooms at each site were randomly assigned experimental or control group status. This resulted in the assignment of six experimental classrooms and six control classrooms at each of the four K–5 sites and two experimental and two control classrooms at the PK–1 site and four experimental and four control classrooms at the 2–5 site, for a total of 60 classrooms. All classrooms received the nonfiction books used in the study as daily read-alouds; however, the control classrooms did not receive any special instruction on how to engage students in using the materials. Teachers in the experimental groups utilized scripted lessons designed to lead to a restructuring of the ways students read and analyzed nonfiction texts, ultimately resulting in an internalization of the process.

Data Collection Procedures

Data collection began in early September 2003 and ended 8 months later, at the end of April 2004. During the data-gathering period, the researchers visited the schools several times for informal conversations with participating teachers designed to allow teachers to share successes and researchers to address any difficulties teachers had in implementing the project. Participants and researchers also communicated via e-mail and telephone as needed. Random observations of lessons assured fidelity of implementation. Teachers also kept daily journals to document that lessons were taught each day. Each day in these journals, teachers answered questions about the effects of each lesson on students' learning, as well as questions regarding the ease/difficulty level of teaching that lesson.

All students in both the experimental and control classrooms were tested with both norm-referenced and criterion-referenced tests. Comprehension and vocabulary sections of the Stanford Achievement Test–9 (SAT–9) were administered in September 2003, prior to the study, in order to provide baseline reading data. An alternate form of the SAT–9 was administered in December 2003, at the end of the intervention period, in order to monitor improvement in comprehension achievement. The last administration of the SAT–9 occurred in April 2003 to assess retention.

On Friday of each week of the intervention period, teachers also administered criterion-referenced, content-specific tests that had been developed by the researchers. These tests were designed to measure students' comprehension of the material presented in that week's expository read-aloud. The tests were also designed to provide the researchers with insights into the types of access features and metacognitive processes on which students most often relied in their reading.

Additional data were obtained from the three focal students in each classroom. Teachers pulled aside these students and asked them to read an unfamiliar nonfiction text each week. The teachers took notes on the actions of the readers in order to determine whether or not they were independently employing any of the comprehension strategies modeled in the interventions.

Intervention Procedures

Three metacognitive building strategies were used as interventions. Each strategy was comprised of several comprehension processes that worked synergistically. The total intervention period was for 8 weeks—4 weeks per intervention. The first intervention labeled as a treatment was a hierarchical graphic organizer in chart form that is designed to help children visualize the effective comprehension processes that strategic readers employ before, during, and after reading.

The GO! Chart (Benson & Cummins, 2000, 2001; see Fig. 15.3) is a large chart, usually made from bulletin board or butcher paper, approximately 90 inches wide, which has been divided into six columns: Preview/Predict, Vocabulary/Inquiry, Understandings, Interpretations, Connections, and Organizers. Each of these categories encourages dialogue and engages the reader in specific metacognitive processes:

- *Preview/Predict* is designed to help establish or confirm schema/background knowledge for the text. Because the titles of most nonfiction texts are very specific to the content, predictions are often hard to make; therefore, a preview of the access features or other clues within the text is conducted in order to help stimulate thoughts about the text prior to reading. The teacher points out these access features and clues to the students and guides them in making connections to what has been previously studied and/or to students'

Book Title

Predictions/ Previews	Vocabulary/ Inquiries	Understandings	Interpretations	Connections	Organizers
Students' logical predictions of what the text might be about. Predictions are based on the ACCESS FEATURES or other clues about the text. Connect to what has been previously studied and to children's prior knowledge.	Beginning of creating wonder about topic by having children predict kinds of questions the text might answer or questions they would like to have answered. Also introduce key vocabulary needed to understand reading.	Students' responses to specific reflection questions identifying basic understanding of the text or text structure (relationship of ideas). Responses are generated at the knowledge and comprehension level.	Students' responses to specific reflection questions that move beyond basic comprehension levels: application, analysis, synthesis, and evaluation. Application of information to new situation.	Students' responses to specific reflection questions that identify connections to the students' own lives, to the world, or to other literature.	GO! maps used to organize the text according to text structure to facilitate the understanding and the organization of information.

FIG. 15.3. GO! Chart: Engaging students in multiple metacomprehension processes before, during, and after reading.

prior knowledge. Students then make logical predictions of what they think the text might be about.

- The *Vocabulary/Inquiry* category is used to help create wonder about the topic by having students explore words used and/or associated with words used in the text, as well as to create wonder about questions the text might answer or questions students would like to have answered, based on the earlier predictions.

- The *Understandings, Interpretations,* and *Connections* categories provide specific reflection prompts designed to stimulate student responses after reading (ultimately during reading mentally) at a variety of comprehension levels. The *Understandings* category reflects a basic understanding of the text or relationship of the ideas in the text as responses are generated at the knowledge and comprehension level of understanding—the facts from the text. *Interpretations* then moves beyond basic comprehension levels as the reflection prompt provided requires the students to analyze, apply, synthesize, and evaluate the information. This section is also designed to help students identify the author's purpose and the structure of the text. The *Connections* category is designed to continue the use of higher order thinking processes as the students connect the new information to their own lives, to the world, or to other literature.

- The last category, *Organizers,* is designed for the development of an appropriate text structure, mind map/graphic organizer that will help readers organize their understandings of the text. This organizer can then be used to assist students in producing a successful retelling, written report, or comprehension assessment.

This graphic organizer system, known as the GO! Chart (Grades K–5), was followed by a strategy called Post-it Noting (Grades K–2) or Bookmarking (Grades 3–5). Experimental students received intervention instruction for approximately 30 minutes per day during the 8-week period. During this 30-minute period, control teachers read the same nonfiction book with their students but without intervention instruction.

A new nonfiction text was introduced each week and portions were read aloud daily to the students. Teachers in all classrooms were provided a script each week in order to guide the interventions in a consistent way across all research sites. The script for the control groups provided basic directions regarding which pages to read daily. The teachers then read the books aloud to the class, with discussions occurring only to the extent dictated by student interest and/or questioning. The script for the experimental group contained the same information as that of the control group, with additional information designed to help guide the teacher in modeling the metacomprehension processes while thinking aloud and eliciting contributions from students. Analyses of variance data analyses and chi-square statistical tests were conducted on 12 classes of student reading test scores to determine short- and long-term effects of these treatments. Teacher data were analyzed through analyses of variance to determine the significance of change in comfort levels and effectiveness that occurred over the 8-week treatment periods. Teacher journals were also analyzed qualitatively.

RESULTS

One piece of data that was somewhat discouraging, yet also enlightening, was that neither teachers nor students were able to accurately graph the total contextual structures used by authors in writing their books. There are two reasons for this finding. First, many texts written for the elementary classrooms are a mixture of genre structures, which makes nonfiction even more difficult for readers to comprehend or for teachers to identify significant textual structures or features that help guide their reading. Second, the metacognition required to keep a large gestalt authorial writing pattern in mind appears to require more time to develop than we were able to invest in our initial study.

Student data analyses demonstrated that teaching several metacognitive strategies together significantly increases students' comprehension (Stewart, Block, & Cummins, 2004). Teacher data also demonstrated that experimental teachers judged their teaching behaviors to have been effective significantly more than control teachers who taught nonfiction through read-alouds, question–answer sessions, and discussions (Block, Cummins, & Stewart, in preparation). Teachers judged the comfort level and effectiveness of each lesson to vary significantly from week to week. The second and third weeks of multiple metacognitive strategy instruction were ranked significantly least comfortable and effective than other weeks of instruction. Weeks 1 and 4–8 were judged as effective instructional weeks, with Weeks 5–8 being judged most effective. Because many teachers reported in their journals that they felt very unsure of themselves in Weeks 2 and 3, data suggest that once the novelty of metacognitive instruction "wears off," many teachers may not continue to teach it.

DISCUSSION

The literacy instruction students receive exerts a powerful influence on the level of comprehension achieved from classroom reading. Due to the limited exposure of many elementary-grade students to nonfiction text, explicit comprehension instruction becomes even more critical when the reading involves expository text. Effective lessons, designed to provide students with a rich experience in learning to read and comprehend nonfiction text, generally require the teacher to draw on a broad knowledge base of textual structures and strategies intended to engage students in interacting with text. Because in the beginning teachers did not have a fully developed understanding or repertoire of strategies concerning ways to teach comprehension with expository text, researchers initially provided a script to guide instruction. From this scripted lesson, we observed that as teachers began to understand how nonfiction works, they began to deviate from the script and take ownership of providing the rich instruction that children needed in the comprehension of nonfiction. Through the GO! Chart, post-it notes, or bookmarks (listing the metacognitive processes in which expert readers engage before, during, and after reading) that we created, students and teachers gained comfort and confidence in incorporating metacognition processes as a part of their reading classes. By packaging these together, we enabled every student to see what it felt like mentally to process through a nonfiction text, truly understanding each aspect of the riches involved in that reading experience.

We determined through an informal survey that the majority of the teachers in participating schools did not fully understand many of the complexities involved in teaching comprehension of nonfiction texts even by the end of Week 8. A general lack of understanding of the importance of helping students identify the author's purpose as soon as possible in the reading was clearly evident. Teachers also demonstrated that they often knew the names of the access features used within the text but did not understand the purposes for which they were designed. Another key area in which teachers needed guidance involved understanding that text structure, global and genre specific, plays an important role in guiding the way a reader reads and organizes information. The results of this survey led the researchers to develop a model and a series of instructional statements that teachers could use in their classrooms to teach children to examine text features and apply metacognitive thought processes using the GO! Chart, post-it notes, and bookmarks to facilitate understanding. The two days of professional development opportunities in these areas were supplemented with very specific guidance provided during the study by scripts and responses to individual questions by researchers. Excerpts from these orientation inservices can be found in Fig. 15.4.

An innovative feature of our teacher development model allowed teachers to experience what it was like to be engaged in complex metacognitive processing of nonfiction text. We found that this intensive professional development was necessary. Researchers provided teacher instruction in real time. Instead of *telling* teachers what to do, we showed them by modeling a lesson. To accomplish this task, researchers used the book, *Manatees and Dugongs* (Cole, 2000). The fact that teachers had very limited background for understanding some aspects of the topic made using this book a good choice. Teachers reported that this modeled lesson was very valuable because it allowed them to engage in activities similar to those they would later implement with their students; it allowed them to question aspects of the lesson at specific points of need, and it allowed them to observe implementation of a successful lesson. The modeled lesson script was de-

Monday

(Predictions/Preview)

The title of our book this week is _Manatees and Dugongs_ .

I know that the title doesn't give us a lot of information but does anyone want to make a prediction about what they think our text might be about? (Record responses on chart.)

Let's look at the cover. Look closely for clues the author might be giving us about the text. Now what do you think the text might be about? (Record responses on chart.)

Look at _the caption on page 8_. *What do you think this information might have to do with what we will read about?* (Record responses on chart [can't see well, run into boats, etc.].)

We can also get more information by looking at _the Table of Contents (read the headings, emphasizing the word "manatees" each time)_ . *Based on this information, do you have anything to add to our prediction column?* (Record responses on chart [Read more about manatees, maybe dugongs extinct, etc.].)

(Vocabulary/Inquiry)

Listen while I read over the great predictions that you made about our text. Based on these predictions, can you think of any key words the author might have to use to help enhance our thinking about _manatees and dugongs_? (Record responses on chart.)

Let's preview some key parts of our text again, this time thinking about key words that might help us think more deeply about our text.

Look at _the word "blubber" on page 8_. *What do you think this word might have to do with our text?* (Add responses to prediction column [They live in cold water, migrate, etc.].)

Look at _the glossary and the word "endangered."_ *What do you think this might have to do with what we are going to read about today?* (Add responses to prediction column.)

Think about these predictions and key vocabulary words. Now, based on this, what questions do you think or hope are answered in our reading? (Record questions on chart under voc.)

****

Wow! You guys did a great job of thinking about _manatees and dugongs_. *Tomorrow we will read to see how accurate we were in our predictions and to see if the author answers any of our questions.*

Tuesday

Very quickly, let's read over the predictions, vocabulary, and inquiry questions that we generated yesterday so we can bring our thoughts about _manatees and dugongs_ *back to a conscious level.*

Now look up here and listen while I read the text aloud. Be listening to see if any of our predictions are accurate and if any of our questions are answered.

(Read over the Table of Contents and then read pages _2–13_ , pointing out the pictures/captions/ diagrams before you read each section.)

FIG. 15.4. (*Continued*)

Well, we learned a lot about manatees today. Let's go back now and look at the predictions we made yesterday so we can confirm or disconfirm our thinking. Now remember that all of our predictions were good yesterday based on the information we had, but now we have more information. (Go through each prediction and check those clearly confirmed or disconfirmed; but since the text was not read in its entirety today, leave any prediction that might not yet have been covered.)

Now let's look at the vocabulary words we listed yesterday. Did we encounter any of these words in our reading today? (Go through each word; and, if yes, go back into text and point it out and clarify meaning; if not, leave until tomorrow.)

What about our questions—were any of these answered today in our reading? (Read each question on chart, have kids tell you if answered and if so give the answer, then check it off. Any not answered, just leave unchecked.)

(Understandings)
Today we read about manatees.

What are some things that you noticed about manatees? (Record and remember to ask for their verification when appropriate. Be sure to pull them back to the predictions and inquiry questions if needed to pull out noticed facts.)

Now, let's read over all of the things you noticed. (Read the listed facts.) *Is there anything else you want to add before we leave our GO! Chart today?* (Record responses on chart.)

Ok, you guys did a great job; we'll read and talk more about manatees and dugongs tomorrow.

Wednesday

Ok, let's start thinking about manatees and dugongs again.

On Monday we made some great predictions and generated some super questions about manatees and dugongs.

Then yesterday we read and confirmed some of those predictions. (Read the ones you checked.)

We also found these words in the text (go over quickly), *and we answered these questions* (read the ones you checked and have students quickly answer them again).

Then after we read you shared some of the things that you remembered or noticed while I was reading. (Read over list in Understanding column.)

Now today we are going to read some more of text to see if we can find out any additional interesting information that will help us know more about manatees and dugongs. Be listening to see if any more of our predictions prove to be accurate and if any more of our questions are answered.

(Read over headings in the Table of Contents and pages 14–23, pointing out photos and captions before reading each section.)

Well, we learned a lot more about manatees and dugongs today. Let's go back now and look at the predictions we made Monday that we haven't yet confirmed or disconfirmed. Now remember that all of our predictions were good Monday when we first started and we had only a little information, but now we have more information. (Go through each prediction and check those clearly confirmed or disconfirmed.)

FIG. 15.4. *(Continued)*

Now let's look at the vocabulary words we listed Monday. Did we encounter any of these words in our reading today? (Go through each word and if yes go back into text and point it out and clarify meaning.)

(Understandings)
Today we read about <u>manatees and dugongs</u>.

What are some things that you noticed about <u>manatees and dugongs</u>*?* (Record and remember to ask for their verification when appropriate. Be sure to pull them back to the predictions and inquiry questions if needed to pull out noticed facts.)

Now let's read over all of the things you noticed yesterday and today. (Read the listed facts.) *Is there anything else you want to add before we leave our GO! Chart today?* (Record responses on chart.)

Ok, you guys did a great job, and we now know quite a bit about <u>manatees and dugongs</u>. *Don't you agree?*

Thursday

(Interpretations)
The last couple of days we have read and talked a lot about something, but if we could put all of this together into one main idea, what would you say was the main content we read about? (Facilitate the conversation pulling them to main idea.) *You are right. The main content the author was sharing was* <u>things about manatees and dugongs</u>. (Write this beside the word content on the chart.)

Ok, let's look at the Understandings column. Here are some of the things that we noticed and now understand about <u>manatees and dugongs</u>. *Based on these facts, what do you think the author's main purpose was in sharing this information?* (Guide them to see the Purpose.) *You are right. Our author* <u>Sally Cole</u>, *wanted to* <u>describe things about manatees and dugongs</u>. (Write this beside Purpose on the chart.)

Let's look at our facts again. Since <u>order doesn't matter in the way we read or remember our facts about</u> <u>(we could have read about dugongs before manatees, etc.)</u>. (Write this by word structure on the chart.) *We could use a* <u>conceptual</u> *or a* <u>hierarchical map</u> *to help us remember our facts.* (Draw a small one of both on chart explaining how you could list facts in any order they remembered them.)

Now another clue that authors give readers to help them better understand the structure of the text, and therefore make reading easier, is the type of language they use.

Listen while I read this sentence in our text on page <u>7</u>, "They use their flippers to steer with when they swim." (Read.) *Did you hear the word* <u>use</u> *in that sentence? The word* <u>use</u> *is present tense, meaning it could happen right now—in the present.*

What about this sentence on page <u>19</u>, "Manatees move slowly and cannot get out of the way of fast boats." (Read.) *Did you hear the word* <u>move</u> *in that sentence? The word* <u>move</u> *is also present tense, meaning it could happen right now—in the present.*

FIG. 15.4. (*Continued*)

The author used language written in the present tense that helps us to better understand how the text is written.

So it looks like the author's purpose for writing this text was to describe things about manatees and dugongs. And since order doesn't matter, either a conceptual or hierarchical graphic organizer could be used to help us organize our facts. We also know now that since the author was describing things about manatees and dugongs and that order didn't matter in how they shared the facts with us and that he used present tense language, that this is a descriptive nonfiction text.

Now, let's look at the questions you generated on Tuesday and Wednesday so we can make sure that they were all answered. (Read each question in the Inquiry column and confirm that it was answered; and if not already in the Understandings column, add it.)

Ok, before we leave our Interpretation column, is there anything else that you are still wondering about? (Record responses. Go into text for answers if there; and if not, then this might be future research.)

(Connections)
Think about all of the questions and answers that we have generated and the information we have read about manatees and dugongs. Does any of this information remind you of anything? (Record responses.)

(Retelling)
Now we only have one category left and our GO! Chart for the book, Manatees and Dugongs, will be complete. Let's look back at our Interpretation column. We said that the author was describing facts about manatees and dugongs and that the order he used didn't really matter so we could use either a conceptual or hierarchical map to help remember the facts.

Today I think we will use a hierarchical map, so let's make one now (draw a hierarchical map on the chart with the main categories). *Our main topic is manatees and dugongs so I will put that right at the top of our chart. We have two main things that we learned about, so I can label our columns manatees and dugongs. Now tell me what important facts you remember from our reading this week* (List these under the correct category—be sure to have children provide their rationales if needed.)

Wow, we now know a lot more about manatees and dugongs than we did on Monday. All of you did a great job of helping me work our way through this text.

Friday

Pass out weekly assessment pages and instruct students to complete to the best of their ability. (Pull and assess the focal students one at a time during this time or at another time of the day.)

FIG. 15.4. Sample professional development program (GO! chart lesson plan to be used by experimental group, grade 5, week 3).

signed to develop students' metacognitive processing from the beginning to the end of the book.

DIRECTIONS FOR FUTURE INSTRUCTION

This research study provided participating teachers with new methods of teaching students to internalize and transfer metacognitive processes, but there are still many questions regarding implementation and usage of the interventions that need to be answered:

1. *How do teachers gradually release students from the visual scaffold in the form of GO! Charts, post-it note prompts, and bookmarks to create less artificially imposed, and more self-initiated instances of metacognition by their students? How can the GO! Chart, post-it notes, and bookmarks facilitate total transfer of responsibility for the utilization of the metacognitive processes?* When children are able to complete it easily and comfortably, and teachers begin to notice students utilizing some of the processes in their independent reading, then may be the time to scaffold some of the responsibility for the completion of the GO! Chart, post-it notes, and bookmarks. This initial scaffolding can be done by utilizing a "ping-pong" technique. This simply means that the teacher begins to allow students to take over some of the responsibility for writing their responses on the chart, post-it notes, or bookmark. This ping-pong technique is then followed by providing students with even more responsibility. One way to do that is to provide individual GO! journals, post-its, and bookmarks that students complete in conjunction with the class's chart. Students complete a section on their own and then bring it to the whole group. This ping-pong technique would continue until less and less support was required and students were able to complete their own metacognitive thoughts entirely on their own. Eventually, there would be no need for a GO! Chart, journal, post-it note, or bookmark as the students would be utilizing the processes mentally every time they picked up a nonfiction book. This process, not initiated in the study due to time limitations, is being tested in classrooms across the United States.

2. *Where does this complex instructional process fit in normal classroom instruction?* The GO! Chart, post-it notes, and bookmarks should be used to help students delve more deeply into texts in order to reach higher levels of comprehension. In the study, the text was part of the daily read-aloud period and each book was completed over a one-week time period. In a regular reading class, this is generally done with that one text that is used as the "reading text" for the week. If trade books are used as the reading materials in the reading program, then teachers can begin to use them immediately by supplementing some of their fictional texts with nonfiction texts. If basals are the only reading materials utilized in the

classroom, then one or all of these multiple metacognitive process instructional strategies can be used anytime a nonfiction selection is provided in the basal. Informational trade books can and should also be used as supplemental sources.

3. *How long should it take? When should we start teaching metacognitive processes in the school year?* Implementation of a multiple metacognitive process instructional strategy should begin at the beginning of the school year; however, depending on the age of the students, certain categories might be eliminated until students become comfortable with the process. Ideally, instruction should take about 20–30 minutes per day. This will vary depending on the students' participation and the complexity of the nonfiction text. The process will take longer initially because students are often not accustomed to interacting with text at the depth of metacognitive comprehension.

This study was an initial voyage into investigating how teachers can assist students in developing metacognitive processing of nonfiction texts. This "maiden voyage" provided participating teachers with a wealth of new strategies for using nonfiction texts in comprehension instruction, yet it was also a voyage in which they were learning about the complexities of nonfiction text and the role these played in comprehension. This was a major limitation of the study. In the future, a replicated study needs to be conducted in which teachers are provided with more intense instruction and understanding of genre structure, particularly the specific characteristics of the genres, as well as the intricacies of each intervention. Their increased knowledge of nonfiction and their own internalization of these processes should facilitate an even better transfer and internalization for their students.

CONCLUSIONS

We are presently analyzing additional data from six elementary schools that have followed this process of building children's metacognition with nonfiction text. We know that teachers and students have grown in their abilities from the first day through the 8 weeks they taught these instructional processes. We found that as teachers grew in expertise in facilitating the strategy, students' questioning ability increased significantly, the amount and the quality of their answers expanded, the number of connections students were able to retain increased, and the ease with which they could pick up a novel nonfiction text and begin to comprehend it from page 1 has grown significantly. We also found that when predicting occurs during the reading, as well as before reading, students revisit the information from the book more often and are more accurate in their recall.

In addition, we found that most of the participating teachers wanted to continue this process of instruction after our study ended. Teachers and students alike enjoyed and profited from comprehension instruction that utilized several processes simultaneously. We also know that teachers felt that the level of reading ability of their children did not affect the time it took for them to integrate this process. This is a phenomenal occurrence in instruction. We will continue to document the statistically significant effects of this study.

METACONNECTION FOR CHAPTER 15

In the next section of the book, Duffy offers the reader a view of visioning as a foundation of metacognitive teaching as well as suggestions for how the expert role might shift in supporting teacher development. In chapter 17, Risko, Roskos, and Vukelich turn our attention from visioning to reflection.

REFERENCES

Anderson, R. C., & Pearson, P. D. (1984). A schema-theoretic view of basic processes in reading. In P. D. Pearson (Ed.), *Handbook of reading research* (pp. 255–291). New York: Longman.

Baker, L. (2001). Metacognition in comprehension instruction. In C. Block & M. Pressley (Eds.), *Comprehension instruction: Research based practices* (pp. 274–289). New York: Guilford.

Benson, V., & Cummins, C. (2000). *The power of retelling: Developmental steps for building better comprehension.* Bothell, WA: Wright Group/McGraw-Hill.

Benson, V., & Cummins, C. (2001). *Nonfiction retelling: Teaching literacy skills through informational texts* [text available in conjunction with workshop of same title]. Bothell, WA: Wright Group/McGraw-Hill.

Block, C. C. (1993). Strategy instruction in a student-centered classroom. *The Elementary School Journal, 94*(2), 137–153.

Block, C. C., & Pressley, M. (Eds.). (2002). *Comprehension instruction: Research-based best practices.* New York: Guilford.

Block, C. C., & Israel, S. (2004). The ABC's of performing highly effective think-alouds. *The Reading Teacher, 57*(2), 81–99.

Block, C. C., Cummins, C., & Stewart, M. T. (in preparation). *How long does it take teachers and students to internalize and transfer specific combinations of comprehension processes* [tentative title of qualitative analysis].

Brown, A. L., Collins, A., & Duguid, D. (1989). Metacognition: Effects on academic achievement. *Journal of Educational Psychology, 81*(3), 403–419.

Cole, S. (2000). *Manatees and dugongs.* Bothell, WA: Wright Group/McGraw-Hill.

Duke, N. (2000). 3.6 minutes per day: The scarcity of informational texts in first grade. *Reading Research Quarterly, 35*(2), 202–224.

Duke, N., & Pearson, P.D. (2002). Comprehension instruction. In A. Farstrup & S. J. Samuels (Eds.), *What research has to say about reading instruction* (2nd ed., pp. 103–129). Newark, DE: International Reading Association.

Durkin, D. (1978–1979). What classroom observation reveals about reading comprehension instruction. *Reading Research Quarterly, 14,* 481–533.

Fielding, L. G., & Pearson, P. D. (1994). Synthesis of research: Reading comprehension: What works? *Educational Leadership, 51*(5), 62–67.

National Reading Panel (2000). *Report of subsection IV: Comprehension instruction.* Washington, DC: National Institute for Child Health and Human Development.

Pearson, D. (1985). Changing the face of reading comprehension instruction. *The Reading Teacher, 38*(8), 724–738.

Samuels, J. (2002). Fluency instruction. In A. Farstrup & J. Samuels (Eds.), *What research has to say about reading instruction* (2nd ed., pp. 347–369). Newark, DE: International Reading Association.

Stewart, M. T. (2004). Early literacy instruction in the climate of No Child Left Behind. *The Reading Teacher, 57*(8), 732–753.

Stewart, M. T., Block, C. C., & Cummins, C. (2004, December 4). *Evidence-based research: Internalization and transfer of comprehension processes.* PowerPoint session presentation, National Reading Conference Annual Conference, San Antonio, TX. (Available from M. T. Stewart, LSU, EDCI, 223 Peabody Hall, Baton Rouge, LA 70803)

Trimble, S. (1994). The scripture of maps, the names of trees: A child's landscape. In G. P. Nabhan & S. Trimble (Eds.), *The geography of childhood: Why children need wild places* (pp. 15–32). Boston: Beacon Press.

IV

Metacognition and Professional Development

As Duffy (chap. 16, this volume) points out in the opening chapter of this section, the principles of metacognition have not typically been applied to the realm of professional development of teachers. The goal of this section is to encourage the reader to explore how professional development of teachers can be viewed from a metacognitive perspective. Part IV provides a framework and practice-based examples of how the theoretical principles of metacognition can be applied to teacher learning.

One prevailing criticism of current professional development opportunities for practicing teachers is that it is often superficial and disconnected from the reality of teaching and student learning. Critics of preservice teacher preparation programs also point to the inadequacies of preservice experiences that are not clearly and tightly grounded in what teachers must know and be able to do. The chapters in Part IV acknowledge the complexity of teaching and provide suggestions for how to design and implement high quality professional development.

One consideration that can contribute to high quality experiences for both preservice and inservice teachers is to approach teaching and learning from a metacognitive perspective. Like learners, teachers are more likely to be accomplished if they approach tasks with awareness and self-regulation. The chapters in this section illuminate the possibilities of examining professional development from a metacognitive perspective.

In chapter 16, Duffy describes how *visioning* can be seen as one foundation of metacognitive teaching, and proposes four shifts in the expert's role in professional development. Risko, Roskos, and Vukelich (chap. 17) juxtapose reflection, a cornerstone of teacher preparation, and the principles of metacognition. In chapter 18, Bowman, Galvez-Martin, and Morrison extend this analysis offered by Risko et al. through an examination of guided reflection based on one research study. Just as reflection as a metacognitive process holds promise for professional development, so does a structured analysis of teaching in a coaching context. Rosemary describes in detail a tool for analyzing teaching, the *Teacher Learning Instrument*, in chapter 19. Then Kinnucan-Welsch focuses on coaching and teaching as metacognitive activity in chapter 20, by embedding research incorporating the *Teacher Learning Instrument*.

The authors of the chapters in this section suggest that we have the theoretical base and practical knowledge to design and deliver substantive professional development for preservice and inservice teachers that can impact teaching practice as well as student learning. Research is needed that focuses on the efficacy of the principles outlined in these chapters. There is also a need for research that examines how schools could be structured to support professional development grounded in a metacognitive perspective. This is a challenge, to be sure, but one that holds promise to shape education in the 21st century.

16

Developing Metacognitive Teachers: Visioning and the Expert's Changing Role in Teacher Education and Professional Development

Gerald G. Duffy

University of North Carolina–Greensboro

I see professional development as an essential focus area, as I fulfill my duties in the role of a Literacy Coach. Teachers do not always understand "what it is and why it is" they teach, if the materials and methods they are using for instruction are appropriate, and how to design instruction to fit the diversities of every learner. At this point, I wonder, should not all classroom teachers become Reading Specialists? A question I still have is: Does professional development fit into the traditional school day/calendar and what is the motivation for teachers to be involved?
—Pamela Groach, Literacy Coach for Grades K–6, Ohio

Metacognition, with its emphasis on self-conscious action, is not normally associated with teacher development. Instead, the talk is about "teacher *training,*" which carries the implication that teaching is a mechanical matter of implementing technical acts in a predetermined manner.

Training, however, seldom works because classroom teaching cannot be predicted in advance. There are no certain answers, knowledge is situational, and teachers must make "on-the-spot" responses to students' emerging understandings. Effectiveness in such a fluid environment requires teachers to "know where to be and what to do at the right time" (Berliner, 1994), an ability Bransford, Brown, and Cocking (2000) called "adaptive expertise." It is a particular state of mind—a feeling of "being in charge." It is, in short, metacognitive.

However, because little is known about how to develop such a state of mind in teachers, this chapter suggests what could be done to develop metacognitive teachers. Three questions serve to guide the reading:

1. What characterizes a metacognitive teacher and why is it a viable alternative to training?
2. Why is visioning a necessary prerequisite to metacognitive teaching?
3. How must teacher educators, staff developers, and other experts change their professional development practices in order to develop metacognitive teachers?

METACOGNITION AND ADAPTIVE TEACHING

Teaching is a dilemma-ridden endeavor (Buchmann, 1990; Windshitl, 2002). Teachers face a continuous stream of problematic, ill-defined, and multidimensional situations. There are no easy answers; instead, teachers must adapt "on-the-fly" to pupils' developing understandings and to opportunities for situating instruction in motivating tasks. Consequently, instruction is not a tidy endeavor that can be predicted in advance. As Spillane, Reiser, and Reimer (2002) pointed out, the nature of teachers' work "involves unpredictable human relations not reducible to programmatic routines" (p. 390). It is demanding work.

This is especially so in reading. Cultural differences make for a diverse clientele; basic skills are not the end goal, but just a foundation for developing more important outcomes such as comprehension, higher order thinking, and the ability to prevail in a complex society; and accountability pressures are more intrusive than ever (see, e.g., Miller, Heafner, Massey, & Strahan, 2004). Ambiguity prevails; certainty is rare.

Succeeding in this environment requires that teachers take charge of their work and be adaptive decision-makers. Training, however, seldom helps teachers feel like they are in charge. Instead, training tends to emphasize passive assimilation of knowledge and compliance with experts' recommendations, which in turn causes teachers to construct the understanding that they are expected to be followers who should not "think-on-their-feet." In fact, some programs even have "program police" that visit classrooms to ensure that teachers are doing exactly as they were told. What such approaches encourage is passive compliance; they do not encourage thoughtfully adaptive responses to children and creation of inspiring learning opportunities.

Metacognition offers a more promising alternative. Often described as "thinking about thinking," metacognition emphasizes conscious, mindful action as opposed to technical compliance. Two components are essential: being aware of one's knowledge (i.e., knowledge about task variables and strategies) and control and self-regulation of one's knowledge (i.e., monitoring and controlling one's cognitive activity) (Hofer, Yu, & Pintrich, 1998; Paris & Winograd, 1990).

In reading instruction, metacognition is associated with comprehension strategies (see, e.g., Brown & Pressley, 1994; Duffy, 2003; Garner, 1987). That is, good readers are conscious of when a text makes sense, and when it does not they impose conscious control over the situation by accessing and using a strategy to repair the difficulty. Hence, comprehension is metacognitive; readers must be aware of knowledge (in this case, of how to be strategic) and must accept the responsibility of "thinking-on-your-feet" with that knowledge (i.e., they must self-regulate and apply that knowledge adaptively as opposed to procedurally).

The same idea is applicable to teachers. They, too, must self-regulate if they are to respond differentially to children and situations. For instance, when teaching a comprehension process that cannot be broken down into tangible parts and taught by drill and repetition, self-regulated teachers access knowledge (in this case, professional knowledge about comprehension and teaching), "think-on-their-feet" as they implement that knowledge (in this case, adapt it to fit different children and different textual situations), and repeat the process in a fluid, ever-changing cycle as teaching situations change. Such autonomous instructional behavior is often associated with exemplary teaching (see, e.g., Block, Oakar, & Hurt, 2002; Duffy, 1991, 1993; Wharton-McDonald, Pressley, & Hampston, 1998).

Hence, effective teachers tend to exhibit metacognitive behaviors. They orient their actions toward the attainment of a goal (Schunk & Zimmerman, 1994), use feedback from their performances to make adjustments during instruction (Zimmerman, 2000), abandon routinized procedures when they fail (R. Kanfer & F. H. Kanfer, 1991), and transfer knowledge from one situation to another without prompting (Smith, 2003).

Interestingly, however, such metacognitive action is more than just "cognitive." It is also affective. That is, metacognitive people self-regulate doubts and fears and other emotions about specific performance contexts (see, e.g., Pintrich, 1995; van den Berg, 2002; Zimmerman, 2000). This aspect of metacognition is especially relevant to teachers. Schooling generally and literacy instruction particularly does not occur in cool, quiet cloisters but, rather, in the heated atmosphere of classrooms where instruction is more demanding than ever, the uncertainties more prevalent than ever, the pressures heavier than ever, the curricular goals more complex than ever, and the stakes higher than ever. To self-regulate in these highly charged environments, teachers must control emotional as well as cognitive aspects of teaching.

In sum, metacognition offers an alternative to "training." Rather than creating passive users of knowledge who apply what they know in procedural ways, metacognition offers the possibility of creating teachers who possess the proactive state of mind and the emotional strength to "take charge." The question is, "How do we develop such a 'state of mind'?"

VISIONING AS THE FOUNDATION OF METACOGNITIVE TEACHING

The distinguishing feature of a metacognitive state of mind is a propensity to act on one's own authority. You decide, rather than waiting for someone else to decide for you. Doing so, however, involves both mental and emotional strength. But where does the strength come from?

I believe it is rooted in a sense of independent spirit that I call "visioning" (Duffy, 1998, 2002). That is, to impose control over one's work, especially given the pressures teachers face today, one must have a strong sense of personal mission. This sense of mission is an internal voice that reminds teachers that teaching involves inspiring and enlightening children as well as teaching basic skills and competencies. One of my former students who is now teaching describes it as "my ideal. It's what I'm setting out to accomplish so that despite the politics of the job, I ask myself, 'What's the essence of my being here?' " (Duffy, 2002, p. 339).

Visioning is my term, but others describe a similar characteristic using different terms. For instance, Greene (1991) talked about "personal reality," that is, a "particular standpoint, a particular location in space and time" (p. 4); Feiman-Nemser (1990) emphasized "personal orientation"; Van Manen (1977) referred to an orientation to what a teacher "believes to be true, to be valuable and to be real" (p. 211); Garrison (1997) cited "practical reasoning"; Rosaen and Schram (1998) talked about "the autonomous self"; and Bandura (1997) emphasized "self-efficacy."

Regardless of label, the focus is teachers' conscious sense of personal stance and values about teaching generally and about literacy in particular. For some teachers, the higher mission is to empower students to rise above circumstances and difficulties; for others, it is to develop a sense of what it means to be human; for still others, it is to prepare citizens who will engage in social change. The specifics vary from teacher to teacher, but a vision always goes beyond the visible curriculum of teaching decoding and comprehension and identifies a larger goal that becomes a "hidden curriculum" reflecting a teacher's highest ideals about teaching and literacy. As another of my students has said, "If you have an idea why you're teaching, you can hold everything up to that. It's your touchstone. You won't allow things that go against that" (Duffy, 2002, p. 339).

Vision, then, serves as a "moral compass." When inundated with the "dailiness" of teaching and with the seemingly stifling directives from higher authority, a teacher's vision points the way to doing more than just raising test scores and managing behavior. It is this "moral compass" that provides the psychological strength to continue the effort to be in self-regulatory control and to rise above the difficulties of day-to-day teaching. In the absence of a vision, on the other hand, directives from higher authority are a teacher's only compass.

Consequently, visioning is an antidote for the intrusive nature of today's policy initiatives. When teachers have a clear vision of their mission, they are better able to control the affective doubts and fears that accompany pressure-filled mandates, and are more likely to persevere in pursuit of complex curricular goals in the face of tests that emphasize low-level skills. In short, when teachers are consciously aware of their visions, they are more likely to be metacognitive.

In sum, visioning and the sense of personal agency that results is the wellspring from which metacognitive teaching flows. To self-regulate, teachers must have a sense of what is right and good, and criteria that can be used to decide how to respond to the ambiguous and often conflicted situations typical of classroom life. Visioning, therefore, transcends the visible curriculum and helps teachers understand that their role is more than technical compliance with policy mandates.

But visioning is not easy to develop. It requires that experts resist the temptation to create disciples. The very essence of visioning is that teachers must act on their own authority, not on someone else's. Therefore, experts must ensure that teachers develop their visions, not the expert's vision.

TEACHER DEVELOPMENT THAT PROMOTES METACOGNITIVE TEACHING

Teacher education and professional development have traditionally been based in rational-linear models. Visioning or self-regulating one's own instruction were not emphasized. Now, however, the bar has been raised because of society's need for all children to achieve high forms of literacy. And that goal requires thoughtfully adaptive teachers. Developing such teachers, in turn, requires a more dynamic, sociocultural approach to the teaching of teachers (van den Berg, 2002).

These more dynamic approaches vary one from another, but all take a flexible, developmental approach (Richardson & Placier, 2001). Randi and Corno (2000) called it "collaborative innovation," R. Kanfer and F. H. Kanfer (1991) called it "participatively-set goals," Smith (2003) called it "flexible delivery," and Hawley and Valli (1999) called it "collaborative problem-solving."

All are based in constructivist ideas. Just as we know that children construct new knowledge and understandings about reading and how to read based on what they already know and believe, teachers also construct new knowledge and understandings about how to teach based on what they already know and believe. Just as we must pay attention to pupils' incomplete understandings, misconceptions, and naïve understandings and be responsive in helping them create more mature understandings, we must similarly attend to teachers' incomplete understandings, misconceptions, and naïve understandings and be responsive in helping them become better teachers.

However, constructivist approaches to teacher development are not easy. Both teachers and experts have difficulty. Teachers, for instance, often resist, apparently because of the "apprenticeship of observation" phenomenon (Lortie, 1975) in which, based on their 13 years as students, they assume they already know how to teach (see, e.g., R. Kanfer & F. H. Kanfer, 1991; Kennedy, 1999; Spillane et al., 2002). So when urged to employ recent research findings, they engage in what Windschitl (2002) called "additive" change and what Huberman (1995) called "tinkering"—that is, they insert minor changes into their existing practices or, as Levin (2003) suggested, do not immediately implement what was emphasized. The problem for teachers is further compounded by pressure to have pupils score well on low-level tests, thereby encouraging passive compliance rather than metacognitive control.

But experts also have difficulty. The criterion is no longer fidelity to what experts say (Garet, Porter, Desimone, Birman, & Yoon, 2001; Hiebert, 1998) and teachers, not experts, assume the lead. This results in four shifts in the expert's role in teacher development.

The First Shift: The Goal Experts Seek to Achieve

Visioning and the development of an independent spirit in teachers is a priority goal. Consequently, the expert's first and foremost task is to promote personal agency. This means that teachers must be freed of the traditional expectation that experts will provide answers. Instead, the priority task is to establish that teachers must self-regulate and make their own decisions, and to do so they must know what they stand for and what their personal touchstone will be when they encounter the daily uncertainties that are the essence of teaching. That is, teachers must identify their "moral compass."

Various educators suggest various ways to do this. I have my students develop "vision statements" (Duffy, 2002); Connelly, Clandinin, and He (1997) worked on "teachers' personal practical knowledge," Anders and Richardson (1991) had teachers explore their beliefs, and Collay (1998) used teacher narratives and life histories. But, whatever method is used, the goal is to have teachers develop a mental model in which they see themselves as being "in charge." The teacher's vision counts, not the expert's vision, because today's teaching demands teachers who make their own decisions rather than looking to an expert for an "answer."

The Second Shift: Experts' Roles as Leaders

A second change is the expert's leadership role. In traditional models, professors, inservice speakers, and other experts make a presentation about what to do, and teachers follow. In a collaborative model, in contrast, teachers decide on goals, on how to proceed with implementation, and on how to evaluate their efforts. Although experts retain a responsibility to ensure that professional development does not turn into "the blind leading the blind," their role is much more subtle and flexible than when acting as trainers.

And because their leadership role changes, the experts' physical position in the gathering of teachers changes. Instead of being "stand-up-in-front" authorities, experts work within a "learning community" (Englert & Tarrant, 1995) or an "intellectual community" (Duffy, 1993). The community may be a primary wing of a building, or a grade level group, or two teachers working together in coaching pairs, or some other combination. Whatever the form, experts provide coaching and support (Dole, 2004). And, in contrast to training models, teachers are invited and, indeed, are expected to mediate recommendations of experts.

The Third Shift: The Expert's Curricular Responsibility

Traditionally, experts have been expected to disseminate professional knowledge. However, self-regulated teachers do not simply use knowledge, they adapt it as they teach. Consequently, whereas content knowledge is often associated with successful professional development efforts (see, e.g., Garet et al., 2001), raw knowledge alone is not enough. Knowledge dissemination must also emphasize the adaptation of knowledge or, as Shulman (1990) said, the "transformation of knowledge" to fit different demands in different situations. Hence, the expert's curricular responsibility is to develop teachers' abilities to transform knowledge, not simply to "know."

At first glance, a judgment-focused curriculum looks like standard teacher education curricula in that the usual forms of professional knowledge are disseminated, including the importance of language structure, text-rich environments, classroom management, high time on task, child development, learning theory, explicit teaching, and other "best practices." Such knowledge remains important because you cannot self-regulate knowledge you do not possess.

But, additionally, teachers must develop the ability to "transform" knowledge. To learn to do so, they must have experience performing academic tasks rich in self-regulatory possibilities (Pintrich, 1995; Randi & Corno, 2000). That is, they must have tasks that require them to transform what they know. Just as children build their understandings about the nature and purpose of literacy based on the kinds of tasks they are asked to complete (Doyle, 1983), teachers build their understandings about the need to transform professional knowledge only if their tasks require transformation of knowledge. Consequently, reading teachers should experience tasks such as the following:

- When learning about a new method, teachers are required not only to "know" the method in the usual sense, but are also expected to modify the method to fit nonstandard situations.
- When learning about informal assessment devices, teachers not only "know" how to use these in standard ways, but also are given academic tasks that require varying the administration of the assessment to fit varying conditions.
- When learning about an instructional technique, teachers not only learn the technique, but are also given academic tasks requiring them to modify the technique to fit unanticipated situations.
- When examining a particular commercial reading program, teachers not only learn how to use the materials in standard ways, but also are given aca-

demic tasks that require them to modify program prescriptions to accommodate certain children.

In sum, an expert's objective is not to present authoritative certainties about
how to teach; rather, it is to prepare teachers to "move outside supposed certainties into the less secure, more tentative and problematic arena of complexities,
instability and value conflict" (Smyth, 1989, p. 195), and to accept what Garrison (1997) called the "uncertainty, mystery, doubt and half-knowledge" (p. 85)
of teaching. In short, in developing adaptive teachers (i.e., teachers who are in
metacognitive control of their work), we must convey not only standard professional knowledge but also an understanding that the best teachers are "method-
ologically eclectic" (Shanahan & Neumann, 1997). That is, they are not locked
into a single method, technique, or set of materials but, instead, impose self-
regulatory control over instruction, select from among practices, and transform
knowledge to fit specific situations.

The Fourth Shift: The Expert's Role at the Practice Site

Finally, the expert–teacher relationship shifts at the practice site. As Elmore, Peterson, and McCarthy (1996) pointed out, teachers are unlikely to change their
practices "without some exposure to what teaching actually looks like when it's
being done differently and exposure to someone who could help them understand
the difference between what they were doing and what they aspire to do" (p.
241). But experts play new roles in such practice situations.

First, teacher-led collaboration and reflection prevails. The authenticity of
the classroom is desirable but, as Ball and Cohen (1999) pointed out, the hurly-
burly nature of classroom life can interfere with opportunity to learn. So there
must also be quiet reflection. But the reflection is teacher led, not expert led.

Second, and despite the previous caution, extensive time must be devoted to
practice in real teaching situations. Metacognitive teaching is a subtle and essentially artful process because every instructional situation is unique in one way or
another. Consequently, practice must be longitudinal. That means staff developers cannot just come in, make a presentation about how to improve instruction,
and then leave. They must stick with teachers over the long haul.

Third, practice must occur in the context of teachers' real situations. Simulations, peer teaching, and other nonclassroom activities tend not to be effective
because teachers see them as artificial and not representative of their realities. As
Schmoker (2004) pointed out, practice must be situated in ground level complexities that cannot be anticipated in advance (see also Hoffman, 1998). Consequently, successful implementation depends on experts being in the trenches
where teachers encounter contextual barriers that often block application of
seemingly sensible research and theory, and where they can assist teachers in

making "on-the-spot" adjustments and transformations that make innovations possible.

Finally, and even though their roles are collaborative rather than directive, experts provide explicit assistance. That is, teacher educators and staff developers immerse themselves in the messiness of day-to-day teaching, doing demonstration lessons to model the thinking involved, providing scaffolding and coaching as teachers attempt to implement, and assisting as teachers evaluate the effectiveness of their efforts. This may seem counter to conventional views of constructivism, given that constructivist approaches emphasize that learners build their own knowledge. However, as Bransford, Brown, and Cocking (2000) pointed out, constructivism does not mean that experts should never state anything directly. Instead, it means that experts take care to determine when to directly intervene, when to collaborate, and when to simply observe and listen.

In sum, developing self-regulated teachers requires a field-based situation in which experts are "on site" enough to ensure that teacher learning occurs in the context of the real classrooms, that assistance is provided over time, and that teachers reflect on their practice experiences. When experts do this, together with developing teachers' psychological strength, being supportive rather than directive, and emphasizing transformation of knowledge, teachers have a chance to become metacognitive.

DEVELOPING METACOGNITIVE TEACHERS AT PRESERVICE AND INSERVICE LEVELS

Emerging ideas about teacher development are most often associated with inservice efforts rather than with preservice teacher education (see, e.g., Anders & Richardson, 1991; Birdyshaw, Pesko, Wixon, & Yochum, 2002; Duffy, 1993). There are three reasons. First, inservice teachers are assumed to have the experience to be independent. Preservice teachers, in contrast, are often immature teenagers who, it is assumed, would be overwhelmed with the task of being metacognitive. Second, university rules and expectations often impose limitations that constrain preservice teacher education. For instance, the curriculum is dictated by university course requirements and state certification, the schedule is driven by university calendars, and teacher educators are seldom rewarded for helping teachers in classrooms. Finally, the university is isolated from the reality of classrooms. Consequently, it is difficult to achieve conceptual congruity between what happens in preservice teacher education courses and what happens in field experiences, with the result that a mini-power struggle develops between university professors and cooperating teachers regarding whose views will prevail.

Despite these difficulties, however, if we want metacognitive teachers, we must deliver the same message throughout a teacher's preparation. Setting the expectation during preservice teacher education that teachers should follow the lead of experts and then expecting them to switch to metacognitive teaching when they become inservice teachers means unlearning one mental model and substituting a different mental model. Doing so is a difficult proposition. Consequently, the development of metacognitive teachers must begin at the preservice level.

Application at the Preservice Level

Preservice teacher education is different from inservice professional development. It must be more directive, more closely tied to the academic life of the university, and responsive to university policy more than to school policy. However, because preparing teachers to assume metacognitive control is still the goal, the differences between preservice teacher development and inservice teacher development is one of degree, not of spirit.

For instance, the ultimate mission of developing metacognitive teachers prevails, but is tempered by the reality that neophytes must learn more professional knowledge than inservice teachers. Consequently, the expectation is not that teacher candidates will be fully metacognitive in their first teaching position; instead, the expectation is that they will have the propensity to approach their work that way and, hopefully, they will end up in a teaching situation that allows them to fulfill that expectation (see, in this regard, Grossman et al., 2000).

Further, whereas the university's course structure and semester system dominates, the tenor of instruction is nonetheless collaborative rather than directive. That is, visioning is developed, professors create various kinds of communities, academic tasks emphasize judgment and collaborative problem solving, and teacher candidates are authorized to be autonomous.

Finally, there is a heavy field-based component. It is characterized not only by extensive time, but also by congruence between what is emphasized in methods courses and what student teachers see cooperating teachers doing. That is, cooperating teachers are themselves metacognitive teachers who have a clear vision of what they are about, who approach teaching as a judgment-based endeavor as opposed to a technical task, and who apply principles and techniques from methods classes to classroom instruction. To maintain that congruence, teachers, professors, and student teachers work together to build a sense of partnership, to improve instruction, and to further cement conceptual congruence between the school and the university.

Applications at the Inservice Level

At the inservice level, development of metacognitive teachers can occur in both small group and schoolwide settings. In the small group model, teachers and administrators may form small study groups to explore professional problems and meet occasionally to discuss those problems. Often these are grade level teams, coaching pairs, or triads or, sometimes, simply likeminded teachers in a building. Participants define a problem, share ideas, and provide feedback on efforts to experiment in their classrooms. The agenda for meetings is flexible, meetings are organized around conversations and discussion, and the criterion for success is student achievement. Experts may be brought in as a resource to the group, but their role is supportive rather than directive.

Schoolwide professional development includes all members of the school staff in an effort to create and implement instructional improvements throughout the building. Again, the effort focuses on student achievement, and the spirit of teacher-driven change prevails. However, because the numbers tend to be large, an organizational structure is often imposed. This structure may include all-staff meetings, grade level meetings, and a representative committee formed to coordinate across grade levels. But, like the small group model, and consistent with constructivist views of teacher development, teachers' views are valued, the goals are teacher determined, the implementation occurs in teachers' classrooms, student data are used to evaluate effectiveness, and revisions are applied in classrooms again. And, of course, experts consult and support, but do not direct.

Whether staff development efforts occur in a small or large group setting, the goal remains the same. That is, the intent is to create teachers who can, by virtue of being in metacognitive control of their work, adapt instruction to fit the fluid situations that characterize classroom life, the diverse student clientele found in today's classrooms, and the more challenging curriculum in the 21st century.

Central to the task is the surfacing of teachers' visions and the creation of the independent spirit. Consequently, there is a prevailing sense of teachers being in personal charge. Accomplishing this requires that experts stay on site at schools for long periods of time, involve themselves in the day-to-day application in real classrooms, and encourage teachers to reflect and evaluate in an ongoing process. It is not a one-shot deal but, rather, an ongoing developmental process.

NEEDED RESEARCH

The debate over teacher development is heated (see, e.g., Cochran-Smith & Fries, 2001). There is a growing political tendency to replace university-based teacher education with "quick fix" (and cheaper) routes to certification. For instance, both Texas and Georgia passed legislation that allows anyone with a bachelor's degree to teach without any pedagogical preparation whatsoever. The voiced rationale for this is that there is no "scientifically based research" (i.e., experimental research) establishing the effectiveness of university-based teacher education.

This is a classic Catch-22 situation. Given human-subject restrictions, it is impossible to do true experiments in teacher education because we cannot do randomized trials. What school district, for instance, would agree to hiring randomly assigned teacher education graduates without any say in the matter, and then agree to keep those teachers for the several years it would take to determine if they were effective or ineffective? But authorities at the federal level apparently ignore this and, instead, say that the absence of experimental evidence means teacher education is ineffective!

The situation is maddening. However, just as we want teachers to impose self-regulatory control over their work and teach to higher ideals despite current pressures, researchers must assume self-regulatory control over teacher development research and conduct studies consistent with our ideals. In short, we must conduct research that is driven by our visions. By doing so, we will "get smarter" about how to develop thoughtful teachers, which will, in the long run, prove to be a more productive approach to literacy reform than the "anybody-can-teach" approach that currently seems to be in vogue.

In that spirit, therefore, I offer some research questions. First, we need to do follow-up studies of teacher education graduates to establish that teacher education graduates do indeed succeed in increasing pupil achievement and are, therefore, more effective than teachers who teach without any prior pedagogical preparation. As already noted, these studies cannot be true experiments. However, it is possible to design quasi-experimental studies that will provide the necessary data. Consequently, the first important question is:

- Are graduates of teacher education institutions effective in increasing pupil achievement when they become employed?

Beyond that input–output question are more substantial concerns about teacher education processes that are more closely related to the content of this chapter:

- Are preservice and inservice teachers who are adaptive (i.e., in metacognitive control of their instruction) more effective in creating achievement gains, especially among high poverty children, than teachers who are trained to follow prescriptive programs, materials, methods or approaches?
- How do teachers who are adaptive in balancing the immediate pressures of accountability tests and the long-term goals associated with higher level learning manage to do so?
- Do collaborative models of teacher development result in teachers who are effective in creating achievement once they are on the job?
- Are collaborative models of teacher development effective at both the preservice and the inservice levels?

At a still finer-grained level, research is needed to answer questions, such as:

- Is visioning an essential first step in creating independent spirit, propensity to assume self-regulatory control, and ability to be adaptive?
- To what extent is the development of visioning associated with adaptive teaching and improved pupil achievement?
- What are the adaptive judgments teachers make during instruction that relate to pupil achievement and pupil motivation to read?
- Is there a developmental progression that preservice and inservice teachers follow when learning to be adaptive teachers?
- To what extent does Lortie's (1975) "apprenticeship of observation" influence teacher development, or is Levin (2003) correct in stating that what is learned in teacher education does not wash out and, in fact, continues to be foundational to teachers' thinking?
- Are graduates of programs that assign preservice teachers to cooperating teachers who are in conceptual congruence with teacher education content more effective when employed than graduates of programs that assign preservice teachers to cooperating teachers having no special knowledge of the content of the teacher education program?

Although those of us who believe in the importance of professional development often resent the implication from policymakers that teacher education is superfluous, the fact is that, until recently, very little research has been conducted on the effectiveness of teacher education and professional development. Consequently, it is important that we do rigorous research to establish that professionally developed teachers are effective and to pinpoint what processes determine such effectiveness.

CONCLUSIONS

There can be little doubt that a teacher's ability to self-regulate thought and action is a key factor in effectively teaching literacy in today's classrooms. It is, therefore, crucial that we learn how to develop such teachers.

According to Sparks (as cited by Schmoker, 2004), the key lies in abandoning a belief in "experts" who "deliver" knowledge of good teaching. Instead, developing thoughtfully adaptive teachers requires that we authorize them to fulfill their own personal commitment and mission in teaching and to base professional development in communities where experts and teachers work in a collaborative fashion to improve instruction. Establishing the effectiveness of this approach to teacher development and identifying how best to accomplish it is by far the most important teacher development issue.

METACONNECTION FOR CHAPTER 16

In chapter 16, Duffy offered the reader a view of visioning as a foundation of metacognitive teaching as well as suggestions for how the expert role might shift in supporting teacher development. In chapter 17, Risko, Roskos, and Vukelich turn our attention from visioning to reflection.

REFERENCES

Anders, P. L., & Richardson, V. (1991). Research directions: Staff development that empowers teachers' reflection and enhances instruction. *Language Arts, 68*, 316–321.

Ball, D. L., & Cohen, D. K. (1999). Developing practice, developing practitioners: Toward a practice-based theory of professional development. In L. Darling-Hammond & G. Sykes (Eds.), *Teaching as a learning profession: Handbook of policy and practice* (pp. 3–32). San Francisco: Jossey-Bass.

Bandura, A. (1997). *Self-efficacy: The exercise of control.* New York: Freeman.

Birdyshaw, D., Pesko, E., Wixon, K., & Yochum, N. (2002). From policy to practice: Using literacy standards in early reading instruction. In M. L. Kamil, J. B. Manning, & H. J. Walberg (Eds.), *Successful reading instruction: A volume in research in educational productivity* (pp. 75–99). Greenwich, CT: Information Age Publication.

Berliner, D. C. (1994). Expertise: The wonder of exemplary performance. In J. N. Mangieri & C. C. Block (Eds.), *Creating powerful thinking for teachers and students: Diverse perspectives* (pp. 161–186). Ft. Worth, TX: Harcourt Brace College.

Block, C. C., Oakar, M., & Hurt, N. (2002). The expertise of literacy teachers: A continuum from preschool to grade 5. *Reading Research Quarterly, 37*, 178–206.

Bransford, J. D., Brown, A. L., & Cocking, R. R. (Eds.). (2000). *How people learn: Brain, mind, experience and school.* Washington, DC: National Academy Press.

Brown, R., & Pressley, M. (1994). Self-regulated reading and getting meaning from text: The transactional strategies instruction model and its ongoing validation. In D. H. Schunk & B. J. Zimmerman (Eds.), *Self-regulation of learning performance: Issues and educational application* (pp. 155–180). Hillsdale, NJ: Lawrence Erlbaum Associates.

Buchmann, M. (1990). Beyond the lonely, choosing will: Professional development in teacher thinking. *Teachers College Record, 91*, 481–508.

Cochran-Smith, M., & Fries, M. K. (2001). Sticks, stones and ideology: The discourse of reform in teacher education. *Educational Researcher, 30*, 3–15.

Collay, M. (1998). Recherche: Teaching our life histories. *Teaching and Teacher Education, 14*, 245–255.

Connelly, F. M., Clandinin, D., & He, M. (1997). Teachers' personal practical knowledge on the professional knowledge landscape. *Teaching and Teacher Education, 13*, 665–674.

Dole, J. A. (2004). The changing role of the reading specialist in school reform. *The Reading Teacher, 57*, 462–471.

Doyle, W. (1983). Academic work. *Review of Educational Research, 53*, 159–199.

Duffy, G. G. (1991). What counts in teacher education? Dilemmas in educating empowered teachers. In J. Zutell & S. McCormick (Eds.), *Learner factors/teacher factors: Issues in literacy research and instruction, 40th Yearbook of the National Reading Conference* (pp. 1–18). Chicago: National Reading Conference.

Duffy, G. G. (1993). How teachers think of themselves: A key to creating powerful thinkers. In J. Mangieri & C. C. Block (Eds.), *Creating powerful thinking in teachers and students: Diverse perspectives* (pp. 3–26). Fort Worth, TX: Harcourt Brace College.

Duffy, G. G. (1998). Teaching and the balancing of round stones. *Phi Delta Kappan, 79*, 777–780.

Duffy, G. G. (2002). Visioning and the development of outstanding teachers. *Reading Research and Instruction, 41*, 331–344.

Duffy, G. G. (Ed.). (2003). *Improving comprehension: 10 research-based principles.* Washington, DC: National Education Association.

Elmore, R. F., Peterson, P. L., & McCarthy, S. J. (1996). *Restructuring the classroom: Teaching, learning, and school organization.* San Francisco: Jossey-Bass.

Englert, C. S., & Tarrant, K. L. (1995). Creating collaborative cultures for educational change. *Remedial and Special Education, 16*, 325–336.

Feiman-Nemser, S. (1990). Contexts and models of teacher education. In W. R. Houston, M. Huberman, & J. Sikula (Eds.), *Handbook of research on teacher education* (pp. 212–234). New York: Macmillan.

Garet, M. S., Porter, A. C., Desimone, L., Birman, B. F., & Yoon, K. S. (2001). What makes professional development effective? Results from a national sample of teachers. *American Educational Research Journal, 38*, 915–945.

Garner, R. (1987). *Metacognition and reading comprehension.* Norwood, NJ: Ablex.

Garrison, J. (1997). *Dewey and Eros: Wisdom and desire in the art of teaching.* New York: Teachers College Press.

Greene, M. (1991). Teaching: The question of personal reality. In A. Lieberman & L. Miller (Eds.), *Staff development for education in the 90's: New demands, new realities, new perspectives* (pp. 3–14). New York: Teachers College Press.

Grossman, P. L., Valencia, S. W., Evans, K., Thompson, C., Martin, S., & Place, N. (2000). Transitions into teaching: Learning to teach writing in teacher education and beyond. *Journal of Literacy Research, 32*, 631–652.

Hawley, W. D, & Valli, L. (1999). The essentials of effective professional development: A new consensus. In L. Darling-Hammond & G. Sykes (Eds.), *Teaching as a learning profession: Handbook of policy and practice* (pp. 127–150). San Francisco: Jossey-Bass.

Hiebert, J. (1998). Relationship between research and the NCTM standards. *Journal for Research in Mathematics Education, 30*, 3–19.

Hofer, B. K., Yu, S. L., & Pintrich, P. (1998). Teaching college students to be self-regulated learners. In D. H. Schunk & B. J. Zimmerman (Eds.), *Self-regulated learning: From teaching to self-reflective practice* (pp. 57–85). New York: Guilford.

Hoffman, J. V. (1998). When bad things happen to good ideas in literacy education: Professional dilemmas, personal decisions and political traps. *Reading Teacher, 52*, 102–113.

Huberman, M. (1995). Networks that alter teaching: Conceptualizations, exchanges, and experiments. *Teachers and Teaching: Theory and Practice, 1*, 193–211.

Kanfer, R., & Kanfer, F. H. (1991). Goals and self-regulation: Application of theory to work settings. In M. L. Maehr & P. R. Pintrich (Eds.), *Advances in motivation and achievement* (Vol. 7, pp. 287–326). Greenwich, CT: JAI Press.

Kennedy, M. (1999). The role of preservice teacher education. In L. Darling-Hammond & G. Sykes (Eds.), *Teaching as the learning profession: Handbook of policy and practice* (pp. 54–85). San Francisco: Jossey-Bass.

Levin, B. B. (2003). *Case studies of teacher development: An in-depth look at how thinking about pedagogy develops over time.* Mahwah, NJ: Lawrence Erlbaum Associates.

Lortie, D. C. (1975). *Schoolteacher: A sociological study.* Chicago: University of Chicago Press.

Miller, S., Heafner, T. L., Massey, D., & Strahan, D. B. (2004). *Students' reactions to teachers' attempts to create the necessary conditions to promote the acquisition of self-regulation skills.* Unpublished paper, University of North Carolina, Greensboro.

Paris, S. G., & Winograd, P. N. (1990). How metacognition can promote academic learning and instruction. In B. Jones & L. Idol (Eds.), *Dimensions of thinking and cognitive instruction* (pp. 15–51). Hillsdale, NJ: Lawrence Erlbaum Associates.

Pintrich, P. R. (1995). Understanding self-regulated learning. In P. R. Pintrich (Ed.), *Understanding self-regulated learning* (pp. 3–12). San Francisco: Jossey-Bass.

Randi, J., & Corno, L. (2000). Teacher innovations in self-regulated learning. In M. Boekaerts, P. R. Pintrich, & M. Zeidner (Eds.), *Handbook of self-regulation* (pp. 651–685). San Diego, CA: Academic Press.

Richardson, V., & Placier, P. (2001). Teacher change. In V. Richardson (Ed.), *Handbook of research on teaching* (pp. 905–947). Washington, DC: American Educational Research Association.

Rosaen, C. L., & Schram, P. (1998). Becoming a member of the teaching profession: Learning a language of possibility. *Teaching and Teacher Education, 14,* 283–303.

Schmoker, M. (2004). Tipping point: From feckless reform to substantive instructional improvement. *Phi Delta Kappan, 85,* 424–432.

Schunk, D. H., & Zimmerman, B. J. (1994). Preface. In D. H. Schunk & B. J. Zimmerman (Eds.), *Self-regulation of learning and performance: Issues and educational applications* (pp. ix–xi). Hillsdale, NJ: Lawrence Erlbaum Associates.

Shanahan, T., & Neumann, S. B. (1997). Conversations: Literacy research that makes a difference. *Reading Research Quarterly, 32,* 202–211.

Shulman, L. (1990, April). *The transformation of knowledge: A model of pedagogical reasoning and action.* A paper presented at the annual meeting of the American Educational Research Association, San Francisco, CA.

Smith, P. I. (2003). Workplace learning and flexible delivery. *Review of Educational Research, 73,* 53–88.

Smyth, J. (1989). A "pedagogical" and "educative" view of leadership. In J. Smyth (Ed.), *Critical perspectives on educational leadership* (pp. 179–204). London: Falmer.

Spillane, J. P., Reiser, B. J., & Reimer, T. (2002). Policy implementation and cognition: Reframing and refocusing implementation research. *Review of Educational Research, 72,* 387–431.

van den Berg, R. (2002). Teachers' meanings regarding educational practice. *Review of Educational Research, 72,* 577–626.

Van Manen, M. J. (1977). Linking ways of knowing with ways of being practical. *Curriculum Inquiry, 6,* 205–228.

Wharton-McDonald, R., Pressley, M., & Hampston, J. M. (1998). Literacy instruction in nine first-grade classrooms: Teacher characteristics and student achievement. *Elementary School Journal, 99,* 103–128.

Windschitl, M. (2002). Framing constructivism in practice as the negotiation of dilemmas: An analysis of the conceptual, pedagogical, cultural, and political challenges facing teachers. *Review of Educational Research, 72,* 131–175.

Zimmerman, B. J. (2000). Attaining self-regulation: A social cognitive perspective. In M. Boekaerts, P. R. Pintrich, & M. Zeidner (Eds.), *Handbook of self-regulation* (pp. 13–39). San Diego, CA: Academic Press.

17

Reflection and the Self-Analytic Turn of Mind: Toward More Robust Instruction in Teacher Education

Victoria J. Risko
Peabody College, Vanderbilt University

Kathleen Roskos
John Carroll University

Carol Vukelich
University of Delaware

. . . to brush history against the grain . . .
—Benjamin (1969, p. 257)

When I think of reflective metacognition, I think of teachers who continuously evaluate what they're doing and why, adapting their practice to meet students' needs. This could occur throughout the day or be documented in journal format. Can you teach educators to be reflective? Metacognitively aware? How do you know they're not just going through the motions to get renewal credit for professional development? How can you "make it stick" so it's applied thoughtfully, forever?
—Roya Leiphart, Kindergarten Teacher

Asking prospective teachers to reflect on their learning and teaching decisions is a common goal of teacher education programs. Reflection is valued by teacher educators for its power to invite critical thinking about one's beliefs and developing knowledge and its potential for providing markers of conceptual change (J. Brooks & M. Brooks, 1993; Clift, Houston, & Pugach, 1990). What is meant by engaging in reflection and how to help prospective teachers deliberate on their learning varies across teacher education settings, but typically teacher educators want future teachers to engage in actions commonly associated with metacognitive activity, which requires self-analysis and taking control of one's own learning.

Over a century ago, James (1890) referred to the importance of introspection to guide meaningful learning. Although current psychologists believe that James' use of this term was not associated with analytic thinking, James' attention to one's own control of information seeded questions pursued decades later about how individuals develop "knowledge of [one's own] knowledge" (Tulving & Madigan, 1970, p. 477). In the early 1900s, for example, learning theorists such as Dewey (1901/1933) and Huey (1908/1968) described learning as involving goal setting, checking progress in attaining goals, and evaluating outcomes of learning activities. Later, developmental and cognitive psychologists examined how students' learning in academic contexts and reported self-monitoring affected comprehension of discourse, either the discourse of instructional conversations or the discourse of instructional (written or multimedia) texts (e.g., Baker, 2003; Baker & Brown, 1984; Brown, 1978; Flavell, 1976; Flavell & Wellman, 1977). Similarly, educational psychologists and teacher educators (e.g., Van Manen, 1977), influenced by ideas on reflection posed by Dewey (1933) and Schon (1983), focused their attention on the mental processes of future teachers and the impact of self-analysis on the learning-to-teach process.

Noting similarities across these lines of inquiry, the goal of this chapter is to show the mutuality between metacognition and reflection on at least two levels: as *acts of thinking* and as *goals of instruction*. As teachers, we want students to think about their own thinking in the discipline because it can benefit their overall learning of content. As teacher educators, we want preservice teachers to think about their own thinking about teaching, because it strengthens their professional learning of teaching practice—it helps them to become "students of pedagogy." What we know about metacognition can inform reflection, and vice versa, on both these complex levels.

Our particular passion, however, is with reflection and how we can better develop this kind of "thinking about thinking," or self-analysis in the pedagogic context. Thus, this chapter reports what we know about reflective thinking with links to metacognition and also about how to teach it, which lags behind what we know about how to support metacognition more generally.

First, what is the mutuality between metacognition and reflection as acts of thinking and what have we learned from research examining methods for fostering reflective thinking in general education and in teacher education more specifically? Next, what instructional features can be gleaned from the reflection research that hold promise for improving reflection instruction on a broader scale in teacher education? Last, what implications for instruction-oriented research are useful (and desperately needed) if we expect teacher educators to adequately prepare new teachers who are thoughtful, committed, and just?

METACOGNITION AND REFLECTION: NOTING THE INTERSECTS

Definitional Attributes

For some researchers, the terms *reflection* and *metacognition* are overlapping constructs—both involving deliberate, evaluative, and constructive activity. For example, Baker (2003) described metacognition as involving the ability to "reflect" on one's own thinking. Earlier, Brown (1978) and Flavell and Wellman (1977) signaled changes in "self-reflection" as markers of metacognitive development. As a construct, however, metacognition has definitional attributes that are more uniformly associated with those associated with the act of reflection.

Metacognition is most typically described as an act of self-monitoring and self-regulation; and thus, it is achieved when learners ask themselves if they understand the meaning of the content under study (self-monitoring) and generate appropriate strategies to eliminate confusions and/or seek additional information (self-regulation). Successful monitoring requires learners to understand themselves as learners (e.g., what they know and don't know, their previous experience with the target content), the characteristics and requirements of the criterial learning tasks, and the strategies that may be optimal for aiding their comprehension (Baker, 2003).

Numerous researchers have described specific mental acts that are fundamental to metacognition. Typically, these acts are situated within a problem-solving framework and are applied to academic tasks (e.g., comprehending text, solving math problems, deriving scientific principles). Following a problem orientation, learners are expected to identify and define the problem situation; determine what is known, unknown, and required for problem solving; plan steps for problem solving; and evaluate progress and performance (Baker & Brown, 1984; Davidson, Deuser, & Sternberg, 1994; Flavell, 1976; Newell & Simon, 1972). During the process of problem identification and goal setting, Davidson et al. (1994) argued that metacognition is aided when learners generate "mental maps" of the problem elements and relationships among these elements and to their prior knowledge. These mental maps are useful for helping the learner organize sets of information that may seem unrelated, especially elements of ill-structured problem situations. Further, they contended that these mental representations change and deepen as students construct and reconstruct potential relationships of ideas and learn to select the most relevant information for problem identification and problem solving.

Metcalfe and Shimamura (1994), although supporting the descriptions of the mental acts required for problem solving and for forming mental representation of ideas, argued that too often this mental activity is reduced to behavioral and observable (and, thus, measurable) descriptors (e.g., generating questions to guide self-analysis, setting goals for learning outcomes). And whereas such descriptions are useful for assessment and instruction, on the whole, such specification underrepresents the active, intentional, and "conscious acts" (that are more difficult to operationalize and measure) that are essential for developing the habits of mind required for metacognitive actions (p. ix).

In contrast, the definition of reflection and associated mental acts are less precise. For example, many teacher educators provide rich descriptions of multiple cognitive processes, usually described in general rather than observable actions.

Thus, they describe reflection as involving actions such as problem solving, comparing and contrasting competing perspectives, and deriving reasoned instructional decisions (e.g., Korthagen, 1985, 1988; Korthagen & Wubbles, 1995; MacKinnon, 1987; Ross, 1989). With attention to the act itself as a catalyst for thought, other teacher educators describe reflection as a tool for engaging future teachers in examining their prior experiences and beliefs in light of new learning, resolving conflicts, and drawing connections between theory and practice (Bainer & Cantrell, 1992; Galvez-Martin, Bowman, & Morrison, 1998; Gore & Zeichner, 1991).

Similar to metacognition research, studies of reflection activities focus on mental acts associated with the process or act of reflection. These descriptions, unlike those associated with metacognitive activity, are typically not situated within a problem-solving framework (a notable exception is the problem-solving framework proposed by Korthagen and his colleagues). Instead, they are associated with levels of thinking, as classified by Van Manen (1977) or Zeichner and Liston (1985). These systems are used by researchers and teacher educators to describe their students' level(s) of thinking when engaged in reflection activities (e.g., writing in journals, evaluating lesson plans, discussing teaching events). These mental acts, then, describe possible ways of "knowing" and "thinking" while engaged in the act of reflection. Van Manen (1977) focused on levels of deliberate reasoning that include: *a technical accuracy level*, where the focus is on procedural aspects of teaching and the accuracy of techniques; *a reasoning level*, at which there is an expectation that prospective teachers will provide a rationale for instructional actions and their reasoning about appropriateness of choice and outcomes; and *a critiquing level*, which focuses on both the analysis of taken-for-granted thoughts and feelings, and the critique of equity issues associated with the teaching practices. And Zeichner and Liston (1985) described four levels of reflective thought: *factual* (focusing on facts and procedural steps), *prudential* (focusing on evaluation of teaching experiences and outcomes), *justificatory* (providing rationales for actions), and *critical* (focusing on the underlying assumptions of actions that impact on social justice).

Similar to Metcalfe and Shimamura's (1994) firm conviction that "intentionality" matters for successful metacognition, teacher educators (e.g., Hatton & Smith, 1995) insist that movement in reflective capabilities requires "deliberate" and focused thinking.

Instructional Supports

Researchers across both lines of inquiry indicate that the deep thinking associated with metacognition and reflection is difficult to attain. Baker (2003), for example, observed that students of all ages are "poor" at monitoring their understanding of text and generating effective comprehension strategies to correct their problems. In our review of the reflection research (between 1985 and 1999) and our own research, we concluded that prospective teachers' reflections were frequently shallow and subjective (i.e., referring to their own [often limited] personal history or experiences related to teaching rather than new information to analyze educational issues and dilemmas). Although teacher educators want their prospective teachers to adopt critical stances for analyzing inequitable situations in classrooms and schools, researchers indicate that this kind of reflection is difficult to foster (Roskos, Vukelich, & Risko, 2001). And when asked to keep reflection journals in our respective methods courses, students reflected largely at the factual and technical levels and rarely did they provide reasoning for their instructional choices or analyze their decisions (Risko, Roskos, & Vukelich, 2002).

Researchers provide a strong case for developing either metacognition or reflection as a social practice and refer to the mediated learning strategies proposed by Vygotsky (1978). Recognizing that each act is influenced by individual differences, they argue that the mental processes associated with metacognition and reflection can be deepened through interactions with knowledgeable others, including instructors, peers, and mentor teachers. How they go about implementing such recommendations differs across the two sets of research.

Metacognitive researchers have established a long history of instructional research that prepares students for self-analysis and monitoring of their own learning. We speculate that this research has benefited greatly from the work of theorists and researchers who have conceptualized and specified explicitly the mental acts associated with metacognition—these mental acts would include the specific ones used for problem solving, as described earlier (e.g., Baker & Brown, 1984; Flavell & Wellman, 1977), the mental mapping of comparisons and contrasts (Davidson et al., 1994), and the active, conscious acts described by Metcalfe and Shimamura (1994). And, once identified, researchers have demonstrated the benefits of teaching these acts within carefully guided instructional contexts, such as the reciprocal teaching activities of Palincsar and Brown (1984), where the teacher guides and demonstrates strategic actions, and the peer collaborative exchanges of Champagne and Klopfer (1991), where students critique and guide each other's learning.

Multiple research studies have demonstrated the positive impact of guided metacognition instruction for enhancing self-monitoring and text comprehension. Baker's (1991) instruction provided think-aloud activities to identify text characteristics (e.g., misleading statements, use of ambiguous referents) interfering with comprehension, and the modeling of questions students can ask themselves (about prior knowledge, about what is known and not known, about misconceptions); both activities were associated with gains in self-assessment and comprehension. Similarly, comprehension improved within formats designed by Linn, Songer, and Eylon (1996), in which students generated their own questions and critiqued each other's questions (strategies that can be modeled initially by the teacher), and by Klingner and colleagues, who taught the use of a set of comprehensive and mutually enabling strategies, such as how to preview text, identify misunderstandings, and apply fix-up strategies (Klingner & Vaughn, 1999; Klingner, Vaughn, & Schumm, 1998).

Heeding the concerns of metacognitive researchers, we recognize that it is "hard work" to foster metacognition (Baker, 2003). Yet, the instructional research in this area has established sufficient evidence for at least four components. These include a provision of *learning goals and outcomes that are made explicit* to both the teacher and the students, an *instructional process that is intentional* (the teacher models and engages students in active development and use of learning strategies), a learning environment that encourages *dialogic conversations* and *students to scrutinize their own understandings*, and *demonstrations of self-assessment* for monitoring learning.

Conversely, teacher education researchers focusing on reflection have paid less attention to the forms of guided instruction that may be needed to scaffold prospective teachers' reflection. Zeichner and Liston (1985) identified six basic instructional frameworks in teacher preparation supportive of reflection development and learning, including reflective teaching, action research, ethnography, writing, curriculum analysis and development, and expert–novice supervision. In the ensuing years, different instructional techniques (e.g., journal writing, portfolios, video critiques) have been variously employed within these macro-frameworks for the purposes of describing and improving students' reflective abilities. One of the more popular, journal writing, is now commonplace in teacher education, and in its various forms offers students the opportunity to practice reflection (see, e.g., Spalding & Wilson, 2002).

It has been difficult, however, to determine the efficacy of these reflection approaches and instructional techniques in the teacher education classroom for a host of reasons. Research reviews point out the methodological problems associated with defining reflection as a research construct; employing rigorous research designs to test instructional approaches; adequately specifying instruction and linking it to reflection development; and developing sound assessment measures of reflection concepts, skills, and dispositions (Rodgers, 2002; Roskos, Risko, & Vukelich, 2001). Despite these challenges, however, the past 2 decades of largely descriptive research have surfaced several instructional features that appear especially supportive of preservice teachers' reflection development and learning. And, as shown later, teacher educators have employed these different features to create more powerful instructional approaches and techniques that support and push reflection development forward.

SOME PROMISING FEATURES
OF REFLECTION INSTRUCTION

What has research revealed about reflection instruction that might make a difference in teaching quality? Among the "this and that" of descriptive evidence, a few features emerge as characteristic of potentially effective instruction in reflection at the preservice level and are also coincident with strong features of metacognition instruction. (See Fig. 17.1.)

- A well-articulated definition of reflection
- Clear instructional goals
- Stated criteria for judging reflection performance
- Multiple, multilayered opportunities to learn
- Compelling content for reflection

FIG. 17.1. Promising features of reflection instruction.

One of these, and perhaps the most fundamental, is a *well-articulated definition* of reflection that serves to theoretically ground and guide instruction. Definitions, when well-crafted, can literally map the reflection concept by describing what it is (e.g., a process, a disposition), its properties or attributes (e.g., deliberate thinking, open-mindedness), and its purpose or function in the teaching experience (e.g., to direct instructional activities with foresight, to plan with ends-in-view). For example, Winitzky (1992) defined reflection as "the ability to retrieve appropriate knowledge, to apply that knowledge in perceiving and analyzing causal relationships in classroom management events, and to connect such knowledge to larger social issues" (p. 3). Here we learn that reflection is *an ability* (a cognitive skill). We learn that its purpose in teaching practice is *skilled use of knowledge* to understand relationships in classroom events. We are alerted to the defining attributes of the thinking skill—*retrieve, apply, perceive, analyze,* and *connect.* And we are made aware that the *use of knowledge must extend* to larger social issues beyond the immediacy of local classroom events. Whether or not we agree with the definition, it explains the concept well enough to map out an instructional route for engaging students in reflective thinking.

A closely related feature and one similarly found in the metacognition instructional research is *clear instructional goals* that set the direction for teaching and learning action. In general, a teacher educator's instructional intentions may be aimed at discovering what students already know and can do as reflectors, improving their reflective abilities, or a combination of both. What matters is that educators' instructional intentions are represented by clear expectations that follow from a well-articulated definition (the "what") and stay true to their course. Korthagen and colleagues, for example, set out to foster an inquiry-oriented attitude in prospective secondary mathematics teachers along with sharper analytic abilities to design creative solutions to teaching problems. They defined reflection in a parsimonious manner as "the mental process of structuring or restructuring an experience, a problem or existing knowledge or insights" (Korthagen & Wubbels, 1995, p. 55). Within this framework they designed a cyclic five-step process model (Action, Look Back, Awareness of Features, Create Alternatives, Try) that repeatedly and recursively engaged students in reflective activity oriented to inquiry and analysis—their stated instructional goals. The crux of instruction occurred in the Awareness of Features phase of the spiral model where students were confronted with new, challenging information (e.g., the role mathematics academic content standards in planning instruction) that motivated processes of inquiry and analysis.

A third feature, also apparent in the metacognition research base, falls into the realm of assessment. It involves the use of *stated criteria* against which the instructor might examine or judge students' reflection performances in oral and/or written contexts. A well-marked trajectory of reflection development in preservice teachers does not presently exist, but there are research-based markers that can be used to gauge cognitive and dispositional growth. In the reflection literature, cognitive growth is frequently measured (largely qualitatively) along a continuum of progressively more difficult levels of reflective thinking—from technical to critical, for example, or from literal to more justificatory and critical forms of discourse as previously stated (Van Manen, 1977; Zeichner & Liston, 1985).

Dispositions associated with reflection, however, are much harder to track; far less is known about how these habits of mind evolve into more mature forms across the preparatory years. Working from Dewey's criteria for reflection, Rodgers (2002) proposed the following indicators of attitudinal growth: *wholeheartedness*, or an enthusiasm and curiosity toward one's subject matter; a *directness* toward teaching and learning measured in the degree to which one is more or less self-aware in helping learners and their learning, not totally self-absorbed with content and the teaching of it; *open-mindedness* to new ways of seeing and understanding one's teaching and subject matter; and *responsibility* for one's thinking in real-life action and personal change. Reflection instruction becomes more strategic when assessment information on students' reflection performances is compared with these kinds of cognitive growth "benchmarks" and attitudinal indicators.

Although it is difficult to capture preservice teachers' thinking and attitudes, and even more difficult to notice small changes over time, applying principles of dynamic assessment may be useful. Dynamic assessment is directed toward the catching of "learning" and "thinking" while in process, and an analysis of the instructional tasks. Described by Newman, Griffin, and Cole (1989) as "assessment by teaching," the instructor orchestrates carefully a progression of tasks (e.g., the prospective teacher is asked to analyze a child's oral reading miscues), evaluations of performance (e.g., what does the prospective teacher know and what additional information is needed; how are miscues judged), and analyses of teaching methods used to support learning (e.g., how new information about the miscues is presented). Progression through these cycles helps the instructor to identify if students are independently applying target concepts, the areas of conceptual development requiring additional instruction, and the form of instruction that may be most optimal.

A fourth feature, and a consistent theme in the research base, is one of *multiple, multilayered opportunities to learn* reflection concepts, skills, and dispositions in challenging yet achievable ways. Opportunities to learn are the result of well-organized instruction that engages students in rigorous ways of thinking in interaction with others and neatly layers procedures to help them become "better" at reflecting. Strong instructional designs reflect an interrelated network of settings (whole-group, small group, individual), learning processes (e.g., reframing to see problems from different perspectives), and instructional techniques (e.g., dialogic journals) that work together to advance students' reflective abilities toward desired goals.

A final feature to emerge from reflection research is that of *compelling content* found in coursework and clinical or field experiences. This goes beyond considering questions of whether or not a teaching practice is working—a kind of reflective thinking that can be immediately satisfying but too often shallow and intellectually weak. Instead, instruction that pulls preservice teachers into considering how certain practices work, for whom, and under what conditions demands more disciplined ways of thinking that exercise and stretch their reflective abilities. Pushing students to critically examine the inherent values in their thinking as well as the larger societal goals for schooling (e.g., academic, social efficiency, humanistic, social reconstructivist; Zeichner & Liston, 1996) also leads to higher quality reflection that is intellectually significant and worthwhile.

Reflection instruction that includes many of these features appears to get better results in terms of the amount and quality of students' reflective thinking about teaching practices. In our own preliminary review of instructional designs across a set of 54 reflection studies conducted between 1984 and 1999, we noted that those incorporating these features into more complex designs (i.e., employing an interrelated set of activities and including deliberate strategy instruction in reflection) did influence students' reflective abilities more substantively and in more varied ways than those studies with less complex reflection instruction (Roskos, Risko, & Vukelich, 2003).

ROBUST REFLECTION INSTRUCTION

We now turn to a few abbreviated examples of what is termed *robust* reflection instruction. Robust means that the instruction includes many of the promising features just described and also coordinates them in ways that both support and pull forward students' reflective abilities to higher levels of performance. This kind of reflection instruction does not stop at discovering what students can do, but intervenes to show students how to do what they must if they are to become reflective practitioners in the truest sense.

Given space constraints, two examples are provided, although other fine examples can be found in the literature (e.g., Cruikshank, 1985; Korthagen & Wubbels, 1995; Ross, 1989). These examples show evidence of promising features at work in instruction, and also provide some practical information for teacher educators seeking to improve their own instruction in reflection.

A Typology of Reflective Practice

A typology of reflective practice (Jay & Johnson, 2002) was developed in the Teacher Education Program (TEP) at the University of Washington in the late 1990s (Hess, 1999; McKenna, 1999). Anchored in the theoretical ideas of reflection giants (e.g., Dewey, Schon, and Zeichner and Liston), the typology profiles three dimensions of reflective thought—descriptive, comparative, and critical. Its primary function is to provide "a framework through which a structure for reflection can be created . . . an outline in which the discourse of individuals or groups may be articulated and examined" (Jay & Johnson, p. 81). The typology, in short, supplies a structure for deep thought.

The typology's structure has as its base a well-developed definition of reflection that also serves as a good road map for instructional action. The definition states that "reflection is a process (thus not a specific skill nor a disposition), both individual and collaborative, involving experience and uncertainty" (p. 76). The reflection process is specified as "identifying questions and key elements of a [significant] matter" (p. 76), then dialoguing with oneself and others about them. (This lays out the task at hand.) Insights gained are evaluated with reference to "(1) additional perspectives; (2) one's own values, experiences and beliefs; and (3) the larger context" (this raises the "ante" on the mental work required) to achieve "newfound clarity" for action and change (p. 76). (The reflection, in short, should move an individual from one level to another in their thinking and action.)

This is a hefty definition, but not a fuzzy one. It outlines what is expected, that is, what students should know and be able to do as a result of the instruction— namely, to focus on some aspect of their teaching, to see it from a variety of perspectives using strategies of reframing and reflective listening, to engage in dialogue independently and with peers, and to state a goal of action or change arising from new understandings.

The typology, by its very structure, leads students through three progressively more difficult levels of reflection. (See Fig. 17.2.) First, they must describe the matter taken up for reflection arising out of their experience (e.g., a thought-provoking article, a classroom observation, a simulated teaching experience, a video excerpt). Next, they must reframe the matter for reflection taking into account alternative views, others' perspectives, research, and so on. For beginners in pedagogic reflection, this is difficult because they need to know and acknowledge their own positions and then be willing to hold them at bay while seriously "entertaining" other perspectives. They need to, in a turn of phrase, "walk around the matter," taking different perspectives and considering them, which sounds easy to do, but is not. Finally, after active, careful consideration of the implications in the matter, they are to establish (as in set out) a renewed perspective that shows change from where they were (intellectually) before they considered the matter.

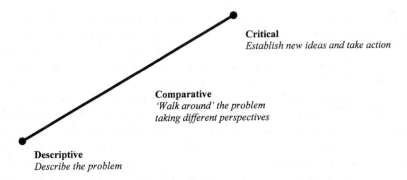

FIG. 17.2.   Levels of reflection.

Teacher educators use the typology as a teaching tool in reflective seminars where they model and encourage reflective thinking through talk as the primary means of expression. The use of oral language within the typology's framework helps students to develop a mental script or register for reflection that they can use to guide and monitor their own personal reflecting done collaboratively with peers. Students also use the typology as a writing "template" to describe, interpret, and evaluate their portfolio artifacts. Writing as a medium forces students to frame language and thereby their thoughts in new ways that promote deeper understandings of decisions, choices, and actions related to teaching work.

The typology is an instructional framework with a high probability of making a difference in students' reflection development because it supports many of the promising features of high quality reflection instruction found in the knowledge base. Aligned with a well-articulated definition, it makes the expectations for reflection clear and provides frequent opportunities to exercise multilevel reflective thinking in different learning contexts and settings. Although the typology does not make the standards for reflection explicit, it does provide a means for teacher educators and students to monitor the quality and logic of reflective discourse in oral and written language. Lastly, it fully engages students with the "puzzles of practice," thus enlivening the content of the teacher education curriculum, which helps students to internalize its essential concepts and skills.

Guided Reflection in the Zone of Proximal Development

Guided reflection, as described by Reiman (1999), is an instructional procedure that applies Vygotsky's zone of proximal development (ZPD) to adult development (Vygotsky, 1978). It is used mostly in the learning contexts of dialogue journals and portfolios where written discourse is the primary cognitive "tool" used to make meaning out of experience, although oral discussion between teacher and student often surrounds the written discourse.

The teacher educator's goal, as the more informed other, is to match support (encouragement) to the adult learner's current level of reflective abilities, and to provoke new learning that improves and advances these abilities. Through careful reading of preservice teachers' written reflections, the teacher educator works to scaffold thinking to more complex levels of reflection through a process of "graduated mismatching" when current ideas on a matter are stable or comfortable (p. 604). The mismatching is intended to create disequilibrium in students' thinking thereby creating a learning opportunity for considering alternatives that may, in turn, incite changes in thought and potentially in teaching action. The teacher educator's statements, however, are *gradually* mismatched to the students' current thinking, first to create instabilities and then to *scaffold* the reorganization of thinking toward a desired goal, in this case, more powerful levels of reflection. The design of the instructional technique, therefore, combines a Piagetian theory of development (cognitive dissonance) and a Vygotskian theory of learning (assisted performance in the zone of proximal development).

Guided reflection rests on a straightforward definition of reflective teaching as a problem-solving process (thus not a skill nor disposition, but a set of dynamic interactions) that involves the mental skills of reconstructing meanings and making judgments (critical thinking skills that confront egocentric thinking) while engaged in authentic activity (the realities of teaching work). As a result of the technique, preservice teachers should be able to analyze their own teaching actions (self-assess); reconstruct their professional and personal knowledge to accommodate new information (self-organize); and make judgments to adapt practice toward better support of learner needs (self-regulate). Guided reflection, in sum, develops the abilities to engage in self-organizing processes that produce changes and growth in individual reflection development.

In the contexts of journal writing or portfolio construction, the teacher educator employs a range of seven response strategies to scaffold the student's reflective abilities from existing to higher levels. (See Fig. 17.3.) Four of the strategies indirectly build the key problem-solving skills of reconstructing meanings and making judgments by accepting feelings, praising thinking, acknowledging and clarifying ideas, and prompting inquiry. Three other strategies develop these skills more directly by providing information, giving directions, and helping students accept responsibility for their thought and actions. The teacher educator deliberately manipulates these strategies in response to the students' current level of critical thinking.

For example, if the preservice teacher expresses self-doubt when trying new instructional strategies, the teacher educator responds with an indirect strategy by offering frequent encouragement in writing and in follow through discussions. When the preservice teacher rarely considers the implications of classroom events, the teacher educator indirectly prompts inquiry by asking probing questions and calling for reasoning about the implications of events (e.g., What is being taken for granted? What are implicit assumptions?). When the preservice

Indirect Strategies	Direct Strategies
o Accepts feelings	o Provides information
o Praises; encourages	o Gives directions
o Acknowledges; clarifies ideas	o Addresses problems
o Prompts inquiry	

FIG. 17.3.   Guided reflection response strategies.

teacher disdains theory and remains rooted in personal feelings, the educator is direct in offering information, linking what the student knows with new experiences, and reviewing research-based approaches and positions. When the preservice teacher demonstrates a high degree of responsibility for his own teaching rationales and actions, the educator is also direct in accepting feelings and thoughts and acknowledging the essential skills and dispositions of professional responsibility and ethics.

Consistent and strategic use of the seven response strategies in written language contexts attempts to influence the students' thinking in ways that foster reflective abilities, such as analysis (clarity, accuracy, precision), interpretation (relevance, depth, breadth), and evaluation (logic, significance, fairness), and in effect "to lead from behind" (as Bruner would say). This approach to reflection instruction, although highly student centered, is also heavily dependent on the teacher educator's expertise and deftness at using the response strategies to promote the preservice teacher's self-organizing processes for producing more mature reflections. But the investment of time and energy in effective strategic responding may be well worth it in that students develop their self-regulatory capacities for reflection, which ultimately can strengthen reflection as an intrinsically motivated activity in teaching practice.

Guided reflection is another instructional procedure likely to make a difference in preservice teachers' reflection development when properly used. It derives from a practical definition that focuses squarely on reflection as a problem-solving process that involves critical thinking skills and authentic activity as the instigators of developmental change. Starting from where students are, it aims to advance their reflective thinking toward fairly well-defined cognitive skills (e.g., analysis) and dispositional indicators (e.g., fairmindedness; responsibility for one's own thinking). Whereas the technique does not lay out explicit criteria for judging reflective performances, it does tend to hold students accountable to an implicit set of intellectual standards, such as accuracy, relevance, depth, logic, and so forth. It builds a scaffolding system into the journal or portfolio activity as a medium for instruction and applies it to content that arises out of real teaching experience.

Guided reflection is a demanding but very rich technique that offers both support and challenge in preservice teachers' reflection development. It also has the advantage of being adaptable to more structural approaches to reflective journal writing. Spalding and Wilson (2002), for example, used a research-based coding system to identify levels of reflection (R = reflection in/on action; P = personalistic; D = deliberative; C = critical) in journal writing and also taught the preservice teachers to do the same. Using these categories, they observed increasing ability to distinguish narration from reflection, to write all four types of reflections, and to link course reading and discussion to observation and experience. Guided reflection strategies can complement structural approaches such as this to more accurately begin where preservice teachers are and build their capacity to reflect more substantively on relevant experience.

Our gain from these two examples of robust instruction is twofold. They alert us to some promising features of instruction that teacher educators can begin to use in their planning to improve reflective abilities, as well as some emerging benefits of the last few decades of reflection research. Also, some potentially strong pedagogic links are indicated between reflection and metacognition that could lead to better reflection instruction in teacher education classrooms and spur progress in reflection instructional research. Although sketchy at this point, descriptive evidence from reflection research suggests that the instructional components of *explicit learning goals, intentional instruction, substantive dialogue,* and *assessment for self-regulation,* already established in the metacognition instruction literature, are worth pursuing as essential elements of an effective *pedagogy of reflection.*

RESEARCH WE NEED TO IMPROVE REFLECTION INSTRUCTION FOR ALL PROSPECTIVE TEACHERS

Some hopeful direction for reflection instruction has been reported in this chapter, but we also do not want to create a false sense of security that all is well and good in the complex endeavor of preparing teachers for reflective practice. It's not. Certainly appealing, the promising features described must nevertheless be handled with care, because some things are clear about developing reflective abilities for educational work, but much is still missing.

For example, we know that writing dominates as the preferred mode for eliciting and documenting reflective thinking in the professional education context. Teacher educators ask preservice candidates to keep journals, respond in writing to portfolios, react in writing to videos, prepare written summaries, develop written plans for professional growth, and so on. As a mental tool for reflection, writing is effective for several reasons (Hoover, 1994). It encourages connection making between current ideas and new experiences; it permits re-thinking and revision of thought; it presses for making tacit knowledge and beliefs explicit.

However, at the level of instruction, where we are trying to help students become better at reflection, it is not clear how writing ability interfaces with reflective ability. Just as writing may jumpstart reflection, it might in fact constrain reflection, making it more difficult for preservice teachers to express their thinking, to clarify their positions, and to entertain alternative perspectives. Research, however, is seriously lacking as to the viability of writing as an instructional medium for developing reflection. No research has examined the comparative impact of monologic and dialogic writing journals on preservice teachers' reflective abilities, for example, nor have empirical studies been conducted that test the use of particular writing tools (e.g., journals, portfolios, responses to questions) for possible differential "reflective outcomes" of selected instructional tools.

In the plus column, reflection research has yielded some information about the interplay between person–context variables on preservice teachers' reflection performances. Preservice teachers' own beliefs about classroom management, instructional practices, tensions between theory and practice, and their unique individual development interact in complicated ways with features of their teacher education program and related field experiences. But this research has not gone far enough to offer specifics about how to cope with these complexities, leaving teacher educators uncertain about how to scaffold preservice teachers' reflection efforts. As it stands, techniques such as peer coaching, journaling, e-mail discussions, and case study analyses have not proven very effective in ratcheting up students' thinking from procedural concerns to critical analyses of teaching problems and dilemmas. More powerful techniques in more varied combinations are needed to move the hearts and minds of individual students.

Relatedly, we have some research evidence of the tremendous influence that personal characteristics (emotional traits not excepted) can have on individual engagement in reflective thought. Students who tend to be externally driven, for instance, appear to require more cues and direction for substantive reflection than those more internally driven, who seem more skilled at setting and monitoring their own learning goals (Korthagen, 1988). Unfortunately, there is not enough research-based information to differentially guide reflection depending on preservice teachers' individual needs, propensities, and investigative tendencies. Along this line, however, coaching is emerging as a viable technique for helping individual students improve their reflection, operating on the fundamental principle of start where the learner is. Still, the very how of coaching is not yet sufficiently described in enough detail, that is, the specifics of the interaction that help the a specific learner under a specific set of circumstances identify the problem, consider alternatives, see theory represented in real practice, and evaluate consequences of action beyond the immediate context.

To further fill the gaps in reflection instruction, researchers should heed and follow the trail of critical observations and insights from recent metacognition instruction studies. For example, some forms of instruction are more optimal than others. Bjork (1994), for example, reported advances of problem-based learning activities that presented obstacles and dilemmas to overcome while learning new information. Activities that engaged learners in problem solving with feedback on performance and opportunities for self-assessment held predictive power for learning and use of information in new contexts. Conversely, less promising for learning impact were activities that are oriented toward accelerating the rate of learning with insufficient attention to instructive formats, required the learners to judge their own learning without instructor feedback, and showed lack of congruence between learning conditions during instruction and conditions where the learner is expected to apply what has been learned.

Another is the value of a prepare for future learning (PFL) model advocated by Bransford and Schwartz (1999). In addition to developing content (what to teach) and procedural knowledge (how to teach), a teacher education program should emphasize the problem-solving acts that teachers will need to use independently to resolve the unpredictable problems they will face. Bransford and Schwartz argued that the goal of teacher educators is to prepare future teachers as future learners—individuals who know how to approach and analyze difficulties, who can access and organize relevant resources, and who can generate reasoned and appropriate resolutions to the problems they face. Preparing teachers as "future learners" involves multiple opportunities to ask questions about issues and dilemmas, opportunities to study a wide variety of problems and contrasting issues and perspectives, and opportunities to receive focused and specific feedback on their progress.

A third involves new ideas about expert learning, as described by Alexander and her colleagues (2003). Their careful analysis of how expertise develops has direct implications for expectations about the learning trajectory of prospective teachers for at least two reasons. First, Alexander and her colleagues indicated that early learning in a new domain is "fragile" and requires an interactive learning environment, with well-supported opportunities for thinking to be strategic within domains of knowledge and for pedagogical considerations. Second, they realized the importance of motivation for aiding intentional activity. They drew attention to a need for synergy among the factors of learning new knowledge, becoming strategic, and making connections to personal experiences and interests. Prospective teachers need to be prepared well in domain and pedagogic knowledge, the use of strategies for posing and investigating their own questions, and the usefulness of forming personal connections between what they are learning and what interests them about teaching.

CONCLUSIONS

Waller (1961) once asked: "What does teaching do to teachers?" And, in light of the goals of this chapter, rooted in instruction, we could recast that question to ask: What does engaging in reflection do for teaching? We agree with Britzman (2003) that reflection, as the self-analytic turn of mind, unlocks personal understanding of "the contradictory realities, indeed, the conflicts and crises that structure the work and narratives of learning to teach" (p. 11). It gives voice to our "private struggles" as professional educators. It is for this reason, then (the "giving of voice"), that future teachers deserve the best reflection instruction so they might speak, hear, read, and write well in the professional life they have chosen. There is a need for more and better informed research on reflection development and learning in order to provide just that.

METACONNECTION FOR CHAPTER 17

In chapter 16, Duffy suggested that we consider how visioning connects the teacher with a moral compass that can guide decisions in the classroom. In this chapter, the authors provided a substantive analysis of reflection as a metacognitive process. In chapter 18, Bowman, Galvez-Martin, and Morrison will provide an example of how one group of preservice teachers responded to guided reflection.

REFERENCES

Alexander, P. A. (2003). The development of expertise: The journey from acclimation to proficiency. *Educational Researcher, 32*(8), 10–14.

Baker, L. (1991). Metacognition, reading, and science education. In C. M. Santa & D. E. Alvermann (Eds.), *Science learning: Processes and applications* (pp. 2–13). Newark, DE: International Reading Association.

Baker, L. (2003). Reading comprehension and science inquiry: Metacognitive connections. In E. W. Saul (Ed.), *Crossing borders in literacy and science instruction: Perspectives on theory and practice* (pp. 239–257). Newark, DE: International Reading Association.

Baker, L., & Brown, A. L. (1984). Metacognitive skills and reading. In P. D. Pearson, R. Barr, M. L. Kamil, & P. Mosenthal (Eds.), *Handbook of reading research* (pp. 353–395). New York: Longman.

Bainer, D. L., & Cantrell, D. (1992). Nine dominant reflection themes identified for preservice teachers by a content analysis of essays. *Education, 112*, 571–578.

Benjamin, W. (1969). The work of art in an age of mechanical reproduction. In H. Arendt (Ed.), *Illuminations* (pp. 217–252). New York: Schocken.

Bjork, R. A. (1994). Memory and metamemory considerations in the training of human beings. In J. Metcalfe & A. P. Shimamura (Eds.), *Metacognition: Knowing about knowing* (pp. 185–205). Cambridge, MA: MIT Press.

Bransford, J. D., & Schwartz, D. L. (1999). Rethinking transfer: A simple proposal with multiple implications. In A. Iran-Nejad & P. D. Pearson (Eds.), *Review of research in education* (Vol. 24, pp. 61–100). Washington, DC: AERA.

Britzman, D. P. (2003). *Practice makes practice: A critical study of learning to teach.* Albany, NY: State University Press.

Brooks, J., & Brooks, M. (1993). *The case for constructivist classrooms.* Alexandria, VA: Association for Supervision and Curriculum Development.

Brown, A. L. (1978). Knowing when, where, and how to remember: A problem of metacognition. In R. Glaser (Ed.), *Advances in instructional psychology* (Vol. 1, pp. 77–165). Hillsdale, NJ: Lawrence Erlbaum Associates.

Champagne, A. B., & Klopfer, L. E. (1991). Understanding science text and the physical world. In C. M. Santa & D. E. Alvermann (Eds.), *Science learning: Processes and applications* (pp. 64–73). Newark, DE: International Reading Association.

Clift, R., Houston, W., & Pugach, M. (Eds.). (1990). *Encouraging reflective practice: An examination of issues and exemplars.* New York: Teachers College Press.

Cruikshank, D. R. (1985). Uses and benefits of reflective teaching. *Phi Delta Kappan, 66*, 704–706.

Davidson, J. E., Deuser, R., & Sternberg, R. J. (1994). The role of metacognition in problem solving. In J. Metcalfe & A. P. Shimamura (Eds.), *Metacognition: Knowing about knowing* (pp. 207–226). Cambridge, MA: MIT Press.

Dewey, J. (1933). *How we think.* Lexington, MA: Heath. (Original work published 1901)

Flavell, J. H. (1976). Metacognitive aspects of problem solving. In L. B. Resnick (Ed.), *The nature of intelligence* (pp. 231–235). Hillsdale, NJ: Lawrence Erlbaum Associates.

Flavell, J. H., & Wellman, H. M. (1977). Metamemory. In R. V. Kail & J. W. Hagen (Eds.), *Perspectives on the development of memory and cognition* (pp. 3–33). Hillsdale, NJ: Lawrence Erlbaum Associates.

Galvez-Martin, M. E., Bowman, C. L., & Morrison, M. A. (1998). An exploratory study of the level of reflection attained by preservice teachers. *Mid-Western Educational Researcher, 11*(2), 9–18.

Gore, J. M., & Zeichner, K. M. (1991). Action research and reflective teaching in preservice teacher education: A case study from the United States. *Teaching and Teacher Education, 79*(2), 119–136.

Hatton, N., & Smith, D. (1995). Reflection in teacher education: Towards definition and implementation. *Teacher and Teacher Education, 11*(1), 33–49.

Hess, D. (1999, April). *Developing a typology for teaching preservice teachers to reflect: A case of curriculum deliberation.* Paper presented at the annual conference of the American Educational Research Association, Montreal, Canada.

Hoover, L. A. (1994). Reflective writing as a window on preservice teacher's thought process. *Teaching and Teacher Education, 10*, 83–93.

Huey, E. B. (1908/1968). *The psychology and pedagogy of reading.* New York: Macmillan.

James, W. (1890). *Principles of psychology.* New York: Holt.

Jay, J. K., & Johnson, K. L. (2002). Capturing complexity: A typology of reflective practice for teacher education. *Teaching and Teacher Education, 18*, 73–85.

Klingner, J. K., & Vaughn, S. (1999). Promoting reading comprehension, content learning, and English acquisition through Collaborative Strategic Reading (CSR). *The Reading Teacher, 52*, 738–747.

Klingner, J. K., Vaughn, S., & Schumm, J. S. (1998). Collaborative strategic reading during social studies in heterogeneous fourth-grade classrooms. *The Elementary School Journal, 99*, 3–22.

Korthagen, F. (1985). Reflective teaching and preservice teacher education in the Netherlands. *Journal of Teacher Education, 36*(5), 11–15.

Korthagen, F. (1988). The influence of learning orientations on the development of reflective teaching. In J. Calderhead (Ed.), *Teachers' professional learning* (pp. 35–50). New York: Falmer.

Korthagen, F. A., & Wubbels, T. (1995). Characteristics of reflective practitioners: Towards an operationalization of the concept of reflection. *Teachers and Teaching: Theory and Practice, 1*(1), 51–72.

Linn, M. C., Songer, N. B., & Eylon, B.-S. (1996). Shifts and convergences in science learning and instruction. In D. C. Berliner & R. C. Calfee (Eds.), *Handbook of educational psychology* (pp. 438–490). New York: Macmillan.

MacKinnon, A. (1987). Detecting reflection-in-action among preservice elementary science teachers. *Teaching and Teacher Education, 3*(2), 135–145.

McKenna, H. (1999, February). *A pedagogy of reflection: Pathfinding in a time of change.* Paper presented at the annual conference of the American Association of Colleges of Teacher Education, Washington, DC.

Metcalfe, J., & Shimamura, A. P. (1994). Foreword. In J. Metcalfe & A. P. Shimamura (Eds.), *Metacognition: Knowing about knowing* (pp. vi–x). Cambridge, MA: MIT Press.

Newell, A., & Simon, H. A. (1972). *Human problem solving.* Englewood Cliffs, NJ: Prentice-Hall.

Newman, D., Griffin, P., & Cole, M. (1989). *The construction zone: Working for cognitive change in school.* New York: Cambridge University Press.

Palincsar, A. S., & Brown, A. L. (1984). Reciprocal teaching of comprehension-fostering and comprehension-monitoring activities. *Cognition and Instruction, 1,* 117–175.

Reiman, A. J. (1999). The evolution of social roletaking and guided reflection framework in teacher education: Recent theory and quantitative synthesis of research. *Teaching and Teacher Education, 15,* 597–612.

Risko, V. J., Roskos, K., & Vukelich, C. (2002). Prospective teachers' reflection: Strategies, qualities, and perceptions in learning to teach reading. *Reading Research and Instruction, 41,* 149–176.

Rodgers, C. (2002). Defining reflection: Another look at John Dewey and reflective thinking. *Teachers College Record, 104*(4), 842–866.

Roskos, K., Risko, V., & Vukelich, C. (2001). Reflection and learning to teach reading: A critical review of literacy and general teacher education studies. *Journal of Literacy Research, 33*(4), 595–635.

Roskos, K., Risko, V., & Vukelich, C. (2003, April). *Reflection instruction for prospective teachers: Where theory and research lead us.* Paper presented at the annual conference of the American Educational Research Association, Chicago, IL.

Ross, D. (1989). First steps in developing a reflective approach. *Journal of Teacher Education, 40*(2), 22–30.

Schon, D. (1983). *The reflective practitioner: How professionals think in action.* New York: Basic Books.

Spalding, E., & Wilson, A. (2002). Demystifying reflection: A study of pedagogical strategies that encourage reflective journal writing. *Teachers College Record, 104*(7), 1393–1421.

Tulving, E., & Madigan, S. A. (1970). Memory and verbal learning. In P. H. Mussen & M. R. Rosenzweig (Eds.), *Annual review of psychology* (pp. 381–391). Palo Alto, CA: Annual Reviews.

Van Manen, M. (1977). Linking ways of knowing with ways of being practical. *Curriculum Inquiry, 6,* 205–228.

Vygotsky, L. S. (1978). *Mind in society: The development of higher psychological processes* (M. Cole, V. J. Steiner, S. Scribmer, & E. Souberman, Eds. and Trans.). Cambridge, MA: Harvard University Press. (Original work published 1934)

Waller, W. (1961). *The sociology of teaching.* New York: Russell & Russell.

Winitzky, N. (1992). Structure and process in thinking about classroom management: An exploratory study of prospective teachers. *Teaching and Teacher Education, 8,* 1–14.

Zeichner, K., & Liston, D. (1985). Varieties of discourse in supervisory conferences. *Teaching and Teacher Education, 1*(2), 155–174.

18

Developing Reflection in Preservice Teachers

Connie L. Bowman
University of Dayton

Malena Galvez-Martin
University of South Florida

Margaret Morrison
The Ohio State University

Students often feel as if they are "walking the plank" when they dare to share a reflection of their thoughts and thinking processes in the classroom. Teachers must create a safe environment in which students can freely express their ideas and where students and teachers have a mutual respect for one another. It is only in this place that students will continually open up and give educators a true picture of their metacognitive processes. A question that remains is, "How do you ensure that each student has ample opportunities for sharing?"

—Stephanie Osborne

As this entire book has described, a critical challenge facing all educators is empowering students to be purposeful learners. One avenue for achieving this goal is the teaching of metacognitive skills and strategies. Flavell (1985) viewed metacognition as having two components: metacognitive knowledge (self-knowledge and task knowledge) and experiences (the ability to monitor, reflect, and regulate strategies and attitudes). These metacognitive processes allow students to become more strategic and thoughtful learners (Williams, 2000), just as they allow teachers to become more strategic and thoughtful about their teaching (Pultorak, 1993).

Moreover, in order to help students develop these skills, teachers themselves must come to understand the language of thinking. Although it is possible to develop proficiency with specific facets or skills of critical thinking over a period of days or weeks, development of metacognition is a long-term developmental process, and must be approached as such both with students and with teachers.

Although metacognitive goals for young students have been at the foundation of reading instruction for many years, they are now, appropriately, central among the goals identified by school systems for all students (Davis & Rimm, 2004). However, researchers have found little evidence that most teachers are equipped to implement, or that they are implementing, metacognitive teaching strategies with their students (Boekaerts, 1999; Fisher, 2002; Niemi, 2002). The question is, why? Or, more aptly, why not? What is the difference between teachers who encourage and build metacognitive skills in their students, and those who do not? Is it primarily a difference in preservice training methods? Is it a difference in teachers' comfort level and knowledge base concerning specific metacognitive strategies so that they feel competent teaching them?

Boekaerts (1997) found that in order for students to develop inquiring skills and to learn to reflect, teachers must learn how to guide the learning process. This can only occur when metacognitive strategies are modeled by the teacher (Fisher, 2002). Teachers must be aware of these processes in themselves before they can adeptly model for students.

The research reported in this chapter investigated the development of reflection, a component of metacognition, in preservice teachers using the following questions: What levels of reflection are achieved over time by preservice teachers, with and without training in reflection? And, what is the content of reflections over time? These findings, coupled with our experiences with preservice education, lead us to offer at the conclusion of this chapter recommendations for both future research topics and preservice teacher preparation strategies.

HISTORICAL PERSPECTIVE
AND LITERATURE REVIEW

A variety of definitions have been offered for the metacognitive skill of reflection or reflective thinking about teaching. Shulman (1987) defined it as "a process that involves reviewing, reconstructing, reenacting, and critically analyzing one's own and the class's performance" (p. 15). Reflection is viewed as an essential component of preservice teacher education programs because it is seen as the primary means by which preservice teachers become thoughtful about their experiences (Pultorak, 1993). Reflection is the means for turning experience into learning (McAlpine & Weston, 2000; Sternberg & Horvath, 1995). Reflective practitioners are viewed as those who link theory to practice, balance learning and teaching styles with content, question and analyze their own practice from multiple perspectives, make decisions grounded in knowledge, and evaluate alternatives for future applications (Kember, 1997; McAlpine & Weston, 2000; Reagan, 1993; Roth, 1989; Rust, 1988; Schön, 1987; Sparks-Langer, Simmons, Pasch, Colton, & Starko, 1990).

Reflective Abilities and the Reflective Practitioner

Several researchers consider reflective abilities to be critical to the development of preservice teachers (Korthagen & Verkuyl, 1987; Richards, Gipe, Levitov, & Speaker, 1989; Ross, 1989; Roth, 1989; Rovegno, 1992; Tsangaridou & O'Sullivan, 1994). However, there is no consensus in the field as to the definition of the best method of developing these abilities. Reflective abilities have been examined in studies that employed a wide variety of reflective exercises (Kuhn, 1986, 1991). We do know that regardless of the method used to develop reflecting, student teachers will be more reflective if the experiences on which they are expected to reflect are real and anchored in teaching action (McAlpine & Weston, 2000). Building on the importance of experience, Roth (1989) suggested that in order to develop greater reflective teacher capabilities, preservice teachers need to have opportunities to reflect on their observations during field experiences and in real school settings. As early as a century ago, this hypothesis was being explored. Dewey (1904) conjectured that it could be even more important to prepare preservice teachers to think about their work than to teach them teaching strategies.

Until the research reported in this chapter was conducted, asking *why* events occurred (Sparks-Langer et al., 1990), and helping preservice teachers describe what happened, the rationale for why it happened, and how it could be improved, were the major strategies used to build reflection (Cruickshank & Applegate, 1981; Roth, 1989; Smyth, 1989; Van Manen, 1991).

A Model of the Reflective Process

The research reported in this chapter incorporated a model for supporting reflection among preservice teachers developed by Boud, Keogh, and Walker (1985) called the Model of Reflection in the Learning Process, as well as Dewey's (1933) description of the reflective activity process. These models have three broad components: experiences, reflective processes, and outcomes.

The "experiences" component is the antecedent stimuli for reflection, and includes such things as behaviors, ideas, and feelings. The "reflective processes" component has three stages: returning to experience, attending to feelings, and reevaluating experience. The first stage, *returning to experience*, involves remembering, reviewing, and reconstructing one's experience. This experience is described in detail, in written form, without judging. The preservice teacher is expected to view the experience from different perspectives and be open to new information (Boyd & Fales, 1983) from internal and external sources. This is when intervention and training can occur.

The second stage, *attending to feelings*, is the essential second phase in a teacher's reflective process. Feelings are viewed as promoting affective and cognitive learning. Positive feelings enhance learning, whereas negative feelings are obstacles to learning and hinder reflection. Therefore, negative feelings need to be removed or transformed for learning to take place. Writing can be a powerful tool at this stage to discharge negative feelings (Rainer, 1980).

The third stage, *reevaluating experience*, is vital because it includes association, integration, appropriation, and validation. Each of these thinking processes are needed to determine the depth of meaning that the experience will have for the individual. At this stage, resolution also must occur, as the individual arrives at an adequate solution or a change in perspective (Boyd & Fales, 1983).

The "outcomes" component constitutes the end of the reflective process and prepares one for a new experience. Therefore, the outcome "may include a new way of doing something, the clarification of an issue, the development of a skill or the resolution of a problem. A new cognitive map may emerge, or a new set of ideas may be identified. The changes may be quite small or they may be large. They could involve the development of new perspectives on experience or changes in behavior" (Boud et al., 1985, p. 34).

Assessing Reflection. Researchers have developed a variety of assessment tools for determining to what extent, or at what level, this reflection model has been employed by teachers. For the purposes of the study reported in this chapter, three frameworks (representing a broad context of reflection) were used to assess the levels of teacher reflection. These contexts were the amount of metacognition that teachers experienced through silent reading (Zeichner & Liston, 1985), class discussions (Zeichner & Liston, 1985), and field experiences (Galvez, 1995; Van Manen, 1991; Zeichner & Liston, 1985). The frameworks applied to these contexts are described later.

Zeichner and Liston's (1985) conceptual framework for discourse analysis uses a continuum to assess what they referred to as four "major logical categories" of discourse (i.e., factual, prudential, justificatory, and critical). Their analysis is based on rationales given by student teachers. Level one is the *factual discourse*, or a description of the situation presented by the preservice teacher. In the next level, *prudential discourse*, the preservice teacher makes suggestions and/or provides advice about the situation. Next on the continuum is *justificatory discourse*, where the preservice teacher identifies reasons and rationales for specific situations. The highest level is *critical discourse*, assessing the rationales of the pedagogical practices.

In contrast, Van Manen's (1991) framework, Levels of Reflectivity of Deliberative Rationality, examined the practice and meaning of pedagogical experiences. This framework is expressed in three levels: *technical*, the effectiveness of the teaching strategies and student achievement; *practical*, the application and analysis of the teaching strategy; and *critical*, the attempt to make sense of past experiences in reference to societal issues.

TABLE 18.1
Galvez' Assessment for Levels of Reflection

Scale	Levels of Reflection
0	No mention of pedagogical concepts or skills. Comments based on self and feelings.
1	General explanation of instructional/non-instructional events in terms of personal experiences without analyzing or predicting consequences based on teaching behavior/performance.
2	Retelling of instructional/non-instructional events in a technical way without analyzing teaching performance or the rationale behind it.
3	Focus on one aspect of teacher behavior and implication.
4	Critique of teaching behavior from one perspective in terms of its impact on students, learning outcomes, and behavior.
5	Analyzes, in detail, teaching behavior as being effective or non-effective from the teacher's perspective during instructional and/or non-instructional time, as well as the behavior of the students and how to deal with similar situations in the future.
6	Acknowledges that instruction is based on objectives, students' characteristics, and that a variety of teaching strategies would be used to match the students' different learning styles. Analyzes students' progress and its implications related to teaching behavior, instruction, students' characteristics and learning styles.
7	Evaluates instructional/non-instructional events from multiple perspectives. Provides recommendations/suggestions for improvement and for future implementations.

Note. Adaptations made from Smith and Pape (1990) and Ross (1989).

A third framework to assess reflection on real classroom settings from single to multiple perspectives was proposed by Galvez (1995). Assessment for Levels of Reflection is an adaptation of earlier frameworks developed by Ross (1989) and Smith and Pape (1990). This alternation was necessary because no framework could be identified that would allow assessment of reflection on real classroom settings from multiple perspectives. Several authors feel that viewing experiences from multiple perspectives is critical in the reflective process (Boud et al., 1985; Boyd & Fales, 1983; Ross, 1989). Galvez offered ratings on a 0- to 7-point scale, moving from reflections on self, to reflections from a singular perspective, to reflections from multiple perspectives (teacher, student, parents, community). These levels of reflection are presented in Table 18.1. It is interesting to note that these levels of reflection are parallel, but each has an increasing and deepening level of metacognitive awareness.

WHAT WE LEARNED ABOUT REFLECTION AS A METACOGNITIVE ACTIVITY

Our study was designed to explore and compare changes in preservice teachers' reflective thinking over a three-quarter period. One group of preservice teachers received training in reflection and the other group received no reflective training. During the study, both groups kept reflective journals covering class readings, class discussions, and field experiences.

By the third quarter, a majority (81%) of the preservice teachers not trained in reflection remained at the lower levels on each of the three assessment frameworks. This means that the control students' responses were in the factual level. They only gave a description of what happened from one perspective, usually their own; retold without providing any type of justification for their ideas; or talked about the teaching strategy they had used to teach students.

The experimental group, trained in reflection and reflective thinking, achieved significantly higher levels of reflection on all the frameworks used to assess the reflection entries. These preservice teachers were able to identify reasons and rationales related to specific situations. They asked the *why* question and attempted to respond to it using research and their limited experiences. They viewed teaching as an action to address student needs and how this new learning could be used in the future. These preservice teachers also looked at societal issues and multiple perspectives (the student, the parents, the teacher, the administrator, and the community) and their effect on the child's learning.

Consider an example of a reflective entry for class discussions:

> We discussed many different kinds of teaching methods and strategies. We discussed such things as collaborative learning, in which students work together to come to the answers to their questions. The best thing I learned last week was how to set up and apply learning centers in the classroom. I really think that small group instruction is very important in the classroom. I think that small group instruction is a good way to break up the boredom of lecture classes. For the students, small group instruction gives them an opportunity to learn from and be supported by other members of their group. Another issue discussed last week that I plan to implement in my classroom is learning centers. If I had room, I would like to have permanent learning centers around the room. Learning centers can give students interesting and fun ways to reinforce and provide practice for some issues.

There was support for the finding that training in reflecting makes a difference in preservice teachers' reflectivity (Troyer, 1988). It is important that preservice teachers understand the purposes of reflecting on class readings, class discussions, field experiences, and the relevance of reflecting on one's own teaching to set the stage for the journal. Reflecting on three types of experiences seems to have enhanced the preservice teachers' overall reflectivity. We found that guided reflection over a long continued practice is important for the skill development (Ericsson & Smith, 1991; McAlpine & Weston, 2000; Troyer, 1988), and training in reflection should be introduced early in the professional education component of teacher education programs if we want our preservice teachers to begin their professional careers as reflective practitioners. Further, in this study, these reflective exercises gained more value when the reflections moved from the readings and class discussions (the theoretical) to the field experience (the practice).

It seems when preservice teachers are reflecting about their work, considering both theory and practice, their reflective capabilities are strengthened and their critical reflective thinking skills are developed (Bolin, 1988).

The trained group did not attain the highest levels as was anticipated. This result may be explained in several ways. One explanation may be that more time was needed for them to consolidate their reflective thinking, or perhaps they needed follow-up training each quarter. Another possibility is that some cooperating teachers could have encouraged the participants' reflective capabilities and others did not. As Boekaerts (1997), Fisher (2002), and Niemi (2002) found in their research, perhaps the cooperating teachers were not equipped to assist in reflection or did not know how to engage in reflection themselves. The findings suggest several implications for preservice preparation programs.

SUGGESTIONS FOR PRACTICE IN PRESERVICE TEACHER EDUCATION PROGRAMS

With the current reform movements, No Child Left Behind, and standards-based education with emphasizing outcomes, it is imperative that teacher education programs produce reflective thinkers who are capable of modeling metacognitive skills, and directly teaching those skills to students, thus empowering students in the classroom to be reflective thinkers. Reflective practitioners are able to connect theory to practice and critical inquiry. As researchers have evidenced, reflection is a learned process (Ellsworth, 2002). It develops from deliberately planned programs beginning with the first professional education course that the preservice teacher takes and continues to student teaching.

According to Martin-Kniep (2000), certain conditions must be met to assist students in developing reflective practices. Interestingly, these recommendations parallel in many ways the recommendations for classroom teachers to promote thinking and metacognition in their classrooms (e.g., Costa, 2003; Davis & Rimm, 2004; DeBono, 1986; Udall & Daniels, 1991). First, an environment that permits reflection needs to be established. Furthermore, purposeful reflective activities must be incorporated into preservice education experiences. This is an ongoing process that requires models, prompts, practice, application, and time. Following are suggestions for assisting preservice teachers in the development of metacognitive skills, and in particular, reflection.

Setting the Stage: Environment

Students, including preservice teachers, need to feel safe in their learning environment. They need to experience and know how to create a class climate that promotes learning. One way to achieve this safe environment is to have a common language where all stakeholders in schools use the same terminology and share the same vision and goals. The field experience can be a frightening and devastating experience for preservice teachers when all the significant players are on different pages. By having university liaisons, professors, and cooperating teachers using a common framework for conversation and a collaborative approach to supervision, preservice teachers will feel more comfortable in sharing experiences.

Portfolio

From the first course taken, preservice teachers need to be introduced to a common framework for assessing performance. For example, in Ohio, the framework is PRAXIS III (Educational Testing Services, 2001). This introduction must be purposeful and meaningful in the class and for the student. The first year begins the professional journey for preservice teachers as they collect evidence for the four domains of the PRAXIS III: organizing content knowledge, creating an environment for student learning, teaching for student learning, and teacher professionalism. The conversations in the early classes are devoted to teaching and learning through readings and observations. The portfolio also becomes a purposeful collection of evidence connecting the framework, the standards, and theory. The portfolio provides evidence of the preservice teacher's growth and understanding of self and students. As preservice teachers write rationales for the evidence collected and offer views on educational issues, they have the opportunity to broaden their perspective on student learning and teaching. This assignment models, for the preservice teacher, a strategy for engaging future students in reflective thinking through the use of the portfolio.

At different intervals during the program, preservice teachers need to meet with professors to share the portfolio and engage in dialogue about their growth and development as a teacher. The preservice teacher reflects on why certain artifacts are present in the portfolio and their connection to student learning and outcomes. This is an opportunity for the preservice teacher to gauge personal growth as evidenced by conversations with the faculty member.

The final portfolio conference is at the conclusion of the student teaching experience where students meet with their cooperating teacher and university liaison to share their experiences. Throughout the 4-year program, the preservice teacher has learned how to use the portfolio in the classroom to help students to become more thoughtful in selecting and analyzing work samples as well as giving rationales for their inclusion.

Case Studies

Another way of helping students with reflection is through the use of models and prompts (Fisher, 2002; Kuiper & Pesut, 2003; Martin-Kniep, 2000). At some point in the preservice program, preservice teachers are engaged in connecting field experiences to case studies. Preservice teachers are able to connect theory to practice by using a problem-based model. This process begins the journey of thinking like a teacher. Here the preservice teacher reflects on the problem-based activities and learns to identify the different parts of a problem: givens, goal, and obstacles (Anderson, 1985). Metacognitive processes allow the individual to identify and work strategically through each part of the problem, leading to multiple solutions for the problem. This brainstorming process permits the preservice teacher the opportunity to look at the givens from multiple perspectives and then weigh the consequences for each possible solution. Through discussion, the preservice teacher is able to determine a viable alternative. Each time the preservice teacher is challenged to think about the process and reflect on its consequences from multiple viewpoints. These strategies become part of the preservice teacher's repertoire for planning and evaluating curriculum, discipline procedures, and instruction.

Guided Reflection

During the internship, a common framework is also used for the postlesson observation conference, in which the preservice teacher, the cooperating teacher, and the university liaison reflect on the preservice teacher's performance. This framework (again, PRAXIS III) gives specific prompts and questions to guide reflection assisting the preservice teacher to focus on awareness of self, the learner, and the task. The prompts themselves serve as a scaffold for the student to move from the lower levels of reflection (from Galvez, 1995, Table 1, Levels 0–3) to higher levels of reflection (Levels 4–7). To assist educators in prompting preservice teachers to these higher levels of reflection, we have aligned suggested prompts with the levels of reflection (see Table 18.2). This table can be used as a guide to scaffold preservice teachers in developing reflective thinking.

The process of guided reflection has been supported in previous research (Galvez, 1995; Glaze, 2001). It also has been found that structured reflection seems to be beneficial to less experienced practitioners because the requisite skills to analyze or reflect on a situation may not be in place (Risko, Roskos, & Vukelich, chap. 17, this volume). When the preservice teacher has structured questions, specific areas are targeted for reflection. Following is an example of a postconference guided reflection between a university liaison (UL) and a student teacher (ST) using the PRAXIS III framework:

UL: *How did the lesson go?*

ST: *Well.*

UL: *What evidence do you have to support this?*

ST: *The students were able to explain the process for a bill becoming a law. I guided them through the various stages, but their homework, the flow chart, will be the proof.*

TABLE 18.2
Guided Reflection Using Prompts to Scaffold Reflections

Level	Prompt
0	How do you think the lesson went today?
1	What evidence do you have to support your belief?
2	What were your learner outcomes? Did you meet them? What evidence do you have to support this?
3	What teaching methods did you select? Were they successful? What evidence do you have to support this?
4	What student activities did you select? Were they successful? What evidence do you have to support this?
5	If you were to teach this lesson again, what would you do differently? Why? What would you keep the same? Why?
6	Who did you think excelled today in class? Why do you think the student was successful? Who did you think struggled in class today? Why do you think one student had difficulty and the other excelled? How can you assist all students in the learning process?
7	Using the evidence and data collected about your teaching methods, student's performance, and learning outcomes that occurred today in your class, what will you do tomorrow? Why?

Note.   Adaptations made from the ETS Pathwise and Praxis III series.

UL: *Were your objectives met? And what evidence do you have to support this?*

ST: *Yes. The lesson's goals were for students to explain how a bill starts, identify who is involved in the process of making a law, illustrate the different routes a bill can take, and apply the process to a real law. The students were able to explain the process and identify who was involved in the process. They were able to help each other when someone was uncertain of the response, and they applied the process to a simulated experience.*

UL: *Were your teaching methods effective? And what evidence do you have to support this?*

ST: *Yes. There was a mixture of songs, video, demonstration, teacher-directed instruction, and role playing. All of these supported the content being learned. I was meeting the needs of the visual, auditory, and kinesthetic learners. Students were singing along with the video and later sang a part of the song when we were discussing the process.*

UL: *Were your activities effective? And what evidence do you have to support this?*

ST: *Yes. Students were actively involved in the bill making process. They were walking through each of the committees and role playing what would be involved in this process. Students were getting involved in negotiating between parties and Houses to get the bill into a law.*

UL: *Based on what happened today, what will you do tomorrow?*

ST: *Based on today, I feel the majority of students got it. So, tomorrow the first 15 minutes of the class, I will give the students a real case of a bill becoming a law and all that it went through. They will role play the process. I will be able to see if they really get it. I will also look at the flowcharts; if they didn't understand the process, there is no way they can complete the assignment. Following the simulations, we will have a discussion of what happened and why, and I will fill in any missing pieces.*

Prior to the guided reflection, the preservice teacher often gave "yes or no" responses with little elaboration. Using the framework as a guide, the preservice teacher was asked to support the responses with evidence from the teaching episode. The last question encourages the preservice teacher to tell what the plan of action is for the next day based on the reflection. This is the critical component of the guided reflection. It compels the preservice teacher to evaluate all the evidence and answer the "so what" question.

Preservice teachers are introduced to this model of guided reflection early in their educational program, and have continuous opportunity to engage throughout their program: journal writing (responding to the questions, or writing rationales for evidence), case studies or vignettes, peer coaching (peers viewing videotapes together and posing the Praxis III questions to the preservice teacher engaged in the teaching episode), mock interviews conducted by educators, and small group discussion (sharing portfolio with peers, solutions to problems, or responding to prompts).

Through this process of guided reflection, the preservice teacher is developing the metacognitive strategies to think about intentional teaching actions. As a parallel process, the preservice teacher is also supporting prekindergarten–12 students in developing awareness of their own learning and thinking processes through prompts. These prompts may be in the form of exit slips distributed at the end of the class asking students to identify one thing they learned, something that confused them, or a question for the teacher to be turned in at the end of the class. This allows the teacher to take the pulse of the class by seeing if goals and content were met and understood. The teacher can use this evidence in planning for the next day's lesson.

The KWL comprehension strategy (What I Know, What I Want to Know, and What I Learned) promotes metacognition that connects the student's prior knowledge with questions they want answered, and for evaluating the learning process. Here students are able to see the recursiveness of learning—that information sparks more questions for exploration and inquiry. By the preservice teacher using the model of think-alouds, students are able to hear how to implement this strategy into their learning processes. The discussion web is another method of thinking aloud where students can express the pros and cons of a situation and then come to a solution based on input from all participants in the group. By using these strategies, the preservice teacher is developing a learning community where students are given time and opportunity to reflect through journals and discussions.

Mentoring

Cooperating teachers play a critical role in developing reflection among preservice teachers. Their training and experience prepares them to use the common
language of established frameworks to mentor the preservice teacher into the
profession of teaching. Giebelhaus and Bowman (2002) found that preservice
teachers whose cooperating teachers (mentors) were trained using a common
framework (PRAXIS III) for discussion demonstrated more complete and effective planning, more effective classroom instruction, and greater reflectivity on
practice than those whose cooperating teachers were not trained in a common
framework. This research was corroborated by a state study conducted by Bendixen-Noe and Giebelhaus (2003), who surveyed 896 entry-year teachers (EYTs)
and concluded that there were differences in the domain scores of the performance assessment between mentored and nonmentored EYTs. The researchers further concluded that the universities and colleges preparing preservice teachers
were addressing the requisite knowledge and skills measured by the state-man-
dated assessment.

Action Research

The empowering of preservice and mentor teachers in reflection is seen through
the action research permitting preservice teachers to ask questions and look for
answers in a systematic manner. Action research, according to Bissex and Bullock (1987), permits the teacher to be "an observer, a questioner, a learner, and a
more complete teacher" (p. 4). The preservice teacher and the mentor teacher
work together as teacher-researchers on questions that are meaningful to them.
Together they identify a problem or situation, formulate specific research questions, determine the method and procedure for investigating the question, conduct research (collect and analyze data), reflect, and make decisions based on the
results of the research. This process is recursive and may repeat multiple times
based on the reflections of the preservice teacher and the cooperating teacher.

IMPLICATIONS FOR FUTURE RESEARCH

When thinking about where to go from here, one conclusion can be gleaned from
the literature: More studies are needed on the impact training has on reflection
and preservice teacher learning. Further empirical studies are needed to measure
achieved levels of reflection over a longer period of time. Such studies would also
help to determine whether the growth rate continues when preservice teachers
are given opportunities to reflect with and without training. Related studies are

also needed to investigate possible relations among cognitive developmental maturity, critical thinking skills, and achieved levels of reflection over time.

CONCLUSIONS

At every level of professional development of educators, from preservice throughout inservice, the typical approach for teaching reflection is to introduce the importance of reflection, involve participants in some form of practice (usually journaling), and then send them out with the hope of reflection on teaching and practice occurring. Such expertise is rarely mastered at the preservice level, and reflection is typically addressed, if at all, as only one of many topics in school district inservice training programs. Even within graduate programs, there is a limited time span for teaching reflection and how to assist students to be reflective thinkers, such as those described in *The Thinking Classroom* (Tishman, Perkins, & Jay, 1995). Reflection must be an ongoing process, deliberate and opportunity laden. This involves all participants in preservice programs explicitly modeling, providing guided prompts, and giving ample opportunities for practice in multiple venues permitting transference of modeling from our preservice teachers to their classrooms.

METACONNECTION FOR CHAPTER 18

In chapter 17, the authors provided an extensive review of the literature on reflection in teacher preparation as well as two examples of reflection instruction. In this chapter, Bowman and her colleagues offered research findings and practice-based examples that support the power of reflection in preservice preparation programs. In the next chapter, Rosemary will turn your attention to a related but distinct approach to metacognitively oriented professional development.

REFERENCES

Anderson, J. R. (1985). *Cognitive psychology and its implications*. New York: Freeman.

Bendixen-Noe, M., & Giebelhaus, C. (2003, October). *Mentoring*. Paper presented at the annual meeting of the Mid-Western Education Research Association, Columbus, OH.

Bissex, G. L., & Bullock, R. H. (1987). *Seeing for ourselves: Case study research by teachers of writing*. Portsmouth, NH: Heinemann.

Boekaerts, M. (1997). Self-regulated learning: A new concept embraced by researchers, policy makers, educators, teachers, and students. *Learning and Instruction, 7*(2), 161–186.

Boekaerts, M. (1999). Self-regulated learning: Where we are today. *International Journal of Educational Research, 31*, 445–457.

Bolin, F. S. (1988). Helping student teachers think about teaching. *Journal of Teacher Education*, 39(2), 48–54.

Boud, D., Keogh, R., & Walker, D. (1985). Promoting reflection in learning: A model. In D. Boud, R. Keogh, & D. Walker (Eds.), *Reflection: Turning experience into learning* (pp. 18–40). New York: Nichols.

Boyd, E. M., & Fales, A. W. (1983). Reflective learning: Key to learning from experience. *Journal of Humanistic Psychology*, 23(2), 99–117.

Costa, A. L. (2003). In the habit of skillful thinking. In N. Colangelo & G. A. Davis (Eds.), *Handbook of gifted education* (3rd ed., pp. 325–344). Boston: Allyn & Bacon.

Cruickshank, D. R., & Applegate, J. H. (1981). Reflective teaching as a strategy for teacher growth. *Educational Leadership*, 38, 553–554.

Davis, G., & Rimm, S. (2004). *Education of the gifted and talented* (5th ed.). Boston: Pearson.

DeBono, E. (1986). *CORT thinking skills program.* Oxford, England: Pergamon.

Dewey, J. (1904). The relation of theory to practice in education. In C. A. McMurry (Ed.), *The relation of theory to practice in the education of teachers* (pp. 9–30). Chicago: University of Chicago Press.

Dewey, J. (1933). *How we think: A restatement of the relation of reflective thinking to the educative process.* Boston: Heath.

Educational Testing Services. (2001). *PRAXIS III: Classroom performance assessments orientation guide.* Princeton, NJ: Author.

Educational Testing Services. (2002). *PATHWISE: Classroom observation system orientation guide.* Princeton, NJ: Author.

Ellsworth, J. Z. (2002). Using student portfolios to increase reflective practice among elementary teachers. *Journal of Teacher Education*, 53, 342–355.

Ericsson, K., & Smith, J. (1991). Prospects and limits of the empirical study of expertise: An introduction. In K. Ericsson & J. Smith (Eds.), *Toward a general theory of expertise: Prospects and limits* (pp. 286–300). Cambridge, MA: Cambridge University Press.

Fisher, R. (2002). Shared thinking: Metacognitive modelling in the literacy hour. *Reading Literacy and Language*, 36(2), 63–67.

Flavell, J. H. (1985). *Cognitive development* (2nd ed.). Englewood Cliffs, NJ: Prentice-Hall.

Galvez, M. E. (1995). *The improvement on preservice teachers' reflection through content-specific reflective teaching.* Unpublished doctoral dissertation, Ohio State University, Columbus.

Giebelhaus, C., & Bowman, C. (2002). Teaching mentors: Is it worth the effort? *Journal of Educational Research*, 95(4), 246–254.

Glaze, J. E. (2001). Reflection as a transforming process: Student advanced nurse practitioners' experiences of developing reflective skills as part of an MSc programme. *Journal of Advanced Nursing*, 34, 639–647.

Kember, D. (1997). A reconceptualisation of the research into university academics' conceptions of teaching. *Learning and Instruction*, 7, 255–275.

Korthagen, F. A. J., & Verkuyl, H. S. (1987, April). *Supply and demand; towards differentiation in teacher education based on differences in learning orientations.* Paper presented at the annual meeting of the American Educational Research Association, Washington, DC.

Kuhn, D. (1986). Education for thinking. *Teachers College Record*, 87, 495–512.

Kuhn, D. (1991). *The skills of argument.* Cambridge, MA: Cambridge University Press.

Kuiper, R., & Pesut, D. (2003). Promoting cognitive and metacognitive reflective reasoning skills in nursing practice: Self-regulated learning theory. *Journal of Advanced Nursing*, 45, 381–391.

Martin-Kniep, G. (2000). *Becoming a better teacher.* Alexandria, VA: Association for Supervision and Curriculum Development.

McAlpine, L., & Weston, C. (2000). Reflection: Issues related to improving professors' teaching and students' learning. *Instructional Science, 28,* 363–385.

Niemi, H. (2002). Active learning: A cultural change needed in teacher education and schools. *Teaching and Teacher Education, 18,* 763–780.

Pultorak, E. G. (1993). Facilitating reflective thought in novice teachers. *Journal of Teacher Education, 44,* 288–295.

Rainer, T. (1980). *The new diary.* London: Angus & Robertson.

Reagan, T. (1993). Educating the "reflective practitioner": The contribution of philosophy of education. *Journal of Research and Development in Education, 26*(4), 189–196.

Richards, J. C., Gipe, J. P., Levitov, J., & Speaker, R. (1989, March). *Psychological and personal dimensions of prospective teachers' reflective abilities.* Paper presented at the annual meeting of the American Educational Research Association, San Francisco, CA.

Ross, D. D. (1989). First steps in developing a reflective approach. *Journal of Teacher Education, 40*(2), 22–30.

Roth, R. A. (1989). Preparing the reflective practitioner: Transforming the apprentice through the dialectic. *Journal of Teacher Education, 40*(2), 31–35.

Rovegno, I. (1992). Learning to reflect on teaching: A case study of one preservice physical education teacher. *Elementary School Journal, 92,* 491–510.

Rust, F. O. (1988). How supervisors think about teaching. *Journal of Teacher Education, 39*(2), 56–64.

Schön, D. (1987). *Educating the reflective practitioner.* San Francisco: Jossey-Bass.

Shulman, L. S. (1987). Knowledge and teaching: Foundations of the new reform. *Harvard Educational Review, 57*(1), 1–22.

Smith, L. C., & Pape, S. L. (1990, November). *Reflectivity through journal writing: Student teachers write about reading events.* Paper presented at the 40th annual meeting of the National Reading Conference, Miami, FL.

Smyth, J. (1989). Developing and sustaining critical reflection in teacher education. *Journal of Teacher Education, 40*(2), 2–8.

Sparks-Langer, G. M., Simmons, J. M., Pasch, M., Colton, A., & Starko, A. (1990). Reflective pedagogical thinking: How can we promote it and measure it? *Journal of Teacher Education, 41*(4), 23–32.

Sternberg, R. J., & Horvath, J. A. (1995). A prototype view of expert teaching. *Educational Researcher, 24*(6), 9–17.

Tishman, S., Perkins, D., & Jay, E. (1995). *The thinking classroom: Learning and teaching in a culture of thinking.* Boston: Allyn & Bacon.

Troyer, M. B. (1988). *The effects of reflective teaching and a supplemental. theoretical component on preservice teachers' reflectivity in analyzing classroom teaching situations.* Unpublished doctoral dissertation, Ohio State University, Columbus.

Tsangaridou, N., & O'Sullivan, M. (1994). Using pedagogical reflective strategies to enhance reflection among preservice physical education teachers. *Journal of Teaching in Physical Education, 14*(3), 13–33.

Udall, A., & Daniels, J. (1991). *Creating the thoughtful classroom: Strategies to promote student thinking.* Tucson, AZ: Zephyr Press.

Van Manen, M. (1991). Reflectivity and the pedagogical moment. The normativity of pedagogical thinking and acting. *Journal of Curriculum Studies, 23,* 507–536.

Williams, M. (2000). The part which metacognition can play in raising standards in English at key stage 2. *Reading, 34*(1), 3–8.

Zeichner, K., & Liston, D. (1985). Varieties of discourse in supervisory conferences. *Teaching and Teacher Education, 1*(2), 155–174.

19

Teacher Learning Instrument: A Metacognitive Tool for Improving Literacy Teaching

Catherine A. Rosemary
John Carroll University

> *When I taught kindergarten, a lot of my students could read by the time they went to first grade. However, I didn't see some of the things that I clearly see now as a literacy coach; namely, how to fine tune instruction. A literacy coach can enhance the process of reflection for the teacher by helping her see the nuances of effective instruction. My question is: How do you help teachers analyze their instruction in order to grow metacognitively?*
> —Bhavna Shah, Literacy Coach for Grades K–6, Ohio

Educators, researchers, and policymakers alike recognize the need to develop a highly knowledgeable and skilled teaching force for excellent education in the 21st century (Darling-Hammond, Wise, & Klein, 1999; Ferguson, 1991; Sykes, 1999). Toward this aim, professional development needs to go beyond traditional approaches that are narrowly focused and disconnected from local contexts of classroom life. Rather than amassing strategies and activities that have little to no impact on teaching and learning, teachers can become serious learners in and around practice through substantive professional learning experiences (Ball & Cohen, 1999; Sykes, 1999).

A primary goal of substantive professional development is to develop teachers' awareness of their own teaching, apply this knowledge to improving, and continue to develop and share this knowledge through collaborative inquiry (Hiebert, Gallimore, & Stigler, 2002). Research on high quality professional development points to design principles to guide the delivery structure and the learning activities that will improve pedagogical knowledge and teaching skill. In professional development that takes an inquiry approach, participants develop a professional stance of critiquing their own teaching as a means to improving practice (Crockett, 2002; Goldenberg & Gallimore, 1991; Hawley & Valli, 1999; Mariage & Garmon, 2003; Richardson, 1994).

Teachers need many types of intellectual tools to assist them in this kind of investigation (Ball & Cohen, 1999). Teaching is cognitive activity; it is thinking in action. Intellectual tools that bring into focus the connection between teaching practice and student learning include examination of student work (Crockett, 2002; Little, Gearhart, Curry, & Kafka, 2003), lesson study (Chokshi & Fernandez, 2004), and analysis of videotaped (Roskos, Boehlen, & Walker, 2000) and audiotaped teaching episodes (Kucan, 2001; Rosemary et al., 2002). All of these tools press for deeper understanding of content and pedagogy. Research has shown that teachers who engage in systematic inquiry about their teaching (e.g., analyzing student work or video or audio examples) become more aware of their actions and, over time, show more intentional and precise teaching, which in turn positively affects student performance (Crockett, 2002; Joyce & Showers, 1988; Rosemary et al., 2002; Roskos et al., 2000). In other words, teachers become more metacognitively aware of self as a mediator of student learning. Given the powerful teacher influence on student achievement, it is wise to develop teachers' metacognition through an inquiry approach to professional development using high power intellectual tools.

The focus of this chapter is on the Teacher Learning Instrument (TLI) (Rosemary & Roskos, 2001), a metacognitive tool to deepen understanding of literacy teaching and heighten awareness of the teacher's role in student learning. According to Flavell, P. H. Miller, and S. A. Miller (1993), metacognitive activity refers to "any knowledge or cognitive activity that takes as its object, or regulates, any aspect of any cognitive enterprise" (p. 150). The TLI zeroes in on teaching as an object of cognitive activity, holding it out for close examination from multiple angles: the teacher, the student, the interaction. Through collaborative problem solving, a literacy coach, defined as a teacher with extensive educational background and experience in literacy, and a primary grades teacher engage in multiple cycles of systematically analyzing and interpreting lesson transcript data, reflecting on the teaching–learning process, and using what is learned to make changes in practice that will lead to improved student performance. Four questions are addressed in this chapter:

1. What is the TLI?
2. How does the TLI engage teachers in metacognitive inquiry?
3. What are considerations in using the TLI?
4. What are directions for further research on inquiry tools for professional development?

The first section describes the theoretical roots of the TLI and highlights findings from research on the use of the TLI in various educational settings. The second section illustrates through examples of transcript data the metacognitive processes and substantive dialogue that participants engage in when using the instrument. The third section closes the chapter with considerations for using the TLI and suggestions for further research.

GROUNDING OF THE TEACHER LEARNING INSTRUMENT

Theoretical Roots

The TLI is rooted in Vygotsky's sociocultural theory (1978), premised on the idea that knowledgeable and skillful teachers are powerful mediators of student learning. Central to this theory is the zone of proximal development (ZPD), which is the concept of the cognitive distance between what a child can do with support from the environment, from others, and from self, and what a child can do proficiently on his own. A teacher's skillfully employed actions, carried out in the children's ZPD, serve as a scaffold, assisting their performance with a challenging task until they reach a level of independent performance (Berk & Winsler, 1995; Wood, Bruner, & Ross, 1976).

The TLI is also grounded in the work of Tharp and Gallimore (1988), who applied Vygotsky's ZPD to a school context in their longitudinal work in the Kamehameha Elementary Education Program (KEEP). They described the everyday life of the school in terms of activity settings, the contexts that provide the social scaffold for achieving a shared goal. These contexts of assisted performance occur whenever people intentionally come together in designated places and interact in ways that are culturally bound. In the coaching context of the TLI, assisted performance functions on two levels, a teacher assisting students during instruction, and a coach assisting a teacher to improve assistance to the students. The goal for all involved in the triad is skillful performance: for the coach, successfully moving teachers toward more skillful teaching; for teachers, successfully moving students toward independence in learning; and for students, showing independence in the use of skills and strategies.

The TLI takes into account research syntheses on literacy teaching and learning (Adams, 1990; National Institute of Child Health and Human Development, 2000; Snow, Burns, & Griffin, 1998) and research on teaching strategies shown to be effective in boosting literacy development (see, e.g., Beck, McKeown, Hamilton, & Kucan, 1997; Brown, Pressley, Van Meter, & Schuder, 1996; Liberman, Shankweiler, Fischer, & Carter, 1974; Ogle, 1986; Palinscar & Brown, 1984; Samuels, 1979). One assumption is that the teaching actions characteristic of effective strategies can be explicated. For example, Ogle's (1986) K-W-L begins with the teacher focusing students' attention on the topic of study, drawing out their background knowledge, and engaging students in purposes for reading. Next, reading occurs and is integrated with the teacher helping students to see what they learned in relation to what they wanted to learn.

Likewise, fundamental teaching actions, or protocols, are found in other research-based strategies. Although specific teaching strategies vary depending on students' needs, learning goals, and instructional focus, they all have salient features that can be explained and applied. Through teachers' understanding and practice in implementing protocols embedded in effective strategies, they can develop more skillful performance. Effective strategies research also underscores the importance of scaffolding student learning through teacher–student interactions that are integral to the teaching. Taken together, an analysis of protocol and scaffolding embedded in teaching can provide a critical lens through which teachers can determine ways to improve instruction.

Research on the Teacher Learning Instrument

Research on the TLI has examined the viability of its use as a professional tool to improve literacy teaching. The findings reported here are summarized from a series of preliminary studies that have focused on various aspects of the tool and its use.

From an investigation of the TLI in a variety of teaching contexts, findings showed that both inservice and preservice teachers changed toward a more intentional approach in their teaching and greater awareness of how to scaffold student learning with use of the TLI. Later lessons showed stronger evidence than earlier ones in the teachers' skillfulness in scaffolding students toward achieving instructional goals. As teachers developed more skill in transcript analysis, they focused on specific ways to scaffold student learning based on what they observed in their teaching from the previous lessons (Rosemary et al., 2002).

Findings from follow-up studies (Freppon & Feist-Willis, 2002; Kinnucan-Welsch, Zimmerman, & Campbell, 2002; Rosemary & Grogan, 2002) provide additional support to the TLI as a tool that assists teachers' change toward more skillful practice. Findings on what teachers learned was shown in their talk about themselves and about the children they taught. Conversations focused on four topics: instructional goals (e.g., to improve students' fluency), analytical process (e.g., how to code the transcript), appropriateness of materials (e.g., text difficulty), and student performance (e.g., how well the students accomplished the task). Little to no deviation from those topics was evidenced. This finding is important in that it shows the potential of inquiry tools to focus teachers' thinking on themselves as mediators of student learning to engage teachers in self-monitoring in a supportive professional context in ways that can lead to improved student learning.

From an analysis of the TLI process based on activity setting framework (Tharp & Gallimore, 1988), structural elements of the TLI that support a context for assisted performance were identified (Kinnucan-Welsch et al., 2002; Rosemary & Grogan, 2002). These included focused conversations embedded in teachers' everyday work, planning guide and lesson transcripts that provided tangible records for mediating coach–teacher conversations, and positive human relations that developed through structured, collaborative problem solving. The TLI process called for teachers' increased control over the process of analysis and refinement of teaching, which was evidenced in a comparison of early and later debriefing conversations.

DESCRIPTION OF THE TEACHER LEARNING INSTRUMENT AS A METACOGNITIVE TOOL

The cognitive task central to the TLI is a close analysis of lesson transcripts to determine what works in a lesson, what does not, and to identify ways to improve the lesson based on the critique. Throughout a school year, a literacy coach and teacher come together regularly around the shared goal of improving literacy instruction. Using various strategies, the literacy coach and teacher keep track of how well they are meeting the cognitive goal of the analysis, namely, to understand how a previous lesson was taught and use that knowledge to make improvements. The coach assists the teacher in better understanding the lesson and achieving more skillful teaching. Transcending the goal, the coach and teacher engage in the TLI to improve student learning.

Procedures for the Teacher Learning Instrument

Planning the Lesson. The teacher and coach plan a literacy lesson using a planning guide similar to the one illustrated in Fig. 19.1. They begin by identifying the instructional focus (e.g., phonics, fluency, comprehension, phonemic awareness) and a teaching strategy for improvement (e.g., repeated reading, word sort, K-W-L). They discuss the strategy in terms of when to use it, with whom, and why, and then outline the teaching actions or protocol for implementing it. They also discuss how the teacher may support students' learning using the scaffolding components as described by Berk and Winsler (1995). With each lesson, the scaffolding components are listed on the planning guide. The protocol is also listed, and at times, adjustments are made to the action steps based on decisions that arise from the coach–teacher conversations.

Teaching the Lesson. In preparation for audiotaping the lesson, the teacher places a microrecorder in a pocket and clips a lavaliere microphone to clothing so it is close to the face in order to assure clear audio. The teacher then implements and audiotapes the lesson.

Focus of instruction: Phonics

Specific strategy identified for improvement: <u>Word Sort</u>

Protocol Features (Bear, Invernizzi, Templeton, & Johnston, 2000):	Scaffolding Features (based on Berk & Winsler, 1995).
P1 Focus attention on the task (e.g., read words/name pictures).	S1 Joint problem solving (involve children in meaningful activity; helping children learn by doing)
P2 Explain the categories for sorting.	
P3 Model how to analyze words (pictures) according to feature (e.g., sound; sound and pattern).	S2 Intersubjectivity (coming to a shared understanding; working toward a shared goal)
P4 One word at a time, read and place word (or picture) card under appropriate category.	S3 Warmth and responsiveness (creating a positive emotional tone; providing verbal praise; attributing competence to child)
P5 Encourage talk about why the word (picture) fits the category.	S4 Staying in ZPD (organizing activities that are challenging for children, but achievable by them with assistance; using talk that prompts them to talk, encourages them to tell more, and adds to their thoughts and ideas)
P6 Reread words (name pictures) when finished sorting.	
P7 Restate the categories.	S5 Self-regulation (stepping back to let children take control of own activity; providing assistance to support children's problem-solving)
P8 Provide opportunities for children to practice sorting on their own.	

FIG. 19.1.   Sample planning guide for word sort strategy.

Analyzing the Lesson. The teacher listens to the lesson and transcribes a 10-minute segment containing ample teacher–student interactions. This process of transcribing, although relatively tedious and time consuming, calls for close listening, pausing and writing it down, and so forth. This iterative process serves as a powerful mediator for reflecting, looking back at what was said by whom and propels the teacher's thinking about teaching. The transcription process launches the self-analysis process.

The teacher next makes a copy of the transcript for the coach and keeps the original. The first time that the TLI process is used, the coach codes the transcript (in Fig. 19.1, P followed by a numeral designates a specific protocol step, e.g., P1 is *focus attention on the task*; S followed by a numeral designates a specific scaffolding feature, e.g., S3 is warmth and responsiveness) and models for teachers how to proceed with the process. In subsequent lessons, the coach and teacher independently code their own copy of the transcript before coming together to discuss the lesson.

After coding, teachers write statements summarizing their analysis. These may relate to how often some codes are used (e.g., "The scaffolding feature I used the most was warmth and responsiveness"), patterns observed in the teacher's talk (e.g., "My questions were mostly yes or no type questions or required very short responses to answer"), and the student's talk (e.g., "The student started the session with some expanded responses but reverted back to short answers toward the end of the session"). Other elements of instruction may also be discussed, such as the lesson (e.g., "At the beginning of the lesson, I reminded the students of the previous lesson and our continuous focus on fluency"), text, grouping arrangement, student materials, or props.

Reflecting on the Lesson. In addition to writing a summary of the analysis, the teacher writes a reflection on the lesson, which sounds and looks like the following:

> I think that the materials I chose this time lent itself to Readers' Theater. I feel that I did a better job of incorporating the scaffolding features this time. I know there is still room for improvement, but I think that just being aware of the features helped me to improve my use of them. For example, I didn't use a lot of specific verbal praise in lesson one, but noticed it a lot more in this lesson. I also tried to do more joint problem solving and come to a shared understanding (S1, S2). I know what my intentions were, but sometimes I'm not sure it is clear on the tape for reading the transcript. For example, I was attempting to provide self-regulation when I put them in teams and moved around to assist. It's not so much what I SAID [emphasis in the original] during that time as it is that I structured the time in a way to provide small group time to get teams to work and regulate their own and each other's practice of the material. (Third grade teacher's reflection after the third lesson on fluency using the TLI process)

The written summary and reflection are important parts of the TLI process. Whereas coding is a microanalysis to identify protocol and scaffolding features in the actual teaching compared to the intended teaching actions listed in the planning guide, the written summary and reflection show the teacher's articulation of what she understands about her teaching—a macrolevel synthesis of what is learned about teaching.

Discussing the Lesson. Within about a week of the lesson, the teacher and coach meet to discuss the lesson. They bring their coded transcripts along with any relevant artifacts of the lesson to their meeting. These conversations take the independent analyses to a level of collaborative problem solving. It is in the postlesson conversation that metacognitive processes are exposed—the thinking aloud about one's thinking that creates dialectic in search for deeper understanding about how to improve teaching and learning.

During the TLI process, the teacher and coach focus on one strategy at a time for improvement and engage in three repetitions of the TLI cycle before focusing on another strategy. The TLI process of plan–teach–analyze–reflect–discuss allows the teacher to systematically hone instruction with the support of a knowledgeable and trusted coach. In the follow-up conversation, the teacher receives feedback from the coach and from self-analysis and reflection on how to improve teaching. Thus, the TLI process nudges the teacher toward becoming more self-critical about teaching, which can lead to greater self-monitoring and self-evaluation in the act of teaching.

In the next section, examples of coach–teacher conversations following lessons expose metacognitive processes that the dyad engages in during this part of the TLI process. The examples are excerpts taken from transcripts used in research on the TLI (Rosemary et al., 2002, 2003). Table 19.1 provides a profile of the teaching contexts for these examples. The teaching context, TLI transcript number, and line numbers of the transcript identify each excerpt.

TABLE 19.1
Contextual Variables of TLI: Grouping, Coach–Teacher Ratios, Number
and Grade Level of Students, and Focus of Instructional Improvement

Setting	Coach–Teacher Ratio	Number/Grade Level of Students	Focus of Instructional Improvement: Strategy
A—Pull Out 1 on 1 Reading Intervention	1:1	1: third	Fluency: Timed Repeated Reading
B—Pull Out Small Group Intervention	1:1	7: first	Oral Language: Retelling
C—Classroom Whole Group Instruction	1:1	17: third	Fluency: Reader's Theater

TRANSCRIPT AS MEDIATOR
OF METACOGNITIVE ACTIVITY

In the TLI process, the learners—in this case a literacy coach and teacher—employ metacognitive knowledge of themselves in their respective roles, of the task and its demands, and of strategies to accomplish the goal (Flavell et al., 1993). The coded transcripts mediate the postlesson conversations. The coded transcript serves not only as an object of inquiry, but also as a mediator of deeper discussions about teaching and learning.

Planning: Getting Started on Talking About Teaching

The coach and teacher use the coded transcript as an entré into their conversation about the lesson. The initial postlesson conversation usually begins with a brief discussion of how to begin and then proceeds with the discussion around the coded transcript. Before talking about the lesson specifically, the coach and teacher establish the procedures for how to go about the conversation. As seen in the next few examples, they establish who starts and how to use the coded transcript:

Example 1:

    Coach: *Let's look at your transcript and we can compare our notes. You be the teacher and I'll be the student, and then we'll share coding.*

   Teacher: *Okay.* [begins to read the lesson transcript]. (Third-grade intervention, TLI time 1, lines 14–16)

Example 2:

    Coach: *I will, I started out with . . . now, do you want to take it line-by-line or*

   Teacher: *We can go line by line.* (First-grade intervention, TLI time 1, lines 7–75)

Example 3:

    Coach: *Here's your protocol. Remember this? I thought we could go over it today as well and go over the transcript and my coding. I went ahead and coded it. By the last lesson, you will be doing the coding. I will tell you what I coded and why and that kind of stuff and then if you have any questions we will talk about them.*

   Teacher: *Okay.*

    Coach: *I was trying to note their responses, what they were doing, but there were more expressions than words. Just a note that they were engaged. And then, oh, all of the Ts are you, well they stand for "teacher." If I knew their [students' names], I used their initials. But in most cases I put C for "child."* (Third-grade classroom, TLI time 1, lines 1–15)

After the coach and teacher agree on the rules of the conversation, they proceed with comparing and contrasting how to code particular utterances. Understanding how the utterances were coded is central to reaching the goal of understanding how the lesson was executed.

The next section contains examples that illustrate how the coach and teacher arrive at a shared meaning for what had occurred in the lesson and then use this knowledge to plan what to do next time to better support students' learning. Their metacognitive processes are revealed in the explaining, clarifying, questioning, and justifying that they engage in as they try to make sense of the teacher–student talk they observed in the lesson transcript.

Analyzing: Thinking About Thinking in Teaching

Through the structured conversation that is focused on their coded transcripts, the coach and teacher take the analysis to a deeper level when they share their findings (coding) and explain their thinking. The following example illustrates the conversation between a third-grade classroom teacher and his coach after teaching his second lesson on fluency using the TLI process. The teacher expresses confusion about how to interpret the protocol and scaffolding codes in relation to the utterances observed in the transcript. His coach tries to assure him that it is through the conversation about the coding that they will both come to better define what the codes mean.

> *Coach:*   Let's turn our attention to the actual teacher and student responses. Let's see if we can come to agreement on what we found. Do you want to go first or should I?
>
> *Teacher:*   Okay, and to be honest, I could see some of the protocol as I read. They [protocol codes] seem easier to identify, but I am not sure. Well, I didn't even really try looking for or thinking about the scaffolding as I read. I still feel like I need to better understand those.
>
> *Coach:*   Okay, and that isn't surprising. There isn't exactly a right or wrong code. The reason for these conversations is so that we can better define both the protocol and the scaffolding before the next lesson. (Third-grade classroom, TLI time 2, lines 7–15)

This next excerpt from the end of this postlesson conversation illustrates how the teacher realizes that his explicitly stating that he is "not going to say anything" as the students' practice reading is a conscious move on his part toward promoting independence in his students. He expresses, also, that some individuals will continue to need his support. The teacher also explains how he came to differentiate between the meanings of scaffolding and protocol. *Scaffolding* refers to how a teacher interacts with students to support learning and *protocol* is what teachers do in carrying out a strategy. In his coding of the transcript, the teacher figured out that he needed to focus on one level of analysis at a time rather than try to make sense of both what he was doing (protocol) and how he was supporting students' learning (scaffolding) at the same time:

Teacher: I figured this part [refers to section of transcript] would be self-regulation since I say specifically, "I am not going to say anything as you read." I really tried not to, but at times they needed some individual support. That really happened later, but since I pointed it out here, I put S5 [promote self-regulation] so I wouldn't forget. I put P1 for syntax [focus attention on the syntax of the sentence] in several places. Here on this page, and here [refers to sections of the lesson transcript]. It almost seems easier to go through and look for just one thing and then go through and look for another instead of looking for all things as you read it.

Coach: Is that what you did as you read it?

Teacher: No, not really, I just noticed that it seems easier to do that as I was looking over it now. . . . I feel like I'm starting to figure out the Ss [scaffolding] or at least I'm not always sure which one it is, but I definitely know if it is an S or not, or the difference seems clearer between protocol and scaffolding. In some ways, everything you say or do could be one or the other. It's just a matter of if you are doing a good job of it or not, or whether or not what you say or do is effective in actually problem solving with kids or just trying to, or actually helping them to self-regulate or just trying to, or actually encouraging their talk or just trying to.

Coach: Sometimes it's a judgment call. Well, I mean you may know what your intentions were as the teacher, but I guess the trick is to be objective enough when reading the transcript to tell if the evidence is clear or not as to whether or not you actually exhibited a certain scaffold or protocol. (Third-grade classroom, TLI time 3, lines 21–41)

As observed in the last few lines of the transcript, the coach builds on the teachers' understanding that his careful self-analysis helps him see that his intentions are made explicit to the students, that he moves beyond "trying to" to "actually helping them" achieve more skillful performance. Put another way, the coach explains that objectivity is needed in the self-analysis in order to find evidence that the intended teaching actions were actually executed.

What has been discussed so far is how the TLI process engages a coach and teacher in metacognitive activity. On a procedural level, their conversations illustrate their thinking about how to accomplish the cognitive goal of coding a lesson transcript. After this task is accomplished, the coach and teacher establish rules of conversation around the transcript. Once they gain control over the cognitive task of coding and how to proceed in talking about it, they delve into what their analyses (coding) means, and in doing so deepen understanding of the lesson.

Coding utterances in the lesson transcripts involves metacognitive activity that requires the coders to interpret the actions they observe in the transcript and compare them to the teacher's intended actions as listed in the planning guide. Coding for the scaffolding components functions the same way, requiring coders to think about the meaning of scaffolding as defined on the planning guide while also interpreting the transcript to determine if and how the teacher evidenced support in interactions with students.

Figures 19.2 and 19.3 illustrate the multilayered analysis of the TLI. Figure 19.2 shows a third-grade teacher's second TLI plan using the repeated reading protocol, which the coach and teacher co-constructed at the end of their postlesson conversation about the previous lesson on fluency. Figure 19.3 shows part of the coded lesson transcript that was discussed in the postlesson conversation. The codes closest to the text are the coach's; those in circles are the teacher's, which the coach added to her copy during the postlesson conversation. The following text is an excerpt of the postlesson conversation in which the coach and teacher shared their independent coding and grappled with understanding the intent of the teacher's specific actions in helping the student succeed with the task:

Teacher: He said "prosody." I said, "We are looking at prosody. What is prosody?" So here I said that I responded to his prosody, his answer prosody, and then I encouraged to tell more, which is an S4 [staying in the ZPD, prompt to tell more]. [reads the transcript] What is prosody?

Coach: Okay, and I again I saw it as focusing on task [coded P1], which is fluency. But we, yeah . . .

Teacher: Okay.

Coach: And you have S3 [warmth and responsiveness].

Teacher: and S4 [staying in ZPD]. [reads the transcript] Look back at the chart for Jonathan Bing when you have read the poem before. Now you had rated yourself as needs improvement the first time you read it and the second time you rated yourself good. What are you saying you are good at?

Coach: [Reads the transcript as the student]. My reading. I am not saying it word for word, I am saying it like I'm saying it, like I'm talking to someone.

Teacher: Okay, and I put that as S4 [staying in ZPD] and S2 so we're working toward a shared goal of what is prosody and also that I'm scaffolding. I'm trying to use more instructional talk to prompt him to tell more.

Coach: And I put P1 [focus attention on the task] and S1 [joint problem solving].

Teacher: You like those P1's. He's focused on the task, he knows.

Teacher Name:

Literacy Specialist's Name:

Teacher Learning: Procedures and Coding Guide for:
Audiotape record the lesson. (Use a lavaliere microphone for clear audio.)

- Transcribe a 10-minute segment of the lesson.
- Using the codes listed below, code the teacher's talk in two ways: first) code the protocol features; second)code the scaffolding features. (Note: The codes may not apply to all instances of the teacher's talk; and more than one code may be applied to some instances of the teacher's talk.)
- Write statements summarizing your analysis of the transcript.
- Write a 1-page reflection on the lesson.

Protocol Features for:
Fluency - Rereading Strategy
Focus of instructional improvement

P1 Focus Attention on Task
P2 Teacher explains Purpose: rate, accuracy, prosody
P3 Teacher models
P4 Student reads silently
P5 Student reads aloud
P6 Teacher reviews time, errors, wpm,
P7 Student records time, errors, wpm
P8 Student reviews records: prosody
P9 Student rereads at a later time

Scaffolding Features

S1 Joint problem solving (involve children in meaningful activity; helping children learn by doing)

S2 Intersubjectivity (coming to a shared understanding; working toward a shared goal)

S3 Warmth and responsiveness (creating a positive emotional tone; providing verbal praise; attributing competence to child)

S4 Staying in ZPD(organizing activities that are challenging for children, but achievable by them with assistance; using instructional talk that prompts them to talk, encourages them to tell more, and adds to their thoughts and ideas)

S5 Self-regulation (stepping back to let children take control of own activity; providing assistance as needed to support children's problem-solving)

FIG. 19.2.   Third-grade teacher's planning guide for repeated reading strategy.

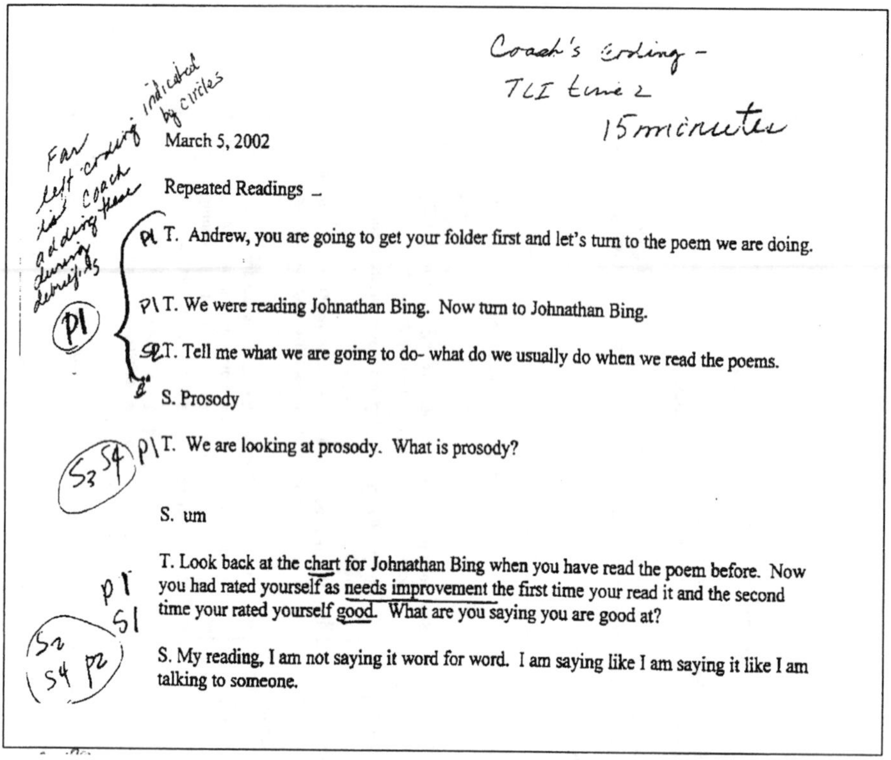

Coach's coding –
TLI time 2
15 minutes

March 5, 2002

Repeated Readings

P1 T. Andrew, you are going to get your folder first and let's turn to the poem we are doing.

P1 T. We were reading Johnathan Bing. Now turn to Johnathan Bing.

S2 T. Tell me what we are going to do- what do we usually do when we read the poems.

S. Prosody

P1 T. We are looking at prosody. What is prosody?

S. um

T. Look back at the chart for Johnathan Bing when you have read the poem before. Now you had rated yourself as needs improvement the first time your read it and the second time your rated yourself good. What are you saying you are good at?

S. My reading, I am not saying it word for word. I am saying like I am saying it like I am talking to someone.

FIG. 19.3. Coach's coded lesson transcript of third-grade teacher's second lesson using repeated reading strategy.

Coach: *But even if you're focused on the task, sometimes, and maybe I could put S4 there, but before you go into the lesson as I feel, you really want the child to know the overall goal.*

Teacher: *That would be explaining the purpose. That would be P2.*

Coach: *And that's part of it.*

Teacher: *That should be P2 then.* (Third-grade intervention, TLI time 2, lines 72–92)

Their discussion is detailed and specific, as seen when they go back and forth between role playing the lesson transcript line-by-line and periodically stopping to discuss their analyses and interpretations of the talk observed in the transcript. In this example, the postlesson conversation is a fine-grained analysis of teaching. The coach and teacher challenged each other to explain their thinking around the codes, especially when they disagreed. The dissonance that sometimes occurred in their talk about the coding provoked a deeper understanding of fluency and how to teach it. They were focused heavily on the teacher's actions, and on a metacognitive level, the teacher's intentions based on what she was trying to get the student to understand and be able to do. In this case, the TLI process set up a collaborative inquiry between colleagues who were both well-versed in reading content and pedagogy and who found themselves learning even more about fluency as one component of literacy instruction.

Reflecting: Thinking About Learning in Teaching

The coded lesson transcripts, as tangible records of the teaching, serve to mediate the teacher's awareness of student learning. In moving closer toward the goal of using the TLI process to improve teaching and, in turn, boost student learning, a coach employs strategies to prompt the teacher to think about the students. The coach may ask the teacher to review the learning goal, the strategy, and the rationale for using the particular strategy for the particular group of students. In the following excerpt, the coach presses the first-grade reading intervention teacher to explain her thinking about a lesson on retelling. The teacher verbalizes her thinking about her own and the students' actions. She uses details of the lesson transcript to illuminate her new thoughts about what had occurred and how she could change her instruction next time to improve the lesson:

> Coach: *Would you please refresh my memory about some of the things we had talked about in the first lesson and how you were going to make the changes with this next lesson.*
>
> Teacher: *All right, first of all the material was too difficult for students. It was a story that, although I was familiar with it, the students weren't. The dialogue did not happen even with repetition of it, so, it was difficult for them to catch on to the phrasing. I drove the majority of the entire play by jumping in and trying to get them the language, feed them the directions and so forth, primarily driven by myself. So spending time doing the [retelling] protocol, I chose Three Little Pigs trying to give them a more familiar story [in this lesson]. I still found myself jumping in and providing dialogue, providing transitional phrases, hoping they would do more on their own. But they still weren't quite there.* (First-grade intervention, TLI time 2, lines 2–12)

After the third lesson on retelling and the teacher making adjustments in her instruction, the coach asks the teacher to explain what made the third lesson more successful than the other two:

Teacher: The text was much more appropriate, the dialogue was repetitive and eas-
          ier for them to remember and again, I modeled the story using the puppets
          and I read it first and then I gave it to them to rehearse so they had a lot
          more repetition. (First-grade intervention, TLI time 3, lines 80–82)

Ultimately, the shared goal of the coach and teacher in using the TLI is to
make adjustments in teaching that will result in improved student learning. The
conversation that surrounds the analysis of the transcript can result in deep understanding of the interplay between teaching and learning.

This next example illustrates a third-grade intervention teacher's understanding about her student's need for fluency development, her use of a repeated reading strategy, and how to shift her teaching to better support his learning:

Coach: Were you able to discern if the student understood the goal. Was it evi-
           dent?
Teacher: Yes, I think the students understood the goal, although he had difficulty at
           times recalling and using the language we use in the classroom even
           though we have done this now [repeated readings] for many weeks. He's
           still having some difficulty with what does prosody mean and those terms
           that we do use and we do rate and he rates himself.
Coach: Do you use synonyms for prosody?
Teacher: We talk about it's a conversation, when it sounds like conversation or
           reading word by word, and he does pull that out later in this lesson, but it
           takes him a while, the processing for him seems to be slower. And I
           stepped back a little to let him because we've done this lesson before, take
           control of the activity. He knew what to look for next and I let him do
           that, and recall what he was during and why he was doing it, which I did
           not do on the first one.
Coach: Did he need a lot of prompting?
Teacher: He still needs prompting throughout of what's next and what to do and
           where do we record. Some modeling is still being done, but not as much as
           the first lesson. So he's taking more and more control of his repeated read-
           ing.
Coach: Is there carryover in the classroom?
Teacher: I do not know.
Coach: Okay, because we want to know if he's able to read content area with as
           much fluency as he does the activity that you have here.
Teacher: His teacher has responded that she thought his fluency was better.
Coach: Oh, okay.
Teacher: However, does she track it like we track it? No.

Coach: Right, no.

Teacher: But we certainly do see results. I mean, and you'll see in this lesson, he went on with the reading of this poem. He was at 149 seconds to read a poem of 139 words and then he went down to 88 seconds and then the third reading he went down to 77. He sees that and the importance of him reading a second and third time the same things. Hopefully when he's reading something in the content area he realizes the first time isn't going to be fluent and that he needs to go back and reread it for fluency. (Third-grade intervention, TLI time 2, lines 17–47)

It takes more than the TLI process for teachers to know how to adjust instruction to meet students' needs. Although the process can help teachers "see" themselves as mediators of student learning, they need to also gather information about students' needs directly through appropriate assessments, and know how to analyze and interpret data. The TLI process coupled with the teacher's knowledge of the students may even better serve to scaffold teachers' toward more skilled teaching.

These examples and descriptions show that the TLI process creates a context for self-examination of practice with the explicit goal of improving teaching in ways that will improve student learning. The TLI's structure requires intentional thinking on the part of the coach and teacher at every phase, from planning a lesson and identifying a specific protocol (teaching actions embedded in effective teaching strategies) and scaffolding strategies that the teacher intends to implement, to the coach–teacher conversation following the lesson. The TLI sets up a structure for the coach and teacher to think about teaching as cognitive activity through the transcript coding process and the conversation that follows. The coded transcript, always present in the coaching conversation, serves as a mediator of metacognitive processes. Together the coach and teacher learn how to learn about teaching by learning how to talk about their analyses of teaching. They become self-aware of their thinking in their conversation about the lessons and regulate their cognitive processes to accomplish the shared goal.

CONSIDERATIONS FOR USE

The extent to which teachers know how to think about their own teaching and how they can apply what they know to self-regulate their thinking should be useful higher order knowledge in the context of their own instruction (Forrest-Pressley, MacKinnon, & Waller, 1985). There is some research to suggest that the TLI is a viable inquiry tool for assisting teachers in developing a self-monitoring stance toward their own teaching. However, the following cautions should be considered based on the collaborative studies on the use of the TLI in multiple instructional contexts (see also Rosemary et al., 2002):

1. The TLI process can better serve as a tool for teaching improvement when the literacy coach has a solid grounding in research-based reading strategies and a firm grasp of the concept of scaffolding.

2. The process of transcript coding is in itself a cognitive activity that may need to be scaffolded by a more knowledgeable other. The coach–teacher conversations rely heavily on the coded transcript, and thus, the conversation that surrounds the transcript can only be as keen as the observers.

3. The additional time and effort required for transcribing needs to be considered. Transcribing even 10-minute excerpts from lessons is additional work for the teacher. In university clinical settings, this work is typically an assignment. For classroom teachers, ways to support them in this process need to be considered. For example, a coach may assist by taking the teacher's class (some coaches did so in this research).

4. Fundamentally, the teacher–coach relationship must be collaborative and built on mutual trust.

DIRECTIONS FOR FURTHER RESEARCH

The TLI provides a social learning context for collaborative inquiry in the authentic contexts of school life (Feiman-Nemser & Beasley, 1997; Rogoff & Lave, 1984; Tharp & Gallimore, 1988). Two educators, one called a literacy coach and one a primary grades teacher, engage in multiple cycles of analyzing lessons and using what is learned to make changes in practice that will lead to improved student performance. The role of the educator identified as a coach, however, is not well researched. Although descriptions of the coach role, different from that of the traditional role of a reading specialist, may be helpful in guiding professional development at school levels, research on the efficacy of the coach role and what particular functions, if any, may be more important than others, is warranted (Dole, 2004; International Reading Association, 2004).

Studies of the TLI contribute more information about teaching teachers. Its aim is to contribute to teacher education and professional development that is realized in improved classroom practice through our most valued resource—the teacher. In working with the TLI, practitioners have opportunities to put under close scrutiny the product of prior mental activity (lesson transcript) for the purpose of deepening their understanding of teaching. Further development of this tool, as well as other inquiry tools, is greatly needed. To achieve the high quality professional development that will result in greater educational success for all students, more needs to be learned about the content, delivery structure, and learning activities that impact teacher practice.

METACONNECTION FOR CHAPTER 19

In chapter 18, we saw how guided reflection in one teacher preparation program based on models of reflection contributed to the learning of preservice teachers. In chapter 19, Rosemary described the *Teacher Learning Instrument*, a tool that can be useful to coaches and teachers in systematically analyzing and improving teaching. In the next chapter, we examine coaching and teaching from a metacognitive perspective.

REFERENCES

Adams, M. J. (1990). *Beginning to read: Thinking and learning about print.* Cambridge, MA: MIT Press.

Ball, D. L., & Cohen, D. K. (1999). Developing practice, developing practitioners. In L. Darling-Hammond & G. Sykes (Eds.), *Teaching as the learning profession: Handbook of policy and practice* (pp. 3–32). San Francisco: Jossey-Bass.

Bear, D., Invernizzi, M., Templeton, S., & Johnston, F. (2000). *Words their way: Word study for phonics, vocabulary, and spelling instruction.* Upper Saddle River, NJ: Merrill.

Beck, I. L., McKeown, M. G., Hamilton, R. L., & Kucan, L. (1997). *Questioning the author: An approach for enhancing student engagement with text.* Newark, DE: International Reading Association.

Berk, L., & Winsler, A. (1995). *Scaffolding children's learning: Vygotsky and early childhood education.* Washington, DC: National Association for the Education of Young Children.

Brown, R., Pressley, M., Van Meter, P., & Schuder, T. (1996). A quasi-experimental validation of transactional strategies instruction with low-achieving second grade readers. *Journal of Educational Psychology, 88,* 18–37.

Chokshi, S., & Fernandez, C. (2004). Challenges to importing Japanese lesson study: Concerns, misconceptions, and nuances. *Phi Delta Kappan, 85,* 520–525.

Crockett, M. D. (2002). Inquiry as professional development: Creating dilemmas through teachers' work. *Teaching and Teacher Education, 18,* 609–624.

Darling-Hammond, L., Wise, A. E., & Klein, S. P. (1999). *A license to teach: Raising standards for teaching.* San Francisco: Jossey-Bass.

Dole, K. (2004). The changing role of the reading specialist in school reform. *The Reading Teacher, 57,* 462–471.

Feiman-Nemser, S., & Beasley, K. (1997). Mentoring as assisted performance: A case of co-planning. In. V. Richardson (Ed.), *Constructivist teacher education: Building a world of new understandings* (pp. 108–126). Washington, DC: Falmer.

Ferguson, R. (1991). Paying for public education: New evidence on how and why money matters. *Harvard Journal on Legislation, 28,* 465–498.

Flavell, J. H., Miller, P. H., & Miller, S. A. (1993). *Cognitive development* (3rd ed.). Englewood Cliffs, NJ: Prentice-Hall.

Forrest-Pressley, D. L., MacKinnon, G. E., & Waller, T. G. (Eds.). (1985). *Metacognition, cognition and human performance: Vol. 1. Theoretical Perspectives.* New York: Academic Press.

Freppon, P., & Willis, J. F. (2002, December). *Efficacy of the teacher learning instrument.* Paper presented at the 52nd annual meeting of the National Reading Conference, Miami, FL.

Goldenberg, C., & Gallimore, R. (1991). Changing teaching takes more than a one-shot workshop. *Educational Leadership, 49*, 69–72.

Hawley, W. D., & Valli, L. (1999). The essentials of effective professional development: A new consensus. In L. Darling-Hammond & G. Sykes (Eds.), *Teaching as the learning profession: Handbook of policy and practice* (pp. 127–150). San Francisco: Jossey-Bass.

Hiebert, J., Gallimore, R., & Stigler, J. (2002). A knowledge base for the teaching profession: What would it look like and how can we get one? *Educational Researcher, 31*(5), 3–15.

International Reading Association. (2004). *Standards for reading professionals.* Newark, DE: Author.

Joyce, B., & Showers, B. (1988). *Student achievement through staff development.* New York: Longman.

Kinnucan-Welsch, K., Zimmerman, B., & Campbell, L. (2002, December). *What literacy coaches and teachers learned about the teaching–learning process through self-examination of practice.* Paper presented at the 52nd annual meeting of the National Reading Conference, Miami, FL.

Kucan, L. (2001). Transcript analysis project (TAP): An opportunity for student teachers to engage in practical inquiry into classroom discussions. *National Reading Conference Yearbook, 50*, 346–355.

Liberman, I. Y., Shankweiler, D., Fischer, F. W., & Carter, B. (1974). Explicit syllable and phoneme segmentation in the young child. *Journal of Experimental Psychology, 18*, 201–212.

Little, J. W., Gearhart, M., Curry, M., & Kafka, J. (2003). Looking at student work for teacher learning, teacher community, and school reform. *Phi Delta Kappan, 85*, 185–192.

Mariage, T. V., & Garmon, M. A. (2003). A case for educational change: Improving student achievement through a school–university partnership. *Remedial and Special Education, 24*, 215–234.

National Institute of Child Health and Human Development. (2000). *Report of the National Reading Panel: Teaching children to read: Reports of the subgroups* (NIH Publication No. 00-4754). Washington, DC: U.S. Government Printing Office.

Ogle, D. M. (1986). K-W-L: A teaching model that develops active reading of expository text. *The Reading Teacher, 39*, 564–570.

Palinscar, A. S., & Brown, A. L. (1984). Reciprocal teaching of comprehension fostering and monitoring activities. *Cognition and Instruction, 1*, 117–175.

Richardson, V. (1994). Conducting research on practice. *Educational Researcher, 23*, 5–10.

Rogoff, B., & Lave, J. (1984). *Everyday cognition: Its development in social context.* Cambridge, England: Cambridge University Press.

Rosemary, C. A., Freppon, P., Kinnucan-Welsch, K., Grogan, P., Feist-Willis, J., & Zimmerman, B. (2003, April). *Honing the teaching of reading through structured collaborative inquiry.* Presented at the 2003 annual meeting of the American Educational Research Association, Chicago, IL.

Rosemary, C. A., Freppon, P., & Kinnucan-Welsch, K. with Grogan, P., Feist-Willis, J., Zimmerman, B., Campbell, L., Cobb, J., Hill, M., Walker, B., Ward, M. (2002). Improving literacy teaching through structured collaborative inquiry in classroom and university clinical settings. *Yearbook of the National Reading Conference, 51*, 368–382.

Rosemary, C. A., & Grogan, P. (2002, December). *Relationship between teachers' learning and students' learning in teachers' self-examination of practice.* Paper presented at the 52nd annual meeting of the National Reading Conference, Miami, FL.

Rosemary, C. A., & Roskos, K. A. (2001). *Teacher learning instrument.* Unpublished manuscript, John Carroll University, University Heights, OH.

Roskos, K., Boehlen, S., & Walker, B. J. (2000). Learning the art of instructional conversation: The influence of self-assessment on teachers' instructional discourse in a reading clinic. *Elementary School Journal, 100,* 229–252.

Samuels, S. J. (1979). The method of repeated readings. *The Reading Teacher, 32,* 403–408.

Snow, C. E., Burns, S., & Griffin, P. (Eds.). (1998). *Preventing reading difficulties in young children.* Washington, DC: National Academy Press.

Sykes, G. (1999). Teacher and student learning: Strengthening the connection. In L. Darling-Hammond & G. Sykes (Eds.), *Teaching as the learning profession* (pp. 127–150). San Francisco: Jossey-Bass.

Tharp, R., & Gallimore, R. (1988). *Rousing minds to life: Teaching, learning, and schooling in social context.* Cambridge, England: Cambridge University Press.

Vygotsky, L. S. (1978). *Mind in society: The development of higher psychological processes.* Cambridge, MA: Harvard University Press.

Wood, D. J., Bruner, J., & Ross, G. (1976). The role of tutoring in problem-solving. *Journal of Child Psychology and Psychiatry, 17,* 89–100.

20

Coaching for Metacognitive Instructional Practice

Kathryn Kinnucan-Welsch
University of Dayton

Reflective metacognition is thinking and going over what you know about your own learning and understanding on a certain topic or task. This can be a professional development tool because you know how much work or effort a task will take. You will be better able to manage your time and know if you will need additional help.
—Regina Jackson

Teaching is a complex activity. As a teacher educator, I experience the complexity of teaching everyday through the struggles, dilemmas, and triumphs of preservice and inservice teachers with whom I work. As I peruse the 51 chapters of *Handbook of Research on Teaching* (Richardson, 2001), I am struck by the breadth and depth of what teachers must know and be able to do, and how this is represented in an extensive knowledge base.

This knowledge base is often overwhelming in the field of literacy instruction. The research on reading and writing, and the contexts that influence how children learn to read and write, has been extensive (Flood, Lapp, Squire, & Jensen, 2003; Kamil, Mosenthal, Pearson, & Barr, 2000). When one considers the high stakes connected with literacy development for children, families, teachers, and school district administrators, what teachers know and can do is a focal point for how we judge the effectiveness of our schools (Taylor & Pearson, 2002). What teachers know and can do becomes apparent in the literacy development of each learner. One goal for the research on literacy processes and instruction is to support all learners, young and old, as literate, participating members of community.

As authors in this volume have suggested, one way to identify students who are becoming accomplished readers and writers is to observe the degree to which they exhibit metacognitive processes while engaging with text. To what extent are they aware of what they are reading? To what extent do they recognize when comprehension breaks down? How do they go about approaching text strategically so they can better comprehend? Answers to these questions indicate evidence of whether or not children are self-monitoring, self-regulating readers, which is one of the primary goals of literacy instruction.

The purpose of this chapter is to describe how teachers can become more adept, intentional (i.e., more metacognitive), and skilled in instruction that supports literacy development. I am suggesting that ongoing professional development through coaching is one critical aspect of helping teachers become more aware, and therefore more skilled, in their instruction.

This chapter offers two vignettes of coaching that will assist teachers, coaches, administrators, and teacher educators in designing professional development. These vignettes are then analyzed for examples of how the coaches supported teachers in accessing what the teachers needed to know, in using what they knew to provide powerful instruction, and in monitoring and self-regulating their instruction in light of student needs. In other words, it examines coaching through a metacognitive lens (Flavell, 1977; Hacker, 1998). Because coaching occurs within the context of classroom practice, I will also incorporate principles that acknowledge that learning is social and embedded in activity (Moll, 1990; Rogoff & Lave, 1984; Tharp & Gallimore, 1988). This chapter, then, brings together the perspectives of individual awareness of one's own thinking and acting and how individuals learn from others in the context of practice.

This chapter addresses the following questions: What role does professional development play in literacy learning? In what ways does coaching represent one venue for professional development for teachers? How does coaching support teachers in becoming more metacognitive in their instructional practice?

LITERACY LEARNING AND PROFESSIONAL DEVELOPMENT

Children become accomplished readers and writers through literacy instruction based on what we know about the reading process and on pedagogy that leads and supports children toward becoming more expert in processing text. One of the challenges, however, has been to prepare teachers to teach in ways that children are more likely to become accomplished in reading and writing. Compelling research in teacher preparation for teaching reading is sparse (Anders, Hoffman, & Duffy, 2000), but emerging (International Reading Association, 2003).

Furthermore, it is well documented that substantive professional development for practicing teachers is sadly lacking (Ball & Cohen, 1999; Richardson, 2003). Even when teachers are well prepared through effective preservice programs, practicing teachers do not have access to the context-embedded and carefully designed professional development experiences that take them beyond what they know and can do as novice teachers (Hawley & Valli, 1999; Richardson, 2003). Schools have not been designed as places where teachers continue to learn.

Many educators have called for an overhaul of professional development that not only enhances the knowledge base of teachers, but also connects the deepening knowledge base to the daily practice of teachers (Ball & Cohen, 1999; Garet, Porter, Desimone, Birman, & Yoon, 2001; Hiebert, Gallimore, & Stigler, 2002; Wilson & Berne, 1999). One venue for professional development that is receiving increasing attention in the literature and in the daily reality of schools is coaching.

Coaching can be defined as the intentional assistance to teachers by an accomplished or expert other. Tharp and Gallimore (1988) defined assisted performance as "what a child can do with help, with the support of the environment, of others, and of the self" (p. 30). They noted that identical processes can be identified in the learning adult. Therefore, I define coaching as providing assisted performance to teachers in the context of the activity of instruction. Some refer to this assistance as *mentoring* (Feiman-Nemser & Beasley, 1997).

The current research and literature on coaching is somewhat thin, but is generating more interest in the current climate of accountability. Many have called for policies and structures that support ongoing, locally generated, context-specific professional development (Ball & Cohen, 1999; Elmore & Burney, 1999), and coaching represents one option for teachers. Indeed, some have noted that the role of the reading specialist in prekindergarten–12 schools is expanding beyond providing direct support to struggling readers to include an emphasis on coaching teachers (Bean, Cassidy, Grumet, Shelton, & Wallis, 2002; Dole, 2004; International Reading Association, 2004).

Comprehensive descriptions of professional development often include examples of coaching (Lyons & Pinnell, 2001; Robb, 2000; Rodgers & Pinnell, 2002; Sweeney, 2003). In these descriptions, one can find some common contexts that provide opportunities for the coach to provide assistance to the teacher. These include leading discussions on topics related to student learning, instruction, and assessment; engaging in joint planning and coteaching; modeling instruction; and observing teaching and providing feedback. Despite the descriptions of coaching as a process available in the literature, we still have much to learn about how coaches coach. We need to be able to identify what coaching processes support teachers in becoming aware of what they know, of what they can do well, and how to improve what they do not do as well as they must to support accomplished readers and writers. In other words, how can coaching support teachers in being metacognitive about their teaching? The research reported in this chapter contributes to a deeper understanding of coaching for metacognitive instructional practice.

COACHING IN TWO SETTINGS

The examples of coaching presented in this chapter are taken from my research as a participant in a statewide literacy professional development initiative: the Literacy Specialist Project (Kinnucan-Welsch, 2003a, 2003b; Rosemary, Grogan, et al., 2002). The central aim of the Literacy Specialist Project, launched in 2000 by the Ohio Department of Education, is to provide professional development to educators in the state of Ohio that supports enhanced understanding in the teaching of reading and writing. The professional development incorporates foundational knowledge of literacy processes and pedagogy represented in a series of professional development sessions known as *Teaching Reading and Writing: A Core Curriculum for Educators* (Roskos, 2000). In 2002–2003, 158 literacy specialists worked with over 1,100 teachers in 79 districts using the Core Curriculum materials.

I am one of 13 field faculty representing 8 universities directly involved in the initiative. We work with the literacy specialists through monthly meetings and site visits to support them in their sessions with teachers and in coaching. The vignettes about coaching presented in this chapter are taken from this initiative.

Coaching for a District Focus on Spelling

Donna is a literacy specialist in a small district in a rural, but growing, area of Ohio. After her first year as a literacy specialist, she worked in the second year of the project with a group of three second-grade teachers, Judy (in her 5th year of teaching), Terry (in her 6th year), and Fran (in her 11th year; all names are pseudonyms). They met monthly for full-day meetings during the 2001–2002 school year. Donna had written a grant that provided for substitute teachers. The district had decided to focus on improving spelling instruction for this academic year, so Donna immersed her teachers in reading, videos, demonstration lessons, and student data that pertained to writing, word study, and spelling.

In addition to the focus on spelling instruction, the teachers each selected a child from their class and administered several informal assessments, including oral reading of leveled text, writing sample, and spelling/word knowledge. Based on the assessment data, the teachers decided on an instructional focus, planned instruction, and monitored student progress toward the instructional goal. The agendas for the monthly meetings included deepening the teachers' knowledge base about spelling and writing instruction, as well as discussions about the case studies of the individual children they had chosen.

The vignette I have chosen to share is from one of the all day meetings with the teachers on March 27, 2002. I was able to attend part of the meeting, so I was able to participate in the discussion and gather artifacts that indicate what they were learning. The agenda for the March 27, 2002, meeting is in Fig. 20.1.

```
                          Core Curriculum
                          March 27, 2002

  I.      Housekeeping/Updates
          A. How's it going?
          B. Teacher information survey

  II.     Continuing the Assessment Cycle
          A. Ongoing assessments - analyzing and interpreting the data
                  Reading           *Running Records
                  Writing           *Writing Samples
                  Spelling          *Writing Samples/Weekly Assessments

        · B. Planning and Evaluating Further Instruction
             Protocols/Tapes/Transcripts
             What have we learned? Where do we need to go next?

          C. Periodic Assessments - Planning
                  Reading           *DRA/Off grade Reading Proficiency
                  Writing           *Writing Proficiency Benchmark Assessment
                  Spelling          *DSA [Developmental Spelling Assessment]

  III.    Taking Another Look at Spelling/Word Study
          A. Reading - "Word Walls that Work', Janet Wagstaff
          B. Linking Spelling and Writing - How are we doing?
          C. Video - "Learning about Writing", Linda Dorn
          D. Developing mini-lessons to teach spelling and writing strategies

Lunch
P.M. John Smith Elementary School
I.V. In the classroom
      A. Lessons
Terry and Judy: Will you get together and plan your afternoon schedule for the sub
so we can have a block of time in each of your classrooms to work with some
individuals or small groups, including your case study child? The rest of the class will
need to be doing something fairly quiet. Plan for about 30 minutes in each classroom.
I will teach a minilesson and you will teach another similar lesson immediately
following mine. Fran can be the observer this time. We will debrief afterwards in
the center room. If you have specials that interfere let me know so we can work out
something else. Donna
```

FIG. 20.1.

This agenda provides a glimpse of how Donna's plan for the day with her second-grade teachers incorporated many of the aspects of what coaches do. First, Donna had told me in a previous conversation that the teachers began the year with little knowledge of how to assess and appropriately instruct students based on spelling assessment data. Donna purchased *Word Journeys* (Ganske, 2000) for the teachers, and they had spent considerable time in previous sessions learning the Developmental Spelling Assessment (DSA) and designing instruction based on where children were in spelling development. Judy, one of the participating teachers, told me during the meeting that at the beginning of the year she was a bit apprehensive about implementing this approach to spelling instruction. She said, "We all had the DSA on our shelves, but we have 10 other books to read also."

Donna was aware of their apprehension, and acknowledged that they were aware of the gaps in their knowledge base. She devoted considerable time in the second-grade classrooms modeling how to assess the children and followed up during their meetings to explain how to interpret the data. On March 27, after 6 months of support from Donna, the teachers came with data from their case study children that included data on spelling development.

A second aspect of Donna's coaching evident from this agenda is that she supported the teachers in understanding how student data should drive instruction. One of the characteristics of accomplished teachers is that they know what children know and can do, and how to teach them (assisted performance) so that they reach the next level of accomplishment. Donna wanted these second-grade teachers to design instruction for children based on what they can do and what they need to learn. The teachers each chose a child, assessed the child using several informal instruments at the beginning of the school year, and designed and implemented instruction with Donna's support. During the March 27 meeting, the teachers brought their case study data and a brief summary of where their child was at this point in time. Judy's summary of her second-grade child follows[1]:

> Jordan came to me reading at a "G" level. He is now reading at a 92% at the level "M." Hopefully, he will hit benchmark by the end of the school year. He is writing and has improved. At the beginning of the year, his writing consisted of short sentences. His stories did not have a beginning, middle, or ending. Now his writing has a title, beginning, middle, and ending, in addition to a problem and solution. He still struggles with his spelling, though he has improved in this area from the beginning of the school year. He began spelling in the Letter Name stage and is now transitioning into the Within Word stage. Some of his spelling concerns are related to his speech.
>
> I will continue to work with Jordan in all these areas. In reading, I want him to become more fluent and not depend so much on his strategies. His strategies are interfering with his fluency. I want him to continue to use his strategies when stuck on words, in a quick manner so it does not interfere with the meaning of his writing. I would like to see more detail. I want him to continue to emphasize the visual part of the word. This visual part is the manner in which he can picture what a word looks like when he goes to spell the word.
>
> Overall, Jordan has improved in all three areas. My main goal for him is to be reading at grade level by the termination of the school year. It looks promising that he will attain benchmark status for second grade. His writing and spelling have some areas of concern. Jordan is a hard worker who wants to succeed; he has come a long way this year. (Judy, case study summary, 3/27/02)

---

[1]For specific details on the reference to spelling levels, refer to Ganske (2000).

The teachers shared, in turn, their case study summary. The conversation focused on what instructional strategies would support each child to progress in literacy development. Next is a brief excerpt of the conversation. Judy is describing how she had engaged Jordan in a repeated reading to improve his fluency. During the reading, she had called Jordan's attention to how he was reading like a robot. Notice how Donna gave Judy some feedback on her instruction:

Judy: [referring to repeated reading] And this is kind of like the next step. [recalling what she said to Jordan] "Let's try and make it sound not like a robot." He said it perfectly, so it was interesting to see if this repetition works and to not let it go but to do it again you don't really have to spend that much time each time you do it.

Donna: And even with some of the phrases that he did, it comes natural. They don't realize that they know they start with part four for some reason and it sounds right. So we just hope that they continue to carry that over. I really did like too the way you noticed he had slipped back into the robot reading. And that you caught him right away. (coaching meeting, 3/27/02)

The aforementioned excerpt, although brief, does provide a glimpse of one of the more powerful aspects of coaching. Donna had suggested to Judy during a previous session that Judy try repeated reading of familiar text with Jordan. Judy was able to monitor Jordan's progress in fluency, and Donna also plays a role here in monitoring Judy's progress. Donna had addressed the topic of fluency in previous meetings with the teacher. As coach, Donna's role was to ask what does Judy know about fluency? What does she still need to learn?

I have described how Donna provided resources for the teachers that deepened their knowledge about literacy assessment and instruction. I have also described through Judy's summary and a brief excerpt of a coaching conversation, how analyzing student assessment data can be a powerful coaching context. Now I would like to turn to how Donna provided a scaffold for the teachers to more systematically design and implement instruction.

After the teachers and Donna had talked about the case study data, they turned to a focus on instruction. One of the professional development resources that Donna used with the teachers to help them improve instruction was the video *Learning About Writing* (Dorn, 1999). Donna showed excerpts from this video and the teachers talked about how the instruction that was modeled in the video could be adapted to their classrooms. Donna, realizing that teachers often have difficulty transferring what they see in videos to their own classrooms, brought a minilesson organizer that she had adapted from *Snapshots* (Hoyt, 2000), one of the resource books she had purchased for the teachers. Using the mini-lesson organizer as a guide (See Fig. 20.2), Donna and the teachers co-planned a lesson focused on writing. Following the planning in the morning session, Donna taught the lesson in Fran's classroom, providing a model of instruc-

Gradual Release of Responsibility
Mini-lesson Planning Organizer

Teachers Name_____ Date_____
Subject_____

GRR Model	Mini-lesson components
Introduce the Topic/Strategy Explain the goal to your students. Tell them what they will learn.	
Model the use of the strategy Talk out loud about what you are doing. Tell the students what you are thinking. Explain why you are doing what you are doing and how you decide when and if to use the strategy. The goal is to make your thinking as transparent as possible so the students will understand how to use and apply the learning.	
Provide guided practice Work with your students to practice the strategy. This is often a good time for partners, cooperative groups, or teams to work together and support each other while you act as coach, praising appropriate use of the strategy and assisting those who need additional help. This is also a good time to assess how well your students understood your demonstration.	
Offer independent practice Children work independently using the strategy in their personal work. This is a second opportunity to assess understanding, support appropriate uses of the learning, and re-teach as needed.	
Encourage self-reflection Students now have a chance to stop and consider: What did we just learn (the content)? How did the strategy work for us (the process)? How else might we use the strategy?	

FIG. 20.2.   Adapted with permission from *Snapshots* © 2000 by Linda Hoyt. Published by Heinemann Publishers, Inc., a division of Reed Elsevier, Inc., Portsmouth, NH. All rights reserved.

tion for the teachers. The group then moved to Terry's classroom, and she taught the same lesson to her children. After a debriefing on Terry's lesson, the group moved to Judy's classroom, Judy taught, and they ended the cycle with a final debriefing. This was a routine that Donna and the teachers had followed all year, as each teacher had the opportunity to teach, observe, and debrief.

According to Tharp and Gallimore's definition of assisted performance (1988), teachers can look for support from the environment as well as from a more expert other. Donna was providing support by co-planning instruction with the teachers that she would model that afternoon. Following the modeling, Judy and Terry taught a lesson that afternoon that was similar to the one Donna modeled. In other words, Donna modeled and provided the opportunity for guided practice for the teachers. Donna also provided a concrete object that became a part of the teachers' environment, the minilesson planning organizer. The teachers would be able to use this organizer in the future as they planned lessons in their grade level team meetings. Planning instruction that takes children from where they are to where they need to be is challenging. A parallel challenge is providing professional development that takes teachers from where they are to where they need to be. The framework of gradual release of responsibility provides a model of assisted performance that applies to all learners, children and adult.

What is also rather striking about this planning tool is that it encourages children to be metacognitive as well. Note the last section, "encourage self-reflection." The questions in that section encourage children to think about their own thinking and to be metacognitive in their use of the strategy. This tool, and the purpose for which Donna used it, provides an example of how to support both teacher and student metacognition.

So, to summarize, I would like to offer a few thoughts about this vignette before turning to the second one. First, Donna was intentional and deliberate about enhancing the teachers' knowledge about the content of literacy instruction. The teachers knew what they didn't know, and Donna provided resources and opportunity to discuss the content and to apply the content in practice.

Second, Donna encouraged the teachers to think about their own thinking and actions during the session discussions. The teachers brought artifacts, including data, case study summaries, lesson plans, and the like, around which the conversations took place. Again, Donna was encouraging the teachers to view teaching from a metacognitive perspective by facilitating discussion, asking questions, modeling instruction, and co-planning. In each of the context-embedded activities, Donna made her thinking transparent to the teachers so they could analyze their own knowledge and actions in the same way. Finally, Donna encouraged teachers to use tools that would assist them in self-monitoring and improving their teaching.

Did the teachers see themselves as being more aware of their teaching actions following these sessions? I conducted an end-of-year interview with Donna and two of the teachers, and comments from this interview indicate that they were more aware:

Judy: I think I am just more aware of their ability and, you know, I'm thinking more [about] DSA. I think I analyzed or just knew more about what to expect and what not to expect and I was able to move students to their appropriate level sooner than I was last year. Actually we would give them spelling assessments and then we would analyze. Okay, this student is ready, this student is not ready. So I felt as a teacher I was able to get them more on the appropriate level and have them be challenged, but also be successful in that area.

Fran: And I think I had kids and I don't know if it was me being more aware
and being more experienced because I had done it a year, but I moved
kids into the next level sooner than I had the year before and I felt
pretty comfortable doing that. I knew they were definitely ready,
whereas last year I was hesitant. I just felt more comfortable with the
program having that year of experience. I felt good about the time I
put into the spelling because I believe in it, it is important, and I just
think the way my kids look at words is totally different than they have
before.

KKW: Do you think your teaching is different in terms of helping kids with
spelling?

Fran: Yes, I think it is more natural now. It's not so much the spelling. We
do spelling for thirty minutes a day or depending on the day. I think it
is more, we integrate it more throughout different subject areas, in the
writing and, because we are more familiar with it, it just comes naturally to teach it more. (end-of-year interview, 5/08/02)

Judy and Fran were able to articulate how they had adjusted their spelling instruction based on what they had learned through the coaching support Donna
had provided throughout the year. In other words, the comments from the interview suggest that coaching had supported these teachers in being more metacognitive as teachers as they identified their intentional decisions regarding instruction and adjusted based on student progress. I would now like to turn to the
second coaching vignette.

Transcript Analysis as a Context for Coaching

This vignette also comes from the Literacy Specialist Project described earlier in
this chapter. I examined coaching conversations that took place over three cycles
using the *Teacher Learning Instrument* (Rosemary & Roskos, 2001; also see Kinnucan-Welsch, 2003a, 2003b, and Rosemary, chap. 19, this volume). The purpose of this research was to examine how coaches coach teachers using an analytical framework for examining teaching, the TLI.

The underlying premise of the TLI is that instruction can be analyzed on two
dimensions. First, each literacy instructional episode should have identifiable, salient features that distinguish that instruction. For example, a word building lesson has features that distinguish it from a word sort. These fundamental features,
or teaching actions, are termed *protocol features* in the TLI. The second dimension of teaching that is analyzed in the TLI is evidence of instructional talk that
scaffolds learning. These features are called *scaffolding features* in the TLI.

To use the TLI, teachers audiotaped three lessons targeting the same student
learning goal, transcribed a segment of the lesson, and analyzed the lesson according to protocol and scaffolding features. Each teacher–literacy specialist

(coach) pair had conversations about the lessons using the analyzed transcript as a guide. The TLI cycle is a context through which coaches support teachers toward more metacognitive instructional practice. The vignette presented is taken from the conversations of one coach–teacher dyad.

Susan (coach) and Connie (teacher) chose to focus on Oral Language: The Language of Literacy. This domain of instruction supports the development of children's oral language, a critical component of literacy development. This protocol was one that was described in the CORE Curriculum materials that the literacy specialists used in their professional development sessions with teachers. The protocol is represented in Fig. 20.3. Because the coach and the teacher each analyzed the transcript using the protocol and scaffolding features as a guide, the conversations contain reference to these features.

Susan and Connie had three conversations over a course of several weeks. Each conversation was focused on an excerpt of a lesson that Connie had taped and transcribed. The focus here is on how the talk between the coach and the teacher about the lesson encouraged Connie to be more metacognitive in her instruction.

The focus of this lesson was fluency. Connie was working with a small group of first-grade children. She read the book *The Elves and the Shoemaker* to them and then distributed stick puppets to help them retell the story. The children became

Protocol features for:	Scaffolding Features
Language of Literacy Protocol: Narrate modeled stories	S1 Joint problem solving (involve children in meaningful activity; helping children learn by doing)
P1 Focus attention on using oral language for a purpose	
P2 Explain the language function (for reading/writing, for inquiry, for social interaction)	S2 Intersubjectivity (coming to a shared understanding; working toward a shared goal)
P3 Model the talk that supports the function	S3 Warmth and responsiveness (creating a positive emotional tone; providing verbal praise; attributing competence to child)
P4 Provide opportunities for practicing language function and related talk	
P5 Give feedback on using oral language for a purpose	S4 Staying in ZPD (organizing activities that are challenging for children, but achievable by them with assistance; using instructional talk that prompts them to talk, encourages them to tell more, and adds to their thoughts and ideas)
	S5 Self-regulation (stepping back to let children take control of own activity; providing assistance as needed to support children's problem-solving)

FIG. 20.3.

rather distracted with the stick puppets and were not very successful in reaching their goal.

Susan opened conversation one by asking Connie to comment on what her overall impression of the lesson was. It is important to note here that Susan made a choice to open with an opportunity for the teacher to provide feedback, a metacognitive task. It is also interesting to note that Susan encouraged Connie to provide feedback to herself, an example of what Tharp and Gallimore (1988) referred to as providing assistance to self:

> **Susan:** I think that the first thing I would like to talk about is your overall impression of how we think this went and take a look at, thinking back, at how you originally envisioned this lesson was going to go and then some of the things that happened as planned and then some of the things that happen as things do when you work with kids.
>
> **Connie:** OK. I had hoped that because I was using what I thought was a familiar story, The Elves and the Shoemaker, and because I was giving them puppets to work with, stick puppets, and because I didn't think they had a lot of opportunity to do something like that, I thought that they would be more engaged, more anxious to retell the story, when in fact, I don't think I ever actually got to a P5.

From that invitation for Connie to provide feedback on the lesson, Susan drew Connie's attention to the main coaching point of conversation one in the TLI series, why the students were distracted and not engaged in the retelling:

> **Susan:** Well, I really think we'll hold off on the protocol thing for a while. What I really wanted to bring to your attention and to our discussion about this lesson is the fact about how well the preplanning went, how your materials were prepared, and how everything there was as you would expect for first grade . . . you know, I thought that all of that was very well planned out in advance, and as we talked while we were transcribing we felt we were having a hard time listening to the children and yourself because things were becoming very frustrating, I noticed, and I don't want to be overly critical at this time.

Susan then commented on the specific student behavior that indicated the students were not focused on the task. Based on that observation, she provided for Connie a specific goal for her next lesson, that is, to establish student engagement:

> **Susan:** Because this is the first time we tried this, but I noticed frustration in your approach and I think the children's frustration came out later when they started to, you know, beat each other up with their

little stick puppets. They probably, at this point, were not catching on . . . at least that's my impression . . . so, let's talk a little bit about that because there were things that did work but there were other things that probably could be adapted a little better.

Connie: I agree . . . Because . . . I wanted to give them encouragement and I wanted to applaud them for their efforts, but I never even had the opportunity to do that. You're right, it was just turning into frustration. So, I tried to pick something that was more challenging and maybe I should have picked a more familiar story so they could have carried the story without my support as much as I did.

Susan: . . . and then they would get an idea of how your language use would build the story and even use a little bit of that metacognition with them, you know "I'm stuck here. . . . I don't know what I should say, but this is what happened in the story" you know, tell them what you are thinking. (TLI, cycle 1, debriefing conversation)

This is a brief excerpt of the first cycle debriefing conversation, but we can see how the coach is assisting performance through the coaching conversation. The transcript of the lesson provided a concrete record of the instruction, and Susan suggested (taking Connie's lead) a specific improvement for her next lesson, modeling a retelling for the children. The coach and the teacher returned to this in the second conversation:

Susan: Overall, though, as I remember, the first lesson was all of you and very little of the children participating. But, in the second one, I see there was more dialogue the children were using. Why do you think they were better able to put the dialogue in this time, other than familiarity? There were some other things that must have happened.

Connie: Well, there was repetition, a lot of repetition, of a story that they were very familiar with. We did rehearse it. . . . I don't think we really rehearsed the story in the first lesson. I was hoping that as part of the lesson that they would be able to retell and recall and they could not do that with *The Elves and the Shoemaker*. This one was a little easier for them to do.

Susan: Talk a little bit about the modeling that might have occurred in this one as compared this one. I think we both talked about that there was a need for you to do more modeling of that language.

Connie: Right, I did. I read the story to them and as I was telling them the story I was acting it out with the puppets so they could actually see what their puppet might be doing while they were speaking and I . . . I guess that//

Susan: So, as I look at the transcript, I do see many more instances of the P2, which is the modeling of the language, so they were hearing from you and then knowing what you were going to expect, and how they were going to participate. What do you think about the ZPD issue, because that was such a big one from last time?

Connie: It's very important that they have to understand the language, understand the story elements, the problem and solution and at the same time have a clear sense of what they are going to be doing. (TLI cycle 2, debriefing conversation)

The exchange, which occurs early in the conversation, does return to what Connie and Susan agreed would be a focal point for Connie to think about her teaching, modeling a retelling. Although the talk does not seem to move below the surface level, Connie is thinking about her teaching and comments on what the students need to know to be able to retell.

These are glimpses of the complete conversations, and I have done a more detailed analysis of coaching conversations within the TLI (Kinnucan-Welsch, 2003b). The point I would like to make for the purposes of this chapter is that structured coaching conversations provide another opportunity for coaches to support teachers in developing a metacognitive orientation to their practice. Susan was able to refer to a concrete record of her teaching over time, the transcript, and that created a context in which the coach–teacher conversation focused on how the teacher can engage in metacognitive processing of instruction. What did I do in this lesson? How can I adjust the lesson the next time that will better meet the demands of the task for the children? What do I need to know about retelling that I might not now embed in my instruction? Some of these questions were asked by the coach, and some were asked by the teacher of herself, which is an indication that she was becoming self-monitoring and self-regulating in her teaching actions.

FUTURE DIRECTIONS

The role of the literacy coach is evolving to meet the demand for high quality professional development that is embedded in the daily work of teachers and teaching. Many districts have allocated resources for this role, and despite the challenge of limited resources, it appears that coaching positions will continue to increase in number.

The role and practice of coaching, however, is still ambiguous and uncertain. It is clear that we do not know what we need to know about coaching as a metacognitive process. Research is needed to determine what effective coaching looks like. Research is also needed to define high quality professional development for coaches. The research is beginning to provide clear descriptions of accomplished teaching in the area of literacy (Taylor & Pearson, 2002). We do not yet have a research base on what accomplished coaching looks like.

A second area of needed research must address the relationship between accomplished coaching, accomplished teaching, and student learning. Sykes (1999) commented that the link between professional development and student learning has not been tightly established. An even more tenuous connection exists between coaching and student learning. As educators, we must begin to explore what the appropriate paths are that will illuminate these questions.

CONCLUSIONS

Hacker (1998) defined metacognition as "knowledge of one's knowledge, processes, and cognitive and affective states, and the ability to consciously and deliberately monitor and regulate one's knowledge, processes, and cognitive and affective states" (p. 11). To summarize this journey into the worlds of two coaches, I would suggest that coaching is an essential and viable professional development structure that can support teachers being more metacognitive about their instruction. Coaching can take many forms, as these vignettes would suggest, and research is needed to shed light on what models of coaching yield the greatest benefits in terms of enhanced practice and greater student achievement. Teachers, like learners who are metacognitive in their actions, are more deliberate, and intentional. Coaching holds promise as one way to support teachers in metacognitive instructional practice.

The current era of accountability is placing increasing pressures on children, teachers, educators, and policymakers. Teachers deserve substantive professional development, just as children deserve effective teachers of reading. Hopefully, insights from future research on coaching, assisted performance, and metacognition will help shape future directions in policy and program development.

METACONNECTION FOR CHAPTER 20

In chapter 19, we learned about the *Teacher Learning Instrument* and how coach–teacher dyads engaged in a cyclical process of planning, analyzing, and improving instruction. In the final chapter focusing on professional development, Kinnucan-Welsch invited the reader into two coaching contexts in which coaches and teachers improved their practice by incorporating metacognitive principles.

REFERENCES

Anders, P. L., Hoffman, J. V., & Duffy, G. G. (2000). Teaching teachers to teach reading: Paradigm shifts, persistent problems, and challenges. In M. L. Kamil, P. M. Mosenthal, P. D. Pearson, & R. Barr (Eds.), *Handbook of reading research* (3rd ed., pp. 719–742). Hillsdale, NJ: Lawrence Erlbaum Associates.

Ball, D. L., & Cohen, D. K. (1999). Developing practice, developing practitioners. In L. Darling-Hammond & G. Sykes (Eds.), *Teaching as the learning profession: Handbook of policy and practice* (pp. 3–32). San Francisco: Jossey-Bass.

Bean, R. M., Cassidy, J., Grumet, J. E., Shelton, D. S., & Wallis, S. R. (2002). What do reading specialists do? Results from a national survey. *The Reading Teacher, 55,* 736–744.

Dole, J. A. (2004). The changing role of the reading specialist in school reform. *The Reading Teacher, 57,* 462–471.

Dorn, L. (1999). *Learning about writing.* York, ME: Stenhouse Publishers.

Elmore, R. F., & Burney, D. (1999). Investing in teacher learning: Staff development and instructional improvement. In L. Darling-Hammond & G. Sykes (Eds.), *Teaching as the learning profession: Handbook of policy and practice* (pp. 263–291). San Francisco: Jossey-Bass.

Feiman-Nemser, S., & Beasley, K. (1997). Mentoring as assisted performance: A case of co-planning. In V. Richardson (Ed.), *Constructivist teacher education: Building a world of new understandings* (pp. 108–126). Bristol, PA: Falmer.

Flavell, J. H. (1977). *Cognitive development.* Englewood Cliffs, NJ: Prentice-Hall.

Flood, J., Lapp, D., Squire, J. R., & Jensen, J. M. (Eds.). (2003). *Handbook of research on teaching the English language arts.* Hillsdale, NJ: Lawrence Erlbaum Associates.

Ganske, K. (2000). *Word journeys: Assessment-guided phonics, spelling, and vocabulary instruction.* New York: Guilford.

Garet, M. S., Porter, A. C., Desimone, L., Birman, B. F., & Yoon, K. S. (2001). What makes professional development effective? Results from a national sample of teachers. *American Educational Research Journal, 38,* 915–945.

Hacker, D. J. (1998). Definitions and empirical foundations. In D. J. Hacker (Ed.), *Metacognition in educational theory and practice.* Hillsdale, NJ: Lawrence Erlbaum Associates. Retrieved from http://emedia.netlibrary.com

Hawley, W., & Valli, L. (1999). The essentials of effective professional development: A new consensus. In L. Darling-Hammond & G. Sykes (Eds.), *Teaching as the learning profession* (pp. 127–150). San Francisco: Jossey-Bass.

Hiebert, J., Gallimore, R., & Stigler, J. (2002). A knowledge base for the teaching profession: What would it look like and how can we get one? *Educational Researcher, 31*(5), 3–15.

Hoyt, L. (2000). *Snapshots.* Portsmouth, NH: Heinemann.

International Reading Association. (2004). *Standards for reading professionals: Developed by the professional standards and ethics committees of the International Reading Association* (rev. ed.). Newark, DE: Author.

Kamil, M. L., Mosenthal, P. B., Pearson, P. D., & Barr, R. (Eds.). (2000). *Handbook of reading research* (3rd ed.). Hillsdale, NJ: Lawrence Erlbaum Associates.

Kinnucan-Welsch, K. (2003a, April). *Coaching as assisted performance.* Paper presented at the annual meeting of the American Educational Research Association, Chicago, IL.

Kinnucan-Welsch, K. (2003b, December). *Coaching for improved teaching: An analysis of assisted performance in a professional development context.* Paper presented at the 53rd annual meeting of the National Reading Conference, Scottsdale, AZ.

Lyons, C. A., & Pinnell, G. S. (2001). *Systems for change in literacy education: A guide to professional development.* Portsmouth, NH: Heinemann.

Moll, L. C. (1990). *Vygotsky and education: Instructional implications and applications of sociohistorical psychology.* Cambridge, England: Cambridge University Press.

Richardson, V. (Ed.). (2001). *Handbook of research on teaching* (4th ed.). Washington, DC: American Educational Research Association.

Richardson, V. (2003). The dilemmas of professional development. *Phi Delta Kappan, 84,* 401–406.

Robb, L. (2000). *Redefining staff development: A collaborative model for teachers and administrators.* Portsmouth, NH: Heinemann.

Rodgers, E. M., & Pinnell, G. S. (2002). *Learning from teaching in literacy education: New perspectives on professional development.* Portsmouth, NH: Heinemann.

Rogoff, B., & Lave, J. (1984). *Everyday cognition: Its development in social context.* Cambridge, England: Cambridge University Press.

Rosemary, C. A., & Roskos, K. A. (2001). *Teacher learning instrument.* Unpublished manuscript, John Carroll University, University Heights, OH.

Rosemary, C. A., Freppon, P., Kinnucan-Welsch, K., with Grogan, P., Feist-Willis, J., Zimmerman, B., Campbell, L., Cobb, J. Hill, M., Walker, B., & Ward, M. (2002). Improving literacy teaching through structured collaborative inquiry in classroom and university clinical settings. *Yearbook of the National Reading Conference, 51,* 368–382.

Rosemary, C. A., Grogan, P. R., Kinnucan-Welsch, K., Zimmerman, B., Campbell, L., Fesit-Willis, J., & Freppon, P. (2002, December). *Scaffolding teacher learning as a scaffold for student learning: An analysis of assisted performance using activity setting framework.* Paper presented at the 52nd annual meeting of the National Reading Conference, Miami, FL.

Roskos, K. A. (2000). *Teaching reading and writing: A core curriculum for educators.* Columbus, OH: Ohio Department of Education.

Sweeney, D. (2003). *Learning along the way: Professional development by and for teachers.* Portland, ME: Stenhouse.

Sykes, G. (1999). Teacher and student learning: Strengthening the connection. In L. Darling-Hammond & G. Sykes (Eds.), *Teaching as the learning profession* (pp. 127–150). San Francisco: Jossey-Bass.

Taylor, B. M., & Pearson, P. D. (Eds.). (2002). *Teaching reading: Effective schools, accomplished teachers.* Hillsdale, NJ: Lawrence Erlbaum Associates.

Tharp, R. G., & Gallimore, R. (1988). *Rousing minds to life: Teaching, learning, and schooling in social context.* Cambridge, England: Cambridge University.

Wilson, S. M., & Berne, J. (1999). Teacher learning and the acquisition of professional knowledge: An examination of research on contemporary professional development. In A. Iran-Nejad & C. D. Pearson (Eds.), *Review of research in education* (Vol. 24, pp. 173–209). Washington, DC: American Educational Research Association.

FINAL REFLECTIONS

Metacognition in Literacy Learning: Then, Now, and in the Future

Michael Pressley
Michigan State University

The editors asked me to read the chapters in this volume and offer an integrative response and commentary. They were aware that, throughout my career, my work has contacted metacognitive theory and many of the major issues covered in this book and continues to do so now. I'll start with a brief, personal, intellectual history, emphasizing aspects of my past work that are relevant to the thinking and research summarized in this volume. Then, I turn my attention to some recent work carried out by my group as I comment on the particular issues covered in the volume.

MY METACOGNITIVE JOURNEY

My senior, college thesis was on memory strategies used by elementary-level students as they tackled laboratory-type memory tasks—learning lists of words. Like others working in that era, I found that children's recall increased with age from kindergarten through the middle and later elementary years, with much of the increase due to developmental increases in the use of strategies, specifically, cumulative rehearsal strategies (i.e., saying the words on the list over and over, saying more and more words as more and more words are revealed by the experimenter). I left this undergraduate experience with deep, personal knowledge of a finding that has stood the test of time (see Pressley & Hilden, in press, for a review): In some laboratory-type learning situations, children are increasingly strategic with increasing age, with the clearest indicator being that the earlier an item appears in a to-be-learned list, the more likely it is to be recalled (i.e., items that can be rehearsed more because they were presented earlier are more likely to be recalled). This research probably contributed to my success in gaining admission to the graduate program in child psychology at Minnesota.

I arrived at Minnesota in September 1973. During my first week on the campus, I read a manuscript that John Flavell and his colleagues had recently completed, which would become one of the most important papers in the history of the field of cognitive development (Kreutzer, Leonard, & Flavell, 1975), entitled "An Interview Study of Children's Knowledge About Memory." They asked children questions, such as whether to dial a telephone number immediately after hearing it or to wait until after getting a drink of water. The claim was that there was a clear increase in understanding of memory across the elementary school years, with older children, for example, more certainly understanding the memorial consequences of waiting before dialing the number.

This interview study appeared at a time when self-reports of all sorts were suspect in the psychological research community, and, frankly, many at Minnesota, including my classmates and I, were not quite sure what to make of it. That Flavell produced it—and John was already seen as a monumental figure in cognitive development—must mean that it was important, but how was it important? I found out during my first year in graduate school, with John requiring that the cognitive development class read *Cognitive Development* (Flavell, 1977), which included a chapter on metacognition. That draft was the first major theoretical effort to make the case that metacognition was important in regulating cognition—specifically, what children know about their memory has much to do with what children attempt to do to remember information. There would be substantial followup inspired by Flavell's perspective on metamemory (see Schneider & Pressley, 1997, chap. 6).

As Flavell's thinking on metamemory emerged, some studies conducted by Markman (1977, 1979) were gaining attention. She read children stories that contained internal contradictions (e.g., a story asserting that snakes do not have ears and later asserting that they can hear insects). The major finding was that children often did not notice the contradictions, with Markman concluding that they did not monitor that the text did not make sense, that there were ideas in the text that clashed. She referred to this as a comprehension monitoring failure. In her integrative writing at the time, Brown (1978; A. L. Brown & DeLoache, 1978), in particular, made the case that monitoring was a particularly critical aspect of metacognition, that online awareness of how thinking is going is critically important in regulation of thinking. The point that deserves emphasis here is that the basic metacognitive framework (in this volume, see especially Griffin & Ruan, chap. 1, as well as Baker, chap. 4) has been around for a quarter century: Metacognition is cognition about thinking, including facts that are known about thinking and the monitoring processes that produce understandings about cognition, understandings that can impact subsequent cognitive self-regulation. Although the very first studies of metacognition were in the area of memory development, beginning with Markman's work, metacognition was a construct that psychologists interested in reading and some reading educators began to consider.

Frankly, during my graduate school years, I was aware of this work on metacognition, and I even carried out some studies involving children's self-reports of their strategies (e.g., Pressley & Levin, 1977) and whether and when children can monitor their memory performances (i.e., predict what they will remember, are aware of what they have remembered; Levin, Yussen, DeRose, & Pressley, 1977), but it was not my central focus. My central focus was on whether or not children could use imagery strategies to understand text and learn vocabulary.

Back then, there were theoretical reasons to believe that young children (i.e., preschoolers through age 6 or 7) might experience difficulties executing imagery strategies (i.e., a direction to make an image of the ideas encountered in a text being read; see Pressley, 1977, for a review). The point that deserves emphasis here is that this research was among the earliest work on teaching the comprehension strategies now commonly taught to children. I recall vividly a Minnesota professor challenging me to justify why it made any sense at all to teach strategies to improve comprehension. That faculty member made the case that reading was about processing words, and, once children could read words fluently, they needed only to listen to themselves read, with powerful language comprehension abilities permitting ready understanding of text. That was the first time I experienced what has become known as the simple view of reading (Gough & Tunmer, 1986).

After graduation, I did a lot of work that somehow was related to metacognition. In the early 1980s, I worked hard to develop understanding of what it meant for learners to realize that the strategies they were learning, in fact, benefited their performances. Such metacognition proved to be a powerful determinant of whether or not students continued to use the strategies they were taught (Pressley, Borkowski, & O'Sullivan, 1984, 1985). Moreover, when students learned when and where the strategies they were acquiring could be deployed profitably, it impacted their strategy transfer (e.g., O'Sullivan & Pressley, 1984). The work of the 1970s and 1980s documenting important interactions between knowledge of strategic procedures, metacognition, and motivation informed a comprehensive model of thinking that I did much to develop, called the Good Strategy User model, which later evolved into the Good Information Processor model (Borkowski, Carr, Rellinger, & Pressley, 1990; Borkowski, Schneider, & Pressley, 1989; Pressley, Borkowski, & Schneider, 1987, 1989). This was the first comprehensive model of cognitive processing to integrate cognitive strategic, metacognitive, world knowledge, and motivational elements, which now are in every credible model of thinking (e.g., those offered in this volume by Baker, chap. 4; Israel & Massey, chap. 10; Joseph, chap. 11; Samuels, Ediger, Willcutt, & Palumbo, chap. 3; Schreiber, chap. 12).

In the early 1990s, I carried out what I consider to be one of my most important investigations (Wyatt et al., 1993), documenting that when skilled readers
read, they are massively strategic and metacognitive. This work led to my reviewing, with Afflerbach (Pressley & Afflerbach, 1995), the entire literature on verbal protocols of reading. We made the case in that volume, *Verbal Protocols of
Reading*, that skilled readers are massively active as they read, continually responding to ideas in text. Skilled readers' verbal reports about what they do when
they read are filled with reports of strategies used but also filled with substantial
evidence that they know a great deal about their thinking and use what they
know about their thinking as part of the decision making about how to read the
text in front of them at the moment.

From the late 1980s to the present, I have been very involved in studies of
both engaging, effective teachers and not-so-engaging ones (for a review, see
Pressley et al., 2003). Just as sophisticated readers know much about their reading, the best teachers have sophisticated understanding of their own thinking
and their students' thinking, and this goes far in driving their instructional decision making. Skilled teaching is heavily metacognitive.

So, I read this volume with some gratitude, informed by living through the
early days of metacognition and strategies instruction and conducting a substantial amount of research in my career that anticipated the directions featured in
this volume. There is a strong sense in the chapters of this book that developing
metacognitive competence in children is a good thing, as is teaching them to use
comprehension strategies. There is also a strong sense that developing metacognitive competence in teachers is a good thing to do, especially developing
their ability to reflect on their teaching (i.e., monitor it) and improve teaching
on the basis of reflections.

You might think that I would be overjoyed that so many prominent workers in
the field have come to embrace ideas I have considered important during my entire career. Well, yes, I am, but I also find myself at least as worried as I am joyful,
although a more constructive way to characterize this emotion is as anticipatory
excitement: There is a lot of research that needs to be done on the important topics covered in this book; this is work that can be informed by the research of the
last 30 years, but it must go well beyond the extant research. The authors of the
various chapters point the way to some of the potential research directions. The
next subsection adds the ones that I feel are very important. I am excited because
there is much important research on metacognition that remains to be done and
many scholars who are interested in embarking on new research adventures.

THE RESEARCH TO COME

The remainder of this chapter touches on each of the research directions suggested by this volume's authors. All of these areas are important, so readers
should note that the order of their coverage has no significance.

Comprehension Strategies Instruction

The chapters in this volume pertaining to comprehension strategies instruction (e.g., Donndelinger, chap. 13; Griffith & Ruan, chap. 1; Israel & Massey, chap. 10; Randi, Grigorenko, & Sternberg, chap. 2; Schreiber, chap. 12; Smith, chap. 14; Cummins, Stewart, & Block, chap. 15) come at a strange moment in history. There is actually legislation in the United States that requires comprehension instruction to occur in schools that receive certain forms of U.S. federal education assistance, that is, the Reading First funds in the No Child Left Behind legislation (107th Congress, 2002). These funds cannot be used to buy reading materials that do not include coverage of comprehension strategies, and, thus, comprehension strategies are included prominently in all comprehensive reading instructional series that enjoy any substantial sales in the United States in 2004 (when this chapter was written). Schools receiving Reading First funds are required to provide professional development in comprehension strategies instruction. The result has been a proliferation of textbooks on comprehension strategies instruction being pumped out by publishers who serve the professional development text market. You would think that I would be thrilled with these developments. In fact, I am very worried.

Many texts targeting the professional development market, in particular, are informed by a very superficial reading of the comprehension strategies instruction literature. Much of this superficiality was prompted, in part, by the section on comprehension in the National Reading Panel (2000; chap. 4, part II), which was the key document informing Reading First as framed in the No Child Left Behind legislation. The panel read the literature on comprehension instruction. Basically, there are many studies of individual strategies that, when taught, can produce increases in understanding or memory of text. These include teaching students to use graphic organizers, constructing mental images representing ideas in text, increasing prior knowledge, question generation and question answering, paying attention to story structures, and summarization. Based on this literature, a case can be made for teaching any of these strategies.

Most of the research on the potency of individual comprehension strategies was carried out in the 1970s and 1980s. It is no longer state of the art/science, with no serious scholar in comprehension thinking that students should be taught only one strategy. I also know of no evidence indicating that it would make sense to teach students to use all of the strategies. Yet, the evidence produced in the studies of individual strategies is now being interpreted by some who write the professional development texts to mean that students should be taught to use all or many of these strategies. I now count more than two dozen such texts that do exactly that. Each of these texts provides tips about how to teach each of these strategies, tips that the authors have gleaned from their own classroom experiences or those of others, who presumably taught strategies to their students. At a minimum, these tips about teaching individual strategies go well beyond the operations in the studies that validated the potency of the individual strategies. For example, in the mental imagery literature, students are instructed to make images in their heads of what is occurring in the story being read. In many of these professional development texts, imagery instruction includes asking students to draw external pictures, which—as far as I know—is nowhere in any of the successful imagery training studies. Much of the instruction recommended in these books has not been validated.

What about the stance in these volumes that students should be taught a large number of strategies to use in repertoire? In fact, the panel was aware of the research on teaching repertoires of comprehension strategies, although it definitely did not do much to highlight it. Panel members were aware of the conclusions of Rosenshine and Meister's (1994) review of reciprocal teaching, which involves teaching students to use four strategies in repertoire: Make predictions about what might be in text, generate questions about information in text, seek clarifications when confused, and construct summaries of the ideas in text. In addition, two very important studies of multiple comprehension strategies instruction were covered in a separate part of the comprehension chapter (part III), which focused on the fact that teachers need a lot of training to teach repertoires of comprehension strategies. In my view, a point of emphasis should have been that, in the two most relevant studies (i.e., the studies most relevant to teaching repertoires of comprehension strategies; Anderson, 1992; R. Brown, Pressley, Van Meter, & Schuder, 1996), students were taught to use small repertoires of strategies (e.g., prediction, questioning, imaging, clarifying, summarizing). The teaching was long term, including much teacher-scaffolded student practice of the strategies, applying them to diverse texts.

That is, when multiple strategies instruction has proven potent in the literature, a few strategies were taught, not the laundry list of comprehension strategies that is possible by listing every individual comprehension strategy ever studied!! In contrast, if you look in those books cranked out for professional development in comprehension strategies instruction, the implication is to teach many strategies and to do so using the teacher tips that overflow these volumes. Note that there is not a single study in the literature validating the professional development advocated in these volumes—not one. That worries me a lot.

With respect to the comprehension strategies repertoires covered in chapters in this volume, my strong advisement is to get busy doing validation work, like that being conducted by Cummins, Stewart, and Block in chapter 15. I hope it proves that some of the specific multiple strategies packages favored in this volume do improve performance, but I want to see the data. I'll add that the more it is obvious that the students are autonomously using the strategies as a function of the instruction they receive, that students are no longer dependent on teacher prompting, the more convinced I will be that the instruction is effective. Moreover, consistent with concerns raised by Samuels, Ediger, Willcutt, and Palumbo (chap. 3, this volume), the more obvious it is that the students are using the strategies with fluency, the better I will feel. Self-regulated, fluent use of the reading comprehension strategies used by the best readers should be the goal of instruction.

If there is one thing I am certain of with respect to comprehension strategies instruction, it is very challenging for teachers to implement, even when they receive excellent professional development and support. Thus, in the early 1990s, when my colleagues and I studied multiple comprehension strategies instruction in schools, we became aware that many teachers who tried the approach dropped it in frustration (see Pressley & El-Dinary, 1997). Recently, Katie Hilden and I have worked with two middle schools as they attempted to jump-start comprehension strategies instruction. There were many challenges, from simply getting the teachers to understand what it means to be an active reader, to finding appropriate practice materials, to getting teachers to commit the substantial amount of class time required for students to become active comprehenders.

More than committing time to comprehension strategies instruction, teachers have to make a commitment to a particular form of teaching that seems to work well for the development of complex skills. In part, this type of instruction is inspired by Vygotsky (1978), in part by Bandura (1986), but in the area of reading, most directly by Roehler and Duffy (1984) and Duffy (2003). Teachers first explain and model strategies use for students, and then require the students to try the strategies, often with much prompting and support. As students become more facile using a procedure, the support fades. Strategies can be introduced one at a time, but as new strategies are added, it is essential for students to use the new strategies in an articulated way with the strategies learned previously. Even teaching a small repertoire of comprehension strategies can take a school year (as shown in Cummins, Stewart, & Block, chap. 15), with several school years of such instruction and practice likely for the students to internalize completely the use of the repertoire of strategies (Pressley et al., 1992). Both Anderson (1992) and R. Brown et al. (1996) used this gradual release of responsibility approach to develop the small repertoires of comprehension strategies in the students they studied (see all Pearson & Gallagher, 1983).

Active comprehension develops over months and years, not days and weeks. Unfortunately, many teachers expect results more quickly, and are ready to move on when they do not get them. I felt as I read this book that more emphasis should have been put on the fact that development of reading skills and the associated metacognition so that the skills learned can be used well takes a long time. But, it is worth it. Why? Because the good comprehension strategy user has learned the strategies that permit the construction of deep understanding of texts read, they have learned how to relate their prior knowledge to ideas in text and that it is important to do so. They have learned to ask questions and look for answers as they read. They have learned that sometimes text is confusing and needs to be reprocessed a few times to make sense of it. They have learned the power of vivid images of the settings, characters, and events in text. And, they know that there are messages in text, that some information is much more important than other information, recognizing that their job as a reader is to leave the text with the information that is most relevant to their reason for reading the text (i.e., their reading goal). In short, good comprehenders have learned how to make great sense of what they read, a decidedly higher order skill that we should want for every student.

Teaching Cognitive Monitoring

That monitoring is important in literacy comes through loudly and clearly in this volume (e.g., in the chapters by Donndelinger, chap. 13; Joseph, chap. 11; Schreiber, chap. 12). Awareness of current cognitive level, which is the product of cognitive monitoring, is critical for adequate regulation of cognitive processes (e.g., students are unlikely to reread and use sophisticated text comprehension strategies during a second reading if they are not aware they did not get it the first time; for a brief review of metacognition and cognitive control issues, see Son & Schwartz, 2002). Researchers and educators were first alerted to children's problems of comprehension monitoring in Markman's now classic work (1977, 1979), which was reviewed briefly earlier in this chapter. A related and important finding was that even adults often fail to notice internal inconsistencies in texts they read (Elliott-Faust & Pressley, 1986).

In fact, adults' comprehension monitoring, and their cognitive monitoring more generally, is much worse than suggested by their failures to detect within-text inconsistencies. Ask an adult to read short passages and summarize the main point of each. In most cases, adults can do this. Occasionally, however, they completely miss the point. What I emphasize here is that when they miss the point, they are just as certain that they understood the text as when they actually did understand the text well enough to state the main idea (Pressley, Ghatala, Woloshyn, & Pirie, 1990a, 1990b). As a second example, adults can be asked to use two different strategies to learn, one very powerful in promoting learning and the other much less so. Thus, Pressley, Levin, and Ghatala (1984) had adults learn vocabulary words, with the participants directed to alternate their use of two strategies, learning every other word with a potent approach and every other word with a much less effective method. While they studied, the adults did not recognize at all that they were learning much more with the more potent approach. In short, adult failures to monitor can be very striking.

One implication of these monitoring failures is that students should be taught to monitor. One of the great disappointments for me in the education psychology literature is that there has not been more work about how to teach monitoring. In my own limited work on the topic, Elliott-Faust and Pressley (1986) taught third-grade students explicitly to compare various points made in text to determine if the text was consistent in meaning or contained internal inconsistencies. Ghatala, Levin, Pressley, and Goodwin (1986) taught primary-grade children to note carefully which of several strategies was producing better learning for them, attribute differences in learning to use of the more effective versus less effective strategy, and to make use of such information as they decided on strategies in the future. In general, such monitoring training paid off. Sadly, no researchers investigated further whether and how to teach cognitive monitoring, or at least not in the analytical fashion that my colleagues and I did. That said, many practitioners, in fact, have some very good ideas about how monitoring might be promoted in students (see Joseph, chap. 11, this volume), and others are attempting to teach students strategies that produce metacognitive information incidentally (i.e., that have a monitoring component).

For example, one of the reasons that the comprehension strategies packages reviewed earlier (i.e., reciprocal teaching, teaching of small repertoires of strategies) may be potent is that they contain at least one strategy with an implied monitoring component: If a reader cannot summarize, then that is a strong signal that text was not comprehended. In addition, these packages also include teaching students to seek clarification, which also requires them to monitor their comprehension well enough to recognize that there are points they do not understand and that require clarification. Even so, the research on these packages has not been so complete to assure just how well students do learn to monitor as a function of learning to summarize and seek clarification. As additional evaluations of teaching comprehension strategies repertoires proceeds, I hope there will be more explicit research attention to how monitoring develops as students learn to use repertoires of strategies as well as more analytical, experimental work on teaching cognitive monitoring very directly.

In summary, there has not been nearly enough nor analytical enough research about how to persuade children or adults to monitor their performances effectively and to make decisions about how to proceed on academic tasks on the bases of information gained through monitoring. (See Schneider & Pressley, 1997, chap. 8, for a review of the work that did occur in the 1980s and 1990s; also Maki & McGuire, 2002.) I'm hopeful that as some of the authors in this volume proceed with their work, they will study much more completely the entire issue of whether, when, and how monitoring skills can be developed, especially during reading, but also in general as students tackle the variety of academic tasks that occur in school. Monitoring is essential to produce metacognitive understandings that can permit intelligent choices about how to proceed with tasks, so that it seems to me that cognitive developmental performances (e.g., reading) will never be as good as they could be until we figure out how to teach students to monitor their thinking and learning well.

Developing Metacognition More Generally Through Instruction

In the late 1970s and early 1980s, I coauthored experiments examining the consequences of teaching information about where and when strategies are useful. Such direct teaching did positively impact transfer of strategies taught (O'Sullivan & Pressley, 1984; Pressley & Dennis-Rounds, 1980). Those studies were exceptionally well-controlled experiments: Experimenters did the teaching, precisely following scripts that conveyed the exact information being manipulated in the study. Athough this work was very good experimental psychology, it was not so great in generating information about real teaching.

In more recent years, I have been studying naturalistic teaching, using qualitative methods to do so. My colleagues and I have sought out excellent teachers and encountered many not-so-excellent teachers along the way. Whether the focus was on teaching of reading strategies, which it was when I was looking at real-school teaching of comprehension strategies (e.g., Pressley et al., 1992), teaching of primary literacy (e.g., Morrow, Tracey, Woo, & Pressley, 1999; Pressley, Allington, Wharton-McDonald, Block, & Morrow, 2001; Pressley, Wharton-McDonald, et al., 2001; Pressley, Wharton-McDonald, Raphael, Bogner, & Roehrig, 2002; Roehrig, Pressley, & Sloup, 2001; Wharton-McDonald, Pressley, & Hampston, 1998), or teaching of elementary students more generally (e.g., Bogner, Raphael, & Pressley, 2002; Dolezal, Welsh, Pressley, & Vincent, 2003; Pressley et al., 2003), excellent teaching always included much modeling and explaining of cognitive processes, with the explanations including much metacognitive information (i.e., much information about how, when, and where to use strategies being taught, and much information about the value of skills taught). Such teaching also included a lot of student practice, providing opportunity for students to see for themselves the value of what they were learning. In short, with the focus on the classroom level, my colleagues and I discovered that engaging, excellent classrooms overflow with metacognitive information and experiences. There was far less metacognitive information in the teaching of less engaging and effective teachers. As the contributors to this volume continue their work, I urge them to be attentive to teacher and classroom differences in metacognitive input. If they do, I suspect the case will be overwhelming that good teaching is very much letting students in on the secrets of effective thinking and learning.

I was particularly struck by Schreiber's (chap. 12, this volume) hypothesis that a variety of reading instructional methods and packages probably promote metacognitive development. I was also struck by one teacher's attempts (i.e., Smith, chap. 14, this volume) to increase metacognitive reflection in her students. I certainly can imagine how many of the programs that Schreiber described could develop metacognition in students, and, in fact, I could think of some additional programs than might do so as well, including the current generation of comprehensive basal reading programs. My guess, however, is that the key is the teacher, with some teachers more faithful to the programs they teach and teaching them in ways that make students' learning more certain, including development of metacognitive understandings about reading. Of course, that the teacher really matters in literacy development goes back at least as far as the classic First Grade Studies (Bond & Dykstra, 1967).

It seems high time for some serious empirical work to determine just how much metacognitive development occurs in the various reading instructional approaches and programs, although I strongly urge careful attention to the possibility that what students get out of a program, including the metacognition that develops, very much depends on the teacher. And, based on my previous work (see Pressley et al., 2003), no matter what the program, the more the teaching resembles the engaging and effective teaching my colleagues and I have documented over the past decade, the more student learning will occur, including the more metacognitive development. There's some really important hypothesis testing that needs to occur with respect to the various approaches and programs now in the reading instructional marketplace.

Comprehension Assessment

Several of the chapters in this volume take up the issue of comprehension assessment (Afflerbach & Meuwissen, chap. 8; Paris & Flukes, chap. 7; Randi, Grigorenko, & Sternberg, chap. 2). It is a topic that has been on many researchers' minds, with an entire volume on the topic due out in the near future (Paris & Stahl, 2005). I should add that there is no question I am asked more often than, "Can you recommend a good comprehension assessment?" My answer, at present, is, "No."

Along with many of the contributors to this volume, my vision of the good comprehender is someone who is, appropriately, very active while reading. When such readers really need to get something out of a text, they scan the text before reading, make predictions about what is going to be in it, connect ideas in text to prior knowledge and make appropriate inferences as they do so, construct images capturing the big ideas in text, ask questions and seek answers to their questions, slow down and seek clarification when confused, skip parts of text that seem irrelevant, focus hard on aspects of text that contain critically important information, and make decisions about text—sometimes deciding it is compelling and interesting and relevant and other times deciding the ideas in a text make no sense, are boring, or are really irrelevant to the reader's purpose. Such readers are really metacognitive, monitoring their reading throughout and making decisions based on their monitoring.

What else do good comprehenders do? They get the big ideas in text and key supporting ideas (see van den Broek, 1994). That is, they have a coherent understanding about what the author has said, although they may also have personal responses and interpretations (Rosenblatt, 1978). Although there is plenty of room for variability in the interpretations made by good readers, their interpretations always map to elements of the text, typically seeming at least plausible to others who have read the same text (Eco, 1990).

I want comprehension tests that make clear whether or not readers are metacognitively active like excellent readers, they extract from text the major ideas and important supports, and they make reasonable interpretations. There is no assessment out there that captures reading comprehension as I think it should be captured.

In contrast, there are lots of standardized tests that require students to read texts and respond to multiple-choice items, typically items with one right answer. When I have looked at these, often I find myself convinced that I could come up with interpretations of the texts presented that would render more than one answer correct. Of course, such active thinking is a certain route to a low score.

Even more disturbing is the development of assessments that send the message that meaning making is not really what reading is about—reading the words and doing so quickly is. Thus, in the United States, the Dynamic Indicators of Basic Early Literacy Skills (DIBELS) assessment (Good & Kaminski, 2002) is being used extensively, especially in schools receiving Reading First funds. On the subscales that require reading of actual text, the most important measure is how many words are read in a minute. The aspect of the assessment with the most relevance to comprehension involves only simple retelling of what was read, with each word retold incrementing the student's score. In fact, the student could recall a jumble of these words—getting none of the relations between ideas in text correct—and have a fairly high retelling score. In recent work with my students evaluating the DIBELS (results being analyzed as this chapter is written), we saw a great deal of such jumbled recall among third-grade students.

So, I was heartened that some contributors to this volume are thinking about alternative comprehension assessments. As they do so, I want to urge creativity in format but conservativism with respect to validation of the instruments. In this world of No Child Left Behind thinking, excellent scientific evidence is embraced. This is a good thing that demands that assessments be rigorously evaluated so that it is as clear as possible what such assessments are capturing (e.g., Campbell & Fiske, 1959).

With respect to the development of comprehension assessment, it means that, at a minimum, such assessments have to be reliable. That is, if teachers are going to administer them, they have to be reliably scorable by teachers. This may be a great challenge. Just think about what kind of data are going to be coming in if a teacher is administering an assessment requiring children to think aloud while reading, to tell the teacher what they are thinking while reading a text. Beyond reliability, the assessments have to be valid. There are various ways to assess validity. For example, consider doing experiments where directions are varied, from directions that should undermine extensive comprehension processing (e.g., a direction to read quickly) to directions that bias in favor of extensive comprehension processing (e.g., a direction to read so that understanding is high). Performance on a measure capturing active comprehension processing should vary as a function of such directions. So, if you developed a stimulated recall measure of comprehension processing (i.e., a measure where learners would watch a video of their reading—perhaps aloud—and report on processing that is occurring), there should be more reports of active comprehension strategy use for readers who were instructed to read for understanding versus those who were to read as fast as possible. Also, look for correlations between the target assessment and other potential measurements of comprehension. So, if you had developed a measure of stimulated recall tapping use of comprehension strategies, then you might look at how such reports correlated with the reader's recall of the text read. Hopefully, the recall of more active readers would be better in some objective ways (e.g., more organized, more complete).

Assessment is expensive. Even if the tests do not have to be purchased (e.g., they are in the public domain and can be downloaded from the Internet), they require time to administer, score, and analyze. For that to be worth it, the assessment should provide information not already known by the classroom teacher. So, for example, as my colleagues and I examine the DIBELS, we are looking at correlations with teacher assessments of student reading (e.g., their subjective evaluations of how well the students read, how fluent they are), as well as correlations between DIBELS and reading series unit tests. If the DIBELS correlates highly with these other assessments, then it probably is telling little beyond what is already known by the teachers. In addition, we are looking at how the DIBELS, teacher assessments, and reading series tests correlate with end-of-the-year performance on a standardized reading assessment. Again, if the DIBELS is no more predictive than the other assessments, then it makes little sense to administer it (i.e., it provides no incremental validity, no unique understanding of student differences in reading).

I am emphatic about the need for rigorous validation of comprehension assessments because reading assessments, in general, have not been validated nearly as completely as they could be (Rathvon, 2004). Consider the DIBELS. Virtually all of the validation data on the DIBELS Web site (http://dibels.uoregon.edu/techreports/DIBELS_References.pdf) are correlations with other measures of reading. As implied in the previous paragraphs, much more analytical validation can be done and should be done before millions of schoolchildren experience an assessment or have their instruction shaped by it. Consider that, in our initial work on the DIBELS, we have found that when third-grade students are asked to read faster, they do so, resulting in fewer students being classified as at-risk than with the standard DIBELS administration. Important instructional decisions are being made on the basis of outcomes produced by the standard DIBELS administration, and we have data that raise questions about those decisions. With more extensive validation, the assessment might have been designed so that young readers know that it really, really matters that they read as quickly as possible, with the result that there would be fewer students considered at-risk based on the measure. The main point here is that any reading assessment should be studied extensively to determine its validity before it impacts the schoolplace.

Metacognitive Assessments

There are a number of metacognitive assessments described in this volume (i.e., in chapters by Block, chap. 5; Cassidy-Schmitt, chap. 6; Paris & Flukes, chap. 7; Afflerbach & Meuwissen, chap. 8; Bauserman, chap. 9). I know some of these measures from encountering them previously. Others are new—or, at least, new to me. My concern for rigorous validation work on these assessments parallels my concern for rigorous validation of comprehension measures. I resonated to Baker's and Donndelinger's (chaps. 4 and 13, this volume) concerns that we do not have adequate tools for measuring metacognition.

In developing any assessment, the developers have to confront an important ethical obligation. If their assessment does get into the schoolplace and become consequential, then it will shape instruction. The evidence is simply overwhelming that many teachers teach to the tests that are used in the school's accountability system. So, test developers have to ask whether or not the test they are developing is encouraging behaviors that should be encouraged. Thinking back to the comprehension assessments, a test requiring students to report their active processing probably is defensible on this count, because all indications are that encouraging such active processing is, in fact, encouraging good reading. What about DIBELS reading? Do we really want students to be able to read quickly regardless of whether or not they comprehend (and my colleagues and I believe that those jumbled retellings that we observed suggest that many DIBELS readers are not comprehending much). I don't think we want to encourage that kind of reading, and hence, that is a huge red flag that should be considered in deciding whether or not to use DIBELS.

As far as metacognitive assessments are concerned, there is much that is metacognitive that can be known about reading and reading strategies. For example, a very important form of metacognition is knowing that words are composed of sounds blended together. That is phonemic awareness. By measuring phonemic awareness explicitly, which has occurred a lot since the early 1990s, teachers have been encouraged to teach it more, which is defensible because increasing phonemic awareness promotes beginning reading competence (National Reading Panel, 2000).

There needs to be some very hard thinking about just which aspects of metacognition should be assessed. What should be assessed is metacognition that, if readers possess it, will cause them to be better readers. So, teaching monitoring makes sense, because monitoring does seem to be part of excellent reading, for example, it is prominent in the verbal protocols of skilled readers (Pressley & Afflerbach, 1995). It is probably obvious by now that I think there should be assessment of students' conscious, self-regulated use of comprehension strategies, with such assessments potentially filled with information about students' metacognitive understandings about reading. If there is more measurement of such active processing of text, then there will be more teaching of it.

That said, as I reflected on the various types of metacognitive assessments proposed by authors in this book, I had a hard time in some cases convincing myself that encouraging the development of the type of metacognition being assessed necessarily would encourage teaching of reading skills that would positively impact reading. I urge all of the authors who are proposing metacognitive assessments to think about them from this perspective. Is this likely to lead to teaching to a test that taps skills that are really essential for students to develop? If the answer is no, then I have my doubts about whether or not educators should expend the money and effort required to administer such an assessment to their students. The ultimate goal of any assessment used in schools should be to improve teaching, and thus, student learning, although there are other ways besides providing tests worth teaching to that can impact better teaching in classrooms.

Improving Teaching

A number of authors in this volume addressed issues of improving teaching, with an implication in many that teachers can be taught to be reflective in ways that will increase their understanding of students and the curricula they are charged to teach. The more such understanding develops, the more likely it is that teachers will teach better (see the chapters by Block, chap. 5; Duffy, chap. 16; Bowman, Galvez-Martin, & Morrison, chap. 18; Kinnucan-Welsch, chap. 20; Risko, Roskos, & Vukelich, chap. 17; and Rosemary, chap. 19). The ideas presented in these chapters deserve serious study in excellent experiments, quasi-experiments, and other research designs. Done well, such studies could go far in identifying how to encourage teacher reflection as well as better understanding the outcomes in the classroom when teachers are reflective versus not so thoughtful.

Based on some of my own work, I think there is an important individual-differences dimension among teachers that may affect their susceptibility to becoming reflective practitioners. Alyssa Roehrig and I (along with other students in our research group) addressed the issue of mentoring, specifically, whether providing beginning primary-grade teachers with mentoring that focuses on the elements of effective teaching can improve teaching (see Pressley et al., 2003, for a complete review). The mentored beginning teachers interacted with very effective, engaging teachers as part of the study. The mentored teachers were taught a variety of instructional tactics used by effective teachers. They were also taught how to motivate students, using a variety of well-validated mechanisms to do so. They received input about effective classroom management. All of this information was provided over a full year of beginning teaching.

Did such mentoring work? The answer is that it worked when the young teachers were open to it. That is, some of the young teachers we worked with were open to improving and others were certain they were already good and did not need to improve. Only those who were open improved their teaching over the year of mentoring. This finding is very much in synchrony with another persistent outcome in a decade's worth of research on the nature of engaging, effective teaching and not-so-engaging teaching (e.g., Allington & Johnston, 2002; Bogner et al., 2002; Dolezal et al., 2003; Morrow et al., 1999; Pressley, Allington, et al., 2001; Pressley et al., 2003; Pressley, Wharton-McDonald, et al., 2001; Pressley et al., 2002; Roehrig et al., 2001; Wharton-McDonald et al., 1998). Invariably, engaging, effective teachers believe they have much more to learn about teaching, despite the fact that they are already pretty good by any objective measure of their teaching. In contrast, less effective teachers are more likely to be comfortable with their teaching, more certain that they are good teachers already and do not need to improve. In short, my colleagues and I have a lot of evidence that openness to improving is a personality variable that is an important determinant of whether or not a teacher will benefit from input. Of course, at the heart of this personality difference seems to be a metacognitive difference: Some teachers have the metacognitive understanding that their teaching can improve and others do not; among those who do not, there is an important metacognitive failure that my colleagues and I observed often: Such teachers often have no clue that they are not very good teachers and their students are not learning much. I hope that as some of the hypotheses advanced in this volume about improving teaching are evaluated, the researchers will do studies that are sensitive to whether or not open-minded and close-minded individuals benefit differentially to the induction and teacher development experiences provided for them.

Many ideas in this volume about development of more competent young teachers deserve careful study in studies that permit cause-and-effect conclusions. As Ingersoll and Kralik (2004) pointed out, most evaluations of approaches on teacher induction have not been done in well-controlled studies, so it is impossible to know if any gains associated with such experiences were actually due to the induction experience or something else. Well-controlled true experiments and quasi-experiments evaluating the ideas about reflection and teacher metacognition advanced in this volume could go far in making an important contribution to the understanding of how beginning teaching can be a more profitable experience for young teachers.

This section on improving teaching concludes by citing what I think is an important omission in this volume. Teachers really need to know much about the minds of their students, both the general facts about and trends in cognitive development, but also much about the individual differences in thinking skills that characterize their students. A hallmark of engaging teaching is that teachers scaffold (Wood, Bruner, & Ross, 1976) a lot for their students, which requires them to monitor children as they work, size up what assistance a child needs at this moment, and deliver just enough help to get the youngster started in the right direction and back on track. Such teaching is massively metacognitive. Weak teachers scaffold much less, and I hypothesize that, as a function of their more distant teaching style, they know little about their students' minds compared to the engaging, scaffolding teacher. My colleague Dick Allington once proposed to me a one-question quiz to give to a teacher to decide whether or not the teacher is effective: Ask the teacher, "Tell me about Johnny's *or* Mary's reading?" Effective teachers go on and on, reporting many details of the skills the student has mastered, the skills in development, and the skills still out of reach. They know the kinds of texts the child likes to read and those the child abhors. They know what the student likes to write about as well as many details about the student's writing skills. In contrast, ineffective teachers offer a short answer: "Johnny (Mary) is one of my best readers" or "Mary (Johnny) needs Reading Recovery."

What I am suggesting here is that engaging, effective teachers have a lot of metacognition about their students, and they use their understanding of the students and the curricular options every single minute of every single hour of every instructional day to make instructional decisions about the students. We very much need to study carefully such metacognition, how it does develop, and how teachers can become committed to teaching in ways that serve children well as they increase young teachers' understandings of their students. I share with Duffy (chap. 16, this volume) the perspective that metacognitively mature teachers develop much of their understanding through actual teaching. A very concrete piece of evidence supporting this is that in 10 years of looking for engaging and effective elementary teachers, my colleagues and I never identified one who had been teaching for less than 4 years.

CONCLUDING COMMENTS

Research events in the year I entered graduate school changed much about the way the world thinks about teaching and learning. In the introduction, I discussed briefly the Kreutzer et al. (1975) monograph on metamemory. I also read another preprint during my first week at Minnesota. The preprint of the LaBerge and Samuels (1974) article made it clear that automaticity in word recognition mattered very much, and stimulated wide-ranging research establishing that cognitive skills work much better when they are automatized than when people have to think hard about what to do and then think hard as they do it.

Beyond increasing the skills that are the focus of this volume, it is essential to determine how use of sophisticated comprehension tactics, as well as cognitive monitoring and other metacognitive processes, can become automatic habits of mind, that is, skills used without learners having to expend much short-term capacity to decide to use them or execute them once decided.

Over the years, I've seen automatic use of sophisticated cognitive strategies. I saw it when Wyatt et al. (1993) studied social scientists reading in their content area. I saw it when I watched fourth and fifth graders, who had experienced several years of very good comprehension strategies instruction, read a complicated chapter book together, habitually reporting the cognitive activity they experienced as they read (Pressley et al., 1992). I've seen it when really excellent elementary teachers teach, with them knowing what to do without thinking about it much, seeming to be able to attend to the needs of several children at once because attention to one of them is not all-consuming (Pressley et al., 2001). Real people can learn to do really important, real-world tasks very fluently.

I was disappointed that the authors in this volume who suggested instructional interventions did not seem to think about issues of fluency development. I think as the interventions proposed in this volume experience additional research and development, fluency should be a major goal.

The directions covered in this volume did get their start more than a quarter century ago. They have proven to be enduring ideas. I suspect they will endure for another quarter century. With a great deal of research effort, the ideas showcased in this volume could go far in defining teaching and learning for the next quarter century. I feel very fortunate to have started graduate school in 1973. It was the dawning of a new age that seems to have the potential at least to span my professional lifetime. My on-time retirement is scheduled for 2016, but I plan to stick it out longer, guessing that when I clean out my last university office desk, there will be some recent papers on comprehension instruction, comprehension assessment, monitoring and metacognition, and teacher improvement that will be part of the final cleanup. Some of the authors in this volume undoubtedly will be some of the authors I am reading during the very last days of my career.

REFERENCES

Allington, R. L., & Johnston, P. H. (2002). *Reading to learn: Lessons from exemplary fourth-grade classrooms*. New York: Guilford.

Anderson, V. (1992). A teacher development project in transactional strategy instruction for teachers of severely reading-disabled adolescents. *Teaching & Teacher Education, 8,* 391–403.

Bandura, A. (1986). *Social foundations of thought and action: A social cognitive theory*. Englewood Cliffs, NJ: Prentice-Hall.

Bogner, K., Raphael, L. M., & Pressley, M. (2002).How grade-1 teachers motivate literate activity by their students. *Scientific Studies of Reading, 6,* 135–165.

Bond, G. L., & Dykstra, R. (1967). The cooperative research program in first-grade reading instruction. *Reading Research Quarterly, 2,* 10–141.

Borkowski, J. G., Carr, M., Rellinger, E. A., & Pressley, M. (1990). Self-regulated strategy use: Interdependence of metacognition, attributions, and self-esteem. In B. F. Jones (Ed.), *Dimensions of thinking: Review of research* (pp. 53–92). Hillsdale, NJ: Lawrence Erlbaum Associates.

Borkowski, J. G., Schneider, W., & Pressley, M. (1989). The challenges of teaching good information processing to learning disabled students. *International Journal of Disability, Development, and Education, 36,* 169–185.

Brown, A. L. (1978). Knowing when, where, and how to remember: A problem of metacognition. In R. Glaser (Ed.), *Advances in instructional psychology* (Vol. 1, pp. 77–165). Hillsdale, NJ: Lawrence Erlbaum Associates.

Brown, A. L., & DeLoache, J. S. (1978). Skills, plans and self-regulation. In R. Siegler (Ed.), *Children's thinking: What develops?* (pp. 3–35). Hillsdale, NJ: Lawrence Erlbaum Associates.

Brown, R., Pressley, M., Van Meter, P., & Schuder, T. (1996). A quasi-experimental validation of transactional strategies instruction with low-achieving second grade readers. *Journal of Educational Psychology, 88*, 18–37.

Campbell, D. T., & Fiske, D. W. (1959). Convergent and discriminant validation by the multitrait-multimethod matrix. *Psychological Bulletin, 56*, 81–105.

Dolezal, S. E., Welsh, L. M., Pressley, M., & Vincent, M. (2003). How do grade-3 teachers motivate their students? *Elementary School Journal, 103*, 239–267.

Duffy, G. G. (2003). *Explaining reading: A handbook for practitioners and researchers.* New York: Guilford.

Eco, U. (1990). *The limits of interpretation.* Bloomington, IN: Indiana University Press.

Elliott-Faust, D. J., & Pressley, M. (1986). Self-controlled training of comparison strategies increase children's comprehension monitoring. *Journal of Educational Psychology, 78*, 27–32.

Flavell, J. H. (1977). *Cognitive development.* Englewood Cliffs, NJ: Prentice-Hall.

Ghatala, E. S., Levin, J. R., Pressley, M., & Goodwin, D. (1986). A componential analysis of the effects of derived and supplied strategy-utility information on children's strategy selections. *Journal of Experimental Child Psychology, 22*, 199–216.

Good, R. H., & Kaminski, R. A. (Eds.). (2002). *Dynamic indicators of basic early literacy skills* (6th ed.). Eugene, OR: Institute for the Development of Education Achievement. Retrieved from http://dibels.uoregon.edu/

Gough, P. B., & Tunmer, W. (1986). Decoding, reading and reading disability. *Remedial and Special Education, 7*, 6–10.

Ingersoll, R., & Kralik, J. M. (2004). *The impact of mentoring on teacher retention: What the research says.* Denver, CO: Education Commission of the States. Retrieved from http://www.ecs.org/clearinghouse/50/36/5036.doc

Kreutzer, M.A., Leonard, C., & Flavell, J. H. (1975). An interview study of children's knowledge about memory. *Monographs of the Society for Research in Child Development, 40*(1, Serial No. 159), 1–58.

LaBerge, D., & Samuels, S. J. (1974). Toward a theory of automatic information processing in reading. *Cognitive Psychology, 6*, 293–323.

Levin, J. R., Yussen, S. R., DeRose, T. M., & Pressley, M. (1977). Developmental changes in assessing recall and recognition memory. *Developmental Psychology, 13*, 608–615.

Maki, R. H., & McGuire, M. J. (2002). Metacognition for text: Findings and implications for education. In T. J. Perfect & B. L. Schwartz (Eds.), *Applied metacognition* (pp. 39–67). Cambridge, England: Cambridge University Press.

Markman, E. M. (1977). Realizing that you don't understand: A preliminary investigation. *Child Development, 48*, 986–992.

Markman, E. M. (1979). Realizing that you don't understand: Elementary school children's awareness of inconsistencies. *Child Development, 50*, 643–658.

Morrow, L. M., Tracey, D. H., Woo, D. G., & Pressley, M. (1999). Characteristics of exemplary first-grade literacy instruction. *Reading Teacher, 52*, 462–476.

National Reading Panel. (2000). *Report of the National Reading Panel: Teaching children to read: An evidence-based assessment of the scientific research literature on reading and its implications for reading instruction: Reports of the subgroups.* Washington, DC: National Institute of Child Health & Human Development, National Institutes of Health.

107th U.S. Congress. (2002). *Public Law 107-110: The no child left behind act of 2001.* Washington, DC: Government Printing Office.

O'Sullivan, J. T., & Pressley, M. (1984). Completeness of instruction and strategy transfer. *Journal of Experimental Child Psychology, 38,* 275–288.

Paris, S. G., & Stahl, S. A. (Eds.). (2005). *Current issues in reading comprehension and assessment.* Mahwah, NJ: Lawrence Erlbaum Associates.

Pearson, P. D., & Gallagher, M. D. (1983). The instruction of reading comprehension. *Contemporary Educational Psychology, 8,* 317–344.

Pressley, M. (1977). Imagery and children's learning: Putting the picture in developmental perspective. *Review of Educational Research, 47,* 586–622.

Pressley, M., & Afflerbach, P. (1995). *Verbal protocols of reading: The nature of constructively responsive reading.* Hillsdale, NJ: Lawrence Erlbaum Associates.

Pressley, M., Allington, R., Wharton-McDonald, R., Block, C. C., & Morrow, L. M. (2001). *Learning to read: Lessons from exemplary first grades.* New York: Guilford.

Pressley, M., Borkowski, J. G., & O'Sullivan, J. T. (1984). Memory strategy instruction is made of this: Metamemory and durable strategy use. *Educational Psychologist, 19,* 94–107.

Pressley, M., Borkowski, J. G., & O'Sullivan, J. T. (1985). Children's metamemory and the teaching of strategies. In D. L. Forrest-Pressley, G. E. MacKinnon, & T. G. Waller (Eds.), *Metacognition, cognition, and human performance* (pp. 111–153). Orlando, FL: Academic Press.

Pressley, M., Borkowski, J. G., & Schneider, W. (1987). Cognitive strategies: Good strategy users coordinate meta-cognition and knowledge. In R. Vasta & G. Whitehurst (Eds.), *Annals of child development* (Vol. 4, pp. 89–129). Greenwich, CT: JAI Press.

Pressley, M., Borkowski, J. G., & Schneider, W. (1989). Good information processing: What it is and what education can do to promote it. *International Journal of Educational Research, 13,* 866–878.

Pressley, M., & Dennis-Rounds, J. (1980). Transfer of a mnemonic keyword strategy at two age levels. *Journal of Educational Psychology, 72,* 575–582.

Pressley, M., & El-Dinary, P. B. (1997). What we know about translating comprehension strategies instruction research into practice. *Journal of Learning Disabilities, 30,* 486–488.

Pressley, M., El-Dinary, P. B., Gaskins, I., Schuder, T., Bergman, J. L., Almasi, J., &Brown, R. (1992). Beyond direct explanation: Transactional instruction of reading comprehension strategies. *Elementary School Journal, 92,* 511–554.

Pressley, M., Ghatala, E. S.,Woloshyn, V., & Pirie, J. (1990a). Being really, really certain you know the main idea doesn't mean you do. *Yearbook of the National Reading Conference, 39,* 249–256.

Pressley, M., Ghatala, E. S., Woloshyn, V., & Pirie, J. (1990b). Sometimes adults miss the main ideas in text and do not realize it: Confidence in responses to short-answer and multiple-choice comprehension items. *Reading Research Quarterly, 25,* 232–249.

Pressley, M., & Hilden, K. R. (in press). Cognitive strategies: Production deficiencies and successful strategy instruction everywhere. In W. Damon (General Ed.), *Handbook of child psychology* (6th ed.). New York: Wiley.

Pressley, M., & Levin, J. R. (1977). Developmental differences in subjects' associative learning strategies and performance: Assessing a hypothesis. *Journal of Experimental Child Psychology, 24,* 431–439.

Pressley, M., Levin, J. R., & Ghatala, E. S. (1984). Memory strategy monitoring in adults and children. *Journal of Verbal Learning and Verbal Behavior, 23,* 270–288.

Pressley, M., Roehrig, A., Raphael, L., Dolezal, S., Bohn, K., Mohan, L., Wharton-McDonald, R., & Bogner, K. (2003). Teaching processes in elementary and secondary education. In

W. M. Reynolds & G. E. Miller (Eds.), *Handbook of psychology: Vol. 7. Educational psychology* (pp. 153–175). New York: Wiley.

Pressley, M., Wharton-McDonald, R., Allington, R., Block, C. C., Morrow, L., Tracey, D., Baker, K., Brooks, G., Cronin, J., Nelson, E., & Woo, D. (2001). A study of effective grade-1 literacy instruction. *Scientific Studies of Reading, 5,* 35–58.

Pressley, M., Wharton-McDonald, R., Raphael, L. M., Bogner, K., & Roehrig, A. (2002). Exemplary first-grade teaching. In B. M. Taylor & P. D. Pearson (Eds.), *Teaching reading: Effective schools, accomplished teachers* (pp. 73–88). Mahwah, NJ: Lawrence Erlbaum Associates.

Rathvon, N. (2004). *Early reading assessment: A practitioner's handbook.* New York: Guilford.

Roehler, L. R., & Duffy, G. G. (1984). Direct explanation of comprehension processes. In G. G. Duffy, L. R. Roehler, & J. Mason (Eds.), *Comprehension instruction: Perspectives and suggestions* (pp. 265–280). New York: Longman.

Roehrig, A. D., Pressley, M., & Sloup, M. (2001). Reading strategy instruction in regular primary-level classrooms by teachers trained in Reading Recovery. *Reading & Writing Quarterly, 17,* 323–348.

Rosenblatt, L. M. (1978). *The reader, the text, the poem: The transactional theory of the literary work.* Carbondale, IL: Southern Illinois University Press.

Rosenshine, B., & Meister, C. (1994). Reciprocal teaching: A review of the research. *Review of Educational Research, 64,* 479–531.

Schneider, W., & Pressley, M. (1997). *Memory development between two and twenty* (2nd ed.). Mahwah, NJ: Lawrence Erlbaum Associates.

Son, L. K., & Schwartz, B. L. (2002). The relationship between metacognitive control and monitoring. In T. J. Perfect & B. L. Schwartz (Eds.), *Applied metacognition* (pp. 15–38). Cambridge, England: Cambridge University Press.

van den Broek, P. (1994). Comprehension and memory of narrative texts: Inferences and coherence. In M. A. Gernsbacher (Ed.), *Handbook of psycholinguistics* (pp. 539–588). San Diego, CA: Academic Press.

Vygotsky, L. S. (1978). *Mind in society: The development of higher psychological processes.* Cambridge, MA: Harvard University Press.

Wharton-McDonald, R., Pressley, M., & Hampston, J. M. (1998). Outstanding literacy instruction in first grade: Teacher practices and student achievement. *Elementary School Journal, 99,* 101–128.

Wood, S. S., Bruner, J. S., & Ross, G. (1976). The role of tutoring in problem solving. *Journal of Child Psychology and Psychiatry, 7,* 89–100.

Wyatt, D., Pressley, M., El-Dinary, P. B., Stein, S., Evans, P., & Brown, R. (1993). Comprehension strategies, worth and credibility monitoring, and evaluations: Cold and hot cognition when experts read professional articles that are important to them. *Learning and Individual Differences, 5,* 49–72.

Author Index

Subject Index

A

A Corner of the Universe (Martin), 171, 174–176
Action research, 346
Adaptive teaching, 300–301, 303, 310–311
Add-A-Word Spelling Practice, 205–206
Advanced organizer, 30
Aesthetic reading, 22, 27
Analytical skills
  componential reading comprehension, 28–30, 31–37
  professional reflective metacognition, 315–316
  self-assessment strategies, 150, 151t, 152
Archival records, 202
Assessment, *see* Metacognition assessment
Assessment for Levels of Reflection, 339
Assisted performance, 380–381
Attention
  automatic metacognition, 43–47, 48–49, 53–55, 56–57
  developmental metacognition, 64–65
  higher order thinking skills (HOTS), 48–49, 51
  interest reading, 9, 41

lower order thinking skills (LOTS), 49
  skilled reading, 5–6
Australia, 127
Authentic reading
  home context, 27–28
  Metacognitive Processes Inventory (MPI), 170
  PROMISE instructional strategy, 242–244
  reading comprehension, 27–31, 36–37
Automatic metacognition
  attention, 43–47, 48–49, 53–55, 56–57
  automaticity theory, 43–44
  cognitive monitoring, 42–43, 53–57
  cognitive psychology, 43–44
  comprehension process, 43–47
  developmental metacognition, 42, 51–52
  distractions, 49
  educational psychology, 43
  higher order thinking skills (HOTS), 48–49, 51
  insights, 49–50, 55
  instructional practice
    developmental metacognition, 51–52
    home context, 51–52
    individual differences, 52–53
    learning disabilities, 52

S